£22—

GERMAN RESPONSIBILITY IN THE ARMENIAN GENOCIDE

VAHAKN N. DADRIAN

GERMAN RESPONSIBILITY — IN THE — ARMENIAN GENOCIDE

A REVIEW OF THE HISTORICAL EVIDENCE OF GERMAN COMPLICITY

FOREWORD BY ROGER W. SMITH

BLUE CRANE BOOKS
WATERTOWN, MASSACHUSETTS

GERMAN RESPONSIBILITY IN THE ARMENIAN GENOCIDE

A Review of the Historical Evidence of German Complicity

by Vahakn N. Dadrian

Second Printing in 1997

First Published in 1996 by

Blue Crane Books
P.O.Box 291, Cambridge, MA 02238

Copyright © Vahakn N. Dadrian, 1996
All rights reserved

Jacket design by Aramais Andonian
Book design, typography & electronic pagination by Arrow Graphics, Inc.
Watertown, Massachusetts

Printed in the United States of America

Library of Congress Cataloging-in-Publication Data

Dadrian, Vahakn N.
German responsibility in the Armenian genocide : a review of the historical evidence of German complicity / Vahakn N. Dadrian.
p. cm.
Includes bibliographical references (p.) and index.
ISBN 1-886434-01-8 (hc)
ISBN 1-886434-02-6 (pb)
1. Armenian massacres, 1915—1923. 2. Germany—Foreign relations—Turkey. 3. Turkey—Foreign relations—Germany. I. Title.
DS195.5.D37 1996
956.6'2015—dc20 96-10409
CIP

ACKNOWLEDGEMENT

This book is the result of a substantial expansion of Chapter 16, "The Issue of German Complicity," of the author's published volume *The History of the Armenian Genocide. Ethnic Conflict from the Balkans to Anatolia to the Caucasus.* Berghahn Books, Providence / Oxford, 1995.

To the memory of the victims of the Armenian genocide
who, in the words of German writer Armin Wegner,
an eyewitness, "died all the deaths on the earth,
the deaths of all ages."

(*Alle Tode der Erde, die Tode aller
Jahrhunderte starben sie*)

CONTENTS

List of Illustrations / *x*

Abbreviations / *xi*

Foreword / *xiii*

Introduction / *1*

PART I

THE GERMAN READINESS TO EMBRACE TURKEY'S ANTI-ARMENIAN POSTURE. THE LEGAL-MILITARY CONSEQUENCES / *7*

- Informal and Secret Methods of Consorting / *13*
- The Legal Perspective: The Bearings of International Law / *16*
- General Bronsart's Foreknowledge of Massacres When Ordering Deportations / *23*
- The Argument of Armenian Provocation Through Rebellion / *25*
- The Purposive Misportrayal of the Van Uprising / *29*

  Some preliminary comments

  The documentary evidence of the outbreak of Van uprising

- The Key Support Role of a German Chief of Staff in the Initiation of the Armenian Genocide / *34*

  The role of the IIIrd Army High Command—Its German Chief of Staff

  The role of the IIIrd Army High Command—Its Turkish Commander-in-Chief and the Pre-designed Wholesale Massacres

  The Role of the IIIrd Army High Command—Its Civilian Commissars as Subordinate Coconspirators

- The Decisive Role of the Special Organization East / *43*
- The Potency of the German Connection to the Special Organization / *49*

  The Artifice of Islam

- Turko-German Joint Initiatives and Their Implications for Ottoman Armenians / *54*
- The Ideological and Instigative Role of Oppenheim / *65*

  His general attitude and motives warranting the adoption of anti-Armenianism

  His espousal of the wartime Turkish anti-Armenian measures

  The indignant but ineffective repudiation of Oppenheim by lesser German officials

  Did Oppenheim consort with the massacrers?

- The Nature and Outcome of German Diplomatic Initiatives—The Quest for Alibis and the Inculpation-Exculpation Stratagem / *81*
- The Issue of Legal Liability Revisited / *89*

PART II

THE POLITICAL DETERMINANTS IN THE INVOLVEMENT OF THE GERMAN MILITARY / *107*

- The Revival of the Armenian Question and the New Turko-German Partnership / *107*
- The Inroads of the German Military Mission to Turkey / *109*
- The Bearings of the German Ideological Perspectives / *112*
- The Complicity of the Military. The Order for the "Deportations" / *116*

  General Major Bronsart von Schellendorf's role

  The genocidal consequences of the order and the issue of legal liability

  General Bronsart's exculpatory rationale blaming the victim after the fact

  Bronsart's protective thrust

  The roles and attitudes of other high-ranking German officers

  - Von der Goltz. Field Marshal
  - Feldmann. Lieutenant Colonel
  - Boettrich. Lieutenant Colonel
  - Guido von Usedom. Admiral
  - Wilhelm Souchon. Rear Admiral
  - Seeckt. Lieutenant General
  - Count Eberhard Wolffskeel von Reichenberg. Major
- The Political Indicators of Complicity / *137*
- An Ambassador and a Marine Attaché: The Issue of Paramountcy in Complicity / *141*

  Ambassador Hans Freiherr von Wangenheim

  Lieutenant Commander and Marine Attaché Hans Humann
- Turkish Assertions on German Complicity / *148*

  The views of Turkish publicists

  The reported disclosure of a former Turkish Foreign Minister

  The intimations of two Turkish deputies—before and after the fact

  The assertion of a Turkish cabinet minister

  A Turkish historian's input

- Incidents of Concealment and Disclosure / *153*

  The deletions in the main foreign office documentary tome

  The issue of financial liability

  The injunctions of German military and civilian censors

  The removal by the Germans of Ottoman General Staff files

  A German document with a revelatory hint

  Disclosure through the medium of two veteran Austrian consuls

- The Anti-Russian Ideology in the Turko-German Partnership and Its Anti-Armenian Repercussions / *165*
- German Political Economists and the Armenian Genocide / *168*
- The Views of German Experts of Criminal and International Law on German Complicity as a By-Product of Militarism / *169*
- The Significance of Emperor William II's Secret Activities / *171*
- The Official Formulas of Subterfuge / *173*
- A Trenchant Rejoinder from a German Newspaper Editor / *175*
- A Final Commentary on the Issue of German Responsibility / *182*

Appendix-A / *199*

The Transition of Prominent German Officials from Service in Turkey to Service in Nazi Germany

Appendix-B / *205*

The Indignity of Decorating the Arch Perpetrators

- The Honorees and their Medals
- The Decorations Given to Dr. Behaeddin Şakir and Talât Paşa

Appendix-C / *223*

The Differential Treatment of the Greeks and the Jews (Against the Background of the Armenian Genocide)

- The Ottoman Doctrine of Domination and the Legacy of Nationality Conflicts—A Historical Perspective
- The Case of the Greeks
- The Case of the Jews

Appendix-D / *263*

The Impassioned Appeal of German Writer Armin T. Wegner, an Eyewitness to the Genocide

Illustrations / *273*

Bibliography / *283*

Other Works by the Author / *293*

Index / *297*

LIST OF ILLUSTRATIONS

Commander Rafael de Nogales / 273

Henry Morgenthau / 273

Marshal Colmar von der Goltz / 274

Marshal Limann von Sanders / 274

General Fritz Bronsart von Schellendorf / 275

General Kress von Kressenstein / 275

General von Falkenhayn inspecting Turkish troops / 275

Baron von Wangenheim / 276

The funeral of Baron von Wangenheim, Istanbul / 276

Dr. Arthur Zimmermann / 277

Dr. Bethmann Hollweg / 277

Enver Paşa and General von Seeckt / 278

The Grand Vizier Talât Paşa / 278

Kaiser William II in Constantinopel in 1917 / 278

Kaiser William II inspecting Turkish Troops / 279

Enver Paşa / 279

Cemal Paşa / 279

Battle Cruiser *Goeben* (Yavuz) / 280

Admiral Souchon / 280

German and Turkish Navy officers on board the *Goeben* / 280

General Seeckt and Hitler / 281

General Seeckt reviewing his regiment on parade / 281

ABBREVIATIONS

AA	=	*Auswärtiges Amt.* German Foreign Office Archives. Political Department 1A (Berlin; presently Bonn)
BA/MA	=	*Bundesarchiv/Militärarchiv.* The military archives of the German Federal Republic, Freiburg im Breisgau
Cong. Rec.	=	Congressional Record
DAA	=	Diplomatic Archives of Austria, 19th Century
DAF	=	Diplomatic Archives of France, 19th Century
DAG	=	Diplomatic Archives of Germany, 19th Century
Doc.	=	Document
DZA	=	Deutsches Zentralarchiv. The archives of the former German Democratic Republic (East Germany), Potsdam
ESCOR	=	U.N.'s Economic and Social Council Official Records
Eur. Parl.	=	European Parliament
FO	=	British Foreign Office Archives
G.A.O.R.	=	General Assembly (U.N.) Official Records
K	=	Botschaft Konstantinopel (German Counsular Files)
N. S.	=	*Nouvelle Série.* French Foreign Ministry Archives (AMAE), Departments Turquie (Arménie) and Jeunes Turcs. Guerre: volumes 887–889, covering events relating to Armenia from August 1914 to May 1918 under the heading Turquie
P.C.I.J.	=	Permanent International Court of Justice
RG	=	*Record Group,* U.S. National Archives, Papers Relating to the Foreign Relations of the U.S. 1915 Supplement. World War I
T.S.	=	Treaty Series
T. V.	=	*Takvimi Vekâyi.* Official gazette of the Ottoman government, whose special supplements covering the proceedings of the Extraordinary Turkish Military Tribunal served as a judicial gazette
U. N. T. S.	=	United Nations Treaty Series

A note on the use of dual track dates:

Because of the prevalence in the respective periods of the 20th century of the 13-day differential (12-day for the 19th century) between the Ottoman calendar, otherwise called *rumi,* Julian, or old style (o.s.), and the European-Western calendar, otherwise called *miladi,* Gregorian, or new style (n.s.), both variants have been adduced in connection with the narration of certain specific events for which purpose the slash mark, separating the two, has been used. See, for example, the August 14/26, 1896 date for the Bank Ottoman raid on page 239 and the January 26/February 8, 1914 date on page 108 for the outbreak of the anti-Ittihadist counter-revolution in the Ottoman capital.

FOREWORD

Turkey's responsibility for the genocide of over one million Armenians during World War I has been well-documented, most notably by Vahakn N. Dadrian in *The History of the Armenian Genocide.* At the same time, there have always been questions about the role Turkey's World War I ally, Germany, may have played in the genocide. Two lines of thought, neither well-substantiated, have existed. The first is that Germany was the instigator of the genocide; the second is that Germany had nothing to do with Turkey's attempt to annihilate a people. Now in this detailed and path-breaking work of historical recovery, Professor Dadrian produces evidence from German and other sources that show that Germany is not free from a measure of criminal, moral, and political responsibility in the genocide. To say this in no way relieves Turkey of its responsibility, and it would be unfortunate if the evidence presented here were used by Turkey as yet another way of pretending to clean hands.

Dadrian does not accuse the German people, but rather officials and the state. Nor does he put forth any doctrine of collective guilt. Instead, he names individuals where possible, and beyond that, points to a more general, legal and political responsibility. Both approaches are important—criminals must be identified where possible; the responsibility of a state, on the other hand, is encompassing, and in the present case is not subject to the test of statutory limitation.

German responsibility in the Armenian Genocide falls into two broad patterns: official policy made at the highest level, and acts of officials—military and diplomatic—that were sanctioned after the fact either through explicit approval or through silence. Some of these policies and acts were immoral, but others were clearly criminal; given the standards prevalent in Western jurisprudence, in either case, the state bears responsibility for them.

There is also an ideological pattern that is suggestive, but its precise influence among both German and Turkish officials is not yet clear. The role of Turkish social theorists in providing an intellectual basis for the elimination of the Armenians has long been documented: Turkey for the Turks, expansion to the East, the pan-Turkic future in Muslim Central Asia. All of these goals were thought to be impossible as long as the Armenian Christians occupied Eastern Anatolia, blocking the gateway to the Muslim East. Such ideologies have been traced in part to Western thinkers, such as Durkheim, who emphasized the need for social cohesion and integration. But several German thinkers and activists, notably Field Marshal von der Goltz, laid out explicitly in the late nineteenth century what became the Ittihadist Turkish ideology. Goltz, who also was a principal reformer of the Turkish army, and professor at Istanbul's military college, put forth a doctrine portending a major calamity for the Armenians in terms of what today would be called "ethnic cleansing." He encouraged the Turks to turn away from Europe and create a new empire in the East. He thought this would provide, as Dadrian notes, "a bulwark against expansionist Tsarist Russia, and a potential springboard for future eastward incursions. But there was an entrenched obstacle, the indigenous Armenian population." Ominously, Goltz projected the forcible evacuation of the Armenian population residing in eastern Turkey. Despite the magnitude of horrors implicit in such a scheme of large-scale dislocations, forced expulsion is, nevertheless, not genocide per se. But given the history of previous exterminatory massacres against the Armenians such ways of thinking were bound to embolden the Turks, historically so predisposed, to seek a total and final solution of what they defined as the "Armenian Problem."

Moreover, Dadrian's book makes clear that, once the genocide began, the refusal to intervene became the focal point of German policy. This policy, explicitly approved by the Kaiser, was publicly justified on the grounds that Germany must retain the "trust" of Turkey as a valuable wartime ally. There is no suggestion in Dadrian's material that Germany was *unable* to restrain Turkey; rather, there is clear evidence that it was *unwilling* to do so in order to further its own interests.

There was also a policy of covering up the genocide. This involved several related aspects, ranging from censorship of the press to dissemination of anti-Armenian Turkish propaganda to the sending of mild notes of protest to the Turkish government. The latter, which were followed by no action, were attempts to exculpate Germany from responsibility for the massacres. As early as August 1915 a White Book was planned that would blame the Armenians, both lament and explain away the atrocities, and indicate that Germany had done all it could to mitigate the suffering through a combination of advice and protest notes; however, these notes were in fact nothing more than pro-forma protest notes intended to serve as alibis.

Finally, abandoning all scruples, the Kaiser and his coterie of German military and civilian leaders, honored many of the executioners of the Armenian people. They conferred upon these executioners a host of decorations, including the Prussian Orders of the Black Eagle and the Red

Eagle, and the military decoration the Iron Cross. Moreover, as Dadrian points out, three high ranking German military officers at the end of the war organized, through a coordinated effort, the clandestine flight from the Ottoman capital, Istanbul, of the seven top Young Turk Ittihadist leaders, who during the war had masterminded the Armenian genocide. Of these, General Bronsart lent his help from Berlin, and General Seeckt, the last German Chief of Staff of Ottoman Armed Forces, and Admiral Rebeur-Paschwitz took care of the logistics of the operation from their headquarters in the Ottoman capital. Most of these "fugitives of justice" found welcome sanctuary in Germany, especially wartime Grand Vizier and party boss Talât, the principal architect of the Armenian genocide; Talât had been honored, with several decorations, including the highest Prussian decoration: The Order of the Black Eagle (March 20, 1917). The attempts of the postwar Ottoman authorities to have him extradited to Turkey for prosecution by the Turkish Extraordinary Court-Martial were rebuffed by then German Foreign Minister Wilhelm Solf who made it clear that Talât could stay in Germany as long as he wanted to stay.

Acts by individuals that were ratified by those higher up include several instances in which deportations, with "severe measures," were ordered by German military officers, resulting in the deaths of tens of thousands of Armenians. The role of General Bronsart von Schellendorf, the German Chief of Staff of Ottoman Armed Forces, is in this respect inculpatory—morally, politically and legally. He was a senior member of the German Military Mission to Turkey (which Emperor William II had personally created) and as such was a high ranking official of the German state system. Operating from the vantage ground of Ottoman General Headquarters, he issued orders for the deportation of the Armenians. In one of these orders he demanded that "severe measures" be applied against already disarmed Armenian labor battalion soldiers most of whom were consequently slaughtered by the gangs of the murderous Special Organization. Others aided and abetted massacres and deportations through suggestion or through approbative passivity. Conscientious German officials, who did object or sought to intervene on behalf of the Armenians, and there were quite a few of them, were reprimanded by their military or diplomatic superiors. Other acts by individuals included vilification of Armenians, thus reinforcing the anti-Armenian Turkish posture. Indeed, the compulsion to accommodate the Turks went so far as to try to impose limits on the raising of relief funds in Germany for Armenians.

There is compelling evidence, then, of significant German state responsibility for the Armenian Genocide in the course of whose enactment not all Germans adhered to the declared policy of non-intervention; nor did they all remain bystanders. In the case of Urfa, for example, German cooperation with the Turks transformed itself into sheer butchery when a German artillery officer, Major Wolffskeel, single-handedly reduced the Armenian section of the city to rubble and ashes. The Turks had readily availed themselves of his skill in the handling of the available canister-shots when regular Turkish infantry, despite several attempts, could not overwhelm the barricaded defenders. Like the defenders of the Warsaw Uprising, the stalwarts of the Urfa defense were desperately resisting the Turkish plan to deport and annihilate the approximately 25,000 Armenians of that city.

As to the issue of punishment, those who committed the criminal acts, incurred moral guilt by rationalizing the enormous crime as a "strictly internal matter," formulated a policy of non-intervention, or engaged in coverup, are no longer alive. Yet, the quest for truth requires that their actions be disclosed before history. Equally, if not more important, however, is the matter of justice.

Indeed, there is already sufficient evidence for Germany to acknowledge such guilt, not as the actual and principal perpetrator of the genocide, but as an accessory to that crime of genocide. Again and again, officials fretted about possible German financial liability in the wake of revelations inculpating German officials on the matter of personally ordering Armenian deportations.

With the advent of the era of Chancellor Adenauer (1949–1963), there emerged a new Germany and a new democracy that may well be acclaimed as a new rampart of Western Civilization. The present pioneering work of historical recovery by Prof. Dadrian, well documented as it is, is germane and persuasive enough. As such, it should afford an opportunity to the heirs of the Adenauerian legacy to redeem themselves once more as they did with respect to the victims of the Jewish Holocaust. They have a chance to demonstrate for all to see that justice delayed is not necessarily justice denied.

Finally, it is important for Germans and non-Germans alike to resist as resolutely as possible any attempt by Turkey to exploit the present study and to shift, or dilute, its overwhelming responsibility for the death of over a million Armenians, a responsibility it has never acknowledged.

ROGER W. SMITH
Professor of Government,
College of William and Mary

INTRODUCTION

One of the main reasons why the World War I Armenian genocide has been dubbed "the forgotten genocide" had less to do with the incidence of poor memory but more with the distribution of power relations in national and international arenas; such distribution generally helps determine the selection of topics on which the public may be sensitized and from the discussion of which public policies may emerge. Impotent or weak constituents are in this respect critically handicapped. This truism is particularly applicable to nations that may become victimized by a powerful perpetrator nation-state. When focusing on genocide, the ultimate form of victimization on a national scale, one cannot help but discern the overarching operativeness of power in this respect. Indeed, power is an essential ingredient for the enactment of genocide as well as for the preemption of effective public debate subsequent to that enactment. It takes ample power, for example, to overwhelm and reduce a victim group targeted for genocide. If, following such victimization, the perpetrator group still enjoys a substantial power leverage, and all other things being equal, the chances are that that leverage will be used to deny, to obfuscate, to coopt potential advocacy groups as abettors, or even intimidate challengers for the sole purpose of consigning the crime to oblivion. The ultimate goal is to impose silence.

This scenario in broad outlines describes the past and current status of the historical reality of the Armenian genocide. The power position of Turkey, past and present, afforded the emergence of a Turkish denial syndrome through which the story of the optimal annihilation of the Armenian population of the Ottoman Empire for more than eight decades has been consigned to oblivion as far as the desiderata of worldwide scholarship, global recognition, and international justice are concerned.

Moreover, the persistence of these Turkish denials, past and present, proved functional at another level, further aggravating the despair of the Armenian survivor population and their progenies. They served to provide a protective shield to Germany, several of whose officials serving in Turkey as wartime allies have been incriminated in a variety of ways. The picture of German involvement as a result remained obscure and vague. In fact it has been reduced to irrelevance on the strength of adamant, and at times truculent Turkish denials of the occurrence of any genocide against the Armenians. But there is the stark evidence of the abrupt disappearance of an entire indigenous population from its ancestral territories and the even more stark evidence of the resort to massive and lethal violence to effect that disappearance. This is the type of *corpus delicti* in face of which denials acquire foremost significance and the quest for uncovering and identifying the arch perpetrators becomes a paramount task. Despite the solemn pledges of the victorious Entente Powers to bring to trial, by way of international justice, the authors of the Armenian genocide, that pledge of justice was sacrificed at the altar of political expediency and economic rapaciousness.

Notwithstanding, there occurred an event in this period that represented a milestone in Ottoman-Turkish legal history and promised to administer retributive justice against the arch perpetrators of the genocide.That event was the establishment and maintenance by successive Turkish postwar governments of a Military Tribunal which, in a period of some eighteen months, tried these offenders, issued verdicts, and rendered sentences. The new Kemalist regime felt constrained, however, to repudiate that tribunal and disclaim any responsibility for its findings, and the feuding and weary victors of the West once more acquiesced to the demands of the Kemalists. Through insurgency and considerable help from the newly established Bolshewiks these Kemalists had managed to convert in less than three years a shattering military defeat (October 1918) to a resounding victory against two lesser enemies, the fledgling Republic of Armenia in the East (November 1920) and a fractured and emasculated Greece in the West (September 1922). The proceedings of the Tribunal proved inconsequential as far as retributive justice was concerned as the trials altogether were jettisoned by the new rulers.

This study represents an effort to remedy, to the extent possible, the ills of this stunted development within the boundaries of historical scholarship. In performing that task material from such ancillary disciplines as international law, political science, and diplomatic history have been utilized as well. Since the topic has been artificially and deliberately reduced to controversy, the greater part of this effort involves documentation. After all, the validity of any analysis and conclusion necessarily hinges on the reliability of the sources on which a study is predicated. The gravity of the crime of genocide and the incidence of complicity attached to it presently mandate that the documentations involved be as compelling as possible. For this very reason the available German official documents have been abundantly used in this study. To underscore authenticity and facilitate source-checking by investigative scholars, extensive use has also been made of the German originals of a plethora of documentary quotations; they have been inserted in parentheses following their English translations.

This study has but one focus: the examination of the role of German officials, military and civilian, in the initiation of those wartime measures that engulfed the Armenian population of Ottoman Turkey during World War I. The relevance of such an inquiry is exceeded only by its overall significance. Imperial Germany and Imperial Turkey were close military and political allies during that war—this is a most relevant fact for the examination of the conditions of the Turko-German cooperation involved. The significance, on the other hand, issues from the cardinal fact that these anti-Armenian measures were intended to, and in fact did, entail the optimal destruction of the victim population, as borne out by the evidence unearthed since the event. The need for such an inquiry is accented further by the consideration that, despite the large volume of research generated in the last eight decades on the fate of the Armenian population, there is hardly any work in the respective literature dealing with this problem-focus. The emergence of this problem-focus was the result of a stream of fragments of evidence that were thrust upon this author in the course of prolonged research activities on the Armenian Genocide in the archives of Europe, especially Bonn and Vienna, and in the published literature of memoirs by a number of Turks directly and indirectly associated with German officials and functionaries serving in wartime Turkey. These fragments of evidence, when interrelated and reconstructed, did yield the contours of certain types of German involvement signaling a measure of complicity, and therefore, German responsibility. After making a judgment that further research was warranted to explore the specifics of that involvement, a concentric effort was made in that direction. The present study is the product of that effort.

I should like to state also that this book is primarily intended for German audiences. Contemporary and recent developments in Germany inspire hope that, notwithstanding the probable displeasure of certain segments of German society, the majority of democratically inclined Germans will read this book with an open mind. This book represents my perception of the constellation of the facts under which the problem of German complicity is subsumed and examined, without disregarding or discounting the benevolent roles of a host of other German civilian and military officials. In fact it is due to the integrity and fortitude of these officials that the Armenian genocide until today remains documented and exposed in German state archives.

Before presenting the findings of the study, however, it may be appropriate to direct attention to a fact that imparts a paradoxical twist to the entire inquiry. It concerns the great contribution German consuls, stationed in wartime Turkey, made in documenting the Armenian genocide. Seemingly unaware of the covert designs and purposes of their superiors in the German Embassy in the Ottoman capital, the Foreign Office, and the German Chancellor's Office in the capital of Germany, these lesser functionaries of the German state literally deluged the former with a stream of reports on the details of the unfolding mass murder; similar reports were sent to the German Military Mission to Turkey by German officers operating in the interior of Turkey. Compared to other state archives in Europe, the depositories of the archives of the German Foreign Affairs Ministry in Bonn are unexcelled in terms of their abundance in primary sources relative to that mass murder. The respective records are preserved, classified, and filed with Teutonic discipline and orderliness. It would be no exaggeration to state, therefore, that through the existence and maintenance of these records, the documentation of the Armenian genocide is elevated to the highest degree of its incontestability.[1] It is not enough to emphasize the alliance factor to explain this fact even though that factor alone would be more than sufficient to warrant the optimal credibility of the sources and the material issuing from them. An equally if not more important consideration in this connection is the fact that these reports, when prepared and dispatched, were not intended for the public but rather for in-house, internal purposes. Nearly all of them were classified with such symbols as "confidential," "secret," or "top secret" (i.e., *vertraulich, geheim, streng geheim)*. Removed from the levers of consultative deliberations and decision making, these subordinate German officials were inevitably confined to the task of reporting on the relevant facts and events they could observe and verify. Their reports essentially focus, therefore, on the levels of organization and implementation of the genocide. Precisely for this reason, their contribution to historical research and, of course, indirectly to the quest for truth, is invaluable. That contribution acquires, moreover, inordinate significance in face of the rather reflexive persistence with which the Turks, with very few muted and timid exceptions, have continued in the last eight decades to deny the occurrence of the enormous crime. Encouraged by the advantages accruing to it as a NATO ally and capitalizing on its economic leverages in terms of rapidly expanding industrial and commercial ties to the West, Turkey presently is pursuing new objectives of obfuscation and denial by "reordering" its archives, by manipulating Western scholars and elites through a mixture of methods of cooptation, cajoling, and intimidation, and by engaging the services of several public relations firms in the hope of influencing the media in the West so that, for example, the term "genocide" is negated by the use of the adjective "alleged" to be placed in front of it.

In this respect alone this study is cast in a discordant role. It seeks to examine the conduct of certain high-ranking German officials suspected of having consorted with Turkish authorities at the peril of the Armenians, at the same time recognizing and applauding the collateral services of other and lesser German officials in helping to expose the crime in all its facets. This paradox is such, however, that it may be bested through the use of a methodological expedient. In the structuring of the study an effort was made to interconnect certain aspects of the crime, as exposed by the German officials described earlier, to its hidden aspects. The purpose was to bring into some plausible relationship the manifest involvement in the enactment of the crime of the Turkish authorities, and the less manifest involvement in it of a class of German officials. The key to this procedure is the harnessing of those components of the official German documents that are implicative in their contents; they suggest covert involvements by actors comprising a broad net of participants.

Foremost among these components are those expressions in the respective documents that are often furtive in texture and as such consist of hints that purposively are not elaborated, thereby suggesting a measure of concealment. Far more implicative in this respect is the resort to outright deletions, omissions, and rephrasing of sentences. In the originals of some documents certain portions are crossed out either at the point of dispatch or of reception in Istanbul or Berlin. Perhaps the most signal resort to concealment is evidenced in the preparation of the massive volume by Lepsius containing the ensemble of German Foreign Office documents pertaining to the World War I Armenian deportations and massacres. Despite the assurances given in the foreword that the presentation of the material is complete and that nothing will be left out that "in any way may incriminate (*belasten*)" German civilian and military officials,[2] the volume is replete with deletions of precisely of those components of the documents that one way or another are incriminatory in this respect. Some of these deletions are singled out and commented upon in Part II, section on "The deletions in the main foreign office documentary tome." They are explained with some further detail in a previous study.[3] The conditions under which Lepsius undertook the selection of the documents and their compilation were fair and liberal, except for one. Foreign Minister Dr. Wilhelm Solf, who previously was Colonial Minister, stipulated that Lepsius endeavor "to justify our conduct" (*unser Verhalten zu rechtfertigen*) in the matter of Armenian deportations and massacres.[4] Dr. Otto Göppert, Privy Legation Councillor in the Foreign

Office, then proceeded to negotiate with Lepsius on this point.[5] The result was that Lepsius felt constrained to be accommodative; he agreed to "exonerate" (*entlasten*) Germany.[6] Of course it can be argued in this connection that the demand for justification and exoneration is not always a type of tactic only guilty defendants are wont to employ in a court of law in order to cover up or deflect from the facts of culpability; it can also stem from a genuine sense of innocence, or relative innocence. In principle, however, the idea of innocence is incompatible with a propensity to "handle" the existing documentary evidence.

In trying to deal with this problem of concealment, bordering on coverup, a need was felt to establish a framework of analysis within a set of indicators signaling reasons and evidence of a kind of involvement that is tantamount to complicity. Motivation was considered one such major indicator calling for probing. The first question to pose in this regard is: Is there any evidence to suggest that certain German authorities, whether in Berlin or in Istanbul, had any interest in seeing Turkey purged of its Armenian population? The following study attempts to answer this question.

Notes to Introduction

1. For a compilation of these documents in terms of their core parts certifying the facts of the Armenian genocide, *see* Vahakn N. Dadrian, "Documentation of the Armenian Genocide in German and Austrian Sources," in *The Widening Circle of Genocide. Genocide: A Critical Bibliographic Review.* vol. 3. Israel Charny, ed. (New Brunswick, N.J., 1994) pp. 77–125. Republished, also in 1994, as a separate entity with additional pp. I–XXVII, containing a Table of Contents, a Foreword and an Introduction.
2. Dr. Johannes Lepsius, *Deutschland und Armenien 1914–1918. Sammlung Diplomatischer Aktenstücke* (Berlin-Potsdam, 1919), vi.
3. Dadrian, "Documentation" [n. 1], 78, 95–5 n. 2.
4. A. A. Türkei 158/21, A54420, p. 5 of Dr. Göppert's December 28, 1918 memo.
5. A. A. Göppert Papers (*Nachlass*) vol. VI, file 5, p. 4 (files 1–8), February 1, 1919.
6. A. A. Türkei 183/56, A20906. The Haag, July 13, 1919.

PART I

The German Readiness to Embrace Turkey's Anti-Armenian Posture. The Legal-Military Consequences

Motivation for a course of action implies—in fact presupposes—a definite interest in the thing toward which the action may be oriented; the more acute the interest may be, the stronger the motivation and the greater the likelihood of the determination to engage in such action. German interest in Turkey evolved, intensified, and eventually culminated in the World War I military and political alliance as a result of a process that was cumulative and distinct. It has therefore a kind of historical dimension that requires dissection in order to assess properly the consequences of that interest for the fate befalling the Armenian population of the Ottoman Empire in World War I.

In its inception German interest in Turkey had a colonialist thrust of which the "Berlin-Baghdad" imagery was emblematic. Moltke dreamed, for example, of a German Palestine. Roscher in 1848 advocated the inheriting of Turkey's realm as a German entitlement. Two years earlier List had proposed the Baghdad Railway and the colonization by Germany of Asia Minor. Despite his disclaiming of interest in Turkish affairs Bismarck in the summer of 1878 ushered in new vistas of such aspirations by performing the role of an "honest broker" at the Congress of Berlin. Within four years after that congress the first German Military Mission arrived in the Ottoman capital with the aim of reorganizing the Ottoman army. Through the assignment of von der Goltz, then a major, as a military instructor in Turkey, the German military tradition gained a foothold in Turkey and with it Krupp became a permanent fixture in the military armament economy of Turkey. In 1886 the Orientalist Sprenger published a book with the title: *Babylonia. The Richest Land of the Past and the Most Remunerative Field of Colonization in the Present.* He broadcast in it the idea that part of Turkey constituted the sole land which was not yet occupied by a Great Power. For his part Kärger advocated Asia Minor as an area ripe for colonization. These espousals coincide with the period when German engineers and emissaries of the Deutsche

Bank were establishing the Anatolian Railway Society and building as far as Konya and Angora (Ankara). As to the contemporary Pan-Germans, they were promoting the idea of German protectorate of Asia Minor and the acquisition of Syria and Mesopotamia. German artillery officer Kannenberg in 1897 published a monograph on Asia Minor's Natural Riches. During his investigations on the ground he was accompanied by an officer of the German General Staff. A year later Emperor William II entered the picture and inaugurated Germany's new policy on the Middle East, but especially on Turkey. It may, therefore, be argued that at the epicenter of this historical process are the powerful exertions of the personality of Emperor William II whose imperious temperament, shifting moods, frequent impulsiveness, punctuated by equally frequent instances of indecisiveness and other idiosyncrasies, are essential ingredients which need to be taken into account. In fact, it may be argued that it was in the volatile configuration of these personality characteristics that began to germinate, mature, and ultimately crystallize the emperor's affinities for Turkey. Given their origin and direction, these affinities became the more or less fixed standards of German policy toward Turkey in the 1888–1918 period, defining the basic goals and interests of Germany in this regard. The efforts of the Germans to ingratiate themselves with the Turks and to win a steady stream of economic concessions began in 1888 when Sultan Abdul Hamit decided to reward William II by granting the Germans the first railway concession, which was followed by subsequent concessions subsumed under the Baghdad Railway Project. These developments were accompanied by the infusion of German capital in Turkish economy and, with it, a steady increment of German political and economic influence at the expense of the British and French. William II gave impetus to the proliferation of German economic designs on Turkey with a view to penetrating it commercially and industrially. Partly out of spite against France and England in particular, the Sultan went often out of his way to facilitate this penetration. The Baghdad Railway Construction project is a case in point. The entire process was decisively accelerated by the two trips the emperor made to Turkey in 1889 and 1898. Equally important, Prussian military officers continued to instruct, train, and rebuild the Ottoman Turkish army.

But the episode that is believed to have exerted a great influence in cementing Turko-German ties of friendship was the German response, or rather the lack of it, to the 1894–1896 empirewide massacres against the Armenians. The crucial role this German attitude played in the unfolding of the subsequent stages of the Turko-Armenian conflict involving aggregate massacres against the Armenians of Turkey cannot be overemphasized. In several respects, one may contend that the World War I Armenian genocide is foreshadowed in the devastating consequences of this German attitude, largely forged and fostered by Emperor William II. A closer examination of the formation and application of this German attitude relative to the Abdul Hamit-era massacres is, therefore, in order; the central issue here is the German response to them. In one major respect that response has a saliency deserving attention. The response was such as to augment the chances of impunity accruing to the Sultan and his coterie of perpetrators. The massacres thus proved affordable, as far as these perpetrators were concerned. Equally important, the uniform attitude of German diplomats, controlled as that attitude was by the emperor, presaged an almost identical German response in connection with the World War I enactment of the Armenian genocide. Here, the German monarch emerges as the functional nexus, interconnecting the two episodes of organized mass murder. Even though there were certain groups in Germany voicing their revulsion and protest against the massacres and against the policy of the German government, the latter almost imperturbably continued to pamper the Sultan through its ambassador Marschall von Bieberstein, who, together with the emperor, was recasting the new German policy toward Turkey, in the process eliciting profuse thanks from Sultan Abdul Hamit. The relish of the Germans in the pomp and ceremony attending William II's second visit to Turkey in 1898, barely two years after the end of the series of the empirewide massacres, when a benumbed Europe was still abhorring them and anathematizing its author, "the Red Sultan," was an indulgence that signaled a German proclivity to condone the butchery of a subject nationality. For this indulgence the emperor was amply rewarded by his host. In the language of French ambassador Cambon, the Sultan proved a veritable "milch cow," dispensing a string of most valuable gifts to his guest.[1] The net result of all these endeavors was the emergence of Germany as the dominant economic factor in the development of Turkish commerce, industry, and military procurement, at the same time displacing France's privileged position in the Near East in general and in Turkey in particular.[2]

The Germans were neither apologetic nor anxious to relent in their efforts to accommodate the Turks in pursuit of their drive to penetrate Turkey still further—both economically and politically. In doing so they did not conceal their disdain for England and France, who continued to press for reforms as part of their mission to pacify Turkey by seeking remedies for the lingering nationality conflicts in that land. The roots of that disdain were planted by Bismarck. Months before the start of the

Congress of Berlin, when the Russian army was still battling against the Turkish army, Paul von Oubril, Russian ambassador to Germany, told Prince Bernhard von Bülow, the German Foreign Minister at the time, that Russia was not fighting with any ulterior motivation but in the name of "humanity" as well as "for the sake of the Christians" of the Ottoman Empire. In responding, Bismarck inserted on the margin of Bülow's report the words: "Why such hypocrisy in the course of a confidential exchange."[3] Emperor William II was even more vehement in his decrial of what he regarded as British resort to hypocrisy in such matters. On the eve of World War I he enjoined his diplomatic and consular representatives to "tear off England's mask of Christian" pretense, denouncing the British as a whole as "a hated, mendacious, unscrupulous nation of hagglers" (*dieses verhasste, verlogene, gewissenlose Krämervolk*).[4] The most dominant thesis in the annals of German public debate on the Armenian Question and the massacres of the era of Abdul Hamit is articulated by Friedrich Naumann, a theologian by training but, by profession, a "political pastor," to use his own description of himself. He had accompanied the emperor on his 1898 trip, thereby spending a month in Turkey. Faithful to the legacy of Bismarck's brand of nationalism but at the same time completely identified with William II's posture on Turkey, Naumann, with brutal frankness, declared that Germany's higher interests require the maintaining of "our political indifference to the sufferings of Christians in the Turkish Empire, painful as these must be to our private feelings." Describing this position as one based "on deep moral grounds," he went on to provide a rationale for the Armenian massacres of the 1894–1896 period.

> Diminishing in numbers, constantly in retreat, the Turk acquired a characteristic which he probably did not possess before. He acquired the cunning of people who at their core are broken people but who want to continue existing as far as the outside world is concerned. Like a small animal which instinctively knows how in all its weakness it can still use its teeth and claws, so knows the Turk also as to when he may once more act as a barbarian and shed blood. The genocide of the Armenians [*Armeniermord*] was the last opportunity affording the act of Turkish barbarism.

In the final analysis this act of "Armenocide" was, according to Naumann, a political event marking Turkey's method of handling "internal affairs" and as such was "a piece of political history, expressing itself in asiatic form."[5]

The import of the publication of this thesis is exceeded only by the articulation of the respective official German position, mirroring more or less an identical thesis. It was framed in the wake of the last phase of the

Abdul Hamit-era massacres (November 1896) by Alfons Mumm von Schwarzenstein, chief advisor for Near East Affairs in the Political Issues Section of the German Foreign Office. The German stance is expounded in a brief, comprising 12 pages, which are written in a succinct and rather blunt style. Three main lines of argument keynote the contents of this document: 1) The Armenians, a crafty and seditious race, provoked the Turks, who became enveloped with a sense of peril to their national existence; 2) Germany has no reason to intervene on behalf of a race in which she has absolutely no interest, nor can it be the duty of German politics to embark upon a crusade against the Crescent for the sake of a Christian people, for the benefit of whom the interventionist Powers last year interceded only to aggravate the plight of that people; and 3) given the dangers that are otherwise threatening the integrity of Turkey and the business interests of numerous Germans in Turkey, the bloodbaths in "Armenia," as regrettable as they are, should be regarded as being the lesser of evils in the overall picture. This policy declaration ends with the conclusion that Germany can but only remain an observer of the scene, avoiding any and all action "which might precipitate matters." After approving it, Foreign Minister Marshal, on the very same day, November 26, 1896, forwarded the position paper to Chancellor Chlodwig Prince von Hohenlohe-Schillingsfürst.[6] The chancellor was actually in agreement with the basic thrust of the paper. He told his sister that the German Parliament, the Reichstag, mindful of Bismarck's famous maxim on the priceless value of the bones of a German musketeer, would resolutely oppose any proposal to move against Turkey for the sake of the Armenians. He then posed the rhetorical question: Why then alienate the Sultan and by the same token forfeit German influence in Turkey?[7]

These postures, adopted in the name of higher German national interests, did not always square, however, with the personal sentiments and persuasions of both Bismarck and William II, as revealed in certain pieces of German diplomatic correspondence. Nor did Bismarck and the monarch absolutely reject principles of humanitarianism. At times both rulers reacted rather vehemently to tales of unspeakable Turkish atrocities. Even Bismarck, the Iron Chancellor, could not contain his indignation in face of "the heinous atrocities perpetrated by the Turks against the wounded and the defenseless. It is difficult to maintain diplomatic quiet in view of such barbarities, and I believe that the sense of indignation is common among all Christian Powers." Bismarck directed these words to his Emperor William I at the time of the 1877–1878 Russo-Turkish war, urging the dispatch, together with the other Powers, of a protest note to Turkey.[8]

More revealing are the frequent outbursts of William II reacting to the ferocity with which the Armenians were being slaughtered in that period. Twice on these occasions he exclaimed "shame on us all" for allowing the perpetration of such horrors.[9] On two other occasions he noted that the only solution to the problem of the massacres was "the deposing" of the Turkish monarch (*man setze ihn ab*).[10] On another occasion he called the latter "a nauseating human being" (*ekelhaft*).[11] In the same vein, he declared that bombarding the Yıldız Palace with cannonballs was the only effective way to get rid of him;[12] he even suggested that the Sultan could be eliminated in the same way as was his predecessor Sultan Aziz,[13] whose ostensible suicide was considered by many a ploy to disguise his murder. At one point William II went even so far as to concede that British Prime Minister Salisbury's proposal to end by force Sultan Abdul Hamit's regime, which at the time he had rebuffed, was an appropriate one.[14]

These mutually incompatible and often out and out contradictory utterances are, beyond the level of an indulgence in royal vagaries, indicative of the range of his idiosyncrasies, signaling at the same time the probability of their intrusion into his political thinking and decision making. More often than not he relied on his imperial ego to resolve his inner conflicts. As Admiral Alfred von Tirpitz, Marine Minister (until 1916) in wartime Germany and the architect of the buildup of German naval power, in his memoirs pointed out, William II more often than not waivered, recoiling before situations requiring resolve and decisiveness.[15]

Nevertheless, Emperor William II weighed his options and in reality decided to stick with the man he in privately circulated documents so repeatedly had castigated and condemned. His government did all it could to suppress efforts of disseminating news and details about the massacres; any expression of criticism of the Turkish government in Germany at the time was considered an expression of hostility to the Reich.[16] The German emperor even called the Sultan and his regime "a blessing for his subjects—except for a handful of Armenians," believing as he did that as a ruler Abdul Hamit could serve as "a model for other countries."[17] When the Young Turk revolutionaries in 1908 did in fact depose the Sultan, William II, by way of a delayed reaction, four years later called for the expulsion from Europe of these revolutionaries for "they dethroned my friend, the Sultan."[18] Defying all manner of public opinion and dismissing the resentment of some of the other Powers still chafing from their knowledge of the horrors of the massacres, William II set out to cultivate the kind of amicable relations with the Sultan that served to strengthen the latter's regime and buttress his policies, and ultimately make the emperor appear to approve of the massacres. That sense of approval is epitomized by the response of Naumann, the emperor's admirer and supporter. In reacting to the horrors of the Armenian massacres of the 1894–1896 period, Naumann, cited earlier, stated that Germany should let these massacres "run their own course" (*eigenen Weg gehen*) and worry only about the task of "binding the wounds of the surviving victims."[19]

When transposed to the level of a broader perspective, this supportive role of the German monarch assumes even greater significance. That perspective encompasses two periods of Turkish history, marking the sway of two distinct and separate regimes, in the careers of which the fact of the continuity of the imperial rule of William II parallels the fact of the continuity of the process of the ultimate obliteration of the Armenians. Given the sustained character of the partnership of Germany with Turkey throughout these periods, William II, with all his pronounced predilections for Turkey, emerges as the functional connecting link between the eras of Sultan Abdul Hamit and the Young Turk Ittihadists (who succeeded him to power), in which eras these processes of destruction unfolded. The manifest nonchalance of the German monarch toward the fate of the Armenians, subjected to exterminatory massacres, at the very least indicates, if not demonstrates, that Germany didn't object to the emergence of a new Turkey that is purged of its native Armenian population.

INFORMAL AND SECRET METHODS OF CONSORTING

The legitimate representatives of any state organization, as a rule, are bound to operate under certain constraints in order to remain accountable for their behavior. When under specific conditions a need arises to avoid being held accountable, however, the resort to secrecy becomes an option. A diplomat or any other governmental functionary may exercise that option by indulging in behavior that may be dubious in nature, or even sinister, but against the negative consequences of which protection may be secured by qualifying the specific indulgence as one that is to be regarded as "off the record." Dubious and sinister acts depend on stealth in order to serve their purposes. Nearly all measures surrounding the lethal aspects of the victimization of the Ottoman Armenians involved a variety of methods of stealth, including conspiratorial schemes through which sovereigns and their coteries could afford to consort at the expense of the potential victim population. In examining the issue of German involvement, certain indicators signaling this type of stealth come to the fore of attention. One may begin with the German monarch. Part of his modus operandi was based on his penchant for utmost secrecy in transactions of dubious character, requiring autonomous decisions and actions. One of the two of Abdul Hamit's most trusted advisors disclosed in his memoirs, for instance that,"on the emperor's initiative and technical assistance he supplied" there was installed in the Yıldız Palace a highly secret equipment for wireless communication; the two monarchs were thus enabled to consult one another, personally and informally. "Neither their Cabinet members, nor their ambassadors knew of this arrangement, and the code key for the exchange of ciphers was kept locked in the office in which his [Abdul Hamit's] most important documents were kept."[20]

Given the nature and implications of this type of interaction between the two monarchs, it becomes evident that there are limits to the task of exploring completely the conditions of political decisions and actions emanating from the regimes these monarchs represented. Official records are part of this problem of limitation and restriction; they do not always tell the whole story. Even Bismarck was not entirely free from this resort to informal and conceivably surreptitious transmission of advice. In the summer of 1896, that is, six years after his retirement from office and amidst ongoing massacres against the Armenians, Bismarck in a private letter to the Sultan advised him to "not be afraid of England whose power is dissipated all over the world," and to "rely on Russia" in opposing the scheme of Armenian reforms as well as other similar projects. The wording of Bismarck's advice was: *Fermeté, pas se laisser intimider.*[21]

In fact, Bismarck, in one of his explanations on the value of communicating secret material, stressed the critical importance of using informal channels as a vehicle of communication; he dismissed official documents as material that is "nothing unusual." As he stated, "the most important [*das Wichtigste*] material consists of private letters and confidentially relayed verbal communications, which do not become part of archival documents."[22]

In April 1915, Wangenheim, the wartime German ambassador to Turkey, expressed himself in the same vein. In a report to German chancellor Bethmann Hollweg he admitted to "often" (*öfters*) using such an informal channel for conveying "material, the transmission of which by me, i.e., through the official avenue, is inappropriate." He was referring to Marine Attaché Hans Humann, a bosom friend of War Minister Enver, as the vehicle for unofficial communications. Wangenheim added that

Enver reciprocated by using the same method, through the same intermediary, and for the same purpose.[23] To return to the array of channels through which the German monarch is seen as an operator consorting with his Turkish counterpart, the account below may be regarded as characteristic. According to material gathered at the time by Russian intelligence (whose agents in the Ottoman capital were not only quite numerous but also were as successful in engaging the services of palace informers as those of England and France), Emperor William II's government: 1) allowed Abdul Hamit to send his secret service agents to Germany who, consorting with German authorities, helped suppress the news of Armenian massacres; 2) instructed its ambassadors in Russia, England, and France to collect information on Armenian nationalists in these countries. "The results of this investigation, contained in voluminous reports, were handed over to Abdul Hamit in Constantinople"; 3) ordered the German consuls, operating in the provinces of Turkey, "to acquaint Abdul Hamit with everything concerning the Armenians living in their districts"; and 4) authorized through a 1898 circular its ambassador in Turkey to exhort the German consuls throughout Turkey not to intercede on behalf of the Armenians; not to be concerned with the manner in which local authorities have been dealing with the Armenians; to prepare a complete list of Armenian merchants, artisans, etc., who live in their districts. Moreover, there were 32 German and Austrian agents who spied on Armenians in Turkey, reporting not only to Abdul Hamit but also to the German Embassy. Equally significant, Abdul Hamit invested huge amounts of money in subventions thereby indirectly, and sometimes directly, bribing several German newspapers, as well as their correspondents in Constantinople through separate monthly allotments ranging from 50 to 100 Turkish pounds.[24] As a rule, intelligence reports of this kind preclude verification. But the picture presented here, even if embellished, fits the overall picture relative to Sultan Abdul Hamit's proclivity to bribe foreign potentates, including editors and correspondents, to stifle adverse publicity against himself and his regime (see note 1). These are the salient features of the relationship between German state policy toward Ottoman Turkey, on the one hand and the exterminatory massacres punctuating the significance of that policy, on the other. It is worth noting in this connection that one of the vocal exponents of that policy, Naumann, saw fit to coin for the first time the term "Armenocide" (*Armeniermord*) to describe the intent and scope of these massacres,[25] thereby in a sense anticipating Raphael Lemkin who on his part coined the analogous term "genocide" in connection with the destruction of European Jews in World War II.

THE LEGAL PERSPECTIVE: THE BEARINGS OF INTERNATIONAL LAW

First to consider is the matter of the specificity and extent of the German involvement at issue here. The term "German" being a general designation, the charge of involvement has the overtones of a blanket accusation. As noted earlier, however, a host of German officials and functionaries are not only to be excluded from any onus of such involvement but also their genocide-resisting role performances call for depiction and emphasis. The introduction of this caveat is a moral imperative that should have its own place in the discussion on the legal ramifications of the problem under review here. Included in this category are the German consuls, vice consuls, gerents, consular agents, and even an ambassador, Count von Metternich, Generals von Lossow and Kressenstein, as well as Colonel Stange. These people often risked their positions, health, and even lives in their efforts to obviate, if not prevent, the carnages occurring in the interior of Turkey and subsequently in certain sectors of Russian Armenia that were occupied at the time by the Turkish army. They were not necessarily Armenophiles but decent and God-fearing servants of the German state who felt trapped in the vortex of a war generating conflicting emotions and loyalties. One of them, veteran Aleppo Consul Dr. Walter Rössler, was observed "weeping bitterly" (*bitterlich geweint*) in face of the inferno of unspeakable atrocities that were being enacted in and around his consular district, one of the epicenters of the Armenian holocaust.[26] These Germans deserve being called the intrepid paladins of outraged humanity.

The specter of that outraged humanity is still looming large in the horizon as the residual perpetrator camp persists, often with truculence, to deny the enormous crime. But a crime is first and foremost a grave violation of the law and the rules of law. It has, therefore, such legal implications as they are attached to the principle of criminal justice, as understood in the West. In the history of human relations the failure to address these legal implications had always had one single corrosive effect: undermining the efficacy of the rule of law and thereby contributing to the growth of systems of human relations in which criminal justice is rendered expendable and, therefore, dysfunctional. All current suggestions, contentions, and notions on the precedential impact of the Armenian genocide on the subsequent incidence of the Jewish Holocaust attest to the plausibility of this argument. The investigation of the problem of German involvement is necessarily an investigation into the problem of German complicity. As such it should not be confined to historical and political considerations but must include a framework of analysis that is predicated upon legal doctrines and principles with a focus on international law. The test of the complicity at issue here is related to the following question: Is there any violation of any international law in the wartime treatment of Ottoman Armenians for which there is credible evidence to inculpate any German official? Such evidence is adduced in the body of this study. There is, for example, the order of General Bronsart, the Chief of the Ottoman General Staff at Ottoman General Headquarters, in which two critical ingredients constitute a basis for the kind of liability that is nothing short of being a criminal liability. First of all he is declaring in it that "the deportation of the Armenian people (*Ermeni ahali*) has been decided (*mukarrerdir*)." This is not an order targeting a segment of the victim population but one encompassing the general Armenian population. Secondly, he is ordering the adoption of "severe measures" of security against clusters of disarmed and isolated Armenian soldiers, classified as labor battalions.[27] By any standard of probing, the question would naturally pose itself as to how totally disarmed and in general emaciated men could be regarded so dangerous as to require the application against them of "severe measures" of security. And then, of course, arises the concomitant question: Were they in fact secured? If so, how is it that tens of thousands of them disappeared without a trace? In the second part of this study, official German documentary evidence is introduced to demonstrate the outcome of the adoption of these "severe measures" of security against these disarmed Armenian labor battalions. In case after case, civilian and military Germans in these documents narrate how the victims in every instance were butchered wholesale in paroxysms of mass execution (see notes 37, 38, 39, 40 of Part II).

The order for general deportation, which comprises the first part of the cipher, has twin implications. One concerns the matter of liability from the vantage point of international law relative to the penal provision "crime against humanity." The other involves responsibility for the liability. Two prominent Turkish leaders, a wartime Grand Vizier and a Prime Minister of the post-war Turkish Republic, in their memoirs emphatically stated that German generals almost "categorically" insisted on the wholesale deportation of the Armenians and of these, Talât, the Grand Vizier, specifically identified General Bronsart as having taken the initiative in this regard (see notes 27, 28, 29, 30 in Part II). Of course, memoirs in and of themselves can hardly serve legal purposes as far as the criterion of probative evidence is concerned. But weighed in conjunction with the admissibility of an official document (the reference is to the Bronsart order described above) that has the character of evidence-in-chief, the relevant piece of information in a memoir acquires some corroborative value. That document, in the framing and issuance of which is lodged the burden of liability, is a principal legal ground for contending German complicity. It clearly indicates German involvement in the decision to "deport the Armenian people," as formulated in the cipher order. It is, therefore, necessary to examine the legality of that order with reference to the rules of international law. On October 18, 1907, the participants of the Fourth Hague Convention (Second Peace Conference) made the following declaration in that convention's preamble:

> Until a more complete code of the laws of war has been issued, the High Contracting Parties deem it expedient to declare that, in cases not included in the Regulations adopted by them, the inhabitants and the belligerent remain under the protection and the rule of the principles of the law of nations, as they result from the usages established among civilized peoples, from the laws of humanity, and the dictates of the public conscience.[28]

As Bassiouni pointed out, however, the juridical roots of the concept of "crimes against humanity" are to be found in the First Hague Convention of 1899 on the Laws and Customs of War where "humanity" is invoked as a general norm and where "the laws of humanity" and "the requirements of public conscience" are identified as a matrix of "the principles of international law."[29]

In January 1919, the Preliminary Peace Congress in Paris established the Commission on Responsibilities and Sanctions. Chaired by U.S. Secretary of State Lansing, its First Subcommission (also known as the Commission of Fifteen) examined, among other offenses, "barbarous and illegitimate methods of warfare." This included the category of "offenses against the laws and customs of war, and the principles of humanity," the adoption of which the French representative of the Third Subcommission, Larnaude, insisted was "absolutely" necessary to ensure human rights. The Commission of Fifteen proceeded in its investigation according to the terms of the Fourth Hague Convention. This convention, part of the 1907 Second Peace Conference, was intended to give "a fresh development to the humanitarian principles [toward] evolving a lofty conception of the common welfare of humanity."[30]

A March 5, 1919 report by the commission specified the following violations against civilian populations: systematic terror; murders and massacres; dishonoring of women; confiscation of private property; pillage; seizing of goods belonging to communities, educational establishments, and charities; arbitrary destruction of public and private goods;

deportation and forced labor; execution of civilians under false allegations of war crimes; and violations against civilians as well as military personnel. The commission's final report dated March 29, 1919 spoke of "the clear dictates of humanity" that were abused "by the Central Empires together with their allies," including Turkey, "by barbarous or illegitimate methods in violation of … the elementary laws of humanity."[31] The report concluded that "all persons belonging to enemy countries … who have been guilty of offenses against the laws and customs of war or the laws of humanity, are liable to criminal prosecution."[32] Prompted by the Belgian jurist Rolin Jaequemeyns, the commission included the crimes perpetrated against Turkey's Armenian citizens.[33] Moreover, when a Committee of Jurists in 1920 was commissioned by the Council of the League of Nations to prepare the Statute of Permanent Court of International Justice, the issues of humanity and civilization surfaced again. Baron Descamps of Belgium, the Chairman, injected into the concept of international law not only such rules as were "recognized by the civilized nations but also by the demands of public conscience [and] the dictates of the legal conscience of civilized nations." After much debate, the committee adopted his revised version, the third point of which referred to "the general principles of law recognized by civilized nations."[34] If one disregards all other offenses associated with the wartime treatment of the Armenians and focuses on the earlier discussion, *the official order to deport them en masse* emerges as a major violation against "the dictates of the legal conscience of civilized nations," in other words, it constitutes a "crime against humanity."

A parallel instance of German complicity is evident in the case of another German officer, Lieutenant Colonel Boettrich, who, like General Bronsart, was on duty at Ottoman General Headquarters in his capacity as Chief of Railroad Services. He too is on record as having issued an order for the deportation of a specific category of victims, namely, Armenian workers, engineers, and technical and administrative personnel engaged in the massive construction of the Baghdad Railway tracks and tunnels. He not only issued the order but also, to the dismay of German Foreign Minister von Jagow, affixed his signature to it. As in the case of victims of general deportation and of the "severe measures" applied against Armenian labor battalions, very few of these railway workers and employees survived the annihilative thrust of the order, disguised as an order for "deportation" (see Part II, the section on Boettrich).

As stated earlier, there are dual channels through which complicity in a crime is legally taken to task. The above discussion addressed one of them: responsibility. German involvement in the decision and initiative to deport the bulk of the Armenian population of the Ottoman Empire is a condition that warrants the assertion of German coresponsibility. The other concerns the matter of specific liability through which the elements of inculpation are identified, explained, and assessed. The two German officers in the Ottoman General Headquarters who are known to have issued deportation orders had an official capacity. They were members of the German Military Mission to Turkey. In the field of interstate relationships, regulated by treaties and subsidiary contracts, the liability for the misdeeds of a given official, representing one of the signatories of the treaties or one of the parties to contract, devolves upon the respective state or party, especially if the misdeed is committed in the name of one of these bodies represented by the offending functionary. The Turko-German political and military alliance was secretly signed on August 2, 1914. The contract, spelling out the terms of the function of the German Military Mission to Turkey, on the other hand, was signed on November 27, 1913 and ratified by the Ottoman government. It was Emperor William II who created, authorized, and instructed the original contingent of the high-ranking Prussian officers comprising the German Military Mission to Turkey of which both Bronsart and Boettrich were members. It was he who gave the final and decisive order to proceed with the formation of the Turko-German military and political alliance, overruling his subalterns, including Ambassador Wangenheim, who had serious doubts about the treaty's utility for Germany.

It should be parenthetically noted in this connection that Marshal Goltz, whose involvement in the decision to deport the Armenian population is acknowledged by Turkish authorities, was a favorite of the emperor. When considering candidates for the post of Reich's chancellor, which in 1909 had become vacant as a result of the resignation of Prince von Bülow, Emperor William II's first choice was Prussian General Goltz. The emperor was the supreme embodiment of the wartime authority of the German state—in a dual sense, that is, civilian and military. Generals Goltz and Bronsart, Marine Attaché Humann and Ambassador Wangenheim, who one way or another contributed to the demise of the Armenian population, were all his subordinates and as such were authorized by him to serve as the officials of German state. (Part II will have details on this).

Returning to the issue of liability relative to the deportation orders of Bronsart and Boettrich, the two German officers serving in the Ottoman General Headquarters, there is one more point needing clarification. In defense of these orders, particularly in defense of the resort to deportation as distinct from an order for massacre, the argument may be advanced that the problem of responsibility should be assessed strictly with reference to an order for deportation and not to the massacres that resulted. The idea here is that the authorities issuing the orders cannot be held responsible for the misdeeds of those authorities who were entrusted with the task of organizing the details of the implementation; in other words, they are not responsible for what the Turks did in the course of executing the orders.

This argument is seriously flawed and is, therefore, untenable, even if one should grant the underlying contention that deportation can be a justifiable wartime measure and as such should not be confounded with massacre, which is mass murder. The argument is untenable for the following reason. The two orders in question bear the dates of July 25, 1915 (Bronsart) and October 3, 1915 (Boettrich). These dates comprise timeframes that were antedated by episodes involving a whole series of foregone massacres—massacres to which deportee convoy after deportee convoy fell victim. What is more, German officials in the Ottoman capital, whether serving in the embassy or the Ottoman High Command, were fully informed about them. In Part II this point has been discussed in some detail in the sections dealing with Bronsart, Marine Attaché Humann, Admirals von Usedom and Souchon, and Ambassador Wangenheim. In other words, by July 25, 1915, not to speak of October 3, 1915, the German military and civilian officials in Istanbul were aware that under the pretense of wartime deportations "the Armenian nation [was being] cruelly destroyed (*die grausame Vernichtung der armenischen Nation*) by the Young Turk government whose barbaric [methods] were such as to outrage to the highest degree all human feelings (*eine barbarische alle menschlichen Gefühle aufs höchste empörende Aktion*).[35] This is the statement of Vice Marshal Joseph Pomiankowski, Austrian Plenipotentiary and Military Attaché, who throughout the war was attached to the Ottoman General Headquarters and was in close contact with War Minister Enver.[36] In prefacing his order with words "The deportation of the Armenian people has been decided," General Bronsart was not only confirming a fact, which was then still unfolding, but also registering his approbation of the very decision associated with that fact.

The German state archives in Bonn are replete with documents clearly demonstrating the fact that at the time Bronsart issued his order the German Embassy was in receipt of a large number of reports sent by German consuls from the interior of Turkey detailing the specifics of the process of destruction. Here are some examples. On June 17, 1915, Ambassador Wangenheim informed Berlin that the Armenians from Diyarbakir who were supposed to be deported to Mosul "were en route all slaughtered."[37] On June 29 he told Berlin that "The deportees are being suddenly set upon and butchered."[38] On July 7, he again reported that "the manner in which the matter of relocation [through deportation] is being handled demonstrates that the government is in fact pursuing the goal of annihilating the Armenian race in Turkey (*die armenische Rasse zu vernichten*).[39] On July 9, he further reported that "The massacres are being carried out by convicts" (*entlassene Sträflinge*).[40] On July 12, he wrote, "The Armenians of the convoy from Mardin were let be slaughtered just like sheep" (*wie Hammel schlachten lassen*).[41] On July 16, he informed again Berlin that "By its policy of deportation and relocation the Turkish government is delivering up the Armenians to [the clutches of] a policy of annihilation (*Vernichtung*)."[42] The litany of the dispatching of these series of reports continued unabated throughout 1915 and up to the end of 1916 when the genocide all but ran its course.

In other words, there were sufficient grounds to contend that the German officers had foreknowledge of the process of annihilation for which deportations were being used as a vehicle. They were, therefore, obligated to refrain from issuing new orders for deportation and by the same principle of constraint they were to try, within the purview of the means at their disposal, to disallow the continuation of the deportations. International bodies, empowered to deal with the juridical aspects of this problem, have consistently maintained—as described earlier—that the absence of universal penal codes at that time was a problem of mere technicality and that there were prevailing rules of international law that were binding; these rules proscribed wholesale deportations, not to speak of other related lethal offenses, and prescribed strict adherence to "the laws of humanity and the dictates of public conscience." Even the Turkish Military Tribunal in its Key Verdict against the principal authors of the Armenian genocide upheld this prescription. In explaining the reasons for that verdict it declared, "… even after news was received of the atrocities, no steps were taken to prevent their repetition … " let alone allow their continuation.[43] The view of Dr. Otto Göppert, the legal councillor in the German Foreign Office, pertaining to this point may be adduced here. Referring to the surge of assertions in the aftermath of the war that German officers were culpable for advising the Turks with respect to the latter's scheme of deportation, Dr. Göppert expressed a measure of anxiety that bordered on apprehension. He declared, "This is a grave incrimination from which we must free ourselves for reasons that are also financial. Otherwise, we will be held liable for damages" (… *eine schwere Belastung … man will uns für den Schaden haftbar machen*)."[44] It is equally significant that Dr. Axenfeld, Göppert's correspondent in this exchange, conceded that insofar as the deportations were founded on military grounds, the belief on the German involvement was "justified; the deportations could not have been carried out without the knowledge of German officers serving in Turkey" (*nicht ohne Wissen der deutschen Offiziere in der Türkei ins Werk gesetzt sein …*).[45]

GENERAL BRONSART'S FOREKNOWLEDGE OF MASSACRES WHEN ORDERING DEPORTATIONS

This raises the question of the validity of the presumption, or belief, that the German military officers, General Bronsart in particular, did have the foreknowledge about the real purpose and outcome of the deportations as reported by the various German consuls. It develops that Ambassador Wangenheim often relayed these reports to the Ottoman General Headquarters for the attention of General Bronsart. In one particular case where a German vice consul had requested permission from Wangenheim to intervene on behalf of the Armenians, who were slated to be deported en masse, Bronsart is on record as not only rejecting the request but also scolding the consul for wanting to help the Armenians. The consul involved was Dr. Max Erwin von Scheubner Richter. In a comprehensive May 20, 1915 report the vice consul had emphasized that the targeted victim population consisted almost exclusively of women and children and as in pitiful condition. He had gone to the spot where they were assembled for the perilous deportation trek. "The misery, despair, and bitterness are great. The women threw themselves and their children in front of my horse, begging for help. The sight of wailing people was pitiful and painful. But even more painful was the feeling of not being able to help" (*Elend, Verzweiflung und Erbitterung sind gross. Die Frauen warfen sich und ihre Kinder vor mein Pferd und baten um Hilfe. Der Anblick dieser jammernden Armen war mitleiderregend und peinlich—noch peinlicher aber war für mich das Gefühl nicht helfen zu können*).[46] Scheubner had also arranged for distribution of bread among the deportees who had received no food and had used the wagons of the consulate for the transport of that bread. Bronsart objected against even this help. Among the handwritten notes he appended to Scheubner's report is this retort, "The consul would do better sending the bread to the Turkish army" (*Das Brot sollte der Konsul lieber der türkischen Armee schicken.*)[47]

Far more significant is another aspect of General Bronsart's campaign against the Armenians. Despite overwhelming evidence that the bulk of the able-bodied Armenian population was conscripted and that there was no possibility of a revolt in Erzurum, for example, the general persisted in arguing in terms of "military necessity" when demanding the expulsion of these multitudes of women, children, and old men. In his report Scheubner had pointed out this fact, indicating that the Armenian male population between the ages of seventeen and forty-eight was in the labor battalions or had already been killed off (*oder bereits umgebracht worden*). He, therefore, went out of his way to impress upon his superior, Ambassador Wangenheim, that there was absolutely no basis to be concerned about any possibility of a rebellion in this district by a defenseless and inoffensive population. On May 16, 1915, he reported to the ambassador, for example, that "There is no possibility of a revolt by the local Armenians … their deportation is groundless" (*Ein Aufstand der hiesigen Armenier nicht zu erwarten … Deportation ist unbegründet*).[48] On June 2, he again stated that there was no reason to reckon with a revolt by the local Armenians.[49] In his very extensive August 5, 1915 report, Scheubner categorically declared, "In my view, there are no proofs whatsoever for a general and set Armenian rebellion" (*Für einen allgemein beabsichtigten und vorbereiteten Aufstand der Armenier fehlen jedoch meines Erachtens jegliche Beweise*).[50]

It should be noted here parenthetically that Scheubner not only incurred the displeasure of General Bronsart in Istanbul for his efforts to mitigate the suffering of the Armenians of his district but also risked his life in that district as a result of his confrontation with General Mahmud Kâmil, the Commander-in-Chief of the Ottoman IIIrd Army, with headquarters in Tortum, near Erzurum. According to the account of Scheubner's adjutant, Scheubner during his meeting with the Turkish commander ridiculed the argument of "military necessity"; he "sneered bitterly" (*lächelt bitter*) at the assertion. How could the general excuse the expulsion of old men, children, and women on grounds of military necessity? The general showed impatience and the meeting ended. In a subsequent meeting with the governor-general of the province of Erzurum, Tahsin, Scheubner is forewarned. Unless he changed his attitude in the matter of Armenian deportations, he, the governor, "cannot guarantee your safety here," in Erzurum. To deal with any eventuality in this respect Scheubner equipped himself with a revolver, which was "ready to fire" (*schussfertig*).[51] This is exactly the illustration of the type of intrepid German consul to whom allusion was made at the start of the section on the Legal Perspective (note 26.) In his August 5, 1915 report, Scheubner made an explicit reference to his willingness to take risks in face of "dangers" (*Gefahren*) that his interventions on behalf of the Armenians entailed. He added that he was assuming that this line of behavior, as long as it was lawful, would place his government on record on account of its goal to secure a "humane and just treatment for the suffering of innocent people."[52]

Bronsart's evident resolve to back up under all circumstances the Turkish leaders in their lethal design against the Armenians assumed a degree of truculence through which he continued to denounce the Armenians in terms that were twisted and perverse. This condition prompted the Swiss author Dinkel to emphasize "the completely false and distorted" picture Bronsart was painting (*vollständig falsches und verzerrtes Bild*) about the Armenians and which condition Dinkel attributed to the general's "outrageous cynicism" (*mit unerhörtem Zynismus*).[53] The ostensible rationale for the display of this type of truculence and enmity against the Armenians was what Dinkel calls "hysteria about rebellion"[54] (*Aufstandshysterie*), which at that time had gripped the officers of the German Military Mission. It is, therefore, appropriate, and even necessary, to examine the circumstances surrounding this "hysteria" in order to adjudge its relationship to German motivation for acts that were clearly incriminatory.

THE ARGUMENT OF ARMENIAN PROVOCATION THROUGH REBELLION

A careful dissection of available documentary material clearly indicates that the targeted victim population was subjected to a steady stream of incremental provocations. Evidently, the plan was to elicit from some members of that population violent reactions that were intended to serve as a basis for charges of rebellion through the mechanisms of embellishment and the issuance of reports inflating the incident. The tactic worked in some instances, and the requisite reports were dispatched to the central government. Vice Consul Scheubner in his May 15 report cites such "isolated" instances as "armed resistance to requisitions in remote villages" and "murder of Turks who demand the delivery of girls and women." He added that there was a pattern of mistreatment of the Armenians by the Turks; "Your Excellency knows well that the Turks constantly made mistakes in the handling of the Armenian question" (... *von türkischer Seite in der Behandlung der Armenierfrage andauernd Fehler germacht worden sind*). It is most significant that in the same report

Scheubner points to the fact that as far as he could determine all house searches in Erzurum ended without finding any "incriminating evidence" against the Armenians.[55] He repeated this assertion on June 2; "In Erzurum and the environs no bombs or anything like bombs could be found and the governor-general has confirmed this fact."[56] In his August 5, 1915 report, Scheubner provides more details about governmentally staged provocations against the Armenians. He declared, the government "threw the gauntlet to a portion of a rightly discontented people by the provocative conduct of its police agencies and the brigands (*çetes*), a conduct capable of unleashing an uprising" (*eine Erhebung ... durch das provokatorische Verhalten ihrer Polizeiorgane und 'Tschättäh' geradezu herausfordert*).[57] Scheubner's December 4, 1916 report, his last, is a summary of all his experiences from which he distills some key judgments about the hidden aspects of the Armenian genocide. The report is addressed to German chancellor Bethmann Hollweg. In a preparatory statement Scheubner explains that he had ample opportunity personally to experience, observe, and learn through "a series of conversations with competent (*massgebend*) Turkish personages" the underlying motives of the Ittihadist Young Turks relative to their exterminatory massacres and other methods of extirpation. He was given to understand that the majority of the Young Turk Ittihadists want to rectify a great mistake of their ancestors. Turkey a long time ago should have been purged of its non-Muslim population either through forcible conversion and Turkification or, failing in this method, through annihilation. The present time is deemed the most propitious to carry out this plan. The first stage of this plan calls for "the finishing off of the Armenians" (*die Erledigung der Armenier*). And here comes the most relevant and significant part as it reveals the depth of Turkish charades and deceptions to justify their crime of genocide. "To those Powers allied with Turkey there will be put forth the excuse of an alleged revolution prepared by the Dashnak party (*eine angeblich vorbereitete Revolution ... vorgeschützt*). Moreover, local disturbances and attempts at self-defense by the Armenians will be embellished and used as a pretext to show just cause for the compulsory transfer of the Armenians from the frontier regions that are threatened (*... Selbstschutzbestrebungen der Armenier wurden ... aufgebauscht und zum Vorwand genommen*). Once en route, the Armenians would be set upon and murdered by Kurdish and Turkish brigands and, at certain spots, by gendarmes also—at the instigation of the Young Turk Ittihadist party" (*Unterwegs wurden die Armenier auf Anstifung des Komitees von kurdischen und türkischen Banden, stellenweise auch von Gendarmen, ermordet*).[58] As if to document the application of an aspect of this sinister scheme Scheubner in the same extensive report recounts an episode from his personal experience. On his way to an insurrectionary undertaking in Persia he and the other cocommandant of the Expeditionary Force, Ömer Naci, a prominent Ittihadist orator and leader, received an order from the VIth Army High Command to storm an Armenian village "in which allegedly rebel Armenians had fortified themselves, and to punish them. I learned in a timely fashion that 'the rebels' were people who from fear of a massacre had entrenched themselves and gladly were prepared to surrender their arms against assurance that their lives would be spared."[59] There are numerous other reports of similar content sent by German consuls who were stationed in the interior of Turkey. But the adducing of another significant testimony may be in order. It originates from Richard Kühlmann, who served in Turkey first as a councillor in the embassy and then as an ambassador before he was promoted to become Foreign Minister of Germany (August 6, 1917–July 16, 1918). In a November 17, 1916 report to Berlin, he berated the Turks for their manufacturing of pretexts in order to justify their deportation of the Armenians. The Turkish authorities had claimed that they discovered bombs in the Armenian cemetery of Smyrna (Izmir). Kühlmann retorted, "The pretext for deportations (*Der Vorwand der Verschickungen*) belongs to the already well-known inventory of the Turkish authorities relative to such pretexts" (*gehört zu dem schon bekannten Inventar der türkischen Behörden an solchen Vorwänden*).[60] These official German documents are confirmed and corroborated by countless pieces of unofficial testimonies emanating from Armenian and non-Armenian eyewitnesses. The few examples below illustrate the range of ploys the Turkish authorities resorted to incriminate falsely their Armenian subjects and thereby also incite the rest of the population, including many unsuspecting officials.

In a report to the Armenian Patriarch on October 13, 1914, the Primate of Bitlis despairs of the manner in which "individually committed insignificant acts" are being exploited. The governor is "cynically" misconstruing them as proof of "general Armenian disloyalty." On November 8, 1914, the Primate of Muş informed the Patriarch that "The times are pregnant with danger. The people are prepared to suffer any kind of privation in exchange for security of life. But the government, which is the source of all the turmoil and evil, is inciting the dark forces and arming them against the Armenians." Another communication from Sıvas, also in the IIIrd Army zone, let the Patriarch know that "In the months of February and March 1915, the government ordered the surrender of all arms, maintaining that it needed them. While those delivered by the

Armenians, (mostly nonprohibited arms) were retained, those delivered by the Turks were handed back to them. The government put on top of these arms a thin layer of its own weapons and had the pile displayed publicly and photographed for the dual purpose of inciting the Turks against the Armenians and of apprising the authorities in Istanbul of an imminent Armenian insurgency."[61] In this connection it is significant to note that a Venezuelan officer, engaged by the IIIrd Army, described in almost identical language another such deception. After completing the massacre of 1300–1500 Armenian labor battalion soldiers, the commander of a gendarmery regiment, "the enactor of the massacre, courteous and cultured … this gentleman overwhelmed me with attentions; and offered me two photographs, showing him and his secretaries aligned behind a stack of arms, which, so Mehmed-Asim [the Commander] pretended, had been found hidden in the houses and even the churches of the Armenians. However, a close contemplation of those interesting photographs revealed plainly that the park therein represented was composed almost entirely of fowling-pieces easily disguised by a thin layer of army guns. I fear very much therefore that all this ostentatious collection [was intended] to mislead and impress the public."[62]

These are some of the devices used to create the requisite environment in which the Armenians could be defined as the internal foe capable of sabotaging the Turkish war effort and altogether representing a threat to the survival of Turkey. The ensuing "hysteria" was but a natural consequence. However, the event that actually catalyzed this development and gave substance to the evolving hysteria was the Van uprising. It was the main animus of the Turkish propaganda campaign through which a whole series of agitations and incitements were launched against the Armenians. The complicitous behavior of the high-ranking German military officers involved is intimately connected with this campaign, which helped pave the ground for the initiation of anti-Armenian measures under the plea of "military necessity"; these measures acquired a semblance of legitimacy and as such were considered affordable and warranted. The Van uprising calls, therefore, for special attention and review.

THE PURPOSIVE MISPORTRAYAL OF THE VAN UPRISING

Some preliminary comments

Of all the German officers serving in the Turkish army in World War I, Dr. Felix Guse, with the rank of lieutenant colonel, was closest to the scenes through which the drama of Armenian deportations and massacres unfolded. From the very start of the General Mobilization (early August 1914), he held the post of Chief of Staff at the headquarters of the Ottoman IIIrd Army. That army's command-and-control zone encompassed those six provinces that contained the greatest concentration of the Ottoman Armenian population and as such throughout modern history had been the centerpiece of the Turko-Armenian conflict in terms of reforms prescribed by treaties but for reasons of state repelled and brushed off by successive Ottoman governments. These provinces were Erzurum, Van, Bitlis, Harput, Diyarbekir, and Sıvas; due to wartime exigencies the province of Trabzon was added to this zone controlled by the IIIrd Army. One of the chief characteristics of the Armenian genocide was the pronounced ferocity with which the victim populations of these provinces were exterminated and destroyed, precisely for the reason described earlier. The killer bands of the Special Organization, consisting mostly of carefully selected convicts adept at bloodthirsty savagery (Turks called them *kanlı katil*),[63] primarily operated in these provinces. In other words, Lieutenant Colonel Guse served in the very epicenter of the Armenian cataclysm.

Three specific facts underscore the critical role Guse played in the vilification of the victim population and the consequent destruction of that population. First of all he vowed that he considered General Bronsart his model (*Vorbild*).[64] He admired him and readily adopted his orientation in the Armenian Question. His decrials of the Armenians as fiendish enemies of Turkey parallel and reflect Bronsart's analogous denunciations. Second, he boasted in his book of the fact that, except for personal and political matters, "all important things passed through my hands" (*alles Wichtige durch meine Hand gegangen*).[65] This is confirmed by Marshal Liman von Sanders, the chief of German Military Mission to Turkey. In his memoirs he states that Guse "was the moving spirit at headquarters"[66] of the IIIrd Army (*die Seele des Oberkommandos* in its original German). The Venezuelan officer Rafael de Nogales who had volunteered to serve in the Turkish army under the tutelage of Bronsart, in his account of the conditions in the headquarters, declared that Guse was allowed "to do things and undo them as he pleased"[67] (*Liess ... schalten und walten*).[68] Third, and most important, it was Guse who first initiated the process of besieging Bronsart, the Chief of Staff in the Ottoman High Command, with reports of Armenian seditiousness, sabotage acts, and rebellion. There is no denial that isolated acts of sabotage and espionage were committed by individuals or groups of Armenians. As Vice Consul and Reserve Captain Scheubner gave his ambassador in Istanbul to understand, such acts, "however deplorable, are to me natural occurrences in those theaters of war which involve border regions containing a population that is oppressed and mistreated by its own government and is, therefore, a disaffected, alienated population ... Such acts occurred in other theaters of war" (*von ihrer eigenen Regierung unterdrückte und schlecht behandelte ... erscheint mir, wenn auch bedauerlich, so doch natürlich und ist auch auf anderen Kriegsschauplätzen vorgekommen*).[69]

Notwithstanding, with a vehemence inconsistent with the stature of a German doctor of jurisprudence and staff officer, Guse lashed out against the Armenians in general as if they were the arch enemies of Germany, which to defend was his supreme duty. He categorically declared that involved in the Van episode was nothing less than "an open revolt"; he insisted "the Armenians have begun the fight with their insurrections" in Van (*Die Armenier haben mit ihrem Aufstand den Kampf angefangen ...*). He further asserted that "the uprising was not the result of a sudden reaction to arrests but rather a carefully prepared undertaking."[70] And how did he arrive at this conclusion? His relevant statement not only provides a clue in this regard but also confirms Scheubner's revelation observed earlier. His Young Turk Ittihadists contacts, "competent Turkish personages," had disclosed to Scheubner that in order to dupe the German ally the Ittihadist power-wielders would broadcast a disinformation about an "impending Dashnak revolt in Turkey." To forestall and preempt this alleged rebellion the Ottoman authorities would have to order the wholesale deportation of the Armenians only to subsequently entrap them en route and exterminate them through massacres organized by the Ittihad party leadership (see note 58 above). This duplicitous ploy, intended to fool not only the outside world in general but also Turkey's most faithful ally, Germany and its governmental hierarchy, was blindly and naively accepted by Guse, in contradiction to the skepticism of many other German civilian and military officials. Like his "model" Bronsart, Guse most likely wanted to believe the products of what Lepsius called "the Turkish factory of lies" (*Lügenfabrik*). He unequivocally and emphatically declared that "the uprising was planned" in connection with the 8th quadrennial Congress of the Dashnak party that had convened in Erzurum in the July 10/23–July 23/August 2, 1914 period. The analysis of the proceedings of this party congress is outside the confines of this study. The only way to test and expose within the framework of this study the falsehood of this irresponsible assertion is through the presentation, based on documents and non-Armenian eyewitness accounts, of the real conditions surrounding the outbreak of the Van uprising.

The documentary evidence of the outbreak of Van uprising

The province of Van had the highest percentage of Armenians compared with other provinces, with the city of Van equaling, or even exceeding, the Turkish population. It was also a border province of the northeastern frontier facing Russian Transcaucasia and Persia. The uprising occurred in the period of April 20–May 17, 1915 (n.s.). The most detailed foreign account is in the volume called *The Tragedy of Bitlis.* Two thirds of it comprises the eyewitness accounts of American nurses Grisell M. McLaren and Myrtle O. Shane, whose description of the Turkish plan of wholesale slaughter, prompting the uprising, is as follows: "On April 19, 1915, a general massacre of the Armenians was planned ... soldiers and Kurds, in some instances taking cannon with them, attacked the smaller towns and villages of the province and met with little resistance because most of the able-bodied men had been drafted into the Sultan's army and those who were left had very little ammunition. Fifty-five thousand men, women and children were slaughtered ... ."[71] Another American, and likewise an eyewitness, offers the following comment. "We have absolute proof that fifty-five thousand people were killed .... There was only one hope for the city; the coming of the Russians—the coming of Russians in time." Dr. Ussher, the eyewitness in question, was a resident physician in the American hospital at Van and conducted negotiations with the provincial governor. The Armenian resistance was on the verge of collapse due to acute shortage of food and ammunition and to decimation when the Russians arrived.[72] The April 20, 1915 entry of Dr. Ussher's wife's diary reads as follows: "The Turks began the struggle by attacking an orphan girl who with several village women was trying to escape to the German premises. The revolutionists fired to protect her and the war was on. This occurred in front of the gate of the German compound; so many were eyewitnesses that the trouble was initiated by the Turks. Although the *vali* (governor) calls it a rebellion, it is really an effort to protect the lives and the homes of the Armenians." After excerpting this entry and using it in his book, another author goes on to state, "But in the defenseless villages the story is very different. There the tragedy is too awful to be described. It is nothing but systematic and wholesale massacre. It is now evident that there was a well-laid plan to wipe out all the villages, and then crush the city rebels."[73] A nurse of the German Mission at Van, Kathe Ehrhold, confirms in almost identical words the precipitation of the Van uprising through this incident. "It happened of all places in front of the windows of our orphanage."[74]

There are several other foreign accounts, including those from other German nurses and the Swiss director of an Armenian orphanage, Spörri. The missionary nature of their work in Van may be viewed by some as grounds for pro-Armenian bias. These doubts are roundly dispelled, however, by the testimony of two officers, one of them attached to the Turkish War Office and the other to the field units. Austrian Vice Field Marshal Pomiankowski described the Van uprising, for example, as an act of "desperation (*Verzweiflung*) on the part of the Armenians who saw that the general slaughter had begun," for which eventuality they were prepared.[75] For his part Erzurum's Vice Consul Scheubner underscored the series of provocations on the part of the Turkish authorities involving especially severe methods of requisitions, the arrest and murder (*Verhaftung und Ermordung*) of notables, including the trapping and murder of Ottoman Deputy Vramian and political leader Ishkhan.[76] The detailed and massive testimony of the above-mentioned Turkish-speaking Venezuelan officer, enrolled in the Turkish army, is perhaps the most pertinent and telling. At Van, he directed the artillery fire against the 500–600 Armenians fighting behind makeshift barricades. According to his own admission, he had launched 16,000 bombshells upon them. His testimony, a rare firsthand account from the Turkish side, is unequivocal. His Turkish aides had averred that on "April 21 the Armenians had attacked the town. … [but], Judge of my amazement to discover that the aggressors had not been the Armenians, after all but the authorities themselves … . The *Belediye reisi* (mayor) who was directing the orgy … astounded me by replying that he was doing nothing more than carrying out an unequivocal order emanating from the governor of the province … to exterminate all Armenian males of twelve years of age and over."[77] De Nogales praised "the heroic city of Van … the intrepidity of its [Armenian] defenders … their invention of a sort of auger" and conceded that "I have rarely seen such furious fighting as took place at Van, it was an uninterrupted combat, sometimes hand to hand or with only a wall between. Nobody gave quarter or asked it … . The Armenians fought with a courage undreamt of by our Circassians … . The resistance of the Armenians was terrific, and their valor worthy of all praise."[78] Yet he berated the Armenians for their strictly defensive posture. "If 30,000 or 40,000 Armenians shut up in Van...had undertaken the offensive, and arming themselves with cudgels if nothing better were available, and axes, and knives, had attempted a sally en masse, who knows if they might not have crushed us at length and perhaps even have obliged us to retire to the province of Bitlis. This would have cut off the retreat of our expeditionary army in Persia and have saved the lives of thousands of their own brethren who were perishing daily in neighboring towns and throughout the vilayet of Van … ." Speaking of a similar mistake at Muş, he again criticized the Armenians as mere defenders: "There the Armenians committed their usual strategic error, entrenching themselves in the principal buildings and in the churches, which naturally the Ottoman artillery speedily reduced to ruins."[79]

These comments aptly testify to the strictly defensive nature of the Van uprising, which was precipitated by the perfidious manner in which two prominent leaders of the Armenian community were trapped and murdered. One of them was Vramian, who, as noted earlier, was a member of the Ottoman Parliament, was trying to placate the authorities in order to reduce tensions arising from the excesses of the police, security forces, and Special Organization units harassing and persecuting the Armenians. He had sent several detailed reports to Interior Minister Talât,[80] pleading with him to intervene and restrain the local authorities. He received no reply; instead, he was invited to the governor's office under the pretense of consultation, was arrested, despite the immunity he possessed as a deputy of the Chamber of Deputies, and was subsequently murdered. The macabre details of atrocities in Van involving "splitting the head of the victim with a *yataghan*, or leaving him stretched on the ground with his throat cut … that bacchanal of barbarity" are graphically described by Nogales, the only military who directed the Turkish artillery against the Armenians but who was a Christian. Calling Governor Cevdet (who was in charge of the overall military operations) "a panther in human form," he related how, when infuriated at "the ferocious Armenian resistance, he ordered the massacre of all the remaining Armenians of the surrounding villages," namely, "only women and children." Their execution was carried out by Major Ahmed with such enthusiasm that "the very Kurds were appalled by his fiendishness."[81]

Nor are Turkish documents lacking to verify the thrust of all these foreign, including German, accounts and testimonies regarding the nature and source of the provocations triggering the Van uprising and the purely defensive and almost desperate character of that uprising.

A Turkish wartime and official document from Van clearly recognizes the destructive Turkish provocations as the cause of despondent Armenian resistance to them. In a May 11, 1915 telegram, Erzurum's governor-general Tahsin (governor of Van until October 1914) responded bitterly to a May 10 communication from Talât, asserting that the Van rebellion had occurred because his advice was not heeded.

> Instead of dealing with the Armenians while the war is going on, and for the good of our army and our country, I believe ... it is better to leave them alone and not force them to rebel (*ihtilâle sevk etmemeyi*) ... We have before us the example of Van (*Işte Van gözümüz önündedir*) ... At the time when the assurance was given that the 33rd Division could be safely withdrawn from Van, I did not see the slightest possibility of an uprising by the Armenians and I took upon myself the responsibility for this decision. That decision merited me your most violent criticism ... We have forcibly created the inextricable situation in which we find ourselves (*Vanda ihtilâl olmazdı ve olamazdı. Kendimiz zorlaya zorlaya şu içinden çıkamadığımız kargaşalığı meydana getirdik ve şarkdan orduyu müşkül mevkiye sokduk*).[82]

This candid admission by a Turkish provincial governor is poignantly substantiated by the equally important admission of Ibrahim Arvas, a Turkish deputy from Van in the Ottoman parliament. In his postwar personal eyewitness account of events in Van, he conceded that "Ittihad was underhandedly instigating the [Turkish] people, prodding them to hurl themselves upon the Armenians" (*el altından halkı tahrik ederek Ermenilere saldırtmış*).[83]

THE KEY SUPPORT ROLE OF A GERMAN CHIEF OF STAFF IN THE INITIATION OF THE ARMENIAN GENOCIDE

In order to obtain optimal results potential perpetrators must have propensities as well as proclivities for conspiracy; their capacity for secrecy must be matched by a corollary gift for cunning and scheming. The discussion in the last two sections above contained some pertinent illustrations in this respect but it lacked a frame of reference in which these examples might be seen as the component elements of a broad conspiracy. Scheubner's December 4, 1916 comprehensive report clearly pointed out some of the elements of this conspiracy (see note 58 above). The discussion below intends to focus on the Ittihadist leaders as the architects of this conspiracy. Before doing so, however, it is appropriate to explore briefly the supportive role certain German civilian and particularly military officers, who were successfully coopted by these leaders, played. Having been virtually reduced to actual props these Germans emerge here as the abettors of the Turks in the realization of that conspiracy.

Be it Ambassador Wangenheim, General Bronsart, or Navy Attaché and Lieutenant-Commander of the Navy, Humann, they all automatically and rather willingly embraced Turkish assertions that the Armenians were plotting and rebelling and that the Armenians were also mercilessly massacring the Muslim population of the regions in question. The Van episode furnished in this regard the needed rationale as well as the excuse to launch draconian measures against the Armenians.

The role of the IIIrd Army High Command — Its German Chief of Staff

With an abandon bordering on recklessness, Colonel Felix Guse, IIIrd Army's German Chief of Staff (see notes 70–74 above), lambasted the Armenians as a people deserving the "punishment" meted out to them by the Turks. He categorically declared, for instance, that what the Turks did to the Armenians was nothing but a "retaliation" (*Ebenso haben die Türken geantwortet*).[84] As indicated earlier, Guse as Chief of Staff of the IIIrd Army was a key player in the campaign to denounce the Armenians as traitors and to revile them. The logical and inescapable consequence of this campaign was the overall identification of the Armenians as "the internal foe." Like in the case of his "role model," General Bronsart, Guse's assessment of the Armenians was shaped by his preexisting negative images of them; he unhesitatingly typecasted them as lowly creatures.[85] He described them as a population harboring "a dangerous mentality" (*eine gefährliche Gesinnung*); this characterization was made in connection with the preparations of the Ottoman IIIrd Army to wage war against Russia in October 1914.[86] His anticipation in this respect was of a kind that had the requisite dynamics to precipitate the fruition of that very anticipation; it had the quality of a prophecy that, through resort to preemptive measures, could be rendered a self-fulfilling prophecy. The designation of the Armenians residing in the command-and-control zone of the IIIrd Army as a dangerous internal foe was the defining moment of the World War I Armenian genocide. It was the alpha and omega of the plea of "military necessity" put forth by the High Command of the Turkish army. It was stated earlier that Guse was allowed to reign supreme in that command (see note 68). The putting forth of the plea of "military necessity" is essentially a task that devolves upon the chief of staff of an army. Guse states in his book that his relationship to War Minister Enver, whom "to know closely was a gift of destiny" (*ein Geschenk des Schicksals*), was such that he, Enver, developed "great confidence in and personal affinity for me" (*grosses Vertrauen und persönliche Zuneigung*). The result was that "my proposals at the very least were given very serious consideration" (*sehr ernstlich erwogen wurde*).[87] These proposals included the alarm he sounded in the General Headquarters about "the severe crisis," "the terrible danger," and "the desperate conditions of the Turks" resulting from the Van uprising of the Armenians.[88] Guse not only justified the draconian measures taken against the victim population of the region—"another solution" (*eine andere Lösung*) was not feasible—but also went so far as to belittle the gravity of "the mass murders" being committed against the Armenians inasmuch as he argued the reports about them were often issued for the purpose of "atrocity propaganda" (*Greuelpropaganda*).[89] A fundamental question arises here. How did Guse learn of the misdeeds attributed to the Armenians? He admits that "there was no German fighting in the area of Van and that besides me none of the few Germans who were on duty in the Turkish Caucasus had the kind of position that might enable him to grasp the gravity of the situation. ..."[90] His position, of course, was chief of the staff of that army, but in order to function as such he was largely, if not exclusively, dependent upon the information fed to him by his Turkish subordinates as well as his Turkish superior, the Commander-in-Chief of the Caucasus, or the IIIrd Army. He had absolutely no alternative or supplementary source to check, modify, verify, or dismiss a flow of information with seemingly actual military implications but in reality with enormous political ramifications.

In brief, Colonel Guse was virtually hostage to a group of people who supplied him the requisite data for decision making and whose overall goals he endorsed. This is the more remarkable when one takes into account his view that as Oriental people the Turks are prone to "lying." One explanation for this is that "Unlike Christendom Islam does not require the truth" (*Islam fordert nicht wie das Christentum, die Wahrheit*). The premium placed on truth by the Europeans is incomprehensible, as is the degree to which one may emphasize that he is telling the truth. "They will often unreservedly admit that lying is all too common a phenomenon among them, will be resentful, however, when someone else will tell them" (*Sie selbst sprachen es ungescheut aus dass bei ihnen viel gelogen wird ...*).[91] Below is an inquiry into the web of a probable conspiracy into the snare of which apparently and on their volition fell a number of Turkophile German officers, including Guse. The focal point of that web is the headquarters of the IIIrd Army and more specifically the Commander-in-Chief, General Mahmud Kâmil.

The role of the IIIrd Army High Command—Its Turkish Commander-in-Chief and the Pre-designed Wholesale Massacres

Shortly after Enver's grand offensive at Sarıkamış faltered and ended in disaster for the IIIrd Army, middle of January 1915, the new Commander Hafız Hakkı succumbed to the then raging typhus epidemic on February 12, 1915. The behind-the-scenes maneuvers in connection with the appointment of a new commander-in-chief were the harbingers of a sweeping storm that was to engulf hundreds of thousands of Armenians trapped in the clutches of that army. Enver offered the job to Vehib with the stipulation that he would be promoted from colonel to major-general; the requisite Imperial written order (*Irade*) was obtained. But the Ittihad's Chief, Talât, and some members of the Ittihad party Directorate insisted on the appointment of Mahmud Kâmil, and they prevailed. Kâmil, along with his deceased predecessor Hafız Hakkı, had been Enver's classmate at the War Academy. On December 20, 1914, Colonel Kâmil had been promoted to major-general and was assigned to the post of Commander-in-Chief of the IInd Army (from that of the Vth Army Corps) with the title of a Paşa. As Kâmil Paşa in February 1915 proceeded to Erzurum for his new duties, Vehib too was promoted to Paşa rank, assuming Kâmil's IInd Army post.

Enver previously had placed much faith in his classmate as a like-minded and loyal acolyte. He let him run the affairs of the War Ministry as undersecretary or councillor (*Harbiye Musteşarı*). But more important than this, M. Kâmil was an ardent Ittihadist and carried great weight in the inner councils of the top Ittihad leadership whose views and aspirations he embodied. Most portentous was his close relationship to Ziya Gökalp, the ideologue of Ittihad, and Kara Kemal, Talât's right hand man. General Kâmil, according to the same source, was eager for war as he was confident of a quick German victory.[92] Both men (Gökalp and Kemal) were major forces in the shaping of Ittihad's anti-Armenian policy. Moreover, according to the deposition of an Ittihadist, M. Kâmil was personally involved in the purge of Ittihad's opponents in the wake of the assassination of Grand Vizier M. Şevket Paşa.[93]

In the list of accusations compiled by the British High Commission at Istanbul in 1919, Mahmud Kâmil is described as having presided over three top-level secret councils in Erzurum "for the purpose of concerting inter-provincial measures for the extermination" of the Armenians. The same document cites him as the authority responsible for having "ordered the massacre of Armenian soldiers. ... Cruel, of the worst moral character, he was the trusted agent of the C. U. P. [Ittihad] for the work of suppressing the Armenians."[94] These top-level conferences involved the convening of the governors of the six provinces, encompassed in the IIIrd Army operational zone, at which Ittihad's scheme of extermination of the Armenians was outlined. General Kâmil proclaimed himself as the superordinate authority over the governors and their subalterns; they had to obey him on matters involving the treatment of the Armenians. Commenting on this arrangement, Erzurum's German vice consul Scheubner referred to "the inhumanity [of the system in accord with which] Kâmil Paşa is sharply intervening in the government of the province."[95] In his report another German officer, Colonel Stange, specifically cited General Kâmil as being a principal authority in charge of the exterminatory undertaking against the Armenians.[96]

Turkish officer Colonel Nusuhi personally testified at the third sitting of the Harput trial series (August 5, 1919), telling the military tribunal that he was reprimanded by General Mahmud Kâmil for suggesting that the women and children, remaining in Bitlis as the only Armenians following the enactment of the general mobilization, were harmless people and as such they in no way could endanger military operations. He further tried to impress upon General Kâmil the critical importance of the fact that the Armenians were needed for harvesting, as the harvest that year was abundant and the army desperately needed provisions. He was rebuffed. When he returned to his unit, Colonel Nusuhi saw Special Organization brigand chief Musa at a site half an hour from Bitlis where Special Organization killer units were dousing gasoline on the bodies of massacred Armenians, some of whom were still alive.[97] Additionally, there is the testimony of Süleyman Faik Paşa, the military commander of Harput and that province's Acting Governor in the summer and fall of 1915. While he was serving as Bursa's postwar Court-Martial President in the aftermath of the war, he told Hayret Paşa, Chief Judge of the Turkish Military Tribunal investigating the massacre of the Armenians, "Mahmud Kâmil Paşa's ciphers, ordering the destruction of the Armenians, are still in my possession" (... *Ermenileri imha ediniz diye vermiş emri telegraflar bende mevcuddur*).[98]

The key indictment of the Extraordinary Turkish Court-Martial has two major references to the role of General Mahmud Kâmil and the IIIrd Army he commanded. In trying to explain why so many of the Muslim population could not extend any help to the Armenians slated for destruction, the Court-Martial produced a July 10, 1915 secret cipher (series 13, document No. 1). Through a proclamation M. Kâmil in it warns the Muslim population as follows: "Any Muslim who dares to harbor an Armenian will be hanged in front of his house which will also be burned down. If the culprit is an official he will be dismissed and court-martialed. If those protecting (*tesahüb*) the Armenians are military people, they will be stripped of their military status and will be handed over to the same Court-Martial." Concluded the indictment: "This violates the Islamic precept 'Don't commit forbidden acts under intimidation and threat' " (*nehy alel-munker emri şeriye*).[99]

In order to understand fully the conditions under which Colonel Guse, General Mahmud Kâmil's Chief of Staff, chose to play a crucial role in legitimizing the Turkish contentions of Armenian treason and rebellion and sanctioning the Turkish measures of deliberate and organized mass murder carried out against the Armenians, especially in the IIIrd Army's zone of jurisdiction, attention should be directed to a method of conspiracy most effectively executed by General Kâmil and his co-conspirators. It is the carefully prearranged pattern of providing to the central authorities in Istanbul grounds justifying the initiation of severe anti-Armenian measures which thus had an appearance of legitimacy and purported to be merely reactive and defensive. It involved the arrangement of a system of dispatching formal reports to the Ottoman General Headquarters depicting the Armenians as saboteurs, spies, and insurgents. Enver's War Office and Talât's Interior Ministry were flooded with such reports in the period immediately preceding the launching of the genocidal scheme. As noted in a previous section, military commanders and governors, presumably under secret orders to perform this function, relayed such reports in which small incidents were amplified, details were embellished and their significance inflated. Many of these incidents were deliberately provoked to elicit from the victims such defensive responses as could be portrayed as armed rebellion; nor were there cases lacking where wholly imaginary stories were concocted to meet the condition of the Ittihadists who were poised to strike. Perhaps the most telling disclosure about General Kâmil's role in this respect was made by Pertev, the Acting Commander of IIIrd Army's Xth Army Corps stationed in Sıvas. "Kâmil has the greatest responsibility for the Armenian massacres. He exaggerated small incidents when reporting them, and blamed the Armenians for Turkish military defeats. I am free of all responsibilities because I have in my possession telegrams ordering massacres."[100] In the British archives at Kew, London, there is a document listing the name of an Armenian, Eghia Bakalian, "who has seen the official order sent by Mahmud Kâmil Paşa and personally heard from the lips of Pertev, the Acting Commander of the Sıvas Division of the IIIrd Army Corps [Army], how fully this order was executed in the vilayet of Erzurum."[101] At the fourth sitting of the Trabzon trial series, in the afternoon segment (April 3, 1919), Colonel Vasfi, Chief of Staff in the Trabzon war zone, testified to the following. He received orders from General Ali Paşa, his commander, to go to Erzurum to investigate reports of massacre but was blocked by General M. Kâmil, who told him in so many words that the matter was none of his business.[102] All this is confirmed by a source identified with the victim population. A surviving Armenian physician from Kâmil's command zone bitterly declared that "*The Armenian soldiers were murdered in batch after batch under the authority of Mahmud Kâmil Paşa* (italics in the original). It was this man who shamelessly reported to the Ittihad headquarters that the Armenians were traitors. One has to be a Turk to concoct such a scheme."[103]

That this mode of operation was part of a general scheme applied everywhere else is attested by German Major-General Kress von Kressenstein, Commander-in-Chief of VIIIth Ottoman Army, Palestine front, and in June 1918, Chief of the German Imperial Delegation in the Caucasus. In a lengthy report dated September 3, 1918, he complained to Berlin about this method being applied in Caucasian Armenia, which in spring and summer 1918 was temporarily occupied by the Turkish army. "How unscrupulously misleading reports are being sent to Istanbul for the purpose of creating there totally exaggerated and untrue picture about the so-called Armenian danger."[104] General Kâmil was arrested on January 19, 1919 by Turkish authorities and was deported by the British to Mudros on May 29, 1919, on charges of complicity in "the Armenian massacres and deportations."[105] While being detained at Malta, along with scores of other Turkish suspects, for later trial before an international tribunal, on September 6, 1921, he broke parole and escaped with a group of fifteen other hard-core accomplices whom a British Foreign Office councillor called "notorious exterminators";[106] that group included another army commander (Ali Ihsan Sabis, a very close friend of General Kâmil and an arch massacrer himself), four governors, one deputy of the Ottoman Parliament, and the Chief of the Armenian deportations, Şükrü Kaya.[107] General Mahmud Kâmil on October 27, 1922 committed suicide.

The Role of the IIIrd Army High Command—Its Civilian Commissars as Subordinate Coconspirators

Under conditions of wartime emergency, civilian administration is often subordinated to military authority consistent with martial law and the state of siege. In the Ottoman state organization the provinces of the empire were administered by governors-general (*vali*) who had their own string of subalterns. It was, furthermore, natural that the governors-general of the six provinces, plus Trabzon, would be subordinated to the supreme authority of General Mahmud Kâmil, the Commander of the IIIrd Army. But, these were not ordinary *vali*s. Postwar documentary evidence revealed that many of them were not only potentates of Ittihad party but were secretly inducted into the Special Organizations, the main instrument for the implementation of the Armenian genocide. At the fifth sitting of the Cabinet Ministers Trial Series (May 12, 1919), for example, Atıf, one of the directors of the Special Organization with headquarters in the Ottoman capital, confirmed that the *vali*s of Trabzon and Erzurum provinces, Cemal Azmi and Hasan Tahsin (Uzer), respectively, were such inductees.[108] Turkish general Ali Ihsan (Sabis) adds two more *vali*s to this list, namely, those of Van and Musul provinces.[109] Many of these governors were vested with military authority by the IIIrd Army High Command; they were in charge of the transport, supplies, and communication lines of that army (*menzil*) and exercised enormous power. The collection and initial transport arrangements of the deportee convoys were largely the task of these *menzil* commanders. In an interview with a newspaper editor, Avni Paşa, who became Marine Minister during the Armistice, complained that as commander of the Trabzon area Costal Defense he could not control Cemal Azmi, the governor, who had the dual status of Military and *Menzil* Commandant; both men ended up having equal status in relation to Commander-in-Chief of the IIIrd Army.[110] Colonel Nusuhi, cited earlier, declared that General Kâmil "also ordered me to comply with every instruction of Muammer, the Governor of Sıvas," where IIIrd Army's Xth Army Corps was stationed.[111] Moreover, in his memoirs General Sabis stated that two powerful representatives of the party at Trabzon, Nail, and Riza, were intoxicated with panturanist designs, and their notion of strategy did not go beyond the realm of guerrilla tactics. Both were implicated in the massacres of Trabzon province Armenians with Nail, Ittihad's Responsible Secretary of the province, having been condemned to death in absentia.[112] Naturally these pervasive influences could only be afforded through the authority of Ittihad's Supreme Directorate dominated by Drs. Nazım, Şakir and the godfather of Ittihadist nationalism, Ziya Gökalp, all of them cohorts of General Mahmud Kâmil. These men were even able to impel Enver and Talât in the formation and implementation of the regime's Armenian policy. The civilian chief of the party yielded to the military when the latter felt strongly about an issue and demanded compliance. This symbiotic relationship, which, despite the incidence of frictions, was essentially sustained, is clearly evidenced in a German document in which Schulenburg, the liaison officer of the German Foreign Office sponsoring guerrilla operations against Russia, complained to the German Military Attaché that instead of intervening or referring the matter to the party Directorate Enver advised the German officer to see the IIIrd Army Commander in order to overcome the obstructions of local party branches in the matter of the Georgian Legion.[113]

The central role the IIIrd Army High Command played in the eradication of the region's Armenian population acquires further significance by the fact that Erzurum was not only the locus of the army's headquarters but was also the locus of the headquarters of the Special Organization East, established, organized, and directed by Dr. Behaeddin Şakir, one of the principal organizers of the Armenian genocide. He was assisted by a coterie of Ittihadist leaders and functionaries as well as by several brigand leaders who were in charge of the Special Organization's killer bands.[114] Foremost among these were the party's inspector of the region, Filibeli Hilmi, and most notably five deputies of the Ottoman Parliament, namely Seyfullah (Erzurum district), Hâlet (Erzincan), Servet Bey (Gümüşane), Naci (Trabzon), and Sudi Bey (Lazistan district).[115] By the admission of these Special Organization leaders, the cadres then formed in Trabzon as well as in Erzurum and Van comprised multitudes of convicts who were released from the prisons of the three provinces for special missions.[116] Nor were these measures limited to the eastern provinces. In his testimony before the Fifth Committee of the Ottoman Chamber of Deputies investigating the wartime misdeeds of the ministers of the two Ottoman wartime Cabinets, Ibrahim, Minister of Justice during the deportations and massacres, conceded that "upon the instance of the military authorities, a large number (*mühim bir yekün*) of felons were released from the prisons of the empire."[117] The measure was approved by the "special dispensation" (*hususi müsaade*) of the Ministry of Justice and Interior.[118] However, as in the case of the launching of the series of Armenian deportations, this administrative approval was, by itself, not legitimate as it preceded by about two years the requisite parliamentary approval, which was enacted on December 12,

1916; by then the genocide was largely consummated.[119] These convicts were often described as *çetes* and were subsumed under the category of *milis* (milice). But this term in fact was used to camouflage the origin and status of the enrollees and, in reality, the designation "milis" by and large was synonymous with that of Special Organization.[120]

All these activities evidently were supervised and facilitated by the Commander of the IIIrd Army. In a Turkish account, quoting from a secret cipher telegram that described these activities, it is revealed that in such cities and towns as Erzincan, Tercan, Kığı, and Bayburt, which happened to contain large concentrations of Armenians, there was being formed a detachment of "Islamic Milice" (*islâm milis*) that was to be led, among others, by Erzincan Deputy Hâlet. What is even more revealing and, therefore, more consequential, however, was the following portion of the cipher in question "The formation of the detachment, 'to be led by Dr. Behaeddin Şakir,' was approved by the IIIrd Army Commander" (*Üçüncü Ordu Kumandanı paşanın tasvibi ile*).[121] From the very inception, the buildup of the Special Organization units in the eastern provinces of Turkey is seen here receiving not only active support but also a measure of authorization by the highest ranking military officer in the region, that is, the Commander-in-Chief of the Ottoman IIIrd Army. Equally significant, the *çete* (brigand bands), consisting of "convicts" (*mahbuslar*), were to be "commanded by regular army officers."[122] In the second sitting (May 4, 1919) of the trial of the two wartime Cabinet Ministers, this fact of army officers being in charge of the brigand units was repeatedly acknowledged.[123]

THE DECISIVE ROLE OF THE SPECIAL ORGANIZATION EAST

The authorization by the Commander of the IIIrd Army, cited above, is most noteworthy in terms of recognizing Dr. B. Şakir as the legitimate chief of the Special Organization East and thereby indirectly validating the sway of civilian personnel in the handling of operations that had a quasi-military thrust. The pivotal role of Dr. Şakir in the conception of, decision making on, organization, and actual implementation of the genocide under review here has been noted and underlined throughout this study, especially in note 114. Official and unofficial Turkish literature almost entirely depicts the Special Organization as a patriotic outfit bent on sabotaging the war effort of England, France, and Russia, the wartime enemies of Turkey and Germany. Superseding that goal, however, were two interrelated objectives, one of which, the Turanist expansion in the direction of Central Asia, was not concealed but the other, the Turkification of Turkey through the liquidation of the Armenians as a primary target, was concealed. The Armenians were considered prime targets not only on account of their heavy concentration in the eastern provinces of Turkey but also because they were geographically interposed between Turkey and the Turkic peoples in the Caucasus and beyond. There is, therefore, an element of ambivalence and confusion regarding the character and actual mission of the Special Organization. A closer scrutiny of the memoirs and confidential exchanges of some of the surviving leaders of that organization clearly reveals, however, that "internal security" designs all but aimed at the liquidation of the Armenians.[124] The testimonies of several of the leaders of the Special Organization who were being tried by the Turkish Military Tribunal in the aftermath of the war confirm the existence of the internal mission of the organization. At the fourth sitting (May 8, 1919), for example, the presiding judge told Yusuf Riza, one of the directors of the Special Organization, about the court's knowledge of these dual functions, stating that "there were two kinds of Special Organization; one of them was subject to the authority of the Ministry of War, and the other to the Ittihad party" (*Teşkilâtı Mahsusiyenin iki şekli olduğu, biri Harbiye Nezaretinin, diğeri Ittihad ve Terakki fırkasının mehsuf bulunduğunu ...*).[125] At the fifth sitting (May 12, 1919) Yusuf Riza, who eventually became member of the Central Committee of Ittihad, confirmed "the existence of a second Special Organization [whose cadres] in certain provinces assisted in the work of the organization involving the deportations from the districts and counties of these provinces" (*Ikinci bir Teşkilâtı Mahsusa mevcut ki bunlar bazı vilayetlerin, sancakların, kazaların bu tehcir işini idare etmek için ...*).[126] Another director, Atıf, at the same sitting admitted to the same fact by referring to "the volunteers of whose means we availed ourselves" (*gönüllüler, onların vesaitinden istifade*).[127] At the third sitting Küçük Talât, a member of the Central Committee, made an even more critical disclosure. He declared in court under cross-examination that there was cooperation between War Minister Enver and Dr. Nazım in the direction of the affairs of the Special Organization, thereby portraying a picture of interaction and possibly even interdependence between the two branches of that organization.[128] At the sixth sitting (May 14, 1919) Atıf again admitted that he utilized local Ittihad Party cells to facilitate the work of the organization and for which purpose he requested the intervention of Midhat Şükrü, party's Secretary-General (*Cemiyetin şubelerinden istifade etmek için Midhat Şükrü Beyden rica ettim*). In the same vein, Atıf confirmed the utilization of convicts, "which was authorized by law" (*kanun yapıldı ve kanun mucibine çıkarıldı*).[129]

Throughout the trials the dual functions of the Special Organization confounded the prosecutors and judges. Whereas the first function mainly devolved upon the War Office and Ministry of Defense, the second was identified with the secret designs and objectives of the Central Committee of the Ittihad party. *These dual functions were not discharged simultaneously but rather in sequence.* When the grandiose panturanist plans of toppling the Russian bear in the Caucasus through a string of local anti-Russian insurrections, to be triggered by Special Organization agents and units, failed, the party leadership activated an ancillary plan to liquidate the Armenian population. This is how the other function of that organization materialized. The available Special Organization contingents, augmented by local milice forces and improvised gendarmery units, all of which comprised multitudes of ex-convicts, were diverted to the task of destroying the Armenian population of Turkey, especially in the eastern provinces. A Turkish Reserve officer, affiliated with the Department II (i.e., Intelligence and Espionage) at the War Office, attests to this fact by citing such a shift of objectives from an external to an internal mission and the attendant diversion of Special Organization brigands from the eastern border zones to areas within the Turkish borders. He refers to *çetes* (brigands) operating in the Bozantı area, forty-five miles northwest of Adana. These men who "under Ittihad's policy of Turanism and Islamic Union were first sent to the Caucasus, were now operating in and around the mountains and forests near Bozantı."[130] The reemployment of these Special Organization units for the destruction of the Armenian population in Turkey's eastern provinces is described by Erzurum's German vice consul Scheubner. In his August 5, 1915 "secret" report he states that the killer bands engaged in "a crusade of destruction against the Armenians" (*Vernichtungsfeldzug gegen die Armenier*) of his district are the same people who earlier had engaged in "unprecedented brutal acts (*beispielloses brutales Vorgehen*) in eastern Turkey against the people of Ardanus, Ardahan, Olti, etc., which they temporarily had occupied."[131] In characterizing the leaders of these bands as the "dark forces of the shadowy Ittihad party" Scheubner notes that the leaders "are through and through Germanophiles" who are basically driven by "personal interest and greed."[132] The cooperation between the military and civilian party officials is most evident in the procedures to have convicts released for enrollment in the Special Organization. For instance, Colonel Behiç Erkin, Deputy Director in Department I of the Ministry of War and in charge of the Procurement Bureau (*Ikmal Şubesi*), who advocated in the Senate the passage of the bill authorizing the release of convicts, on November 25, 1914 had sent a cipher to the Directorate of the Special Organization informing it of a new legislative bill authorizing the release from prisons of convicts "for service in the army." Even though the use of the name of the army was intended to cover up the convicts' actual use for duties in the Special Organization, Colonel Behiç at the end of the text of the cipher requested, for the purposes of secrecy, the return of the cipher.[133] He was supported in his bid to gain Senate approval of the bill by the Legal Councillor of the Ministry of Justice who pleaded with the senators for their approval using patriotic hyperboles. Despite the objection of a lone senator, Ahmed Riza, one of the original founders of Ittihad who subsequently had become an ardent opponent, the Senate approved the bill as "an emergency bill" (*müstaceliyet*). Senator Riza sarcastically but vainly had intoned the words, "We know about the [real] nature of that organization."[134] Two aspects of this bill call for comments. As usual, when the Senate finally enacted the bill on December 12/25, 1916, the authorities had by then almost completed the process of liquidating the victim population; the entire procedure had therefore become both theatrical and farcical. Furthermore, the statements of both Colonel Behiç and Legal Councillor Yusuf Kemal (Tengirşek) in the Parliament to the effect that the convicts were only needed for the army were belied by Colonel Cevad, the wartime military governor (*merkez kumandan*) of Istanbul. Testifying before the Military Tribunal, Cevad on May 4, 1919 declared that "the volunteers" recruited for the Special Organization were involved in operations that were "outside the purview of the military" (*askerlik haricinde*).[135]

Although the relationship between the IIIrd Army High Command and the Special Organization East was not always smooth and occasional frictions strained that relationship, the killer bands were not interfered with as they methodically performed their task in a broad sweep of the eastern provinces containing large clusters of Armenian populations. In the provinces of Bitlis, especially Muş district, Diyarbekir, Harput, and to some extent Trabzon, the perpetrators dispensed with the need of "deportations" by organizing a series of provincial, local massacres that included the methods of burning alive en masse (Muş) and drowning at high seas (Trabzon). In order to achieve this goal, the leadership of the organization had managed to persuade the Central Committee of Ittihad and to secure from it a *carte blanche* for handling the Armenian problem at its discretion. This effort was synchronized with the IIIrd Army headquarters whose Commander, General M. Kâmil, as noted earlier, had prepared the ground for such authorization by a deluge of reports to the General Headquarters through which the Armenians were decried as traitors and as such were defined as an "internal foe" that should be eliminated. The sequence of these moves is narrated by a top assistant of Dr. B. Şakir in an extensive analysis of the field operations of the Special Organization; it was serialized in the 1933–1934 period in a Turkish daily newspaper (see notes 108, 116, 118, 121, 122).

It all started with the arrival in Erzurum of Dr. Şakir in August 1914 to set up his Special Organization headquarters. His arrival coincided with the quadrennial congress of the Dashnak party that was being held in Erzurum also. Claiming that the leaders of the party were secretly consorting with the Russian consul of that city, Şakir issued a secret order to "take care of them" (*çaresine bak*) on their way back home; this was a code word to ambush and destroy them. In his September 3/16, 1914 letter Filibeli Hilmi, Şakir's deputy in the organization, promised the latter that he will try to get hold of the Dashnak leaders and "destroy" them (*imha edilmeleri*) through his *çetes*. It was in this connection that as early as September 1914 (i.e., six weeks before the Russo-Turkish war broke out) the Armenians were defined by these leaders as the internal enemy. In articulating this view Hilmi in his letter wrote, "We are maintaining the standpoint that to the extent to which wc arc pursuing an external objective, to that extent there are inside our country also people who ought to be destroyed" (*Dışarıda takip edilecek maksat kadar içeride de imha edilecek eşhas vardır*).[136] According to a Turkish general, Dr. Şakir left Erzurum for Istanbul at the end of February (o.s.) or middle of March 1915 (new style date) for consultation with the Central Committee of the party.[137]

Prior to his trip to Istanbul, Şakir had convened a meeting of top agents of the organization to prepare a new blueprint for action. Here is the decision.

> It is necessary to render the Directorate of the Special Organization energetic and productive. The preparation of the plans should be left to the local bodies. They should determine upon the methods that are particularly appropriate for the organization. We request that those brigands, persons and units that will be dispatched to the eastern region be subjected to the authority of the Directorate of the eastern branch of the Special Organization.[138]

In other words, complete freedom of action was being sought for Special Organization East under the formula of autonomy. Subsequent events indicate that Şakir was able to persuade the Ittihadist Directorate in Istanbul to grant his request, authorizing the autonomy of the Special Organization East. This is confirmed by Turkish historian Doğan Avcıoğlu.[139] The launching of the major phases of the Armenian genocide coincides with Şakir's return to Erzurum in the spring of 1915. In fact Hilmi, Şakir's deputy, in his telegram to the latter threatened to resign unless Şakir would return to Erzurum with a mandate sanctioning the autonomy of the Special Organization.[140] Upon his return Şakir "decided to relinquish his preoccupation with external enemies and set out to deal with the country's internal enemies."[141] It may therefore be concluded that the decisive phase in the unfolding of the drama of the Armenian genocide was initiated by the return to Istanbul from Erzurum of Şakir on March 13, 1915 (new style). Equally important, Avcıoğlu in the same vein asserts that as far as "the ensuing large-scale and systematic deportations were concerned, which were enacted by the Special Organization, *they were endorsed by the Germans*."[142] (Italics added).

This discussion should not end without a comment on the issue of veracity of Turkish charges leveled against the Armenians as traitors. In many sections of this Part of this study the pattern of deliberate embellishments of small incidents and the allied inflated reports to the central authorities have been noted and emphasized. Another such instance of deceptiveness is at hand with respect to the author on the subject of the field operations of the Special Organization whose serialized articles have been cited in notes 108, 116, 118, 121, 122, 136, 140, and 141. After declaring (note 141) that the Armenians were not much different from an external enemy and should be dealt with as such, the Ittihadist leader A. Mil (most probably a fictitious name) proceeds to illustrate the point. In the consecutive installments, February 10, 11, 12, 1934, installments 98, 99, and 100 respectively, Mil is pretending to be exposing the evidence of Armenian treason. The material in question consists of instructions for the training of Armenian guerrilla units to prepare to fight against the Turkish military and the provincial police units. When introducing the lengthy text Mil states, "By organizing guerrilla bands, the Armenians from within Turkey were trying to threaten the rear of our army and were endeavoring to cut off our lines of retreat." Still insisting that this was occurring during World War I, Mil goes on to declare that the Special Organization agents got hold of these instructions and that he was publishing the text because of "its critical importance." But what are the facts? Involved here is a pamphlet bearing the title: Combat Instructions (*Mardagan Hurahankner*). It was prepared and published in Geneva in 1906 by the Armenian warrior hero Antranig. The purpose of the text consisting of 15 sections was to help create fighting squads, freedom fighters in today's parlance, to prepare for partisan war to combat against the tyranny of Sultan Abdul Hamit in the 1908 overthrow of whom Armenians of all factions had joined hands with the Young Turk Ittihadist revolutionaries. In other words, the pamphlet not only antedated World War I but also had no relationship to the Ittihadist regime. The paramount question poses itself: Without this explanation, how could any Turk, or for that matter any friend or foe, not help himself to be provoked and incited against the Armenian "traitors"? But then that is exactly the function of perpetrators conspiring to commit a crime.

THE POTENCY OF THE GERMAN CONNECTION TO THE SPECIAL ORGANIZATION

The Artifice of Islam

German official documents clearly indicate that the Turkish drive to refurbish and enlarge the existing Special Organization units, the remnants of those which had operated in the second Balkan war in 1913, received a needed impetus from German authorities in Berlin. In their drive to take the country completely under their control in the wake of the January 10/23, 1913 putsch when they reseized power, the Ittihadists overhauled their internal security system. For this purpose the War Ministry activated a "secret" Special Organization surveillance team to gather material on the activities of non-Muslim community leaders, especially Armenians, who were suspected of "subversiveness."[143] According to the statement of a police lieutenant working in the National Security Office (*Emniyeti Umumiye*) of the Interior Ministry, "German secret service agents were entrusted with the task of restructuring the office of the directorate in charge of political surveillance; they were to rely on the state of the art, using the latest technologies available. ... A special bureau was set up to follow developments in the Armenian community and to prepare dossiers on individuals."[144] With the outbreak of the war the twin functions of the Special Organization, internal security within and guerrilla and sabotage acts from without Turkey, more or less became interdependent. The elimination of "the internal foe" became an extension of or a prerequisite for the elimination of the external enemy. Consequently, German support of the latter objective inevitably influenced the ways and means through which the former objective, the elimination of the Armenians, was pursued. That support was particularly consequential for the Armenians when German specialists in military intelligence, at the start of the war, began to cooperate closely with Department II of the Turkish War Office that handled the affairs of Turkish military intelligence. However, this very office is identified in several documents as the instance masterminding the logistics of the Armenian genocide. As Otto von Lossow, the German military plenipotentiary at the German Embassy at the time, reported to the German General Headquarters on November 16, 1916, the "Armenian deportations" (*Armenierverschickungen*) were being handled by Department II at the Turkish War Office; that office was headed by Colonel Seyfi (see Part II, notes 10–14). With the outbreak of the war, German military officers and intelligence agents affiliated with the German office of military intelligence set out to streamline the activities of their Turkish counterparts and to introduce a measure of uniformity and coordination in the respective plans of both outfits. German officers were assigned to Department II at the Turkish War Office, and Turkish officers were dispatched to Germany for appropriate training in this field. "Despite differences of language this mode of cooperation (*Zusammenwirken*) yielded good results."[145] Commenting on this cooperation Talcott Parsons, the former dean of Columbia University's Pulitzer School of Journalism, who was born and raised in Turkey, attributed the efficiency of the massacres against the Armenians to German aptitude for planning. As he declared, "Never has it been practiced with such ruthless efficiency as in the alliance between the Turkish secret Committee of Union and Progress (the Young Turk Ittihadists. V.N.D.) and the Berlin General Staff. Of the schedule of instructions for massacre issued to the military authorities at Kharput, I have had a description from the notes of one who read it. At every point it bears the marks of the methodical labours of the Berlin General Staff."[146] Involved here was a new wartime German policy bent on creating and cultivating a system of top-secret clandestine missions with the objective of crippling the war-making capability of the enemy, especially England. The missions involved the objective of circumvening the battlefronts and targeting the support systems of the home fronts, including the colonies and quasi-colonies of France, England, and Russia.

The policy guidelines for the entire system of such revolutionary initiatives in enemy lands were set as early as July 30, 1914, by Emperor William II. In a marginal note to a cipher sent from Petersburg by German ambassador Count Friedrich von Pourtalés, he instructed his diplomats and intelligence operatives to expose, and inflict upon England, this "hated, mendacious, unscrupulous nation of hagglers (*dieses verhasste, verlogene, gewissenlose Krämervolk*). Our consuls in Turkey and India, agents etc., must inflame the entire Muslim world for ferocious revolt" against it.[147] In this sense, the German assistance to Turkish efforts to form a clandestine outfit for the implementation of secret designs was invested with religious symbolism. The evocation of Islam thus functioned as a religious animus propelling many Muslims to embrace the Ittihadist cause and reinforce its war effort. The authoritative thrust of William II's exhortation in favor of Islam sufficiently influenced General Helmuth von Moltke, the Chief of the German General Staff, to issue his own and almost identical exhortation. In a memorandum to the Foreign Office, Moltke on August 5, 1914 called for a general revolution against England as a colonial power, including one "in the Caucasus [that] is of the highest importance. The Treaty with Turkey will enable the Foreign Office to realize this idea and to arouse the fanaticism of Islam" (*den Fanatismus des Islams zu erregen*).[148] On August 27, the Foreign Office followed suit; it instructed the German Embassy at Istanbul "to ruthlessly and unsparingly carry out (*rücksichtslos und schonungslos durchführen*) the plan for the arousal of panislamic sentiment against England and its colonial possessions."[149] To add particular emphasis to this campaign German ambassador Wangenheim was authorized by Berlin to assure Turkey in writing that Germany undertakes to ensure the rectification of Turkey's eastern borders for the purpose of enabling Turkey to establish direct contact with the Islamic nationalities of Russia (Item five of the written agreement).[150]

Even though none of the component plans to inflame and incite Muslim masses in various colonies belonging to the Entente Powers attained the expected results—and there is general agreement that these plans by and large proved abortive—the Germans and their Turkish allies scored some success in one respect. They were able to motivate select groups of peoples of different nationalities comprising an amalgam of aspiring or self-appointed refugee leaders, swashbucklers, professional soldiers, charlatans, rogues as well as idealist patriots; almost all of them were for one reason or another under the spell of an Islamic revolutionary drive that was being prompted by the Germans. They were recruited; organized; equipped with the requisite weapons, funds, and command structures; and were sent on their secret missions. These overall activities are beyond the purview of this study. When considering some of these activities with respect to their specific impact upon the fate of the Armenians, however, certain problem-foci emerge as relevant. They may be described briefly. The martial and belligerent elements of Islam were ideally suited for galvanizing during a war religiously inclined or indoctrinated multitudes. The Turko-Armenian conflict, which had intensified and escalated in the decades preceding the war, was such as to lend itself to a redefinition by the Muslim Turks as a religiously charged conflict; it could be harnessed to a campaign assuming the dimensions of a crusade against specific targets, that is, hostile "infidels" (*giavurs*).

The proclamation of *cihad* (holy war) on November 11, 1914 was the type of expedient that was to serve this function of harnessing. In essence, however, the proclamation was a subterfuge for selective targeting. As the head of the German Military Mission Marshal Sanders observed, "... it bore the appearance of unreality because Turkey was allied with Christian states and German and Austrian officers and men were serving in the Turkish army."[151] In fact one of the most devastating by-products of their campaign to excite and incite Muslim masses against the infidels within the scheme of a holy war was the common penchant to apply it internally (i.e., against the non-Muslim subjects within the Ottoman Empire), in particular, against the Christian Armenians. In his testimony at the trial in Berlin of Soghomon Teilerian, the "avenger" who had assassinated Talât, Marshal Liman von Sanders declared that the men escorting the Armenian deportee convoys were influenced by the spirit of *cihad* when attacking their Armenian charges as Christians.[152] In his memoirs Sanders describes a scene of destructiveness against the Armenian property in Constantinople immediately in the wake of the declaration of holy war, adding that "as usual the processions were organized by the police."[153] The excitatory features of *cihad,* directed especially against the Armenians, are narrated by a number of other eyewitnesses. A confidential internal memo prepared for the German Foreign Office states that "*cihad* excited the passions of the Turkish people against the Armenians."[154] The Venezuelan officer De Nogales, who as a combat officer fighting under German sponsorship alongside the Turks in the border areas of Turkey had the opportunity to observe the application of *cihad* to the targeted Armenian population of Turkey, reached his own conclusion. "The Holy War, " promoted "under the wing of Pan-Islamism," aimed at "the eventual elimination of the Armenians. ..."[155] What is perhaps most noteworthy is the personal involvement of Dr. Nazım, one of the principal architects of the Armenian genocide. Through a cipher telegram to Zimmermann, undersecretary in the Foreign Office, German ambassador Wangenheim on November 15, 1914 stated that the *fetva,* sanctioning the legitimacy of the proclamation of holy war—according to the canon laws of Islam—was read out loud in the mosques of the land. More than 50,000 Muslims, energized "against the enemies of Islam" and armed with religious and nationalist paraphernalia, proceeded to demonstrate in the streets of the capital. When they arrived at the German Embassy, Dr. Nazım, along with Dr. Weber, the dragoman of the embassy, addressed the crowd. To quote the ambassador, "There was enormous enthusiasm ... interminable cheers for His Majesty, the Kaiser, and for Germany. ... As they snapped out of their phlegm, the people became fanaticized." Fully realizing that the matter was getting out of hand—at the end of that cipher he did mention the attack on the Armenian establishments—the ambassador became apprehensive about the possibility of Germany being held responsible (*verantwortlich*) and promised to avert the occurrence of "a calamity" (*Unheil*).[156] Historian Trumpener pointed to the same problem of "unleashing of religious passions" and the incidence of "anti-Armenian violence" that was associated with the internal application of the injunction of holy war.[157] In fact that violence was perpetrated immediately after the crowd had left the German Embassy grounds and was on its way to the Austrian Embassy.[158] As Liman von Sanders pointed out, many of the bands that were engaged as escort personnel were often under the spell of *cihad* when they were escorting. Therein lies one of the connections between the large-scale plans to incite the Muslim masses and the lethal role performance of the killer bands of the Special Organization—incited and inflamed with Islamic fanaticism. More often than not, the escort personnel were in fact part of the cadres of the Special Organization. In this connection it is worth underlining the fact that one of the salient features of the Armenian genocide relates to the condition under which a certain proportion of Armenians, mostly children, girls, and young women, were spared death and destruction on consenting to embrace Islam. The German and Austrian state archives are replete with accounts documenting this fact, not to speak of the vast corpus of Armenian survivor accounts. In trying to influence and win over potentially "revolutionary" Islamic populations in areas contiguous to Turkey, German authorities in Berlin, Istanbul, and the interior of Turkey in a variety of ways bolstered a string of Turkish initiatives that were inherently perilous for the Armenians. They may be outlined briefly. Before describing them below, however, a brief digression on the critical importance of the factor of Islam and Muslim multitudes, not only for Imperial Germany, but also for its arch enemy England, may serve the purpose of ending this discussion with a highly relevant reference.

As has been observed in note 5 of Part II of this study, the escape of the German armada (the cruisers of *Goeben* and *Breslau*) from the pursuit of British battleships, and their taking refuge in the Bosphorus on August 10, 1914 was perhaps one of the most fateful events of the war, denying the Entente Powers the benefits and laurels of a quick victory against those of the Triple Alliance. Through this naval entry into Istanbul, Germany for all practical purposes forced Turkey to relinquish its tenuous neutrality; within weeks thereafter Turkey was pushed by the Germans into the World War conflagration. While the British Cabinet with considerable hesitation was debating the option of offering substantial concessions to Turkey to avert its joining the camp of the Triple Alliance under German inducements as well as pressures, "the violently anti-Turk" Winston Churchill, who was then Lord of the Admiralty in a "most bellicose" mood urged the sending of a torpedo flotilla through the Dardanelles to sink the two German cruisers.[159] But Kitchener, at the time Secretary of State for War, overruled Churchill arguing that England could not afford to alienate the Muslims by taking the offensive against Muslim Turkey. It was up to Turkey to take the initiative and "to strike the first blow."[160]

TURKO-GERMAN JOINT INITIATIVES AND THEIR IMPLICATIONS FOR OTTOMAN ARMENIANS

The overall futility of these undertakings, including the one involving the proclamation of holy war, was in inverse relationship to the scale of expenditure, organizational effort, and loss of prestige incurred by the Germans—except perhaps with respect to the fate of the Armenians. The prophetic forecast of Marshal Sanders is pertinent here. Speaking of the absurdity of the recourse to holy war, Sanders declared that that recourse conceivably "will have a more serious meaning and find its final expression in massacres of Christians. ..."[161] Since there is no explicit evidence to suggest that such massacres were in fact intended by the Germans involved, it is worthwhile to examine the conditions under which they joined hands with the Turks to launch operations involving the Turkish Special Organization. In general terms, there was a plan to enter Baku and try to cripple the Russian war effort in the Caucasus. Closely allied with this was the plan to enter northern Iran and after further preparations use it as a gateway to India. These operations were to be carried out by Expeditionary Forces led by Turkish and German co-commanders and comprising contingents of military personnel, including Turkish Special Organization bands adept at guerrilla war and acts of sabotage, murder, and plunder. These forces would be assisted in their missions by auxiliary Special Organization Forces operating in and around the Transcaucasus, especially in the area of Batum, the Black Sea port. In fact, these auxiliary forces comprised the bulk of the units of the Special Organization East, led by Dr. B. Şakir, who was assisted by German regimental commander Colonel Stange. Both of them were in turn assisted by two foremost Special Organization leaders from Trabzon, Yenibahçeli Nail and Yusuf Riza, both of whom, as noted earlier, were tried during the Armistice by the Turkish Court-Martial as prime suspects in the crimes committed against the Armenians, with Nail having been sentenced to death in absentia. The two other Expeditionary Forces were recast into one when the plan for Baku fell through as a result of Halil (Kut)'s defeat at Dilman in May 1915. Besides General Halil, involved in these undertakings were Lieutenant Scheubner Richter, Hauptmann Schwarz, Louis Mosel, Oswald von Schmidt, Turkish general Ali Ihsan Sabis, Ittihadist orator and top leader Ömer Naci, and Special Organization commanders Yakub Cemil, "Deli" Halit, Çerkez Ahmed, and Topal Osman.

Two aspects of these enterprises must be singled out: 1) With Trabzon serving as the initial center of command and control for the unfolding operations, massive German assistance in weapons, ammunitions, cash money, and advisors were directed to that port city to help these outfits sustain themselves, given the relative scarcity of these resources in the inventory of the Turkish camps. 2) Without exception, all the Turkish leaders mentioned above played key roles in the destruction of the Armenian population, not only in the eastern provinces of Turkey but also in those areas of the Transcaucasus and Iran that the Special Organization units, commanded by these officers during the initial months of the war, had temporarily occupied. It is therefore appropriate to examine more closely the conditions and mechanisms through which German authorities willingly or inadvertently became indirect accessories to crimes perpetrated by Special Organization functionaries whose overall missions they endorsed, financed to some extent, and shepherded.

The ground for this support was prepared by the Prussian officer Captain Rudolf Nadolny. He was in charge of the planning of subversive and revolutionary activities in the countries of the enemy camp; these activities included espionage, sabotage and other types of hostile forays. He was an official of the German Foreign Office where he served as Chief of the Political Section in the Reserve General Staff (*Sektion Politik IIIb des Stellvertretenden Generalstabes*). As he described in his autobiographical book, "all undertakings in foreign countries, which were supportive of our war effort, were coordinated in this office." He was subject to the direct authority of the Political Section of the General Staff in Charge of the Field Forces (*die Politische Abteilung des Generalstabes des Feldheeres*). "Nevertheless, I had far-reaching power (*weitgehende Vollmachten*) ... could for my ends engage any and all officers and enlisted personnel, and had direct access (*unmittelbaren Vortrag*) to the Chief of Staff of the Field Forces (*Feldheer*). My cumulative experience in this area allows me to observe that it was just touching to see how many Germans at that time were volunteering for the most dangerous missions."[162] In the course of his work he assumed duties involving clandestine work in Persia (Iran) that brought him into a working relationship with Marshal von der Goltz commanding the Ottoman VIth Army and Turkish general A. Ihsan (Sabis) commanding the XIIIth Army Corps.[163] Nadolny proposed first that Major Wolfskeel (whose role in reducing the Armenian quarter of Urfa through artillery bombardments and thereby helping the Turks to massacre and destroy the surviving Armenian population is detailed in Part II, in section on the roles and attitudes of other high ranking German officers) be appointed to the post of Contact Officer (*Verbindungsoffizier*) in Trabzon, the hub of Special Organization planning, recruiting, and logistics activities. The purpose would be to "promote the Caucasian movement," that is, guerrilla and sabotage incursions.[164] But Ambassador Wangenheim turned him down saying that Wolffskeel was needed where he was (he was the chief of staff of the provincial government of Syria);[165] Urfa was then within the military jurisdiction of that district. Nadolny thereupon held a conference in Berlin and decided to propose to the German High Command the dispatch of a team of German operatives under the command of an officer with the rank of captain. Among the men he proposed were Louis Mosel and Oswald von Schmidt. (For Oswald von Schmidt's implicit recognition of German complicity in the destruction of the Armenians see Part II, section on A German document with a revelatory hint, note 189). The High Command agreed and offered to send stockpiles of weapons and ammunition. They reckoned that the initial cost of this undertaking would amount to six million German marks, a cost to be borne by the Foreign Office. Mosel indicated that 6,000 Mauser rifles had been already distributed.[166] The participants, who were led by Captain Schulenburg, were ordered under penalty of court-martial to maintain utmost secrecy about their missions.[167]

In analyzing the consequences of these missions for the Armenian population of Turkey a major fact is noted—a fact that is of signal relevance to the central theme of this study. Whereas some German operatives went out of their way to avoid being drawn into acts that would have been tantamount to complicity, others willingly allowed the Turks to coopt them for the perpetration of acts, thereby inculpating themselves. What is most noteworthy in this connection is the additional fact that the Germans belonging to the latter category had more power, greater authority, and ultimately proved more consequential than those subsumed under the former category. Some illustrations may be in order. Two of the German operatives associated with the Turkish Special Organization plans for guerrilla incursions into the Caucasus joined the Turks in anti-Armenianism and denounced the Armenians in special reports to Berlin. In October 1914 Dr. Paul Schwarz, an oil expert with designs on Baku (he was not only an agent and a captain of the army but also at the start of the war served as German vice consul in Erzurum), prepared a report on "The Situation in Turkish Armenia." In it he told Berlin, including Foreign Minister von Jagow, that unlike the Turks, who were Germanophiles, the Armenians of Bitlis, Van, Erzurum, and Trabzon provinces were hostile to the Germans. He further declared that Russian and British money was being put to good use in Armenia and that Turkish Armenia was an area deserving special attention.[168] Another operative, Louis Mosel, in a March 1915 report titled "The Armenian Movement," blasted the Armenians as traitors and spies. Relying on Turkish propaganda, he ventured to make this general accusation against them, "In my opinion the entire Armenian population in the Ottoman realm is organized, and is awaiting the onset of the successes, namely, the advance of the Russians, in order to rise up against the Turkish domination … I consider the chances of changing their mind-set through persuasion or monetary means nil."[169]

One of the most notable Germans readily accommodating the Turks in their designs against the Armenians was Marshal von der Goltz. When commanding the VIth Army in Iraq he received a request from Ömer Naci, the co-commandant of the Special Organization Persian Expedition, to repress "a rebellion" in the area of Cezire. (Scheubner in his December 4, 1915 report identified the Armenian village Hesak as the locus of "the rebellion," adding that he established there was no rebellion after investigating the matter. "The so-called 'rebels' were people who out of fear of an impending massacre had barricaded themselves and gladly would have surrendered their weapons when only their lives could be guaranteed" (*die angeblich "Aufständischen" waren Leute, die sich aus Furcht vor einem Massaker verschanzt hatten*).[170] The request had two characteristics. It took place when Scheubner was in Mosul to secure quarters for his detachment. Moreover, Naci's request was not limited to the use of his detachment but deliberately included Scheubner's detachment, which contained German officers and soldiers. Without hesitation Goltz "agreed with the request and issued the requisite orders (*daraufhin entsprechende zustimmende Befehle erteilt*), which allowed the temporary engagement of both detachments" (*die zeitweilige Inanspruchnahme der beiden Detachmente*). However, as soon as he learned of this authorization by Goltz, Scheubner intervened and arranged for the immediate dispatch to Mosul of his detachment. As Schulenburg, the author of the report to Berlin, stated, Scheubner "found it not right that members of the German army should participate in the repression of an internal rebellion, a repression whose ramifications were not recognizable" (*dessen Bedeutung nicht zu übersehen war*).[171] Scheubner was not alone in the task of dissuading Goltz. The gerent of Mosul's German Consulate, Walter Hoffmann, who confirmed Goltz's authorization, likewise interceded, arguing that there was no rebellion but a desperate act of defense to escape massacre. It was only then that Goltz agreed to rescind his order and requested that he be informed of the instructions sent to the consuls from the embassy about conduct in such situations.[172]

It should be noted at this juncture of the discussion that Marshal Goltz was one of the ardent supporters of the type of missions with which the Scheubner-Ömer Naci Expedition was entrusted. He believed in revolutionary guerrilla incursions as an extension of regular warfare and his ultimate ambition was to invade India and to inflict a major blow upon England. In connection with the plans to complete the Baghdad Railway he prepared a memorandum in which he contended that with the signing of the August 2, 1915 Turko-German alliance it had become feasible to execute a military incursion into India (*einen Indien-Zug nicht für unausführbar*). In expressing this view he invoked, among others, the name of Tamerlane as a conqueror who had proved the feasibility of such a venture.[173]

There is another instance of resistance by lower echelon German officials to the disposition of their superiors in the matter of Turkish anti-Armenian measures that is worth mentioning. When Aleppo's veteran consul Rössler learned that Major Wolffskeel was accompanying Turkish General Fahri Paşa, whose mission it was to repress two defensive uprisings in Mussa Dagh and later Urfa, he questioned the wisdom of such an act in a report to the German ambassador, with a copy to the German chancellor. "I submit for your esteemed consideration the question whether it is appropriate (*zweckmässig*) to have a German officer take part in an expedition against an internal foe of Turkey." It is necessary to point out once more that this portion too is deleted from the version included in the tome of Lepsius.[174] As has been observed in note 105 of Part II, Rössler's admonition was ignored in both Istanbul and Berlin, and Wolffskeel "came to the rescue of the Turks in Urfa who could not overcome the resistance of the intrepid Armenians until he reduced them with his artillery canister-shots (*da kartäschte deutsche Artillerie alles zusammen*), to quote a Swiss professor.[175]

In the deliberations to mount revolutionary forays into the Caucasus a number of German academic experts, so-called Islamists and Orientalists, were consulted. In fact there is an assertion, as noted in Part II, that in the promotion of the idea of the wholesale deportation of the Armenians some of these academicians were in the forefront. It was during the deliberations (as early as October 1914) that one of them, Islamist Prof. Martin Hartmann, in an article in the *Deutsche-Levante Zeitung* suggested that "it was possible" to invade Russian Armenia and "reach Alexandropol (or Giumri today) and Yerevan."[176] When the fortunes of war subsequently were such as to permit such an incursion, General Seeckt, the Chief of the Ottoman General Staff at the time, not only proposed to issue an order for a march into Yerevan but also provided the rationale for the proposed incursion: "to drive away (or to banish) the Armenians" from there (*um dortige Armenier zu verjagen*). In order to achieve this goal of mass expulsion he ordered the cessation of the operations for the drive to Tiflis and the redirection of the Turkish troops toward southeasterly objectives.[177] As in the other cases cited earlier, the efforts of two other German generals (who at the time were serving in the Caucasus, Kress von Kressenstein and von Lossow) to avert the catastrophe associated with this Turkish invasion were fruitless. General von Lossow protested against the new Turkish intent aiming at "the total extermination of the Armenians in Transcaucasus" (*völlige Ausrottung der Armenier auch in Transcaucasien*)[178] by a new form of mass murder, that is, "the complete encirclement and the allied objective to starve off the entire Armenian nation" (*durch völlige Abschliessung verhungern zu lassen*).[179] For his part General von Kressenstein, Chief of the German Imperial Delegation in the Caucasus, wrote

> The Turkish policy of causing starvation is an all too obvious proof, if proof was still needed as to who is responsible for the massacre, for the Turkish resolve to destroy the Armenians" (*ein zu augenfälliger Beweis für den Vernichtungswillen der Türkei gegenüber dem armenischen Element ... als dass noch Zweifel darüber bestehen konnten auf wen die Massakres zurückzuführen sind*).[180]

In a subsequent report he wrote the following:

> The Turkish policy vis-à-vis the Armenians is clearly outlined (*zeichnet sich klar ab*). The Turks have by no means relinquished their intention to exter-

minate the Armenians (*ihre Absicht ... auszurotten*). They merely changed their tactic. Wherever possible, the Armenians are being aroused, provoked in the hope of thereby securing a pretext for new assaults on them (*Man reizt die Armenier, wo nur irgend möglich, man provoziert sie in der Hoffnung dadurch einen Vorwand zu neuen Angriffen ... zu erhalten*).[181]

His last report is perhaps most telling. It not only confirms the resolve of the Turks to extend the genocide to Russian Armenia in the Caucasus but also exposes once more the consistency with which Turks resorted to the standard tactic of going to any length to provoke an already decimated and exhausted population in order to create an excuse for the planned mass murder. In this very comprehensive report General Kress underscores first the Turkish resort to "unconscionable methods of disinformation about the Armenians by Turkish civilian and military authorities reporting to their superiors in the Ottoman capital. He scorns the use of such clichés as "military necessity, " "threat to our communication and supply lines," and "other similar pretexts," which are being advanced in order "to justify the murder of thousands of human beings." In an appended declaration, cosigned by Austrian diplomat in the Caucasus, Georg Freiherr von Franckenstein, Turkish generals Esad, Şevki, and War Minister Enver's brother Nuri are taken to task for spreading "distorted information" (*entstellte Meldungen*) about Russian Armenia. "The perfidy (*Hinterhaltigkeit*) of General Esad was revealed when his explanations about Armenian refugees, without any danger of being slaughtered, being able to return, proved false" (*unwahr*).[182] Finally, reference may be made to Colonel Ernst Paraquin the German Chief of Staff in 1918 of Turkish General Halil (Kut), who too eyewitnessed the atrocities in Turkey as well as in the Caucasus, especially Baku in September 1918. He wrote:

> With hypocritical indignation (*geheuchelter Entrüstung*) the Turkish government denies all barbarous conduct (*barbarisches Verfahren*) against the Armenians. The evacuation of Anatolia by the Russians furnished the desired opportunity to clear out also the Russian Armenians ... . The annihilation campaign against the Armenians proceeded ... with inexorable ruthlessness ... . The Armenian question was solved through annihilation.

Furthermore, Paraquin lamented that, "... if I am correctly informed, we squandered on the Orientals at least 100 millions of coined gold."[183]

Another subordinate German officer ventilated his frustration and even rage about the inexorable methods with which the Armenians in the eastern provinces were being exterminated and about which he felt completely impotent. The reference is to Colonel Stange. He was involved in

Turkish sabotage and guerrilla activities, organized and financed by the German Foreign Office. As such, he was not only an eyewitness but also had valuable access to the representatives of the Turkish War Office and the top delegates of the Young Turk Ittihad party in connection with the mission of that secret organization, and with the command and control of the operations of his detachment. Equally, if not more importantly, a large contingent of this outfit consisted of ex-convicts, released from prisons by the Directorate of the Ittihad party. The most crucial part of Stange's testimony refers to the employment of the convicts (*Sträflinge*) in the enactment of the genocide. They were part of "The Special Organization" (*Teşkilâtı Mahsusa*), which, after their more or less abortive guerrilla campaign against Russia, were transferred to the command of the killer squads in the campaign of the extermination of the bulk of the Armenians of the eastern provinces. The principal architects of that extermination program during the December 1914–April 1915 period were associated with Stange's high command and after February 15, 1915 were under his direct command. They were Dr. Behaeddin Şakir, his deputy Hilmi, retired artillery major and, subsequently, Central Committee member Yusuf Riza, and Trabzon Responsible Secretary of Ittihad, Nail.[184] Colonel Stange's rather lengthy report, the only one available, is most remarkable for candor, factual grounding, specificity, and broad perspective. In it, Stange offers in his own military style the operative contours of a syndrome of genocide in which ingredients of opportunism, premeditation, decision making, supervision, types of atrocities, and scale and agents of destruction seem to configure in a fitting web of relationships. The report, marked "secret" (*geheim*) and issued from Erzurum, is dated 23 August, 1915 and is addressed to "The German Military Mission," headed by Marshal Liman von Sanders. It is perhaps most significant that Stange prefaced his report with a declaration, underscoring the main reason for preparing that report. He referred to "The endeavor of the Turkish government to conceal or tone down the occurrences" (*zu verheimlichen oder abzuschwächen*), adding: "The situation is as follows" (*Die Lage ist folgendermassen*).

> **Opportunity.** "Military reasons were of secondary importance for the deportation of the Armenians. Mainly, (*hauptsächlich*), an intervention from the outside was not expected" in the undertaking, the purpose of which was "to exploit this favorable opportunity" (*diese günstige Gelegenheit, wo von aussen her Einspruch nicht zu erwarten war, zu benutzen*). "The military considerations and insurgent tendencies in certain parts of the country afforded welcome pretexts" (*willkommenen Vorwand*).

Premeditation. For the destruction of the Armenian population the Turks did have "a plan conceived long time ago." (*einen lang gehegten Plan*).

Decision Making (Intent). "The deportation and destruction of the Armenians was decided upon by the Young Turk Committee in Constantinople." (*Die Austreibung und Vernichtung der Armenier war vom jungtürkischen Komitee in Konstantinopel beschlossen ...*)

Organization and Supervision. "... well organized ... members of that committee are on location for that purpose: Hilmi, Şakir, Deputy for Erzurum Seyfullah ... and Commander-in-Chief (IIIrd Army) Kâmil ..."

Agents of Destruction. They were essentially of two kinds.

a. The military: "With the condoning, even with the assistance of the military escorts" (*Unter Duldung der militärischen Begleitung, sogar mit deren Mithilfe*), and "with the help of the members of the army" (*mit Hilfe von Angehörigen des Heeres*) was the annihilation of the Armenians effected.

b. "The scum" category (*Gesindel*), involving "so-called *çetes*." Focusing on a specific case, "as conceded by the governor" (*Der Wali gab diese Tatsachen zu*), Stange declares: "It is absolutely established (*einwandfrei fest*) that practically without exception the Armenians were murdered in the area of Tercan" by these types.

Types and Techniques of Destruction.

a. "The manner in which the deportation (*Ausweisung*) was carried out by the government, the police officials and their organs, was a typical example (*Musterbeispiel*) of beastly brutality (*tierische Roheit*) on the part of all the participating Turks ... they did everything to amplify the torments of the Armenians" (*die Quälereien der Armenier vermehren*).

b. "In Trabzon men were marched off to a mountain site and slaughtered" (*abgeschlachtet*). Again in the same city, "the Armenians were taken on board of vessels and dumped overboard in the sea" (*Auf's Meer hinausgefahren und dann über Bord geworfen*).[185]

Stange ends his report by identifying those Turks who were responsible for the deportations and accompanying massacres. The two of these epitomize the powerful links binding together the civilian and the military potentates of Ittihad party in the common and superordinate task of destroying the Armenian population. The reference is to Dr. B. Şakir and General Mahmud Kâmil, the Commander-in-Chief of the IIIrd Army (February 1915–February 1916). Stange could protest but could not obviate, let alone prevent, these crimes because he and his VIIIth Regiment were attached to the High Command of the IIIrd Army. As discussed earlier, however, "the moving spirit in the headquarters of that army," "the soul of the High Command" was non other than the German colonel Felix Guse, Stange's military superior and General Kâmil's cohort in the headquarters.

Lieutenant Colonel Felix Guse was not the least interested in hearing about atrocities or measures against the Armenians in the command zone of the IIIrd Army. As far as he was concerned the Turks were simply responding in kind in a life and death struggle. He was so entrenched in this stance that even after the termination of his duties of Chief of Staff he felt constrained to protect the reputation of Turkey. His wife was visiting in Switzerland when she attended a lecture and supposedly heard accounts of "atrocities against the Armenians" (*armenische Greuel*). Guse did not waste any time. He immediately fired off a note of protest from the office of the German Military Mission in Istanbul, only to be informed subsequently that he was misinformed and that in none of the three lectures there was any reference to Armenian atrocities.[186]

In order to understand more fully a critical component in the materialization of the Armenian genocide, namely, German complicity through cooptation by the Turks of certain high ranking German officers, Guse's frame of mind, as revealed in his words, may be reconsidered as a signal factor. Such a frame of mind is particularly telling in relation to Guse's ultimate justification of the sweep and severity of the anti-Armenian measures. When conceding that there was no evidence to prove an impending general "revolt" on the part of the Armenian population of Turkey, Guse injected into the arguments the issue of uncertainty and the model of a preemptive solution to it—namely, the army couldn't wait to see "if in a critical moment the Armenians would be so magnanimous as to remain quiet" (*ob die Armenier im kritischen Moment so edel sein würden*).[187] This is a frame of mind that disallows a judicious separation between actual offenses, on the one hand, and possible or probable offenses, on the other; rather, it allows the leveling of the two categories of conduct in a sweep of indiscriminate targeting under the plea of military necessity. The thresholds of human forbearance, if they exist, are imperceptible. One is dealing here with a frame of mind that goes a long way in according to a potential perpetrator license to reduce the precept of military necessity to a subterfuge that affords criminal conduct in the name of "military requirement." It is most likely that for all these reasons the Swiss author Christoph Dinkel became firmly convinced of Guse's complicitous behavior in this respect when he offered his "conclusion" (*muss man zum Schluss kommen*) in this regard. After maintaining that all evidence points to the pivotal role of General Kâmil, the IIIrd Army commander, in the liquidation of the Armenians through a scheme of "ruthless deportations," Dinkel declares, "Guse in essence did not differ from Kâmil [in attitude] but operating behind the scenes rather supported, perhaps even urged him on" (*nicht wesentlich unterschied sondern im Hintergrunde unterstützte vielleicht sogar drängte*).[188]

Colonel Stange's impotence vis-à-vis atrocities against the Armenians emerges here as a phenomenon that, at the very least, is conditioned by the pro-Turkish indulgences of Colonel Guse, his superior in the IIIrd Army High Command. The same impotence is attributable to Consuls Scheubner and Schulenburg who had twin statuses, that is, military and civilian; they were not only in charge of the German Consulate at Erzurum, the locus of the headquarters of the IIIrd Army, but were also in charge of expeditionary forces involved in guerrilla and sabotage acts in the border regions of wartime Turkey. Scheubner's confrontation with the commander of the IIIrd Army has been described earlier (note 51); Bronsart's admonitions to Schulenburg to refrain from assisting the Armenian deportees, as his predecessor Scheubner had done, has also been noted (Part II, note 36). Dinkel states that in the course of the Armenian deportations Bronsart "intervened at least three times against German officials because in his opinion they had looked too much after the Armenians."[189]

Nor did the other German officers operating in the Caucasus in the spring and summer of 1918 have any better luck. Indeed, neither generals Lossow and Kressenstein, nor Colonel Paraquin, were in a position to prevent the Turkish drive to strangulate and further reduce the remnants of the Armenian people. The authority to do so lay elsewhere, namely, within the purview of the Turkish High Command, in whose General Headquarters at that time Lieutenant General Seeckt functioned as Chief of Staff, as noted earlier, and as such he was empowered to exercise some control. The cipher mentioned above (note 177) demonstrates that he was not only averse to exercising such control but also willing to pave the ground for the carrying out of operations that could only serve to help implement the design of the three Turkish generals to extend the genocide to the Armenians in the Caucasus. It is worth reproducing here the typical Prussian rationale Seeckt adopted in the matter of the wartime treatment of the Armenians. As observed in note 104 of Part II, through that rationale he maintained that "sentiments" and "Christian ideals" merited no consideration when planing and conducting warfare. Yet, he saw fit to continue forsaking such Christian ideals and human sentiments even when the war was all but over. Like General Bronsart, he too offered Enver and Talât, the two principal architects of the Armenian genocide, help to escape justice through an escape from Turkey altogether, for which purpose German military ships were made available.[190]

THE IDEOLOGICAL AND INSTIGATIVE ROLE OF OPPENHEIM

His general attitude and motives warranting the adoption of anti-Armenianism

Max Freiherrn von Oppenheim embodied the type of an operative whose inveterate urge to impress the powers to be with displays of demonstrative patriotism in reality often serves to reduce these operatives to mere caricatures of an actual patriot. Oppenheim's zealousness to please the German emperor and to be of service to the German state was such that he ended up losing a sense of balance and proportion in his assessment of the origin and nature of the lingering Turko-Armenian conflict. He became an opportunist, a careerist and an exceedingly pushy operator, to the point where even the Young Turk Ittihadist leaders began to be repelled by him and went out of their way to urge the German Foreign Office to prevent him from returning to Istanbul in 1916. Foreign Minister Halil (Menteşe), for example, in September 1916 complained that Oppenheim became "entirely impossible."[191] Chargé Wilhelm von Radowitz in October 1916 received complaints from Turks to the effect that Oppenheim was impetuous and intrusive and that he was trying to ingratiate himself with "awkward flatteries." The Grand Vizier was unhappy with him, and Cemal Paşa, the "Viceroy" in Syria, Lebanon, and Palestine, made "very derogatory" (*sehr abfällig*) remarks about him.[192] This is all the more significant when one considers the fact that Oppenheim thought highly of Cemal.[193] In December 1916, Dr. Richard Kühlmann, the new ambassador to Turkey, told the Foreign Office in Berlin that "In view of prevalence of the anti-Oppenheim mood in the ruling Turkish circles, I consider Oppenheim's return to Istanbul inappropriate."[194] Given his original predilections for archeology and research through new excavations, his subsequent decision to embrace politics and get embroiled in international intrigues and manipulations is a development that is emblematic of the pitfalls of self-debasement to which are exposed scholars willing to be suborned by the state for material gains and other non-material rewards. Oppenheim offered his knowledge on the conditions in the Near and Middle East to the German state whose leaders were trying to penetrate these regions for purposes of economic exploitation and political-military hegemony.[195] In the process he became a partisan politician, disposed to substitute for the ideals of "truth and beauty" that of instigative propaganda. In fact he consistently agitated against the Armenians in Germany as well as in Turkey, recklessly compounding the perils hanging over a defenseless population targeted for destruction. It is therefore appropriate to review briefly the highlights of this role performance.

Oppenheim entered into the Prussian State Service in 1883 at the age of 23. This engagement afforded him the manifold opportunities to visit and explore a host of Islamic countries, especially Syria and Mesopotamia. In the 1895–1896 period, coinciding with the empirewide Armenian massacres of the Abdul Hamit era, he visited Constantinople (Istanbul) and the interior of Turkey in the performance of a task that was dubbed project William II. He had a private audience with Sultan Abdul Hamit, which lasted more than an hour.[196] In the 1896–1910 period he served as attaché to the German Consulate General in Cairo and was promoted to the rank of *Legationsrat* (Legation Councillor), then to that of Ministerresident. His mutation from the standing of an aspiring scientist to that of agent gathering and relaying intelligence to his government is evidenced in the series of reports he sent to Berlin from this post in Cairo. In them Oppenheim berates and denounces the Armenians as traitors to the Ottoman state. In his April 29, 1904 report to Chancellor von Bülow, for example, he accuses the Armenian political leaders of Egypt of conspiracy against Sultan Abdul Hamit and belittles or dismisses the significance of the massacres that were ordered by the latter.[197] His followup report of May 3, 1904 contains a repetition of the same allegations.[198] In his April 28, 1909 report, which is a standard intelligence report, Oppenheim depicts Diran Kelekian, a prominent Ottoman Armenian publicist temporarily living in Cairo, as a man sympathetic to England and "full of hatred against Germany." He then identifies him as the man hiding behind several pen names.[199]

But Oppenheim's real role as an instigator against the Armenians took on concrete forms with the onset of World War I. Shortly after the outbreak of that war, Oppenheim, through the submission of two memoranda in which he offered advice as to how to inflame the Muslim masses against England, made himself available for engagement as a propaganda operative; in so many words he was in fact appealing to Chancellor Hollweg to make use of his knowledge of Arabs and Islam. He succeeded. The Foreign Office did engage him. After another memorandum on methods of coopting Persia on the side of the Central Powers, Oppenheim in September 1914 prepared a 136-page memorandum on the ways of revolutionizing those Islamic regions that were controlled by opposing Entente Powers (*Die Revolutionierung der Islamischen Gebiete unserer Feinde*). It was printed in October and distributed to various German agencies participating in the war effort.

There are four items in this memorandum that had serious implications for Ottoman Armenians. First and foremost, Oppenheim suggested that as soon as Turkey intervened in the war (*losschlägt, strikes*), *cihad* (holy war) should be declared.[200] (Citing a personal communication from one of the founders of the Turkish Special Organization, Eşref Kuşcubaşı, and Turkish General Sabis, Stoddard indicates that it was General Goltz as well as General Bronsart who persuaded War Minister Enver about the urgency of such declaration).[201] In any event, this fact adds to the other available indices demonstrating that the idea of holy war was conceived by the Germans as an instrument of war in general and as a resource to incite the Muslim masses in particular. Second, in developing further this idea Oppenheim brings it to bear upon the condition of "the Armenians inhabiting in Asia Minor. Cihad may prove useful in preventing the invasion of that land since their inhabitants, the Armenians, are surely not pro-Turkish"(*sicherlich nicht Türkenfreundlich*).[202] Third, in extension of this argument Oppenheim then proceeds to state that "the decrial of the Armenians as cowards and at the same time great intriguants should not be regarded as an unjust act."[203] Finally, perhaps the most ominous item in this memorandum is the reference to the Turkish Special Organization and its first founder, Major Süleyman Askeri. Oppenheim indicates that this outfit's mission was to "revolutionize the Caucasus."[204] The consequences of that mission for the Armenians is a subject that is being examined through this study. In characterizing his memorandum as the output of an author who "under the spell of the war is driven by sentiments of national exuberance," Oppenheim places a high premium "on the intensive participation of the Turks" as "a principal condition for the revolutionizing of the Islamic regions controlled by our enemies."[205] The German Foreign Office at this juncture of the events was quite accommodating vis-à-vis Oppenheim. On December 12, 1914 Undersecretary of State Zimmermann issued a directive: all telegrams covering the developments in the East were to be shown to Oppenheim.[206]

Oppenheim's overall objective was a composite one. He wanted to be of service to Germany by offering his expertise on Islam, Arabs, and anti-colonial tendencies among a host of peoples in the Middle East dominated, if not ruled, by Britain. But he was also eager to pursue his archeological interests in connection with such service to be rendered.[207] His involvement in acts of propaganda and agitation in Ottoman Turkey in the April–November 1915 period must be assessed in consideration of this fact. When the German Foreign Service finally dispatched him to Turkey to organize propaganda through the dissemination of information and news, Oppenheim had this mixed baggage with him (i.e., a record of achievement in archeological research but also in political activities the covert aspects of which involved conspiracy and espionage). In the June–September 1893 period, for example, he undertook an investigative trip to Syria and Mesopotamia, Mosul and Baghdad, among other places. When a year later he published the results in the proceedings of the German Geographical Society, he recommended the establishment of "garrisons" in this part of the Ottoman Empire to exercise "power" in the region. In 1899 he spent seven months in Homs, Aleppo, Urfa, and Chabur, only to come up with his major archeological discovery, namely, the vestiges of Hittite civilization in Tell Halaf, or Ras-el-Ain, as that city in northern Syria is called today.

There are two striking aspects to these undertakings, especially in view of the fact that many of these localities were visited by Oppenheim during World War I while he was propagating and agitating for the Turks as the allies of Germany. First, these were the very localities that proved to be the apocalyptic valleys of the Armenian genocide, especially the Mesopotamian deserts, Ras-el-Ain and Chabur near Deir-el-Zor. As will be seen, Oppenheim is reported to have had dealings with some of the organizers of the massacres taking place in this region.

Second, the German author Treue makes allowance for the possibility that Oppenheim, through his promotion of the factor of Islam in world politics, might have influenced Emperor William II, who in his famous 1898 Damascus speech embraced and declared himself the champion of the cause of 300 million Muslims.[208] But another German author, renowned historian Fritz Fischer, is more certain. He maintains that Oppenheim's thesis of Islam as an ideology and a socio-political system experiencing "a renaissance of power and vitality" (based on his July 5, 1898 memorandum) inspired the emperor to his Damascus speech. In fact Fischer uses the word "enthused" (*begeistert*) to describe the emperor's response to Oppenheim's thesis.[209]

His political activities involving guile and chicanery generated a dichotomous image about him; he was famous as far as archeology was concerned but infamous as far as diplomacy was concerned. While serving as a diplomat at the German Embassy in Cairo, for example, he is reported to have secured through skullduggery a batch of secret documents. The documents reportedly proved the existence of a wide conspiracy against the Turkish sultan and his government. The German government, so goes the report, sent Goltz, the Prussian officer who had tried to introduce reforms in the Turkish army, to Istanbul to alert the Sultan and "to draw the necessary consequences." Oppenheim's mastery of cunning in escaping Egypt and evading the British counterintelligence agents by artfully organizing his trip for a personal delivery in Berlin of the facsimiles of these documents is in itself a saga illustrating the transmutation of an aspiring scientist into a notorious spy.[210] In fact in a report prepared by the British War Office Oppenheim explicitly is described as a former "spy in Egypt."[211] His first World War I clandestine assignment was a secret rendezvous with the Khedive (Viceroy of Egypt) whom he visited at Hotel Imperial in Vienna under a fictitious name and on behalf of the German Foreign Office.[212]

When Oppenheim returned to Istanbul following his propaganda campaign for holy war in southern Turkey, including Syria, Lebanon, and Iraq, which at that time were still part of the Ottoman Turkey, he was wearing "a Beduin-beard and had at his disposal millions of German gold marks and wagon loads of pamphlets."[213] A German newspaper editor relates in his memoirs that Oppenheim's propaganda output was "much derided by the locals and elsewhere by the non-German populace as *sacs de mensonges*" (bags of lies).[214] There was created in the German Embassy at Istanbul a special section (*Nachrichtenstelle der Deutschen Botschaft*) for the acquisition, marshaling, and distribution of this propaganda material, with the Deutche Orientbank, "very confidentially" (*streng vertraulich*) willing to serve as a transmission belt by way of forwarding that material from Berlin to Istanbul where that bank had a branch.[215] His network of propaganda bureaus in the interior of Turkey included those cities that were the centers of the Turkish genocidal machine, namely, Erzurum, Diyarbekir, Urfa, Adana, Aleppo, and Edirne. These were the conditions against the background of which Oppenheim's specific anti-Armenian acts in the course of the war need to be examined and evaluated.

His espousal of the wartime Turkish anti-Armenian measures

Oppenheim's anti-Armenian acts during the war were a by-product of several trends, personal and impersonal, that imparted to these acts a semblance of validity. He could persuade himself, at face value at least, that in supporting the Turks in their anti-Armenian drive he was on the right track. His prejudicial descriptions of the Armenians in general, which have been noted earlier, were a factor in this regard; they made him amenable to generating outright hostility against the Armenians on the basis of incriminatory information he allowed the Turks to feed him. In other words, he was suitably predisposed to agree with certain calumnies that were being disseminated by the authorities. Furthermore, his identification with two major causes for all practical purposes precluded other alternative course of action. The Christian Armenians were a thorn in the eye of Muslim Turks and Kurds and an obstacle for the unhindered sway in the region of Islam to which he had committed himself as a priority in the pursuit of knowledge and politics. The Turko-German alliance only served to reinforce his posture. Summoning up his sentiments of German patriotism, through the exhibition of which he was most eager to impress the authorities in Berlin, he vowed to do all in his power to help defeat the enemies of Germany and its allies, especially the Turkish ally. The lingering Turko-Armenian conflict, which had intensified in the years preceding the war, the generally pro-Entente mood of the Ottoman Armenians, despairing of their historical misfortunes under oppressive Turkish rule, and the identification by the German and Turkish allies of the Armenian quest for reforms with Russian designs on eastern Turkey, were for Oppenheim considerations favoring the adoption of an anti-Armenian stance. Oppenheim zealously thrust himself into the dynamics of this adoptive stance. But according to the information supplied to British intelligence by a German agent in the pay of the British and working in the Aleppo-Diyarbekir area Oppenheim had personal grudges against the Armenians of those localities. According to this report Oppenheim was eager to expand "his archeological hunting grounds at Ras-el-Ain. ... The Christian landowners, however, always proved obstacles. During the Armenian massacres he revenged himself by egging on the notables ... and rousing their fanaticism."[216]

Whether in Berlin or in Turkey itself, Oppenheim set out to incriminate the Armenians in any way he could. He appealed in Berlin, along with another scholar-agitator, Prof. Dr. E. Mittwoch, to Prof. Dr. Joseph Marquart, a distinguished Armenolog, to translate for him the contents of some private letters written by Armenians and in the possession of Oppenheim. In a pungent negative response Marquart decried such a request as an appeal "to espionage for the benefit of Turkey." He then proceeded to berate his own government for "completely distorted and fabricated Turkish accounts on the ghastly massacres against the Armenians" (*die schauerlichen Metzeleien ... unter den Armeniern in einer völlig entstellten und erlogenen Weise darzustellen*). He likewise denounced the German press for publishing "the most wicked calumnies and most venomous lies about the Armenians who are being treated as outlaws" (*die ärgsten Verleumdungen und gehässigsten Lügen über die vogelfreien Armenier*).[217] In another attempt in Berlin to equip himself with material with a view to taking a position against the Armenians, Oppenheim appealed to Wilhelm von Stumm, the director of the political section of the Foreign Office, for receipt of a copy of the secret report of Lepsius, which the government had banned and went even so far as to bar 191 Reichstag deputies from access to it. Even though the report exclusively deals with the destruction of the Armenian population in Turkey through deportation and massacres, Oppenheim chose to describe it as a pamphlet dealing with "the present Armenian difficulties" (*die gegenwärtigen armenischen Schwierigkeiten*). He promised Stumm "strict confidentiality" in the treatment of the material, adding that he was reluctant to ask Lepsius directly for such a copy.[218]

A few weeks before he undertook his trip to Turkey for his new post there as "handler" of news and information about Germany and Turkey and their significance for Islam and the Muslim masses of the area, Oppenheim on February 24, 1915 in a memorandum to the Foreign Office enumerated the reasons why the Armenians should be regarded as an internal foe of Turkey. He directed attention to the fact that the Armenians in Europe, especially in France and Russia, were aligning themselves with the Entente Powers. Referring to some newspaper accounts, presumably German, he declared that "the Armenians deliberately committed treason (*Verrat*) against Turkey." He concluded with the warning: "It is entirely possible that the Armenians everywhere will want to enlist ... with all their might (*mit allen Kräften*) in the fight against the Turks."[219]

But the most damning evidence on Oppenheim's truculent support of the liquidation of the Armenians is contained in his August 29, 1915 11-page report sent to German chancellor Bethmann Hollweg. The gist of it is that the Turks were justified in this initiative of liquidation and that as the ally of Turkey "we ought not to oppose it" (*als Verbündete der Türken durften wir uns ihnen ... nicht widersetzen*). He characterized the entire episode as a Turkish measure of defense and self-preservation against the incidence of "the Armenian danger" (*die Armeniergefahr*) and pleaded for an understanding of Turkey on grounds of the demands of the role of "statesmanship" (*aus staatsmännischen Gründen*).[220] There are several explanations in the report that together represent the rationale of this stance. Foremost among them is his principal one, which dominates the texture of his antagonism against the Armenians: his very negative judgment about them (*ein sehr schlechtes ... Urteil*) based on his many contacts with them in Turkey during his travels.[221] Thus, once more, one notices the functional operativeness of existing negative images about the Armenians either as facilitators of complicitous behavior or mere rationalizations after the facts. The components of this negative image are: "proverbial cunning in commerce, a passion for intrigue, conceitedness, revolutionary tendencies, above all the usury constantly practiced by them in the environment of which they are part, and the anti-Turkish enmity they lately have been openly displaying."[222] The charges leveled against the Armenians in this report about espionage, sabotage, rebellion, etc., in their ensemble are an exact replica of those leveled by the Turkish authorities. Smugly dispensing with the need to exercise caution, if not suspicion, about the veracity of these charges, Oppenheim embraced them wholeheartedly and tried to make maximum use of them. He had requested and obtained from Cemal Paşa, the Commander of the Ottoman IVth Army and the practical ruler of the areas in Syria and Lebanon where Oppenheim was particularly active, the material upon which he based his report. Not content with this, Oppenheim advised Cemal to assemble in Damascus as well as Istanbul such requisite material against the Armenians as might afford the preparation of a dossier to incriminate the Armenians and thereby exculpate the Turks. Oppenheim went so far as to assert that "... in the interior of Turkey, in the cities of Asia Minor, there was uncovered (*aufgedeckt*) the threads of a militarily organized conspiracy" (*eine militärisch gegliederte Verschwörung*).[223] Oppenheim in an effort to impress his superiors in Berlin prepared a report for Chancellor Hollweg in which he made two important points: 1) he was cooperating with the Turkish Ministry of War as well as with the Directorate of the Ittihad political party and 2) he emphasized the importance of the cooperation with the latter group by describing it as "the most important instance of power beside the actual central government of Turkey" (*hauptsächlichster Machtfaktor ...*).[224]

The indignant but ineffective repudiation of Oppenheim by lesser German officials

By completely adopting the Turkish distortions, half truths, and even falsehoods as instruments of his own propaganda campaign Oppenheim not only abandoned all standards of scholarly objectivity but also patently reinforced the Turkish resolve for optimal destruction of the Armenian population, which was then in progress. To Turkish eyes his elevated official position was such that through his approbation of the anti-Armenian measures he lent the imprimatur of German consent to them. One of the most eloquent rebuttals, however indirect, came from Aleppo's veteran German consul Rössler. After recounting the litany of massacres in the area of northern Syria and Mesopotamia, especially Ras-el-Ain, Oppenheim's focus of interest and attention, Rössler expresses astonishment at the audacity of the Turkish authorities who had declared that "the Ottoman government extended its benevolent protection to all honest and peaceful Christians of Turkey." His ire was directed to the respective propaganda being carried out "in the German press." He asked Chancellor Hollweg whether it was appropriate to allow that press to be a tool of Turkish governmental propaganda and wondered out loud whether thereby Germany's honor and reputation was not being compromised. On June 4, 1915 the Turkish authorities had sent a memorandum to the German Foreign Office in which they claimed that the deportations were a temporary measure of relocation (*übersiedeln*) and that they were being applied only to the war zones. The German newspaper *Norddeutsche Allgemeine Zeitung* (the traditional mouthpiece of the German government) in its June 9, 1915 issue had dutifully reproduced that assertion.The reaction of Rössler to this is noteworthy. "Indeed, I couldn't believe my eyes as I saw this statement" (*Fürwahr, ich habe meinen Augen nicht getraut, als ich diese Erklärung gesehen habe*), and I find no words to characterize the abyss of its untruth" (*und ich finde keinen Ausdruck, um den Abgrund ihrer Unwahrheit zu kennzeichnen*). In refuting this assertion Rössler mentioned several towns whose Armenian populations were deported and asked "Are they really in war zones? Does the presence in them of women and children represent a danger to the state inasmuch as practically all able-bodied men have been recruited?" Pursuant to his determination to expose the fraudulent nature of official Turkish communiqués Rössler reveals in his report the fact that the authorities have been using "convicts who have been released from the prisons (*Sträflinge aus den Gefängnissen entlassen*). They were put in soldier's uniforms and were deployed at spots through which the deportee convoys were to pass." Rössler reveals also that the Circassian-Chechens, Oppenheim's favorite object of concern in Ras-el-Ain, were engaged for the purpose of attacking the Armenians. In a fit of anger, the German consul finally declares in his "confidential" report that the Turks in fact were bent on "resolving the Armenian Question during the war as the government is utilizing the alliance with the Central Powers for this purpose." Accusing the Ittihadist power-wielders of the crime of "the ruination (*Untergang*) of hecatombs of innocent people" he declared the Turks "unworthy" (*unwürdig*) of an alliance with Germany.[225]

Perhaps the most direct and consequential rebuttal and therewith repudiation of Oppenheim as a dangerous propagandist and conspirator came from Hermann Hoffmann, vice consul at Alexandrette and intermittently Interim Consul at Aleppo. In one of the most comprehensive and detailed reports (25 pages) ever written by a provincial German consul Hoffmann tackles one by one the factors that configure in the enactment of the Armenian genocide, namely, motivation, methods of execution, techniques of deception and deflection, scope of losses, etc.[226] In the course of this exposition and analysis he felt constrained to take Oppenheim to task on several aspects of the governmental anti-Armenian measures on which Oppenheim had parroted the Turkish line of misrepresentations and outright falsehoods. He prefaced his report by the statement that it is based on observations he made while he was deputizing Rössler at the German Consulate at Aleppo during the latter's leave in October 1915. A full discussion of the content of the report is outside the framework of this study. Therefore, attention will be focused mainly on the set of facts Hoffmann produces from firsthand knowledge, facts through which anti-Armenian charges of Oppenheim are belied and through which Oppenheim emerges as a reckless and ruthless advocate of a clique engaged in the task of obliterating the bulk of an indigenous population. The central issue tackled by Hoffmann concerns the nature of the few Armenian uprisings in his district and their relationship, if any, to each other. This aspect of the problem bears particular attention because of the key Turkish charge embraced by Oppenheim that there was a widespread Armenian conspiracy bent on a general rebellion that imperiled the safety of the Turkish nation and called, therefore, for draconian countermeasures. Commenting on the uprising in Van, the occurrence which, he argues, "should not surprise anyone, given the prior history of that episode," Hoffmann disputes the validity of a general conspiracy against the Turkish state and in doing so he specifically mentions Oppenheim's adoption of this view.[227] On the basis of evidence available to the German Consulate at Aleppo, of the four small uprisings at Zeitoun (March 1915), Funducak (July–August 1915), Mussa Dagh (August–September 1915), and Urfa (September–October 1915), none had a revolutionary, conspiratorial thrust, stated the vice consul. Since all four localities fell within the jurisdiction of the consulate's district (Aleppo), Hoffmann declared that he could attest to these uprisings having been episodes that were "locally confined (*örtlich beschränkt*) and were not a by-product of a widely laid up conspiracy (*nicht als Ausfluss einer weiter angelegten Verschwörung*). Most important, he categorically stated that all of them "were improvised on the spot and were prompted by the threat of deportation" (*an Ort und Stelle durch die Drohung der Verschickung gereift*). In the same vein Hoffmann invoked the testimony of Turkish military officers denying any evidence of conspiracy in the case of Mussa Dagh and confirming that it was a spontaneously improvised defensive uprising. Nor was there any truth to the official charge that the rescue of the fighters of Mussa Dagh by French warships was a long before arranged undertaking, said the vice consul, again invoking the testimony of "well informed Turks."[228]

Moving from the general to a very specific level of discourse, Hoffmann in detail debunks a Turkish charge of a far-reaching Armenian espionage and sabotage ring near Alexandrette. Oppenheim on pages 4 and 5 in his August 29, 1915 report had chosen to dwell on this. Hoffmann points out that a single Armenian was caught in the vicinity of Alexandrette; he allegedly was put on land by the British cruiser *Doris* at Dörtyol and the authorities had found 40 Turkish or British pounds in his possession. "This is the bare fact; everything else is inflated and embellished" (*Zutat*), wrote Hoffmann, at the same time pointing out the fact that it is nothing unusual for local well-to-do Armenians to carry their wealth in their belts. Hoffmann didn't believe that the British needed the help of a single Armenian to effect railroad derailing. He had evidence that the single act of derailing was the work of the British cruiser *Doris*. These are some of the embellishments: there were many Armenians involved; incriminating papers were found; Armenians have derailed railroads carriages; there exist liaisons between enemy naval commanders and Armenians in the area of the bay of Alexandrette. Hoffmann with explanations one by one denies the veracity of these invented charges with an authority evincing a thorough investigation of the matter on the part of the consular officials. In debunking Oppenheim in particular, he points out that even the Turks didn't go as far as to claim that "as a result of the landing , the railroads at Alexandrette were destroyed and undoubtedly espionage and other services were rendered." Retorted Hoffmann: "Though I am familiar with all the details of the case, I have never heard such an accusation, not even from the Turkish-Muslim camp" (*Ich habe diese Anklage noch nie gehört ... obwohl mir der Fall in allen Einzelheiten bekannt ist*).[229] One is provided here with a portrait of a German official whose penchant to inflate and embellish in order to incriminate the Armenians as gravely as possible exceeds that of the latter's arch enemy, the Turkish officials themselves. To underscore this point Hoffmann adduces another telling example. When describing the Urfa uprising, Oppenheim told Hoffmann that the Armenians' inventory of weapons included machine-guns, presumed to be, of course, of Russian venue; Oppenheim was insistent on this point. He considered it "a fact beyond any doubt" (*über jeden Zweifel*) and proceeded to see in that fact "evidence of conspiratorial ties between the rebellious Armenians of Urfa on the one hand, and Van province and Russia, on the other." But Vice Consul Hoffmann had checked with Major Wolfskeel, the German artillery officer who had reduced the Armenian quarter of Urfa to ruins (see note 142, Part II); Wolffskeel characterized the story of such machine-guns as one belonging to "the world of fable" (*in das Reich der Fabel*). Subsequently, Oppenheim had to correct himself.[230] Finally, Hoffmann directs attention to the highly questionable methods through which the alleged Armenian saboteur Torosoğlu Agop was tried, convicted, and executed on the gallows. "I know of no other trial proceeding in Turkey that is more frivolous than this one" (... *mir selbst in der Türkei kein frivoleres Gerichtsverfahren bekannt geworden* ...).[231]

There are two final points to be made about this report. One reason Hoffmann was anxious to rebut and repudiate Oppenheim was his concern that the latter's conduct reinforced in Turkey the credibility of assertions in terms of Germans having been "the accomplices of the Turks (*Mitschuldiger*), if not the instigators" (*wenn nicht gar Anstifter*).[232] It is likewise most significant that like Oppenheim, Hoffmann, perhaps to a lesser degree, was antipathetic toward the Armenians (*Abneigung gegen die Armenier*) but this did not interfere with "the revulsion" he felt for the atrocities inflicted upon them; he accused the Armenians, for example, of ungratefulness.[233] Yet, in the final analysis, he recognized that the Armenians were victims of their economic superiority in relation to the Muslim Turks who welcomed the Van uprising as a needed excuse to eliminate (*Ausmerzung*) once and for all the Armenian element.[234]

Did Oppenheim consort with the massacrers?

In attempting to answer this question the significance of two factors needs to be taken into account. The act of conspiratorial consorting is intrinsically an act of plotting and needs to be enveloped in secrecy. In the case of a mass murder of gigantic proportions that secrecy is expected to be a most compelling condition. Accordingly, the task of a clear-cut documentation of such consorting more often than not is considerably impaired; one has to rely, therefore, on fragmented and circumstantial evidence. A more crucial factor to consider is the cumulative evidence of the conspiratorial activities of Oppenheim whose propensities for learning and archeological research are seen attended, and often eclipsed, by a proclivity for political agitation, incitement, and intrigue.

In other words, one can hardly afford to depend entirely on official German records in order to assess Oppenheim's responsibility in the enactment of the Armenian genocide. In his evaluation of what the *London Times* called "the notorious Baron Oppenheim,"[235] the German author Treue described the latter as "a politically insignificant man bereft of any critical or influential position."[236] But the official titles of agents can hardly be used as yardsticks to gauge their importance or the significance of their work. It was in the nature of his wartime work to combine his overt activities of propaganda with a greater scope of covert, secretive initiatives. If he were that unimportant, what was he doing in the palace of the Turkish sultan? According to a British intelligence report, he visited the latter on January 10, 1916.[237]

Oppenheim's influence in the determination of the nature of German response to the Turkish onslaught against the Armenian population is accidentally revealed in a particular case handled by Konstantin F. Neurath, the councillor and for a time the chargé at the German Embassy in Istanbul. In his November 20, 1915 communication to German chancellor Hollweg he informed the latter that he decided not to intercede any more with War Minister Enver on behalf of the Armenians with a view to mitigating the harsh conditions that at that time were being inflicted upon them. His sole reason was the receipt from Oppenheim of a report on the Urfa uprising in which "the Armenians are particularly incriminated" (*besonders belastet*).[238] One is dealing here not just with a more or less legitimate influence based on dutiful accurate reporting but guileful and malicious influence based on a mode of reporting that borders on resort to dishonesty. There is extensive literature, supplied mostly by American, British, and Swiss eyewitnesses, demonstrating the extremely dire conditions under which the Armenians of Urfa felt compelled to defend themselves, to sell dear their lives, rather than be deported and face implacable destruction. One of these eyewitnesses, the Swiss pharmacist Jacob Künzler, states in his memoirs that he knew Oppenheim for several years and that in Aleppo he prepared for him a written account on the Urfa episode. This was before Oppenheim composed his own report to be sent to his superiors. Künzler in vain hoped that his account would enlighten Oppenheim and as such prove helpful.[239]

These considerations have a bearing that allow the crediting of the document described below with a high degree of veracity. As noted earlier (note 216), it originates from the Armistice period and is prepared by the British General Staff Intelligence Egyptian Expeditionary Force. In information provided by a German agent working for the British Intelligence and covering the areas in which Oppenheim during the war was active, several organizers of the massacres in these areas were mentioned by name: Abdul Kadir Paşa Gueuze, and his three sons, Khudr Chelebi Komerli, Abdur Rahman Kavas, and Razzuk Chelebi, all of Kurdish extraction. Identified by the code letter N, the agent provides some details about those aspects of the massacres that involved the plunder and appropriation of the possessions and riches of the Armenian victims. It appears that a clique composed of Muslim ringleaders and a German business woman, Martha Koch v. Winckler (whose husband, merchant Carl Friedrich Koch, had a business establishment in Aleppo but who had died during the war), accumulated considerable wealth in connection with these massacres. A "Moslem Committee," operating in Diyarbekir and its satellite district Mardin, was organized by these ringleaders to carry out the massacres as a prelude to the ensuing massive pillage. "The spoils … were sent by Abdul Kadir Paşa to Frau Koch, and jewelry and rich furniture, seized by Reşid, governor-general of Diyarbekir, sent to Constantinople as presents for members of Ittihad." One of the members of this clique was Diyarbekir Deputy Feyzi whose pivotal role in the extermination of the area Armenian population is described in Part II, note 154. According to the report dated December 12, 1918 and signed by E. MacRury, captain in Advantell Central and attached to the British Directorate of Intelligence, Mrs. Koch "was always hostess of von der Goltz Paşa, Baron Oppenheim and Liman von Sanders … she served as intermediary [between] Oppenheim" and the four massacrers mentioned earlier, who "were all friends of Oppenheim." Vast amounts of trade and commerce were transacted by this clique with Deputy Feyzi playing a major role in this respect. "When Feyzi went to Germany early in 1918, he was well received by the Kaiser and decorated with the Iron Cross. The fortune accumulated by Frau Koch is estimated at 3 million Turkish pounds." As to the overall scope of the plunder, this is what is said in the report: "The jewelry, carpets and antiquities plundered in Mardin and Diyarbekir are estimated at 6 million Turkish pounds as well as gold to the amount of 1.5 million Turkish pounds." Diyarbekir governor Dr. Raşid was observed arriving in Aleppo "by a train bound for Constantinople with 48 boxes of jewelry and two cases full of precious stones."[240]

When standing alone and not corroborated by any other source invested with a measure of credibility such intelligence reports are often suspect. This is particularly true in instances where wartime hostilities are still lingering and efforts to revile by all means the enemy camp tend to persist. But this document has a number of items that lend themselves to corroboration and, therefore, validation in general terms. One such item involves the figure 143,000 describing the victims of deportation and massacres in the general area of Diyarbekir. This figure more or less jibes with that provided by the Turkish Military Tribunal investigating the wartime Armenian deportations and massacres. In its Key Indictment it states that 120,000 Armenians were subjected to deportation in Diyarbekir.[241] Another item is the reference to Diyarbekir Deputy Feyzi whose role in the organization of the genocide in Diyarbekir province is amply documented in several sources noted in this part and Part II of this study. Mrs. Koch's wartime traffic with the German military and "the princely" hospitality she extended to her guests are matters that are brought forth in her obituary written by Dr. K. Klinghardt, one of the beneficiaries of this hospitality. He notes with chagrin that following the defeat of Germany "all her possessions were confiscated by the Entente Powers and she was evicted at a very short notice (*das Kochsche Eigentum in Aleppo restlos beschlagnahmt, die Besitzerin kurzfristig ausgewiesen*).[242]

Despite Klinghardt's claim in the obituary that she was not only helpful to the Germans but to "the unhappy Armenians also," Mrs. Koch, her occasional token acts of assistance notwithstanding, was not interested in rendering any appreciable help to the Armenians, and, like her cohort Oppenheim, she was not in the least disturbed that the Armenians were perishing as a nation. Following the example of some liberal Turks, including Aleppo province's Governor-General Hüseyin Celal (who was subsequently deposed by Talât for his resistance to massacres against the Armenians),[243] Frau Martha Koch in a letter from Aleppo (dated July 11, 1915) appealed to the German ambassador at Istanbul to intercede with the Turkish authorities to spare the lives of the Armenian deputies Zohrab and Vartkes. These Armenian community and political leaders (the latter also an ardent Ittihadist) were being sent to Diyarbekir for court-martial; before arriving there, however, they were ambushed by two prominent agents of the Special Organization and killed.[244] In her appeal Koch pleaded for a change of venue from Diyarbekir to Aleppo and for mercy for both men. In the same vein, however, she stated that she "had no reason to plead that the [Armenian] nation be spared" (*...keine Ursache habe zu bitten dass man diese Nation schone ...*). Even more significant is the fact that she made this statement after admitting in the same letter that she "saw with my own eyes the atrocities which were being perpetrated against the Armenians" (*Mit eigenen Augen sah ich an Armeniern verübte Grausamkeiten*).[245]

The most incriminating item in the document, as far as the matter of Oppenheim's complicity is concerned, is the following information:

"Daurri (Dürri) Bey, son of Defterdar Djemal Bey, Turk of Aleppo, was the official High Executioner of the Armenians at Ras-el-Ain. This brute, after robbing them of their jewelry chose the youngest girls of good families and kept them in tents guarded by Circassians. After his numerous daily murders, he violated these girls in turn and finally selected a harem of 15 with whom he lived for 9 months under the protection of Reshid Bey (Governor of Diyarbekir) and Zekki Bey (Mutessarif of Deir-el-Zor). After all the Armenians had been massacred he was called by Talât to Constantinople, but on the night before his departure he lined up the 15 girls against the wall and shot them all himself. Note. Above personalities from Dr. Hyacinthe Farajaliah of Mosul now at Aleppo. While at Ras-el-Ain last month Daurri Bey was pointed out to me at the station by Mr. Avdis, Chief Engineer Baghdad Railway, who mentioned quite independently the incident of the 15 girls. Daurri (Dürri) Bey I am told is a wealthy landowner, e.g. half the town of Membij belongs to him."

Dürri's criminal acts are detailed and independently verified in Aram Andonian's volume dealing with the atrocities at Ras-el-Ain. Evidently Dürri had befriended the district governor Ali Suad, with whom he had set up a farming combine as a business deal. Under the pretext of rescuing them from certain destruction through an exile further east to Deir-el-Zor, he lured a host of Armenian families with attractive young daughters to his farm for employment, only to satisfy his sexual appetite and then dispose of them. Governor Ali Suad, a friend of Dürri's father, is said to have tolerated this modus operandi out of deference to the latter and in further consideration of the fact that Dürri often passed the young Armenian girls to others as gifts.[246] The relevance of this critical piece of information to the issue at hand is provided by Oppenheim. He knew Dürri and appreciated him to such an extent that he gave him an ancillary paid job as director of the Ras-el-Ain branch of the German propaganda bureau *Nachrichtenstelle,* which officially constituted a component of the German Embassy to Turkey. In supplying an account to his superiors of the work of this outfit, directed and supervised by Oppenheim and attaching a list of all the employees he had hired, Oppenheim on February 11, 1916 described "Dürri Bey" as the director (*Leiter*) of his branch at Ras-el-Ain.[247]

There are several questions that pose themselves here. How did Oppenheim come in contact with this arch murderer? On what grounds did he consider him qualified for the job? What was the exact nature of Dürri's contribution to Oppenheim's plan of propaganda and agitation? Did he or did he not know of Dürri's heavy involvement in the crimes of massacre, rape, and pillage? If he did know, or could surmise about their incidence, how did he justify the engagement of such a prima facie suspect? These questions, which presently preclude satisfactory answers, are such as to underscore the difficulties of pinpointing complicity with precision, while at the same time highlighting in general terms the contours of the act of conspiratorial consorting at issue here.

THE NATURE AND OUTCOME OF GERMAN DIPLOMATIC INITIATIVES—THE QUEST FOR ALIBIS AND THE INCULPATION-EXCULPATION STRATAGEM

Despite the political constraints of the Turko-German alliance and perhaps exactly because of that alliance, Germany elected to lodge altogether two separate complaints in the form of memoranda that mildly and politely berated Turkey for the extensive massacres, rapes, and plunders accompanying the Armenian deportations and tried to sensitize Turkey to their future dire consequences in the areas of economics, politics, and international relations. The first memorandum was lodged on July 4, 1915 by Ambassador Wangenheim[248] and the second on August 9, 1915 by Special Ambassador Hohenlohe, who at the time was deputizing for Wangenheim, the latter being on sick leave.[249] Both memoranda were directed to the office of the Grand Vizier, which more or less corresponded to the office of a prime minister. Additionally, German diplomats in Istanbul, including Embassy Councillor Neurath[250] and Ambassador Metternich,[251] upon directives from German chancellor Hollweg,[252] Foreign Minister von Jagow,[253] and Undersecretary Zimmermann,[254] personally appealed to and repeatedly warned the Ottoman government in the same sense. There were a number of subsequent verbal remonstrances that culminated in a January 4, 1917 protest note that essentially focused on the forcible conversions to Islam of select groups of Armenians that were taking place on a massive scale throughout the provinces. The note ended questioning the prudence of these measures that could not be justified militarily or in terms of public security needs. In the text of the August 9 memorandum, a key motive for the production of these official German remonstrances is discernible. The text ends with the expression of an anxiety that "public opinion is swayed by the belief that Germany, as a friendly and allied power, had approved or even inspired these violent acts" (*aurait approuvé ou même inspiré ces actions de violence*). The words "violent acts" are a reference to the charge contained in the first paragraph of the memorandum that the deportations were "attended by massacres and plunders" and that "most deportees perished even before reaching their point of destination" (*la plupart d'eux ont pèri avant même d'arriver au lieu de leur destination*). Finally, the memorandum repeats another charge made in the previous one, dated July 4, namely, that the anti-Armenian measures are not limited to the zones of military operations but are encompassing the rest of Turkey and that "no distinction is being made between the innocent and the guilty." Two days after the issuance of this diplomatic note, on August 11, Ambassador Extraordinary Hohenlohe sent a circular to the German Consulates at Trabzon, Erzurum, Adana, Aleppo, and Mosul advising them to "counteract energetically the view that we are the instigator of these atrocities, a view that is so compromising for us." The Turkish response to the two notes of July 4 and August 9 and indirectly to the other German personal appeals preceding, attending, and following these two formal diplomatic protests, was given on December 22, 1915. It has two major themes.

1. The anti-Armenian measures were dictated by military considerations and represent a means of legitimate defense (*dictées par des raisons militaires et constituent un moyen de légitime défense*).
2. These measures are within the purview of acts that pertain to the country's internal administration (*le domaine des actes d'Administration intérieure du pays*). The validity of these measures is even more accented by the fact that they are bent on repressing a subversive movement launched during a war.[255]

The saliency of an expedient resort to formality in this exchange of notes should not detract from the consideration of more critical issues underlying that formality. In the array of German diplomatic initiatives made in this respect, the urge to focus attention on Turkish excesses, to inculpate solely the Turkish authorities and thereby exculpate Germany, is striking. The inference becomes inescapable that the main, if not only, reason for the delivery of official protest notes was to establish a legal basis for a subsequent exculpation. The insistence and persistence of these protests in German official records, intended to demonstrate innocence, may well indicate, if not betray, the obverse of the condition of innocence. Gertrude, the Queen of Denmark, and Hamlet's mother in Shakespeare's play, was exercising what Nietzsche called "the art of suspicion" when, responding to such demonstrative protests, she intoned "The lady doth protest too much, methinks."[256] When reacting to these protest notes, especially to that of July 4, 1915, American ambassador Morgenthau disdainfully called them "pro-forma" protests; "the only purpose was to put Germans officially on record … at the very moment when Wangenheim presented this so-called protest, he was giving me the reasons why Germany could not take really effective steps to end the massacres."[257] And the gist of these reasons was that he didn't want to help. Morgenthau quotes him as saying "I will help the Zionists ... but I shall do nothing for the Armenians."[258] To the extent that this is an accurate quotation, it patently exposes the real position of the German government, a position that constantly remained camouflaged through recourse to the leeways of diplomatic jargon.

Nowhere is this tendency more evident than in the directive of Undersecretary Zimmermann who in the most critical stage of the enactment of the Armenian genocide, on August 4, 1915, urged the German ambassador to Turkey to assemble material for the publication of a White Book. His guidelines revolved around two major points the ambassador was to expound on, develop, and underscore. 1) "There indeed existed in Turkey a far-reaching Armenian movement that was hostile to the state, and whose repression was warranted by the requirements of self preservation" (*tatsächlich eine weitverzweigte staatsfeindliche armenische Bewegung ... ein Gebot der Selbsterhaltung*). 2) "You have then to demonstrate what we have done in order to avert a very harsh treatment of the Armenians and to mitigate the plight of the victims" (*eine allzu harte Behandlung der Armenier abzuwenden und die Not der Betroffenen zu lindern*).[259] The dubious nature of this two-part directive is exceeded only by the obdurate cynicism underlying it. Zimmermann had at his disposal enough information originating from the German Embassy to recognize the implausibility of his first point and the near-absurdity of the second.

They will, therefore, be taken under a searchlight separately. First to examine is the claim of the existence of a wide-ranging Armenian plot. On a number of occasions Zimmermann was told, officially, that there was neither preparation nor practical possibility for the Armenians of Ottoman Turkey to mount a general rebellion. In his extensive April 15, 1915 report, some pertinent parts of which are deleted in the tome published by Lepsius, Ambassador Wangenheim points out how both sides, Armenians and Turks alike, dispute the accusations made by the other party. He then declares: "In one point, there should be agreement, however. Since the advent of the constitutional regime (the Young Turk Ittihadist restoration in 1908 of the 1876 Ottoman constitution. V.N.D.), the Armenians relinquished the idea of a revolution, and there is no organization for such a revolution" (*den Gedanken an eine Revolution aufgegeben haben, und dass keine Organisation für eine solche besteht*).[260]

The point bears elaboration. In a memorandum to German chancellor Hollweg Dr. Mordtmann, the head of the Armenian desk in the German Embassy, related his exchange with German General Posseldt, at the time the commandant of the Fortress in Erzurum. Posseldt told Mordtmann that "the conduct of the Armenians of Erzurum was above reproach (*tadellos*) and that they remain quiet and peaceful if not oppressed and provoked by the Turks" (*wenn nicht bedrückt und gereizt*).[261] In his May 15, 1915 report to the German Embassy, Vice Consul Scheubner Richter stated that "despite the presence in Erzurum and its environs of negligible Turkish forces, a rebellion by the Armenians is not expected." He then added that despite resolute efforts to incriminate the Armenians, "the house searches, insofar as I know, yielded no incriminating evidence" (*belastendes Material nicht ergeben*).[262] Scheubner repeated this assertion of no possibility of an Armenian uprising in his subsequent May 16[263] and June 2, 1915[264] reports. It appears that the central authorities in Berlin and their military potentates serving in Turkey were in consonance with the prevailing Turkish mind-set that the continuity of the quiet and peacefulness of the Armenians was uncertain and could not be taken for granted and that, therefore, it was necessary to preempt such a contingency by wholesale and draconian measures. This mentality comes to the fore of attention by a remark made by Colonel Felix Guse, the German Chief of Staff of the Ottoman IIIrd Army in eastern Turkey. In his postwar analysis of the fate of the Armenians Guse conceded that even he could not prove that there was a sweeping "uprising" (*Aufstand*) launched by the general Armenian population. But then, as noted above, he smugly argued that the Turkish army could not afford to wait to see "whether the Armenians in such a critical moment could be so noble-minded" as to remain quiet (*ob die Armenier im kritischen Moment so edel sein würden …*).[265]

The devastating consequences for both the perpetrators, the Turks, and the victims, the Armenians, of this mentality were earlier examined in the sections titled The Argument of Armenian Provocation Through Rebellion and The Documentary Evidence on the Defensive Thrust of the Van Uprising. In this connection it is appropriate to refer once more to two important Turkish sources (both eyewitnesses), namely, Van deputy Ibrahim Arvas and Van's and subsequently Erzurum's Governor-General Hasan Tahsin (Uzer). The former explicitly and with emphasis stated that the Van uprising was provoked by the incitations of the Ittihadists who inflamed the Muslim populace and egged it on to attack the Armenians (see note 83). The document issuing from Governor Tahsin not only confirms this fact but also warns Interior Minister Talât not to repeat the mistake committed in Van to "leave them [the Erzurum Armenians] alone, and not force them to rebel ... for the good of our army and our country" (see note 82). In this rare set of authentic Turkish documents is compressed the evidence of the premeditated Turkish design to provoke the Armenians to desperate acts of self-defense only to reverse subsequently and fraudulently the polar roles of agents and victims of provocation and thereby blame the Armenians for the fate befalling them. Assuming that Zimmermann was unaware or ill-informed of this fact, what reasons did he have to discount Wangenheim's report of April 15, *which he had read and initialed*, as well as those of Major-General Posseldt and Vice Consul Scheubner? These two German officials had made known their assessment about the inoffensive attitude of the general Armenian population in a province that was the closest to the theater of military operations and as such for the Turks represented potentially the most dangerous zone of the home front. The likely answer is that he had the type of reasons that required the discounting of such reports made in good faith but which had to be converted into subterfuges before being channeled into diplomatic verbiage.

Zimmermann's second directive to the German Embassy at Istanbul is punctuated with macabre irony. Here was abundant evidence that the bulk of the Armenian people was being mercilessly annihilated, that a mass murder of gigantic proportions was in progress, and yet the architect of German foreign policy, a protégé of the emperor and at the same time his confidant, advised his chief subaltern in Turkey to counsel the perpetrators to relent in their "very harsh treatment of the Armenians" and to try to alleviate the latter's plight. Here, mass murder is described as an operation merely involving "a very harsh treatment" of the victims who, though doomed to perish in the clutches of the Turkish engine of destruction, are nevertheless portrayed as people merely afflicted with a plight (*Not*) and which the embassy should try to "alleviate" (*lindern*). But even this display of compassion and charity, despite its irony, proved to be tenuous, if not dubious. The series of prohibitive exhortations emanating from the embassy and directed against kind German consuls and vice consuls wanting to assist the imperiled deportees in the sense outlined by Zimmermann have been mentioned throughout this study. But strictly at the level of charity through monetary contributions one comes across the same practice of extreme caution and circumspection lest the perpetrators become disturbed or annoyed. The prevalent motto is: Let us not offend the sensibilities of the Turks. The document below illustrates the point. While deputizing as ambassador a day after Wangenheim died, Embassy Councillor von Neurath in a letter to Chancellor

Hollweg proposed that German religious and charitable organizations should be restrained in their drive to raise relief funds for the Armenians. He specified three conditions: 1) the scale of the funds "under no circumstances" (*keinesfalls*) should exceed the prewar scale; 2) the Imperial government ought to exercise "the greatest caution" in assisting in such a drive; and 3) "through suitable administrative measures, and underhandedly, an effort should be made to the effect that the funds collected in Germany for the benefit of the Armenians do not acquire an all too large volume" (*... unter der Hand und durch geeignete Verwaltungsmassnahmen dahin zu wirken dass die Sammlungen für die Armenier in Deutschland keinen zu grossen Umfang annehmen*).[266] Speaking of the pretended need for compassion, the following episode is likewise symptomatic. Beatrice Rohner was a missionary nurse with duties at the Maraş station of the missionary outfit *Deutscher Hülfsbund für christliches Liebeswerk im Orient*. It appears that her chief in Berlin, Dr. Karl Axenfeld, Director of the German Society of Missions, had managed to secure an appointment for her with Emperor William II — a chance for an audience. Upon arrival at the appointed hour, however, one of the emperor's aides-de-camp peremptorily told her that if she came to discuss the Armenians the Kaiser would be unable to see her. The emperor's aids were either misled or there was some confusion at the time the original appointment was made. Anyhow, the audience was cancelled forthwith[267] with a royal confirmation of the sway of a policy that warned: on the Armenian matter *noli me tangere* (touch me not as that matter is tabu around here).

Lest there may by some doubts about Zimmermann's knowledge of the implacable character of the Turkish scheme of destroying the Armenian population, the evidence adduced earlier should be adequate to dispel such doubts. That evidence stems from official German representatives verifying, prior to Zimmermann's issuance of the directive, the exterminatory thrust of the Armenian deportations. In notes 37–42 inclusive, Ambassador Wangenheim was depicted as the main source informing in the June 17–July 16, 1915 period Zimmermann, his superior in the Foreign Office, about these exterminatory massacres and using such terms as *abschlachten* (slaughter), *Vernichtung* (destruction), and quoting Interior Minister Talât as saying that the war afforded him the opportunity to "thoroughly clear Turkey of her internal enemies, namely, the Christians." Wangenheim concluded that "the [Turkish] government is in fact pursuing the goal of annihilating the Armenian race in Turkey" (*die armenische Rasse ... zu vernichten*). (July 7, 1915).

The task of implementing Zimmermann's directive devolved upon Ambassador Metternich. With the help of embassy Assistant von Hoesch, Metternich compiled a 72-page-long prototype of a White Book. It was completed and sent to Berlin on September 18, 1916, 13 months after the directive was issued.[268] In trying to comply with the spirit and letter of the directive from Berlin the ambassador in his detailed and comprehensive representation repeats many of the standard Turkish-German charges leveled against the Armenians. In the course of doing so, however, Metternich in one major respect takes exception to Zimmermann and in several other respects concedes facts and conditions undermining the intent of his superior Zimmermann, namely, the inculpation of the Armenians in general and the exculpation of both Germany and Turkey. Here are the details.

1. Contrary to Zimmermann's claim of the existence of "a wide-ranging" Armenian movement bent on insurrection that the ambassador had to document, Metternich came up with the assertion that there was no integrated and unified Armenian movement in Turkey and there was no valid proof that such an integrated unified rebellion was planned or organized (*Zu einem einheitlichen Aufstand ... ist es nicht gekommen, auch ist vollgültiger Beweis dafür, dass ein solcher einheitlicher Aufstand geplant oder organisiert war, nicht geliefert worden ...*).[269]
2. The deportations were not limited to the war zones but encompassed "practically all of Anatolia, stretching all the way to the outskirts of Istanbul (Izmit) and Smyrna (Izmir)."[270]
3. The provocation of the Armenians in the area of Erzurum started before the Sarıkamış military debacle and the Van uprising; it involved "outrages" (*Ausschreitungen*) against the Armenians.[271]
4. The few local uprisings in the summer and fall of 1915 were strictly defensive, "this point is surely to be conceded to the insurgents" (*wird man den Insurgenten freilich zugute halten müssen ...*). They saw the imminence of their deportation and chose to defend themselves (*vorzogen sich zur Wehr zu setzen*).[272]
5. "The occasional utterances of competent authorities (*gelegentlich von massgebender Seite gefallene Äusserungen*) leave no doubt that certain governmental instances pursued beyond the avowed criterion of military necessity (*über die angegebenen militärischen Notwendigkeiten hinaus*) the objective of once and for all 'rendering harmless,' if not exterminating (*wenn auch nicht auszurotten*), the Armenian people."[273]

Finally, and perhaps most importantly,

6. The Imperial [German] Government was aware of the fact that "one of the principal goals of Turkey in this war was the securing of an absolute freedom of action in the interior [of Turkey], that already in the course of this war it revelled in the realization that it had achieved this freedom (*Sicherstellung ihrer absoluten Handlungsfreiheit im Innern ... im Bewusstsein dieser errungenen Freiheit schwelgte ...*). Consequently Turkey would not allow any intervention in its internal politics.[274]

Like his predecessor, Ambassador Extraordinary Hohenlohe, Metternich paid a price for the degree of fortitude and candor he allowed himself in preparing this report and in his personal encounters with the Turkish leaders. In fact Metternich was chosen as ambassador because these leaders had let it be known that Hohenlohe, who temporarily was deputizing for Wangenheim in the summer of 1915, was not welcome as a new ambassador following Wangenheim's sudden death in October 1915. The reason for this disapprobation was what these leaders described as Hohenlohe's misgivings regarding the Turkish treatment of the Armenians.[275] As soon as Metternich was granted an audience with the Grand Vizier in December 1915, he too raised the issue of the treatment of the Armenians, promptly antagonizing the latter and the coterie of the Young Turk Ittihadist leaders. The resulting tensions persisted for months until in August 1916 the two top leaders of Ittihad, Enver and Talât, jointly signed a memorandum requesting from Berlin the recall of Metternich. In disparaging his stance as inimical to the interests of Turkey, the two leaders specifically complained that Metternich was not appreciative of their Armenian policy, with Interior Minister and party boss Talât averring that "the work that is to be done [the liquidation of the Armenians] must be done *now;* after the war it will be too late" (italics in the original).[276] Berlin acquiesced promptly, and the Turks prevailed once more with ease and speed.

In the light of all these diplomatic exchanges, posturing, confirmations, and denials relative to the genocidal fate of the Armenians, it is necessary to readdress the issue of legal implications.

THE ISSUE OF LEGAL LIABILITY REVISITED

Genocide is a type of crime the preparation and organization of which requires conspiracy. To the extent possible, the perpetrators must remain unidentifiable and undetectable. The victims must be caught unaware, and they need to be trapped. The evidence (i.e., the *corpus delicti*) must either be left sufficiently deformed to conceal the nature and dimensions of the crime or to deflect from the intent of the crime. Successful conspirators must not only be circumspect but also patient; they must bide their time and wait for the onset of a suitable opportunity in order to render the impending perpetration least risky and, therefore, affordable. One of the potent weapons of conspirators of this order is their proclivity to contrive a type of scheme through which they may attempt to deny the crime in the event of detection and apprehension. This point has been made before and it bears repetition. Indeed, it is precisely for the reasons cited earlier and still for some other reasons that the documentation of the crime of genocide is a most cumbersome task. That task becomes almost prohibitive in the case of genocides that are consummated in the course of wars at the end of which the perpetrators manage to emerge victorious. The crime is most likely to be denied, irrespective of the conditions surrounding the evidence.

The present status of the World War I crime against the Armenians is reflective of these conditions. The matter of the culpability of the organizers of the genocide is shrouded in ambiguities and nebulousness; there is no manifestly clear-cut structure to the perpetration of the act. One is, therefore, dependent on fragments of evidence that are often disjointed in relation to each other and require careful evaluation for their suitability for integrative rearrangement; they need to be fitted together to create a framework of configuration in which and through which the suspects are seen inculpated as perpetrators. No matter how ingenious such a design and procedure may be one has to be always mindful of the fact, however, that all this rearrangement of fragments of evidence may be covering only the tip of an iceberg; much more is likely to be doomed to remain indefinitely submerged.

These are the parameters within the restrictive boundaries of which the problem of German complicity (and, therefore, responsibility) is being probed into and demonstrated. It is true that unlike Turkey, which through a combination of factors of luck, a measure of tenacious heroism, and the incidence of fortuitous circumstances had managed to convert a shattering military defeat at the end of World War I into a resounding military victory within two years against two lesser enemies, namely,

Armenia and Greece, Germany itself remained nevertheless a vanquished nation throughout. Yet, until now it also remained somewhat shielded through the protective umbrella of Turkish obfuscations, denials, and coverups.

There are two levels at which Germany may try to marshal a defense against the charge of complicity should this protective shield be removed for the sake of an argument. One of them is the level of official protests through diplomatic démarches. The démarches have been examined earlier. The other refers to the implications of the deportations, as distinct from massacres, and the German involvement in the initiation of these deportations. As has been explained throughout this work the decision to deport the Armenians originated from the Ottoman General Headquarters whose Chief of Staff was German General Bronsart von Schellendorf; the entire enterprise bore a military imprint. Furthermore, the fourth article of the May 14/27, 1915 Temporary Law of Deportation, which is barely mentioned in the literature dealing with the Armenian genocide, stipulates that the deportations fell within the jurisdiction of the military (*meriyeti ahkâm*) and were, therefore, to be administered by military authorities.[277] Two legal issues that are interconnected arise here. First, the deportations did not take place in a political or military vacuum, and Germany was not a neutral state. Were it neutral, it could disclaim responsibility on strictly legal-technical grounds for not having intervened effectively. Germany was not only the political-military partner of Turkey but also the dominant partner, especially in all matters of military nature and consequence. The destruction of the Armenian population resulted from joint Turko-German military deliberations and decision making and as such it materialized under these twin auspices that had the imprimatur of a contractual alliance. The rationale, authorization, justification, and everything else associated with the Armenian deportations were part and parcel of a single defense mechanism: the requirements of the war conjointly being waged by Germany and Turkey as allies. The alleged requirements of Turkish internal national security were inextricably interwoven with the German objectives of warfare conducted in and around Turkey. Consequently, when Turkey defined the Armenians as "the internal foe," in the absence of explicit German objections, they automatically became the foe of the Germans too; within the parameters of this rationale, their destruction was at the very least warranted militarily for both partners—formal German disclaimers by diplomats (but not necessarily by certain German military) notwithstanding. Incidental German appeals to the Turks to spare inoffensive multitudes of women, children, and old men, were not only lame in their thrust but also were markedly perfunctory, therefore, inconsequential.

Another defense argument involves the attempt to differentiate mere deportations from massacres with the former being considered as a legitimate wartime measure whereas the latter are disowned as beyond the responsibility of those authorizing only deportations. Even if for the sake of argument one discounts an array of grounds on which wholesale deportations even in times of war are considered to be grave offenses against humanity, this argument is untenable. In all systems of criminal justice, the stated purpose of an act is not the standard by which it is adjudged but primarily the concrete consequences of that act. The fate of the victim of an act eclipses in import the alleged original objective of the offender who is facing prosecution. Moreover, more often than not in circumstances involving conspiracy the real intent of an act is revealed in the actual consequences of that act; criminal outcomes are intimately associated with covert criminal intent.

As the genocide was beginning, the Allies issued a joint declaration on May 24, 1915 condemning "the connivance and often assistance of Ottoman authorities" in the massacres. "In view of these new crimes of Turkey against humanity and civilization," the declaration continued, "the Allied governments announce publicly ... that they will hold personally responsible ... all members of the Ottoman government and those of their agents who are implicated in such massacres."[278] This declaration had several important features: 1) it was a public and joint commitment to prosecute after the war those responsible for the crime perpetrated; 2) it acknowledged the complicity of Ottoman authorities in terms of "connivance and often assistance"; 3) it acknowledged the legacy of Turkey, involving an established record of past massacres, by appending the adjective "new" to the word "crimes of Turkey"; 4) it created a new framework of international law by ushering in the codification of the term "crimes against humanity"; and 5) that concept was later to serve as a legal yardstick to prosecute under emerging international law the top strata of the Nazi leadership at Nuremberg. Consequently, it was fully embraced by the United Nations, forming the core of the preamble of its convention on the Prevention and Punishment Convention on Genocide (December 9, 1948). Even though the target of this formal proclamation are primarily Turkey and the Turks, its reference to the "agents" of "the Ottoman government" as additional subjects with criminal liabilities implicates German officials cooperating with the Turks in the commission of the crime as candidates for prosecution as well.

Furthermore, there was the problem of "dual positions" (*Doppelstellung*). German generals assisting in the Turkish war effort belonged to two overlapping jurisdictions, German (the German Military Mission to Turkey) and Turkish (the Ottoman-Turkish High Command). As German military historian Carl Mühlmann explained, "this condition of investing a single person with two [disparate] functions (*in eine Hand zwei Dienststellungen legen*) ... from a legal point of view (*vom rechtlichen Standpunkt*) entailed problems and complications. But, almost always the Germans and the Turks accommodated each other, thereby averting major crises, especially at Ottoman General Headquarters." Mühlmann even claims that many orders signed by Enver were drafted by his German Chief of Staff, by General Seeckt, for example; this was due to "Enver's express desire to comply with the instructions of the German High Command" (*in nachdrücklicher Form den Weisungen der deutschen Obersten Heeresleitung entgegentrat*). Mühlmann then raised the rhetorical question whether it would have been right for German officers to disappoint knowingly those Turkish leaders whose trust they were enjoying and to harm their state "whose uniforms of honor they were wearing and whose bread they were eating."[279] It was perhaps in congruence with this sense of honor and gratitude that General Seeckt, according to Dinkel, refused "to permit the return of Armenian refugees to the Turkish-occupied areas of the Russian Caucasus,"[280] thereby further aggravating their plight.

In the legal system of any state organization authority of office carries with it responsibility that is determined by the parameters circumscribing that authority. This attribute of responsibility is susceptible to transformation into liability, however, when authority is abused by crossing the boundaries created by the rules of circumscription. The dual positions of the high-ranking German officers serving in wartime Turkey were a function of the military alliance pursuing military objectives. The treatment of the Armenians, who were defined as an internal enemy, was subsumed under the category of these objectives. The coterie of German officers directly participating or assisting in the realization of the Turkish initiative of "Armenian deportations" almost without exception shared this view and articulated it in a variety of situations that are being examined in this study. These officers are, therefore, liable in a dual sense that corresponds to their dual positions, for they were responsible as German authorities as well as authorities identified with the Turkish military command system. The Turkish Military Tribunal in 1919 tried, convicted, and sentenced to death Enver, the chief of that military command. The principal charge was "the deportation and massacre" (*tehcir ve taktil*) of the Armenians. General Bronsart, Colonels Boettrich and Guse, and others were guilty of the same offense but legally were removed from Turkish jurisdiction according to terms of the contract signed with the chief of the German Military Mission. What is important to consider here is the conjoint role of the German and Turkish military in the commission of the offense and, therefore, the correlative character of the legal liability those officers incurred. Compared to the central significance of this fact, the operativeness of diverse jurisdictions to administer criminal justice is but of incidental import.

The picture changes, however, when one shifts the perspective and the allied framework of analysis from national to international law. The Turkish Military Tribunal relied on municipal laws involving domestic penal codes. Yet, prior to and during the proceedings, several Turkish officials associated with the prosecution, including the monarch, have indirectly invoked international law by describing the charges leveled against the *prima facie* suspects as "crimes against humanity."[281] In an earlier section focusing on the international law ramifications of the problem of German complicity, a detailed explanation was provided as to why and how the German officers and through them Germany might be held responsible for the fate of the Armenians. The fact remains that even if one should disregard their exterminatory outcome, wholesale deportations of large clusters of civilian populations, whether preventive or punitive, in peacetime or wartime, are in themselves a gross violation of basic human rights—as such they represent a crime against humanity as far as the general rules of international law embodying "the dictates of human conscience" and "the usages established among civilized peoples" are concerned (see notes 28–34 inclusive). As explained earlier (p. 18, notes 28, 29, 30), the 1899 and 1907 twin Hague Conventions had set forth a set of standards that have the attribute of "rule of law," in the present case, international law. Included in these standards is the legal norm providing for "general and specific protection of civilian population against deportation."[282] Article 46, which is identical in both Conventions, embodies this rule and, as international law expert M. C. Bassiouni contends, in conjunction with Articles 47–53 of both Conventions provides protections that are extensive. Together, these articles signal a basic principle, namely, "civilian populations are to remain in place and not to be deported."[283] This rule of law was subsequently codified in the Fourth Geneva Convention of August 12, 1949. Article 49 of that Convention "unequivocally prohibited deportation." In proscribing such deportations that article refers to "mass forcible transfers, as well as deportations; [they] are prohibited regardless of their motive."[284]

Moreover, the May 24, 1915 public and formal declaration of the Entente Powers, which has been dissected in connection with note 278 in the preceding paragraphs, specifically extends the burden of responsibility and therewith of liability to all those who functioned as "agents" of "the Ottoman government." As stated earlier, the German officers, in their capacity as the representatives of an allied power, were in fact functioning as the agents of the Ottoman government while serving at the same time German national interests.

Presently, the issue of responsibility and its corollary, legal liability, has been cast into sharp relief in terms of a new codification inaugurated by the United Nations. Perpetrators, past and present, are no longer shielded by any statutory limitations attached to a penal code. Addressing the problem of impunity, the United Nations passed a resolution redefining and indefinitely postponing the criminal liabilities of the offenders on November 26, 1968—the Convention on the Nonapplicability of Statutory Limitations to War Crimes Against Humanity. Article (b) includes the crime of genocide, even if it does "not constitute a violation of the domestic law of the country in which [it was] committed."[285] The convention inspires hopes for ultimate justice, belying the general maxim that justice delayed is justice denied. That hope may carry greater relevance for the position contemporary Germans, officially and unofficially, may take in face of the issues raised in this study. The provision of Article 4 of the German constitution, operative in Imperial Germany at the time, had a stipulation: the accepted rules of international law are binding for the legal system of the German Reich.

This study is not and was not intended to be a strictly legal brief challenging contemporary Germany and its governmental authorities solely on the basis of legal considerations. It is essentially a historical study analyzing the involvement of certain German officials in the Turkish scheme to destroy the Armenians. It attempts to dissect and expose the lethal role performance of these officials who, for reasons of their own, allowed themselves to be coopted by the Turk Ittihadist leaders to aid the executioners of the Armenian people. In this sense the study is also an invitation to consider the entire matter as a challenge to historical truth and, therefore, ultimately treat it as a moral issue.

Notes to Part I

1. Victor Bérard, *La politique du Sultan* 3d ed. (Paris, 1897), 280–90, 346–47. Among the "innumerable gifts" the emperor and the empress collected were, the rugs which he got by "cleaning up the entire factory of rugs, and by pocketing a necklace studded with old diamonds worth 5–600,000 francs. In return, he left as souvenir to his host two small busts of his grandfather and grandmother, made of cheap bronze material, along with another bronze object representing an Arab on horseback; the three objects are worth 7 or 800 francs." *Ibid.*, Moreover, William II was so intoxicated with the "gift" of the Baghdad Railway construction project, extracted from the sultan, that he called it "my railway" (*meine Bahn*). Emil Ludwig, *Wilhelm der Zweite* (Berlin, 1926), 391–92.
2. *The Diplomatic Archives of the Foreign Ministry of Germany (Die Diplomatischen Akten des Auswärtigen Amtes)* Die Grosse Politik der Europäischen Kabinette. 1871–1914. (Hereafter cited as *DAG*) vol. 12, part 2, p. 558. *See also ibid.,* Appendix. Doc. Nos. 3357, 3361, 3362. Commenting on the emperor's trip, the French writer François Coppé declared, "After the Armenian massacres Sultan Abdul Hamit had become odious in the eyes of all mankind. Now that he became the vassal of the German emperor, he has become even more odious in the eyes of the Frenchman." Doc. No. 3370, p. 613.
3. *DAG* [n. 2], vol. 2, Doc. No. 308, February 2, 1878 report by Bülow, p. 179 n. 15.
4. *Die deutschen Dokumente zum Kriegsausbruch 1914* (The German Documents on the Outbreak of the War 1914), compiled by K. Kautsky, ed. by Max Graf von Montgelas and Walter Schückling, 2d expanded ed., vol. 1, Doc. No. 401 (Berlin, 1922), 130 ff. *See also* note 147.
5. Friedrich Naumann, *Asia*, 8th ed. (Berlin, 1911), 2, 134, 137, 139, 145.
6. A. A. Orientalia Generalia. No. 5, vol. 30. The Mumm *Konzept.*
7. Chlodwig Hohenlohe-Schillingsfürst, *Denkwürdigkeiten der Reichskanzlerzeit* (Memoirs from the Time of Service as Chancellor) (Stuttgart, 1931), 264.
8. Anhang zu den Gedanken und Erinnerungen (Supplementary volume to Bismarck's *Gedanken und Erinnerungen*) (Stuttgart, 1901), August 11, 1877 letter, p. 273.
9. *DAG* [n. 2], vol. 10, Doc. No. 2457, Ambassador Saurma's November 11, 1895 report that Armenians in Diyarbekir are being slaughtered like sheep. "And, as Christians and Europeans ... we have to watch these things quietly." The Emperor's marginalia, p. 102; *ibid.*, vol. 12, part 1, Doc. No. 2893, cipher No. 176, Saurma's July 29, 1896 report, in which he was informing Berlin that the Turkish plan was the terminal liquidation of the Armenians as Christians (*für alle Zeiten unschädlich gemacht werden müssen*) William II's marginalia, p. 18. "This means that all Christians are to be slayed."
10. *Ibid.*, Doc. No. 2898. August 28, 1896 cipher. Marginalia. p. 20; Doc. No. 2901. August 29, 1896. Marginalia. p. 22.
11. *Ibid.*, vol. 10, Doc. No. 2482. December 19, 1895. Marginalia. p. 133.
12. *Ibid.*, Doc. No. 2484, cipher No. 177. December 23, 1895. Marginalia. p. 134.
13. *Ibid.*, vol. 12, Doc. No. 2893. July 29, 1896 report. Marginalia. p. 18.
14. *Ibid.*, Doc. No. 2416, cipher No. 117. August 22, 1895. Marginalia. p. 61.
15. Alfred von Tirpitz, *Erinnerungen* (Memoirs) (Leipzig, 1919), 435.
16. Alfred Graf von Waldersee, *Denkwürdigkeiten* (Memoirs) H. O. Meisner ed., vol. 1 (Stuttgart, 1923), 269.
17. Bernhard Guttmann, *Schattenriss einer Generation* (The Silhouette of a Generation) (Stuttgart, 1950), 262.
18. George Alexander non Müller, *Der Kaiser ... Aufzeichnungen des Chefs des Marinekabinetts Admiral G. A. V. Müller über die Ära Wilhelms II.* (Navy Cabinet Chef Admiral Müller's Notes on William II's Era of Rule) W. Görlitz, ed., (Göttingen, 1965), 122.
19. Naumann, *Asia* [n. 5], 140.
20. Tahsin Paşa, *Abdülhamit Yıldız Hatıraları* (Abdul Hamit. Yıldız Palace Memoirs) (Istanbul, 1931), 285.

21. The excerpts from Bismarck's letter to the sultan are from the diaries of Theodor Herzl. The entire letter was read to Herzl by Philip Michael de Newlinski, a Polish-Austrian journalist and political agent, who had managed to befriend Sultan Abdul Hamit and his foremost confidant and adviser Izzet (Arab). Newlinski was very eager to assist Herzl, who was trying to gain fundamental concessions from the sultan for a Palestinian homeland for the Jews. Newlinski, the publisher of *Correspondance de l'Est*, had also befriended two Armenians for this purpose, both of them occupying high positions in the offices of the Ottoman Ministry of Foreign Affairs. Herzl describes Artin Dadian, the Undersecretary, as "a new helper" for the success of his enterprise, and Gabriel Noradounghian, Councillor in the Legal Department of the Foreign Affairs Ministry (whose indentity is concealed by the use of the letter N.), as a man who is "fire and flame" for the proposal made by Herzl, and who is "completely for us" (*ganz für ins*); he "promised greatest help." *Theodor Herzl's Tagebücher 1895–1904* 3 vols., vol.1 (1922), vols. 2 and 3 (Berlin, 1923). The excerpts from Bismarck's letter are in vol. 1, pp. 466, 502, July 22, 1896 diary entry. The comments on Noradounghian are in vol. 1, pp. 152, 440–41, 449, and on Artin Paşa, in vol. 2, 271–72, 312–13. In vol. 1, pp. 396, 464 Newlinski is described as stating that the sultan gave him a confidential mission involving contact with Armenian revolutionary groups in Brussels and as asking Herzl to act as a mediator between the sultan and the Armenians in exchange for cncessions from the former for the cause of Zionism which was being pursued by Herzl. On p. 427 in the same volume Newlinski is likewise quoted as saying that Russia gained the upper hand in the counsels of the Palace, where "First Secretary Izzet favors Russia." June 1896 entry. Equally significant, the May 7, 1896 entry in vol. 1 discloses the fact that already at that time the Palace knew of the assault and expected the Armenians to strike (*losschlagen*), probably a reference to the capture of Bank Ottoman. Newlinski, therefore, proposed to Herzl to try to get the Armenians "to wait for a month" so that he could usefully drag the Armenian issue in order to benefit the Jewish issue" (p. 396).
22. Ernst Jäckh, *Der Goldene Pflug* (The Golden Ploughshare) (Stuttgart, 1954), 9.
23. A. A. *Grosses Hauptquartier.* vol. 187, file Türkei 18/3 and 4, Registry No. AS1705, April 13, 1915.
24. FO 96/211, part VIII, 5 pp. report adapted from the Russian newspaper *Petrograd Bourse Gazette* of World War I vintage.
25. Naumann, *Asia* [n. 5], 134.
26. A. A. Türkei 183/39, A29593. German Journalist Tyszka's October 1, 1915 communication to the German Foreign Office.
27. FO 371/9158/E5523. Ottoman Turkish text is on folio 173, the English translation is on folio 175. This document is part of a batch of other documents British occupation forces, especially the Department of Military Intelligence, had secured "in the early days of the Armistice and which have lain hidden in their office ever since." British High Commissioner Nevile Henderson on May 22, 1923 relayed them to London. *Ibid.*, pp. 106–07. The document was accepted and thereby legitimized by the Turkish Historical Society in whose publication, *Belleten*, it was published. A Turkish historian, Salahi Sonyel, republished it in a separate broshure along with an English text which is not an entirely accurate translation. Dr. Salahi Sonyel, *Displacement of the Armenians. Documents* (Ankara, 1978), 1. Bronsart's order is dated July 25, 1915 and has the following notation in the place intended for signature: "By order of the Chief of Staff (i.e., Bronsart. V. N. D.) of the Interim Commander-in-Chief (i.e., War Minister Enver. V. N. D.). It appears that the person who signed the order on behalf of General Bronsart was a staff officer whose handwriting was illegible and the British authorities simply tried to decipher it and came up with Vervem, which is a non-existent name.
28. Vahakn N. Dadrian, "Genocide as a Problem of National and International Law: The World War I Armenian Case and Its Contemporary Legal Ramifications" *Yale Journal of International Law* 14, 2, pp. 279–80.

29. M. C. Bassiouni, *Crimes Aganist Humanity in International Criminal Law* (Boston, 1992), 166–67. For excerpts from the texts of both Conventions *see* 634–37 (1899 Convention) and 634–41 (1907 Convention).
30. The United Nations War Commisson, *History of the United Nations War Crimes Commission and the Development of the Laws of War* (London, 1948), 24, 25. *See also Final act of the Second Peace Conference, The Hague* (1907) (Cmd. 4175) (1914), reprinted in 36 Stat. 2277, Treaty Series No. 539, with Annex.
31. Carnegie Endowment for the International Peace, *Violations of the Laws and Customs of War: Report of the Majority and Dissenting Reports of the American and Japanese Members of the Commission on Responsiblities at the Conference of Paris, 1919*, Pamphlet No. 32, p. 19.
32. *Ibid.*
33. *See* FO 608/246, Third Session, February 20, 1919, p. 20 (folio 163). It should be noted in this connection that as a result of the Commission's efforts, several articles stiputlating the trial and punishment of those reponsible for the genocide were inserted into the Peace Treaty of Sèvres, signed on August 10, 1920. The Treaty of Peace Between the Allied Powers and Turkey. *American Journal of International Law*. Supplement. 15 (1921): 179; 1920 Gr. Brit. T.S. No. 11. Under article 226, "the Turkish government recognize[d]" this right of trial and punishment by the Allied Powers, "notwithstanding any proceedings or prosecution before a tribunal in Turkey." Turkey under same article was obligated to surrender "all persons accused of having committed an act in violation of the laws and customs of war, who are specified either by name or by rank, office or employment which they held under Turkish authorities." J. Willis, *Prologue to Nuremberg: The Policy and Diplomacy of Punishing War Criminals of the First World War* (Westpoint, CT, 1982), 180–81. Under article 230 of the Peace Treaty, Turkey was further obligated "to hand over to the Allied Powers the persons whose surrender may be required by the latter as being responsible for the massacres committed during the continuance of the state of war on territory which formed part of the Turkish Empire on August 1, 1914. The Allied Powers reserve themselves the right to designate the tribunal which shall try the persons so accused, and the Turkish Government undertakes to recognize such tribunal. The provisions of Article 228 apply to the cases dealt with in this Article." *Ibid.,* 181. The Treaty of Sèvres, therefore, provided the legal basis for international adjudication of the crimes perpetrated by the Ottoman Empire against the Armenians during World War I. These provisions never came into force, however, as political tensions within the Allied Powers and nationalistic passions in Turkey eventually led to the scrapping of this treaty.
34. P.C.I.J., Advisory Committee of Jurists, Procès-Verbaux of the Committee, June 16–July 24, 1920, pp. 310, 318, 331, 344.
35. J. Pomiankowski, *Der Zusammenbruch des Ottomanischen Reiches* (Graz, 1969), 165.
36. *Ibid.,* 13, 196, 206, 230, 234. In his Foreword the Vice Marshal alludes to "the influence" the German military and civilian advisers in Turkey brought to bear upon the Turks, adding that he could "neither excuse nor remain silent over the fact that this influence was not always fortunate."
37. A. A. Türkei 183/27, A19744.
38. *Ibid.*, Botschaft Konstantinopel, or K 169 (No. 3876).
39. *Ibid.*, Türkei 183/37, A21257.
40. *Ibid.*, A21483.
41. *Ibid.*, K 169, No. (4184), folio 162.
42. *Ibid.*, Türkei 183/37, A22210.
43. The verdict was issued on July 5, 1919 and is recorded in the No. 3604 issue of *Takvimi Vekâyi*, the official gazette of the Ottoman government whose supplements (*Ilâve*) were used to publish selected portions of the court proceedings. July 22, 1919, p. 219.
44. A. A. Göppert Papers (*Nachlass*) vol VI, file 5. February 14, 1919 letter of Göppert to Dr. Axenfeld, a leader in the German Evangelical Mission movement. Quoted in Christoph Dinkel, "German Officers and the Armenian Genocide" *Armenian Review*, 44, 1/173 (Spring

1991): 82. The citation in German is culled from the unpublished German original filed with this author.

45. *Ibid.*, 82–3.
46. Dinkel, "*German Officers*" [n. 44], 106. (Botschaft Konstantinopel 168).
47. *Ibid.*, (Dinkel).
48. *Ibid.*, K 168, No. (3007).
49. *Ibid.*, K 169, No. 1 (3361).
50. A. A. Türkei 183/39, A28584. "Secret report No. 23," with 5 enclosures.
51. Paul Leverkuehn, *Posten auf ewiger Wache* (Essen, 1938), 41–42, 44.
52. A. A. Türkei 183/39, A28548, J. No. 580.
53. Dinkel, "German Officers" [n. 44], 107.
54. *Ibid.*, 104.
55. K 168, No. 9 (3224).
56. Dr. Johannes Lepsius, *Deutschland und Armenien 1914–1918. Sammlung Diplomatischer Aktenstücke* (Berlin-Potsdam, 1919), Doc. No. 74, p. 80.
57. A. A. Türkei 183/39, A28584, J. No. 580. Geheim Bericht No. 23.
58. *Ibid.*, 183/45, A33457.
59. *Ibid.*,
60. *Ibid.*, 183/45, A31505, No. 710.
61. Zaven Archbishop. *Badriarkagan Housherus. Vaverakirner yev Vugayoutiunner* (My Memoirs as a Patriarch. Testimonies and Documents), (Cairo, 1947), 52, 70, 71. For a whole string of similar incitements and provocations throughout the other provinces see pp. 51–69. For the most comprehensive compendium of pre-war Turkish abuses and provocations against the Armenians in any language *see* Kevork Mesrob, "Turkahayern u Turkeru (1914–1918). Andeeb u Bashdonagan Pastatoughter" (Turkish Armenians and the Turks 1914–1918. Unpublished and Official Ducuments) *Haygashen Almanac* vol. 1 (1922), 102–164.
62. Rafael de Nogales, *Four Years Beneath the Crescent.* Muna Lee, trans. (New York, 1926), 139–140.
63. Aziz Samih, *Büyük Harpte Kafkas Cephesi Hatıraları* (World War I Memoirs on the Caucasian Front) (Ankara, 1934), 68. On p. 59 the author, who was the Chief of Staff of Reserve Cavallery Army Corps (*Ihtiyat Süvari Kolordusu Erkânıharbiye Reisi*), describes the type of people who enrolled in the ranks of the Special Organization, i.e., highly dubious characters on the retention and use of whom, the author maintains, Dr. B. Şakir, one of the principal architects of the Armenian genocide, adamantly insisted.
64. Felix Guse, "Der Armenieraufstand 1915 und seine Folgen" *Wissen und Wehr* 6 (1925): 55.
65. Felix Guse, *Die Kaukasusfront im Weltkrieg* (Leipzig, 1940), 21.
66. Liman von Sanders, *Five Years in Turkey* (Annapolis, 1927), 106.
67. Rafael de Nogales, *Four Years Beneath the Crescent.* Muna Lee, trans. (New York, 1926), 46
68. Idem, *Vier Jahre unter dem Halbmond* (Berlin, 1925), 36. A major feature of this edition, which by one year preceded the English edition of the original Spanish text, is the magnitude of deletions of portions which depict the Turks, especially War Minister Enver, in unsavory situations.
69. A. A. Türkei 183/39, A28584. "Secret report" No. 23.
70. Guse, "Der Armenieraufstand" [n. 64]: 613, 614, 620.
71. Grace H. Knapp, *The Tragedy of Bitlis* (New York, 1919), 15. For Knapp's accounts *see* Bryce-Toynbee, *The Treatment of the Armenians in the Ottoman Empire 1915–1916* (London, His Majesty's Stationery Office, Miscellaneous No. 31, 1916), 32–47.
72. Clarence D. Ussher (M.D.), *An American Physician in Turkey* (Boston, 1917), 264–65.
73. John Otis Barrows, *In the Land of Ararat* (New York, 1916), 128, 134.
74. Käthe Ehrhold, *Flucht in die Heimat* (Flight into the Homeland) (Dresden-Leipzig, 1937), 10.
75. Pomiankowski, *Der Zusammenbruch* [n. 35], 160.
76. A. A. Botschaft Konstantinopel, K 168, No. 9. May 15, 1915 report.

77. De Nogales, *Four Years* [n. 62], 60.
78. *Ibid.*, 68, 70, 80, 89, 95.
79. *Ibid.*, 76, 135.
80. *La défense heroique de Van* (Van's Heroic Defense) M. G. trans. (Geneva: Droshak, 1916). Vramian's report, undated, is on pp. 13–33. Another such report, dated January 6/19, 1915, is in *Jerusalem Armenian Patriarchate Archive*, series 19, file GH (18th character in the Armenian alphabet), Nos. 417–424, fourteen legal size pages.
81. De Nogales, *Four Years* [n. 62], 85–86. On Governor Cevdet's "traitorous assassination" of the Armenian leaders, *see* p. 56. Austrian Vice Marshal Pomiankowski describes Cevdet as "a genuine monster in human form" (*ein wahres Ungeheuer in Menschengestalt!*) Pomiankowski,*Der Zusammenbruch* [n. 35], 160.
82. *Jerusalem Armenian Patriarchate Archives*, Series 21, file M, Nos. 519–20.
83. Ibrahim Arvas, "Tarihi Hakikatler, Eski Van Mebusu Ibrahim Arvasın Hatıraları," (Historical Facts.The Memoirs of Former Van Deputy Ibrahim Arvas) *Yeni Istiklâl*, April 21, 1965, No. 193.
84. Guse, "Der Armenieraufstand" [n. 64]: 619.
85. *Ibid.*: 609, 620.
86. Idem, *Die Kaukasusfront* [n. 65], 27.
87. *Ibid.*, 54.
88. Idem, "Der Armenieraufstand" [n. 64]: 615, 620.
89. *Ibid.:* 617, 619.
90. *Ibid.:* 614
91. Idem, *Die Kaukasusfront* [n. 65], 107.
92. Ali Ihsan Sabis, *Harb Hatıralarım* (My War Memoirs) vol. 1 (Istanbul, 1943), 48, 79; vol. 2 (Ankara, 1951), 165, 179.
93. FO 37/6500, folio 246. February 28, 1919. British General Staff Intelligence report.
94. FO 371/6500, folios 220–222.
95. A. A., K 170, No. 4674, folio 63. July 28, 1915 report.
96. *Ibid.*, August 23, 1915 "secret" report to the German Military Mission. Registry No. 3841, p. 8 of the report.
97. *Renaissance* (French language Armistice daily in Istanbul). August 17, 1919 issue.
98. *Ibid.*, May 20, 1919. *See also* FO 371/6500, folio 220.
99. *Takvimi Vekâyi* [n. 43], No. 3540, p. 7.
100. *Jerusalem Armenian Patriarchate Archives*, Series 22, file Hee, No. 419.
101. FO 37/6500/5029/A/12, folio 221. Obviously the reference to "the Sıvas Division" is actually meant to be a reference to the Xth Army Corps stationed at Sıvas and that to "3rd Army Corps" is a reference to the IIIrd Army. According to this document, Bakalian somehow had become a friend of Pertev, the commander, who confided in him about this fact.
102. *Renaissance*, April 14, 1919; *Vakit, Sabah* (Turkish dailies) April 4, 1919.
103. *Ariamard* (Armenian daily in Istanbul, the namesake of *Azadamard*) December 10, 1918. The physician was Mihran Norair. The article is titled "Hayatchintch Sarsapneru" (The Horrors of the Armenocide).
104. A. A. Türkei 183/54, A39244.
105. FO 37/6500, folio 219; FO 371/6509, folio 51/10.
106. FO 37/7882/E4425, folio 182.
107. FO 37/6504/E10319; FO 37/6509/E10662, folio 159.
108. *Takvimi Vekâyi* [n. 43], No. 3543, p. 30. *See also* A. Mil, "Umumi Harpte Teşkilâtı Mahsusa" (The Special Organization in World War I) *Vakit,* November 7, 1933, installment No. 6, where details are provided about the induction of governors C. Azmi and H. Tahsin and their participation in Special Organization activities.
109. Sabis, *Harb Hatıralarım* [n. 92], vol. 2, 107.
110. *Vertcheen Lour*, No. 1626, July 19, 1919. Retired Major Ethem, who was Chief of Military Supplies in Trabzon, in his testimony before the Military Tribunal (15th sitting, April 30, 1915), declared that General Mahmud Kâmil had invested vali Cemal Azmi

with inordinate powers. *Renaissance,* May 1, 1919. Like party potentate Nail, governor C. Azmi too was condemned to death in absentia by the Turkish Military Tribunal. *Takvimi Vekâyi* [n. 112].

111. *See* note 97.
112. *Takvimi Vekâyi* [n. 43], No. 3616, p. 3.
113. A. A. *Weltkrieg* IId secr. vol. 6 A21256, pp. 2 and 3 of July 6, 1915 report.
114. For an analysis of Dr. Şakir's role and success in this respect *see* Vahakn N. Dadrian, "The Role of Turkish Physicians in the World War I Genocide of Ottoman Armenians" *Holocaust and Genocide Studies* 1, 2 (1986): 169–173, 184; *idem*, "The Role of the Special Organization in the Armenian Genocide during the First World War" in *Minorities in Wartime*, P. Panayi, ed. (Oxford, 1993).
115. Tarık Zafer Tunaya, *Türkiye'de Siyasal Partiler* (Political Parties in Turkey) vol. III (Istanbul, 1989), 277, note 17.
116. Mil, "Umumi Harpte" [n. 108], November 12, 15, 20, 21, 22, 27, 29, and December 10, 11, 1933 issues; installments 11, 13, 18, 19, 20, 27, 38 and 39 respectively.
117. *Harb Kabinelerinin Isticvabı* (The Hearings on the Wartime Cabinets) Vakit Publication Series on Memoirs and Documents No. 2 (Istanbul, 1933), 537.
118. Mil, "Umumi Harpte" [n. 108], December 10, 1933, installment No. 38.
119. *Meclisi Ayan Zabıt Ceridesi* (Transcripts of the Proceedings of the Senate) Third Election Period. Third Session. vol. 1, 15th sitting. pp. 186–87.
120. Mustafa Ragıp Esatlı, *Ittihad ve Terakki Tarihinde Esrar Perdesi* (The Curtain of Secrecy in the History of Ittihad) (Istanbul, 1975), 460, n. 1.
121. Mil, "Umumi Harpte" [n. 108], November 15, 1933, installment No. 13. The No. 13 is a misprint since the preceding November 14 issue bears the No. 13 also.
122. *Ibid.*, November 15, 1933, installment No. 4.
123. *Takvimi Vekâyi* [n. 43], No. 3543, pp. 26, 27, 28, 29, 30.
124. Dadrian, "The Role of the Special Organization" [n. 114], p. 5 references to Stoddard, Kutay, Hiçyılmaz, notes 1, 2, 3 respectively; p. 8, notes 10 and 13; p. 12, note 35; p. 15, note 49.
125. *Takvimi Vekâyi* [n. 43], No. 3549, p. 59.
126. *Ibid.*, No. 3553 (3554), p. 89.
127. *Ibid.*, p. 86.
128. *Ibid.*, No. 3547, p. 46.
129. *Ibid.*, No. 3557, pp. 103, 104.
130. Ahmed Refik (Altınay), *Iki Komite Iki Kıtal* (Two Committee Two Massacres) (Istanbul, 1919), 36. (Ottoman script).
131. A. A. Türkei 183/39, A28584. *See* especially the No. 2 enclosure.
132. *Ibid.*
133. *Takvimi Vekâyi* [n. 43], No. 3543, p. 29.
134. Vahakn N. Dadrian, *The Armenian Genocide in Official Turkish Records.* A Special Issue of the Journal of Political and Military Sociology containing Dadrian's Collected Essays. vol. 22, No. 1 [Summer 1994], 58, 59.
135. *Takvimi Vekâyi* [n. 43], No. 3543, p. 27.
136. Mil, "Umumi Harpte" [n. 108], November 15 and 16, 1933, installment Nos. 13 and 14, respectively; the quotation in Turkish is from November 15 issue.
137. Sabis, *Harb Hatıralarım* [n. 92], vol. 2, p. 192.
138. Mil, "Umumi Harpte" [n. 108], February 19, 1934, installment No. 107.
139. Doğan Avcıoğlu, *Milli Kurtuluş Tarihi* (History of National Liberation) vol. 3 (Istanbul, 1974), 1135.
140. Mil, "Umumi Harpte" [n. 108], February 9, 1934, installment No. 97.
141. *Ibid.*, February 10, 1934, installment No. 98.
142. Avcıoğlu, *Milli Kurtuluş* [n. 139], 1135.
143. Fethi Okyar, *Üç Devirde Bir Adam* (A Man of Three Eras) C. Kutay, ed. (Istanbul, 1980), 106, n. 1.

144. The police lieutenant, "Komiser Harun Efendi," was a renegade Armenian who not only had joined the Turkish secret service but with great zeal performed his task of preparing lists of Armenian notables targeted for subsequent liquidation. Those hundreds of Armenian leaders who were arrested on April 24, 1915 and largely were destroyed as a prelude to the Armenian genocide were mostly selected by him. Not content with his service to the Turks, with equal zeal he pursued and tracked down several Armenian intellectuals who had managed to evade the Turkish police and were in hiding. He was himself tracked down and executed during the Armistice by an Armenian "avenger of justice." Before his demise, he wrote his memoirs in an Armenian daily newspaper he had established himself and became also its editor. Haroutioun Mugurditchian, "Kaghdniknerou Gudzigou" (The Thread of the Secrets) *Hairenik.* October 28/November 10, 1918 issue, installment No. 1.
145. Colonel Freiherr von der Goltz (not to be confused with Marshal Colmar v. d. Goltz), "Die Spionage in der Türkei" *Die Weltkriegs-Spionage.* Major-General von Lettow-Vorbeck, ed. (Münich, 1931) 507. *See also* Vahakn N. Dadrian, *The History of the Armenian Genocide. Ethnic Conflict from the Balkans to Anatolia to the Caucasus* (Providence /Oxford, 1995), 219–20, 229 notes 5–6, 236–39. The item on Lossow is in *ibid.*, on p. 220.
146. Talcott Parsons, *Turkey. A Wold Problem of To-day* (Garden City, N.Y.), 195–96.
147. Fritz Fischer, *Griff nach der Weltmacht. Die Kriegszielpolitik des kaiserlichen Deutschland 1914/18* (Düsseldorf, 1967), 110. *See also* note 4.
148. *Die Deutschen Dokumente* [n. 4], vol. 4, Doc. No. 876, p. 94.
149. A. A. Der Weltkrieg No. 11, vol. 1, cipher No. 518.
150. Sabis, *Harb Hatıralarım* [n. 92], vol. 1, p. 73; *see also* Trumpener, *Germany and the Ottoman Empire* [n. 157], 28.
151. Liman von Sanders, *Five Years* [n. 66], 35.
152. *Der Prozess Talaat Pascha.* Stenographischer Prozessbericht (Berlin, 1921), 62.
153. Sanders, *Five Years* [n. 66], 35.
154. A. A. Türkei 183/49, August 1917.
155. De Nogales, *Four Years* [n. 62], 13–4.
156. A. A. Grosses Hauptquartier vol. 186, file Türkei 18/2. cipher No. 1342, registry No. 1069.
157. Ulrich Trumpener, *Germany and the Ottoman Empire 1914–1918* (Princeton, 1968), 118.
158. Simon Khoren, "Hishoghutiunner" (Memories) in Teotig ed., *Amenoun Daretzouytzu* (Everyone's Almanac) vols. 10–14, 1916–1920, p. 133.
159. Earl of Oxford and Asquith, *Memories and Reflections* vol. 2, (London, 1928), 26, 28.
160. Général Gallieni, *Mémoires: défense du Paris, 25 Aôut–11 Septembre 1914* (Paris, 1920), 26.
161. Sanders, *Five Years* [n. 62], 135.
162. Rudolf Nadolny, *Mein Beitrag* (Wiesbaden, 1955), 40. In 1929 Nadolny was appointed Ambassador to Turkey.
163. *Ibid.*, 44–46, 60.
164. A. A. Weltkrieg, 11 d secr., vol. 3, A6497. February 20, 1915, "secret" cipher No. Pol.532.
165. *Ibid.*, A6497, No. 437. February 23, 1915.
166. *Ibid.*, Weltkrieg, 11 d, vol. 5, A. S. 1551. April 22, 1915.
167. *Ibid.*, vol. 6, p. 5, folio 184, enclosure No. 2 to No. 432.
168. *Ibid.*, vol. 1. Erzberger's October 26, 1914 report to von Jagow.
169. *Ibid.*, vol. 4, A10339. March 26, 1915, No. 250. Also in Botschaft Konstantinopel 168. Report No. 250.
170. A. A. Türkei 183/45, A33457, or K174, folio 53.
171. A. A. Der Weltkrieg, 11 d secr., A37451, vol. 9, No. 6, folios 118, 119. For the revolutionary activities of this Expedition and its incursion into Persia *see* the rest of the long

report. For a summary of the activities of the Detachment and its eventual dissolution *see ibid.*, vol. 15, No. 431, August 23, 1916 10 pp. report of Scheubner.

172. A. A. Türkei 183/40, A33704, No. 669, enclosure. Neurath's November 12, 1915 report.
173. The memo, dated February 2, 1915, is in A. A. Grosses Hauptquartier. Türkei No. 18, vol. 3, it was sent on February 26, 1915.
174. A. A. Türkei 183/39, A33294. October 25, 1915.
175. The professor is identified as "Professor Ragaz whose witnesses are Swiss engineers who at the time were working on the Baghdad Railway project. A. A. Türkei 183/54, A38243 the September 7, 1918 report to Berlin of Romberg, German ambassador to Switzerland.
176. Martin Hartmann, "Der Krieg und der Orient" *Deutsche-Levante Zeitung* 18/19 (October 1, 1914): 754.
177. A. A. Grosses Hauptquartier 191, Türkei 41, vol. 6, cipher No. 1082, May 27, 1918.
178. A. A. Türkei 183/51, A20698, May 15, 1918 report.
179. *Ibid.*, 183/53, A32123, July 10, 1918 report.
180. *Ibid.*, 158/20, A31679, July 13, 1918.
181. *Ibid.*, 183/54, A34707, August 5, 1918.
182. *Ibid.*, A39244, September 3, 1918.
183. Ernst Paraquin, "Politik im Orient" *Berliner Tageblatt*, the second of the two installments in the January 24 and 28, 1920 issues. *See also* A. A. Türkei 158/24, A1373 for a summary of the two articles. Speaking of "The stream of money, which flowed in milliards from Germany into the country *and into the pockets of the most influential politicians,*" Paraquin related the following episode: "Why?" asked Halil, smiling, "Rich Germany has lent us a great deal of money with which we are employing the Russians and English in Asia. Germany knows that she will never get the money back. But if Germany should try to get anything back by force then" — his fiery eyes flashed — *"Germany is our enemy."* From the January 28, issue. For a more detailed account of the Turkish genocidal campaign against the Armenians beyond the frontiers of Turkey *see* Dadrian, *The History of the Armenian Genocide* [n. 145], chapters 19 and 20.
184. For official German sources covering Stange's activities *see* A. A. Grosses Hauptquartier 186, Türkei 18, vol. 2, No. 1181, December 21, 1914; *ibid.*, 187, Türkei 18, vols. 3 and 4, No. 11, 1915; January 2, 1915; *ibid.*, No. 19, January 3, 1915; *ibid.*, No. 62, January 8, 1915; Sanders, *Five Years* [n. 62], 106. For Austrian sources *see* Austrian Foreign Ministry Archives, P. A. I 942 Krieg 21a Türkei. 79/Pol., November 8, 1914; *ibid.*, 83/Pol., December 12, 1914; P. A. XL.272 Interna Konfidentenberichte 1915, No. 56. February 2, 1915. For Turkish sources *see* Sabis, *Harp Hatıralarım* [n. 92], vol. 2, 184, 191; Mil, "*Umumi Harpte,*" January 27, 1915, installment No. 55; January 28, 1935, installment No. 56; January 29, 1934, installment No. 57.
185. A. A. Botschaft Konstantinopel 170. Secret report No. 3841. August 23, 1915.
186. A. A. Türkei 183/51, A24151, No. 1355, report by Montgelas in Bern to the German Chancellor. June 1, 1918; *ibid.,* A25031, No. 3123, report of Germany's General Konsul at Basel, Wunderlich. June 5, 1918.
187. Guse, "der Armenieraufstand" [n. 64], 615. Quoted in Dinkel, "German Officers" [n. 44]: 101.
188. Dinkel, "German Officers" [n. 44], 108.
189. Dinkel, "German Officers" [n. 64], 105.
190. Frank G. Weber, *Eagles on the Crescent. Germany, Austria, and the Diplomacy of the Turkish Alliance 1914–1918* (Ithaca, NY, 1970), 253.
191. A. A. Türkei 167/12, A25599. Berlin, September 21, 1916.
192. *Ibid.,* (No entry number, with the letter A preceding it, is available), Doc. No. 167.
193. A. A. Türkei 183/38, A27584. Oppenheim's August 29, 1915 report.
194. *Ibid.,* 167/13, A33932. December 13, 1916.
195. Wilhelm Treue, "Max Freiherr von Oppenheim—Der Archäologe und die Politik" *Historische Zeitschrift* 209 (1969): 45, 46, 52.
196. *Ibid.,* 48.

197. A. A. Orientalia Generalia 9 No. 1, vol. 7, A7692, No. 196, pp. 2,3,4 of the report. For the documentation of state organized massacres of the 1894–1896 period *see* Dadrian, *The History of the Armenian Genocide* [n. 145], Chapter 8, pp. 113–163.
198. *Ibid.,* A8048, Doc. No. 198.
199. A. A. Türkei 183/36, A9528. Doc. No. 140.
200. A. A. Der Weltkrieg, 11, vol. 2, p.7.
201. P. Stoddard, *The Ottoman Government and the Arabs 1911 to 1918; A Preliminary Study of the Teşkilâtı Mahsusa* (Ph.D. thesis, Univ. of Michigan, 1964), 185. For the details of the application of *cihad* see pp. 23–45.
202. A. A. Der Weltkrieg [n. 200], p. 50.
203. *Ibid.*, p. 51.
204. *Ibid.*, p. 53.
205. Treue, "Max Freiherr" [n. 195]: 62.
206. *Ibid.*: p. 63.
207. *Ibid.*: pp. 66, 72.
208. *Ibid.*: p. 52. Treue argues that since there is no proof positive (*beweisbar ist es nicht*), this is only a supposition.
209. Fischer, *Griff nach der Weltmacht* [n. 147], 109–110. For the English translation of this work *see Germany's Aims in the First World War.* No translator indicated. (New York, 1967). The corresponding page is 121.
210. Alexander Ular and Enrico Insabato, *Der erlöschende Halbmond. Türkische Enthüllungen* (Frankfurt A.M. 1909), 303–308. The authors claim that the book is the inside story of some of the dealings of the sultan and the Young Turk Ittihadists in the arena of international politics—as revealed by an Albanian prince who was the Assistant of Hilmi Paşa in Macedonia and had intimate contacts with the Palace. (pp. 112–113). Even though the book is not uniformly accepted as entirely trustworthy, the noted author Ramsaur found it sufficiently meritorious to include it in his Bibliography, despite his use of a caveat in the text. Ernest E. Ramsaur, Jr., *The Young Turks. Prelude of the Revolution of 1908* (Beirut, 1965), 79, 167. In this sense it may be worthwhile to inject here the view of these two authors that one reason the German emperor was pandering Sultan Abdul Hamit and perhaps tacitly encouraging the latter's scheme of Armenian massacres was his goal of seeing the elimination of Armenian competition in commerce and business and its replacement by German "financial power" in Turkey, which power "already seven years later became established in consequence of the terrible butcheries in Istanbul. The grandiose upswing of German commerce in Turkey requires this elimination of Armenian competition. In this sense the emperor's intent was political." (pp. 162, 165).
211. *British Foreign Office Archives*. War Office, vol. 106. Directorate of Military Opperations and Intelligence. 1870–1925. file 908, p. 95.
212. Treue, "Max Freiherr" [n. 195]: 51.
213. Lothar Rathmann, *Stossrichtung Nahost 1914–1918* (Berlin, 1963), 189.
214. Dr. Harry Stuermer, *Two War Years in Constantinople.* E. Allen, trans. (New York, 1917), 134–135.
215. A. A. Türkei 183/42, A10143. Bank president Dr. Erich Alexander's letter to Dr. Rosenberg, the chief expert in the New East Department of the Foreign Office, and the respective proposal of Lebrecht, the head of the Istanbul branch of the *Deutsche Orientbank.*
216. FO 371/4172/24597. The February 12, 1919 report prepared by the General Staff Intelligence Egyptian Expeditionary Force and submitted to the British Foreign Office by the Director of Military Intelligence. folio 304.
217. A. A. Türkei 183/39, A29589. October 8, 1915.
218. *Ibid.,* 183/44, A24725. September 8, 1916.
219. *Ibid.,* 183/36, A7070. February 24, 1915.
220. *Ibid.,* 183/38, A27584. August 29, 1915, pp. 9, 10 of the report.
221. *Ibid.,* p. 1 of the report.
222. *Ibid.,* p. 2.
223. *Ibid.,* p. 1, 4.

224. *Ibid.,* 167/10. Doc. No. 114/ March 20, 1916.
225. *Ibid.,* 183/38, A23991. July 27, 1915
226. *Ibid.,* 183/41, A2889. BN 944. November 8, 1915.
227. *Ibid.,* p. 13 of report. *See* Oppenheim's report [n. 220], pp. 4, 7, 8.
228. *Ibid.,* pp. 16–17.
229. *Ibid.,* pp. 13–15.
230. *Ibid.,* p. 17.
231. *Ibid.,* pp. 14, 15.
232. *Ibid.,* p. 20.
233. *Ibid.,* pp. 20, 23.
234. *Ibid.,* pp. 17a, 19.
235. *Times,* September 30, 1915.
236. Treue, "Max Freiherr" [n. 195], 62.
237. *See* note 211.
238. A. A. Türkei 183/40 A34383. B. No. 10. 102. November 20, 1915.
239. Jakob Künzler, *Im Lande des Blutes. Erlebnisse in Mesopotamien während des Weltkrieges* (Berlin-Potsdam, 1921), 13.
240. *See* note 216.
241. *Takvimi Vekâyi* [n. 43], No. 3540, p. 7.
242. Dr. K. Klinghardt, "Frau Koch-v. Winckler aus Aleppo zum Gedächtnis" *Orient Rundschau* XVI,9 (September 10, 1934): 70.
243. *See* two German consular reports from Aleppo in this regard. A. A. Botschaft Konstantinopel. vol. 169, folio 13 (3378), Consul Rössler's June 3, 1915 report and *ibid.,* 169. No. 9, folio 84 (3790).
244. *See* the many details of these twin murders of Ottoman Chamber deputies in Dadrian, "The Armenian Genocide in Official Turkish Records" [n. 134], 118–120.
245. A. A. Botschaft Konstantinopel. vol. 169, No. 4314, folio 192. July 11, 1915. For further correspondence on this topic between Istanbul and Aleppo *see ibid.*, folios 195, 196.
246. Aram Andonian, *Medz Vodjiru* (The Great Crime) (Boston, 1921), 46-49.
247. A. A. Türkei 167/10. Enclosure to J. No: Nst 688/A 14. February 24, 1916, p. 5 of the report.
248. *Ibid.,* 183/37, A21257. *See also* Botschaft Konstantinopel vol. 169, folios 142–146.
249. *Ibid.,* 183/38, A24507, and 183/44, A25749.
250. *Ibid.,* 183/40, A33705. Neurath's December 12, 1915 report regarding the secret Turkish plan to deport Istanbul's Armenian population also.
251. *Ibid.,* 183/40, A37207, and Botschaft Konstantinopel vol. 172/25, No. 725. Ambassador Metternich's December 18, 1915 report.
252. *Ibid.,* 183/39, A33132, Hollweg's November 10, 1915 instruction; Botschaft Konstantinopel vol. 172/25, A30410, Hollweg's November 12 communication to the leaders of the German Protestant Missions, University professors, publicists and deputies who had appealed to him for intervention on behalf of the Armenians..
253. *Ibid.,* vol. 171, No. 855 (6749), Jagow's November 12, 1915 directive.
254. *Ibid.,* 183/38, A27200. Zimmermann's September 22, 1915 instruction.
255. *Ibid.,* 183/40, A37610. December 22, 1915.
256. Hamlet, Act 3, scene 2. *Shakespeare. Complete Works.* P. Alexander, ed. (New York, 1952), 1051, left column.
257. Henry Morgenthau, *Ambassador Morgenthau's Story* (Garden City, NY, 1918), 374–375.
258. *See* Part II, note 130.
259. A. A. Türkei 183/37, A22101. Doc. No. 590. August 4, 1915.
260. *Ibid.,* 183/36, A13922. Doc. No. 228. April 15, 1915. The document is initialed by Undersecretary Zimmermann with the indication that he has "read" it (*gelesen*).
261. *Ibid.,* Botschaft Konstantinopel. vol. 168. Doc. No. 258. April 26, 1915. *See also* Trumpener, *Germany* [n. 157], 203, n. 9.
262. *Ibid.,* vol. 168, No. 9 (3224). May 15, 1915.
263. *Ibid.,* No.(3007).

264. *Ibid.,* vol. 169, No. 1 (3361), folio 10.
265. *See* note 187.
266. A. A. Türkei 183/39, A31729. Doc. No. 634. October 26, 1915.
267. Vahram S., "Ariunod Turvakner" (Bloody Episodes) *Zhoghovourtee Tzain*, p.4. February 25, 1919.
268. A. A. Türkei 183/40, A25749. Doc. No. 567. September 18, 1916.
269. *Ibid.,* p. 14.
270. *Ibid.,* pp. 38, 47.
271. *Ibid.,* p. 52.
272. *Ibid.,* p. 42.
273. *Ibid.,* p. 40.
274. *Ibid.,* pp. 49–50.
275. Trumpener, Germany [n. 157], 125.
276. *Ibid.,* 127.
277. Dadrian, *History of the Armenian Genocide* [n. 145], 221, 235.
278. *Ibid.,* 216.
279. Carl Mühlmann, *Das deutsch-türkische Waffenbündnis im Weltkriege* (Leipzig, 1940), 290, 293–294.
280. Dinkel, "German Officers," [n. 44], 102.
281. In the Yozgat Verdict the panel of judges invoked, among others, the precepts of "humanity and civilization." Dadrian, *History of the Armenian Genocide* [n. 145], 332. In the search for a new legal formula needed to institute court-martial proceedings against the Ittihadist potentates, the sultan likewise invoked "the law of humanity" (*kanuni insaniyet*). Ali Fuad Türkgeldi, *Görüp Işittiklerim* (The Things I Saw and Heard). 2nd ed. (Ankara, 1951), 194.
282. Bassiouni, *Crimes Against Humanity* [n. 29], 302.
283. *Ibid.*
284. *Ibid.*
285. General Assembly Resolution 239 (XXIII), 23 U.N. G.A.O.R. Suff. (No. 18) 40, U.N. Doc. A/7218 (1968).

PART II

The Political Determinants in the Involvement of the German Military

THE REVIVAL OF THE ARMENIAN QUESTION AND THE NEW TURKO-GERMAN PARTNERSHIP

The Turkish impulse to consider the Armenians as an "internal foe" was only in part a reflection of the state of exigencies of the war animating that impulse. More critical in this respect was the political fallout of the revival of the Armenian Question in the period interposed between the first Balkan War and World War I. Furthermore, there was a new lineup among the Powers marking the re-emergence of Russia as the advocate of the Armenian cause that issued from that revival; it was supported in this new role, albeit passively, by England and France. The new alignment was this time free from the cryptic acts of sabotage Russia and, to a lesser degree, France were wont to indulge in during the turbulent era of Abdul Hamit, thereby frustrating England's effort to force the Sultan to carry out the reforms in the provinces.

That legacy of shielding Turkey from the presumed inroads of alien reforms, portending an encroachment on Turkish sovereignty, was borne by Emperor William II's Germany, which for some time had been cultivating a new and invigorated partnership with the Young Turk regime. In this new shift of alignments, the Turko-German common objective was to place constraints on Russian designs of reform, which were suspected to be Russian imperial designs in disguise. The man entrusted with this task was Hans Freiherr von Wangenheim, the German ambassador to Turkey. In the unending chain of ironies, characteristic of the vicissitudes and frailties of diplomacy, Russia was now being administered the same dose of frustration it had administered to England in the 1894–1896 period, especially when Salisbury was in office several times during that period. Ambassador Wangenheim, in a manifest gesture of optimal support of Turkey, went so far as to declare at one stage of the negotiations for Armenian reforms (September 1913) that Germany would agree to the terms of the proposed Reform Agreement act only to the extent to which Turkey itself voluntarily would agree. In the period December 1912–June 1913, Russian diplomacy was actively engaged in efforts to prepare the ground for a new international conference on Armenian Reforms. While encouraging the Armenians to pursue their cause inside and outside Turkey through the media and through appeals to governments and public figures, the Russian ambassador to the Ottoman Empire explicitly warned them to refrain from provocative acts through which their condition could but deteriorate, adding: "It is important that in the eyes of Europe the Armenians appear as victims of Turkish willfulness rather than as political revolutionaries who are out to exploit current Turkish military setbacks with a view to realizing their national aspirations."[1]

Following the dispatch on June 6, 1913 by Neratof, the Deputy Foreign Minister of Russia, of a circular Note to the governments of Europe, a Reform Commission, consisting of the representatives of the six Powers, was set up in Constantinople to come up with a new reform project. In order to accommodate the positions taken by Turkey and Germany, the original terms of the project, which was conceived and elaborated by André Mandelstam, the legal expert of the Russian Embassy, were considerably diluted during a series of grueling negotiations. Having ironed out most of their major differences, the Powers, along with Turkey, finally embraced, through the signatures of the Russian representative and the Turkish Grand Vizier, who were acting on behalf of the two camps separating the Powers, the January 26/February 8, 1914 Reform Agreement.

The relevance of this accord for the present discussion derives from the significance the Russians, the Turks, and the Germans attached to this document. In relaying the news of the completion of the accord to his Foreign Minister, Gulkevitch, the Russian Chargé at the Ottoman capital, was relishing what he considered to be the preeminent role Russia played in forging an internationally binding legal document. He redefined Russia's new Armenia policy as one animated by "an appreciation of the great importance for Russia of the Armenian Question, from the point of view of humanitarianism, as well as of Russian interests." He then for the first time injected into the picture the idea of the urgency of pushing through the reforms, to be executed under Russian or European control, with due regard to such principles as "the integrity of Turkey" (*sans porter atteinte à l'integrité de la Turquie*) and "the Sultan's sovereignty."

From a Turkish and, indirectly, a German perspective, the most ominous element of this new policy declaration was the assertion that the Reform Agreement was an act "preparatory for the occupation of Armenia [eastern Turkey], in the event the reform should fail to materialize in consequence of the inability, or the ill-will, of the Turkish government or, in the event the country should lapse into anarchy, imperilling the security of Russia's neighboring provinces."[2] The acuteness of the need for Armenian reforms was exceeded only by the severity of the dangers this Russian stance signaled as far as the future of Turkey's eastern provinces was concerned, not to speak of the future of Turkey as a whole. By a curious twist of circumstances the Armenian Question had thus become the Russian Question inasmuch as the two questions became entwined, especially in the minds of the Young Turk leaders. The threat, emanating from Russia, the historical nemesis of Turkey, was now, more than ever, intimately associated with an Armenian threat flowing from the urgency of the provisions of the accord, which was more or less masterminded by the Russians.

The German partnership with Turkey, which culminated in the wartime enactment of the August 2, 1914 secret Turko-German military alliance, was the direct result of an evolving, historical process, which was considerably accelerated as a response to the re-emergence of this Russian threat. German national interests tended to converge with Turkish national interests. As determined by William II and his advisers, the Russian threat was to be reckoned with and confronted while the war appeared to be imminent.

THE INROADS OF THE GERMAN MILITARY MISSION TO TURKEY

From a strictly military point of view, the event that catalyzed this confrontation in a rudimentary form was the creation of the German Military Mission to Turkey whose arrival in Turkey (December 1913) coincided with the onset of the very last stages of the negotiations on the new Armenian Reform accord. Essentially led by veteran Prussian officers, the group was to reform and reorganize the Turkish army. This mission was nothing new in the history of Turko-German relations. The German involvement in the task of reforming the Ottoman-Turkish army in modern times dates back to 1882 when then Major von der Goltz was commissioned by Sultan Abdul Hamit to reorganize the Turkish army and the training of its officers corps. From a Turkish point of view the military alliance treaty, which first was proposed by War Minister Enver (July 22, 1914), was almost entirely aimed at Russia. The Turks were seeking German protection, but the Germans, although unimpressed with the

Turkish military potential at the time, insisted on a commitment by Turkey to intervene militarily should a Russo-German war break out. The centerpiece of the treaty was an understanding that the officers of the German Military Mission were to assume responsibility for the operative command of the Turkish army. The passage reads: *influence effective sur la conduite générale de l'armée*.[3]

The acerbity with which the Russians reacted to this arrangement in a sense foreshadowed the Russo-German confrontation that was shaping up at the time. The incremental influx of German military cadres in Turkey eventually led to the cultivation of many connections to the German industrial-military complex, especially Krupp, which became the principal supplier of the munitions and armaments of the Turkish army. German military missions to Turkey thus emerge as special harbingers of German power and influence enveloping a struggling and weary nation-state. The authority of the German Military Mission was further enhanced by the injection in the respective contract of a clause by virtue of which German officers could be entitled to a rank one grade higher in the Turkish army than their grade in the German army. The higher echelons of the German Mission included a Prussian Field Marshal (von der Goltz), two generals, who likewise became marshals, that is, *müşir* (Liman von Sanders and von Falkenhayn), three admirals (Usedom, Souchon, and Merten), and about ten generals (those of lower ranks advancing to the Turkish *ferik* rank of various grades). In 1917 a fourth admiral, Hubert von Rebeur-Paschwitz, was engaged. The original complement of 70 officers of the mission had expanded to such a degree that at the height of its wartime operations the mission had at its disposal 700 to 800 German officers and some 12,000 troops.[4]

The most tangible and consequential influence these German military leaders, especially the admirals, had, was that they preempted Turkey's ability to chart its own course relative to the choice and the exact time of intervening in the war. Indeed, they managed to embroil Turkey in a war with Russia—perhaps too soon and, therefore, prematurely. By launching naval assaults against Russian ships and military installations in and around the Black Sea, without legal authorization by the Turks, they forced the hands of the latter in terms of a precipitate intervention in the war.[5] Another condition of the contract involved the understanding that when a Turkish officer served as field commander of a unit, his Chief of Staff was to be a German, and vice versa.

These descriptions and numbers do not tell, however, the entire story of the German influence at issue here. Superseding them in significance was one factor through which the sway of German influence was not only ensured but also was amplified substantially. That factor involved War Minister Enver's personal relationship to the German emperor, combined with his exaggerated assessment of the potential of the German war machine and his overall admiration of what he perceived to be distinct German attributes, such as organizational skills and military prowess and discipline. While a colonel, Enver in the 1909–1913 period twice served as a military attaché at Berlin. During these terms of service William II at times went out of his way to cultivate a special relationship to him, virtually pampering him, in anticipation of the latter's ascendancy in the ranks of the Young Turk power-wielders.[6]

After having attained that position Enver in many, but not all, respects became a kind of proxy of the German strategists in Berlin and in the Imperial German General Headquarters (*Das Grosse Hauptquartier*). Postwar accounts by several Turkish generals, who were part of the military apparatus, bitterly inveigh against Enver, portraying him as a subservient puppet of the Germans who prematurely dragged Turkey into the war in pursuit of dubious objectives and personal glory.[7] One of these generals even asserts that in private conversations Enver disclosed to him that he was planning to "settle in Anatolia many (*bir hayli*) Germans,"[8] presumably in areas vacated through "the Armenian deportations." Another general, Izzet Paşa, complained that Enver in all of his trips to the front studiously avoided taking along Turkish officers and, except for his adjutants and some secretaries, was always accompanied by high ranking German officers.[9] Still another general, Ismet Paşa, deplored the fact that "The German Military Mission was in a position to follow day by day all that was transpiring in the country," that the Germans were "entrusted with all the secrets of the state, be they political or military secrets."[10] The extraordinary importance of this privileged German position for the present inquiry into the matter of German complicity calls for emphasis. It brings into special relief the import of the role of the Ottoman General Headquarters (*Umumi Karargâh*) in view of the duties assigned to a particular department within those headquarters, namely, Department II, Intelligence (*Istihbarat*). This was one of the few departments that simultaneously was Department II in the setups of both the General Staff and the General Headquarters, thus belonging to two overlaping military jurisdictions with but one identity, function, and staff. It was run by Enver's friend and cohort, Colonel Seyfi, and Seyfi was one of the key organizers of the genocide.

Moreover, according to the account of a Turkish historian, "A German officer was appointed to head Department II, which was the center where all the political and military secrets of the state converged. This was tantamount to surrendering the state to the Germans."[11] The officer in question was Lieutenant Colonel von Thauvenay who, as the new Quartermaster, exercised control over Departments I and II in the Ottoman General Headquarters. Before he was transferred to the post of Chief of Staff of the Tekirdağı Armee Corps, he proved not only "very harsh in his criticism of Turkish officers" (*pek sert Alman tenkidi*) but also placed a higher premium on German interests when discharging his duties in the Ottoman General Headquarters.[12] His successor was Lieutenant Colonel Sievert. One of the functions of Department II was the organization, deployment, and direction of the brigand units of the Special Organization,[13] carrying out the operations in the killing fields. The participation of Colonel Seyfi, the Turkish chief of Department II, in the secret Young Turk Ittihadist conference at which the decision for the mass murder of the Armenians was spelled out in terms of a blueprint is one of the indicators of the nature of that department's involvement in the planning and execution of that mass murder.[14] In a final evaluation of the scope of German control of the Turkish military, Lieutenant General Seeckt, the last German Chief of Staff of the Ottoman Armed Forces, stated, "The Treaty [of August 2, 1914] allowed the Germans to manage practically the entire organization of the [Turkish] army, affording the Chief of the [German Military] Mission intervention (*Eingriff*) in nearly all military matters."[15] Even though this control was neither uniform nor consistent or persistent in face of the vicissitudes of the war and internal Turkish politics, by German political design and administrative fiat that control was never brought to bear upon the activities of those Turkish and German high-ranking officers who directly and indirectly became implicated in the organization of Armenian massacres.

THE BEARINGS OF THE GERMAN IDEOLOGICAL PERSPECTIVES

To the extent that it may be possible to ascertain a degree of German complicity under review here, to that extent an examination of certain underlying attitudes affording such complicity may be warranted. There are a number of categories of attitudes to be considered. One of them refers to those that were vestiges of the Abdul Hamit-era and to the massacres of that era. Two personalities stand out in terms of embodying the legacy of that era inasmuch as that legacy in effect carried over into the era of the wartime genocide. The views of Friedrich Naumann have already been exposed in Part I note 5. But the attitude of the other,

Emperor William II (discussed in the same section notes 9–19), deserves a special review, in particular on two separate but interconnected levels. First to be considered is his general perspective on Islam and Turkey, which gradually evolved and eventually crystallized in the course of his two trips to the Sultan's domain, especially the second one (1898). William II's monarchical affinities for the Turkish monarch sufficiently overwhelmed him and led him to re-examine and recast his views on Islam and on theocracy within a new perspective. Identifying himself with the Turkish sultan in some respects, William II, through this new perspective, came to view the latter as a ruler whose power emanated from and was preordained by God, whose Regent on earth he was, and in whom converged sacred and secular authority in the highest form. Within this perspective he also came to appreciate Islam as a unifying force, beckoning to the true believers with the appeal of a set of ideals, the magnetism of which he compared to the spell of the ascetic virtues of an idealized Prussia. In fact he regarded Turkey as the Prussia of the Orient; he compared the Islamic attributes of self-denial to his notions of Prussian puritanism. His November 8, 1898 Damascus speech, proclaiming his solidarity ("friend forever") with three hundred million Mohammedans worldwide, was emblematic of this seemingly ideological embrace of Turkey, as a theocratic wonderland, committed to the task of consecrating the ideals and aspirations of Islam.

These indulgences in exaltations of religious ideals and puritanism were, however, as liable to transmutation into an indulgence in ferocity as the release of the passions, suppressed by the exertions of such puritanism, whether Prussian or Islamic, would allow. The history of the wartime deportations is but an aspect of this phenomenon of transmutation. By inquiring into the German role in the carrying out of these deportations it may be worth considering some evidence of the German emperor's attitude on the idea of such deportations. Before the occurrence of the German military setback at Marne (September 5–12, 1914), he was seriously considering at the Imperial German General Headquarters the possibility of "clearing" (*evakuieren*) from certain occupied regions of France and Belgium the indigenous populations involved and of "settling [there] (*ansiedeln*) in their stead" "deserving" Germans. Equally significant, his chancellor described the suggestion as "intriguing" and, therefore, worth exploring as one of the dividends of military victory.[16] This penchant for uprooting people en masse was even more pronounced with respect to Alsace. In the April 2, 1915 entry of his diary Admiral Tirpitz writes: "The Kaiser said the other day, that he would have every French man cleared out of Alsace."[17] In other words, the emperor and his coterie of rulers were already toying with the idea of what in today's parlance is called "ethnic cleansing" through wholesale deportations.

The ideological rudiments of the Turkish scheme to divest Turkey of its indigenous Armenian population in this respect bear a German imprint. In the immediate aftermath of the 1894–1896 Armenian massacres General von der Goltz, whom German ambassador Marschall at the time described as the guru of patriotic Turkish officers,[18] in a lengthy article advocated a new doctrine of Turkish national renewal; he indicated the perils for Turkey in the event the latter failed to chart the new course Goltz was expounding. The gist of this doctrine was that Turkey's future lay in the Asiatic part of its empire and that, therefore, it should give up the European part, turn inward, and consolidate herself in Anatolia. The goal is, he said, to transform a weak Byzantine realm into a Turkish one by way of cementing the Islamic ties among the peoples of the regions in question. His advice was: concentrate on the quintessential provinces of Asiatic Turkey to achieve the goal of inner strength.[19] Goltz repeated this view when he stated that "the core of Turkey is to be found not in Europe but in Asia Minor. Turkey has greater chances of military success in Transcaucasia, where Russia is militarily weak, and its ethnic and religious ties with the local Muslim populations would come in handy."[20] A similar view was expounded by German Colonel von Diest, and especially Paul Rohrbach, a champion of the idea of German expansionism in the Near East. Rohrbach is in fact suspected to have been the theoretician who implanted in Turkish minds the idea of the expediency of the evacuation of the Armenians from their ancestral territories in eastern Turkey and their relocation in Mesopotamia for the purpose of populating and cultivating the areas through which the Baghdad Railway system was to be established. French author René Pinon asserted, for example, that in a lecture given in the winter of 1913 Rohrbach proposed this deal as a solution to the lingering Armenian Question by virtue of which the interests both of Germany and Turkey could be served simultaneously.[21] American ambassador Morgenthau, citing the French newspaper *Temps*, made the same attribution to Rohrbach.[22] The Armenian Patriarch of Istanbul made a similar assertion. In a meeting on May 28/June 10, 1915 with Dr. Mordtmann, the head of the Armenian desk at the German Embassy at Constantinople, the Patriarch told the latter that the deportations that the Turkish government was embarking upon at that time were the realization of the Rohrbach plan, which Rohrbach in a lecture to the German Geographic Society had presented sometime ago.[23] Echoing these speculations and adding a new detail, namely, that Rohrbach allegedly made his proposal during a presentation to the German emperor, Germany's vice consul at Erzurum, Scheubner Richter, in a report to Berlin, disputed the allied claim that the deportations were the result of this advice.[24] Perhaps the most plausible speculation attaches to a similar proposal attributed to General von der Goltz. He is reported to have outlined such a proposal in a public lecture in Berlin in Februrary 1914. The lecture was delivered under the sponsorship of the German-Turkish League *(Deutsch-türkische Vereinigung)* and was attended by members of the Turkish Embassy, prominent German public figures, and the members of the League. The League itself, which at the time had 5,000 members, was established by Ernst Jäckh, a Turkophile activist with ties to the ruling circles of Germany, including the emperor. It was created on the instance of the German Foreign Office, with Goltz serving as a member of the Board of Directors. The main points of the reported proposal were:

1. Russia for almost a century now has been intervening in the internal affairs of Turkey under the pretext of wanting to protect the subject nationalities.
2. As a result, all non-Turkish nationalities of the empire have emancipated themselves from Turkish dominion and Turkey's territories shrunk substantially.
3. Exploiting thc Balkan War crisis Russia has recently taken up the Armenian problem and is covertly aiming at the further truncation of Turkish territories by bringing up a new reform project.
4. In order to spare Turkey a new disaster, it is necessary to remove from the Russo-Turkish border areas, once and for all, the half a million Armenians who inhabit the provinces of Van, Bitlis, and Erzurum that are contiguous to these areas. They should be transported to the south and resettled in the areas of Aleppo and Mesopotamia.
5. In return, the Arabs of these areas should be resettled along the Russo-Turkish borders.

The elements of this lecture more or less square with his main thesis, which was expounded in his 1897 article and cited earlier. In addition, the background of the source lends a measure of credence to the veracity of that source. That source is an Armenian priest who at the time was a student of theology at the University of Berlin. A German professor, who had attended the lecture, "confidentially" had apprised him of the contents of the lecture, and he in turn had promptly relayed the information to his superiors at the Armenian Patriarchate at Constantinople.[25] In his memoirs a leader of the Armenian Dashnak party is even more specific. He confirms the proposal made at the *Deutsch-türkische Vereinigung* meeting in Berlin relative to the deportation of the Armenians of eastern Turkey to Mesopotamia, and states that the meeting took place in February 1914.[26]

THE COMPLICITY OF THE MILITARY. THE ORDER FOR THE "DEPORTATIONS"

General Major Bronsart von Schellendorf's role

Despite the lengths to which German authorities in Constantinople and Berlin went to avoid appearing being in any way involved in the launching of the wartime anti-Armenian measures, two sets of evidentiary material attest to such an involvement. The first is contained in the edited memoirs of the Young Turk Ittihadist party chief and boss, Interior Minister, and subsequently Grand Vizier (February 1917–October 1918), Talât. According to this account, in December 1914 General Major Fritz Bronsart von Schellendorf, the Chief of Staff at Ottoman General Headquarters (*Umumi Karargâh*), requested from Enver, War Minister and de facto Commander-in-Chief of Ottoman Armed Forces, that he "convene an emergency, secret conference to be attended by competent Ministers." Attending that conference were, among others, German generals Goltz and Liman von Sanders, and Turkish power-wielders Talât and Enver. Reportedly, the German military at that conference supplied evidence of Armenian acts of sabotage and atrocities committed in the rear of the army; they, therefore, requested the initiation of countermeasures (*tedbir*) to stamp out this danger that avowedly seemed to them to threaten the sinew of the Turkish war effort.[27]

In an earlier volume in which his memoirs came to light for the first time (the end of World War II), Talât revealed that the draft bill, which was submitted to the Cabinet Council for approval and ratification and decreed the wholesale deportation of the Ottoman Armenians, "was prepared at the Ottoman General Headquarters."[28] In his memoirs, Admiral Rauf Orbay (the Turkish naval hero, and in 1918 Minister of the Marine, an Ittihadist, and subsequently Prime Minister in the fledgling Republic of Turkey) for his part disclosed that "three German generals, who commanded three of the existing five Turkish armies [in World War I], warned conjointly, and with a categoricalness, bordering on an ultimatum, the government, insisting upon action" to be taken against the Armenians residing in the theaters of the war (*müşterek ve adetâ ültimatom kat'iyetindeki ikazları ile ...*).[29] In the same memoirs Orbay relates a conversation with Talât, whom he "was consulting daily during the second half of October 1918" when he, Orbay, was conducting his negotiations with the British regarding the terms of the Armistice; in the wake of the signing of it on October 30 Talât and his six cohorts fled Turkey, to escape prosecution on the matter of the Armenian deportations and massacres. During one of these exchanges, the topic shifted to the fate of the Armenians, in reference to which Talât told Orbay that the German generals kept pressing the Turkish authorities to initiate measures against the Armenians whom they branded as the internal enemy, adding, "you don't need any other foe ... they are enough."[30] Moreover, in an interview Talât granted Aubrey Herbert, a member of the British Parliament and an intelligence operative, he made the same assertion, namely, that the Germans had pressed for the initiation of anti-Armenian measures.[31] Without specifying the Germans as the people involved, Said Halim, the Grand Vizier at the time, told the Armenian Patriarch likewise that the deportations were the result of "months of pressure by military authorities"; the Patriarch on April 13–26, 1915 (two days after the mass arrests in the Ottoman capital of the leaders of the Armenian community) was in the Grand Vizier's office to present a petition on behalf of the Armenian people.[32]

The second is an official document, unearthed by the officials of the British High Commissioner's office toward the end of the Turkish Armistice. In it, General Bronsart is seen ordering, in his capacity as Chief of Staff at Ottoman High Command, the deportation of the Armenians, urging that "severe" (*şedide*) measures be applied against those Armenians, who were then part of labor battalions, to prevent their being troublesome in connection with deportation procedures and to keep them under strict surveillance.[33] The significance of this document cannot be overemphasized given the unusual circumspection the Germans exercised in structuring their relationship to the Turkish scheme involving the whole array of anti-Armenian measures. Dated July 25, 1915, the cipher in question has this notation at the end of it: "By order of the Chief of Staff (i.e., Bronsart, V.N.D.) of the Interim Commander-in-Chief." (i.e., War Minister Enver, V.N.D.).This issue of circumspection will be discussed later. What needs to be emphasized at this point is that the document clearly demonstrates *the very direct involvement*, whether intentional or inadvertent, of one of the highest ranking German officers, subject to the jurisdiction of the German Military Mission to Turkey, in the authorization of the Armenian deportations. It also demonstrates something that is critical for understanding the real intent of these deportations: the mutual understanding between the German Chief of Staff and his Turkish cohorts at the headquarters on the need to impose a measure of "severity" in the application of the deportation measures. Ordinarily, the word "severe" could denote the idea of strictness. But in Turkish phraseology, especially adopted and used during the Abdul Hamit-era massacres against the Armenians, it also connoted for the officials the idea of license for lethal violence.[34] It is significant to note in this connection that in reproducing Bronsart's order for deportation Turkish author Salahi Sonyel, apart from deleting some words, incorrectly translated the word *şedide* into the word "necessary", thus divesting the composition of the order of its hidden intimation as described in note 34.[35] Moreover, General Bronsart instructed Count von Schulenburg, who had replaced Scheubner Richter as Germany's consul at Erzurum, not to follow in the footsteps of his predecessor and hence not to intercede on behalf of the Armenians.[36] As will be seen later (and as already noted in Part I, notes 46 and 47), General Bronsart, fully aware of the actual outcome of the deportations he authorized, not only did not express any regret, not to speak of any remorse, but also to the end of his life, with unrepentant truculence, acted as a committed apologist for the Turks.

The genocidal consequences of the order and the issue of legal liability

An order, one way or another intended to authorize the violent elimination of a targeted group, if framed carefully, may be, after the fact, defended on semantic, if on no other, grounds. Implied injunctions or instructions, in substitution of explicit orders, have this function. Indeed, by the nature of things, orders of the latter type are the exception rather than the norm. Even the Nazis relied on the use of the covert term *Unschädlichmachung*, that is, rendering the subject "harmless," to mask the actual liquidation scheme involved. In such situations the test of intent lies in the actual end result of the order, in the simple fact that exterminatory intent is best revealed in outcomes that have exterminatory character. Thus, the nature of an intent cannot be separated from the nature of its consequences. General Bronsart's order had, apart from its reference to "the Armenian people" (*Ermeni ahalinin*), whose wholesale deportation has been "determined upon" (*mukarrerdir*), an ancillary purpose, namely, to target "the Armenians in the labor battalions" who, for security reasons, were to be subjected to "severe" treatment. An inquiry into the fate of these Armenians should provide, for instance, a basis for assessing the purpose of the order. From the welter of available material relating to that fate, the adducing of a few examples may assist in this task; they are furnished by sources that were identified with the German camp and, equally important, were actual eyewitnesses.

In one of his reports to his chancellor in Berlin, Dr. Walter Rössler, Germany's veteran consul at Aleppo, relayed the account of a German captain of cavalry on the murder "through cutting off the throats" (*durchschnittene Hälse*) of countless young Armenians who were part of a labor battalion and whose corpses were strewn on both sides of the road he was riding through on his way from Diyarbekir to Urfa.[37] In another report, Rössler on September 3, 1915 relates the story of "the murder of hundreds of Armenians engaged in road construction" in his district.[38] The account of a Venezuelan officer who, under German sponsorship had volunteered to fight alongside the Turks, personally observed, while serving as a commanding officer in the eastern and southeastern sectors of the war front in Turkey, case after case of systematic destructions of these Armenian contingents of labor battalions. Focusing on a particular case whereby he observed those "thirteen or fifteen hundred unarmed Armenian soldiers, breaking stone and mending road," he declared that shortly thereafter they had become the victims of "a massacre," of a "so hideous a crime against humanity."[39] German state archives are replete with documents with similar testimonies on the near uniformity of this pattern of elimination of the Armenian able-bodied men, namely, conscription, disarming, isolation in "labor battalions," and liquidation.

These testimonies are amply corroborated by the official representatives of the U.S. government, which then was a neutral party in the war. The following account by American ambassador Morgenthau provides a succinct picture of the procedure of extermination.

> Let me relate a single episode which is contained in one of the reports of our consuls and which now forms part of the records of the American State Department. Early in July, 2,000 Armenian "amélés"—such is the Turkish word for soldiers who have been reduced to workmen—were sent from Harpoot to build roads ... practically every man of these 2,000 was massacred, and his body thrown into a cave. A few escaped, and it was from these that news of the massacre reached the world. A few days afterward another 2,000 soldiers were sent to Diarbekir. The only purpose of sending these men out in the open country was that they might be massacred. In order that they might have no strength to resist or to escape by flight, these poor creatures were systematically starved. Government agents went ahead on the road,

> notifying the Kurds that the caravan was approaching and ordering them to do their congenial duty. Not only did the Kurdish tribesmen pour down from the mountains upon this starved and weakened regiment, but the Kurdish women came with butcher's knives in order that they might gain that merit in Allah's eyes that comes from killing a Christian. These massacres were not isolated happenings; I could detail many more episodes just as horrible as the one related above; throughout the Turkish Empire a systematic attempt was made to kill all ablebodied men, not only for the purpose of removing all males who might propagate a new generation of Armenians, but for the purpose of rendering the weaker part of the population an easy prey.[40]

That the arrangement of assigning the Armenians to construction work was not in any way related to insurrections in the rear of the Turkish army, as often claimed by Turkish sources, is indicated by Lieutenant Commander Hans Humann, Marine Attaché to Turkey and a close friend of War Minister Enver. In a report on October 16, 1914 (several weeks before even Turkey entered the war), he disclosed that the Armenians, along with the Greeks, were already being segregated in labor battalion formations—long before the Armenians had either any reason or occasion to think of any insurrection, let alone to mount an insurrection.[41]

Before closing this discussion, a comment or two on the cipher telegram sent by General Bronsart is called for; after all, the consequences described earlier are foreshadowed in the text of that cipher. First, neither Turkish authorities nor Turkish or pro-Turkish authors hitherto disputed the authenticity of it. On the contrary, many of them directly or indirectly accepted or validated it by invoking it, i.e., that document, to prove a certain point or to advance a certain argument. Moreover, the Turkish Historical Society, a quasi arm of the Turkish government, in one of its publications, *Belleten*, reproduced the set of documents, of which the Bronsart cipher is part, and Turkish author Sonyel reworked them in a new pamphlet containing translations of that set in French and English.[42] (See Part I on The Issue of Legal Liability Revisited and on The Legal Perspective.)

Beyond these considerations, there is the fundamental legal issue. By identifying himself as the author of the cipher telegraph in question, the German general assumed a level of responsibility that transcends the political and military ramifications of the problem, posing the problem of the legal liability of office. He was not only the Chief of Staff at the Ottoman General Headquarters and at the General Staff, but also temporarily (during the 1914–1915 Sarıkamış offensive) Chief of Staff of the IIIrd Ottoman Army mounting that offensive. The operations had manifold repercussions for the Armenian population of the six provinces that the IIIrd Army's zone of command encompassed. In addition, as noted in Part I, he was contractually a representative of Imperial Germany. He was first and foremost a member of the German Military Mission to Turkey, to which he was accountable, and through it, to Emperor William II and his military and civilian high command. Indeed, that mission was authorized and sanctioned by the very same emperor who appointed its chief, Marshal Liman von Sanders, investing him with enough of a high level of competency to afford him the privilege to bypass the German Embassy and other intermediary channels and to report directly to the emperor (*Immediatbericht*). As Sanders relates in his memoirs, first he was "authorized by H. M. the Emperor to sign" the contract. Then, in November 1913, "I was called before H. M. the Emperor," who briefed him on the mission. Before his departure for Constantinople General Sanders and the first contingent of German officers, including Bronsart von Schellendorf, was once more called before the emperor to be charged formally with the mission.[43]

General Bronsart's exculpatory rationale blaming the victim after the fact

The attribution of guilt to the Armenians is the basis on which Bronsart predicates his justification of the manner in which they were treated during the war. However, the victims are not only accused of acts of provocation but are also blamed on account of certain negative images, which clearly fall into the category of prejudice and typecasting. According to this rationale, the Armenians deserved the fate befalling them. This posture merits special attention as it sheds light on the social psychological mechanisms through the dynamics of which the act of the complicity in question appears to be generated and subsequently rationalized. It is evident that the general's hostility to the victim population did not only not abate in the postwar years but also was sustained throughout. As if frustrated at the incompleteness of the destruction of that population, Bronsart continued to lash out against the Armenians as a corporate entity. One of the methods he used for this end was to compare them with the Jews, vilifying them both through the assertion

> Namely, the Armenian is just like the Jew, a parasite outside the confines of his homeland, sucking off the marrow of the people of the host country. Year after year they abandon their native land—just like the Polish Jews who migrate to Germany—to engage in usurious activities. Hence the hatred

which, in a medieval form, has unleashed itself against them as an unpleasant people, entailing their murder.[44]

Elsewhere, he called the Armenians "agitators" who rightly were much more hated throughout Turkey than "the worst Jews." Extending his rancor to American ambassador Morgenthau, who had been trying to intercede on behalf of the Armenians, Bronsart disdainfully called him "the Jew Morgenthau." By a pun on words, he also described the United States as "the corrupted United States" (*ver-un-reinigten*) (i.e., by inserting the negative *un* and the letter *r* between *Ver* and *einigten).*[45] One reason for this invective was the fact that Morgenthau in his memoirs had called General Bronsart "the evil spirit," interfering in the affairs of the Turks and influencing some of their decisions.[46]

But under the conditions prevailing in wartime Turkey, no foreign general could venture to interfere without a power base affording such intervention. In his capacity as Chief of Staff at Ottoman General Headquarters, Bronsart had that base. His close personal ties with Enver, War Minister and de facto Commander-in-Chief of Ottoman Armed Forces, served to solidify that base. As noted earlier, the power emanating from that base included the power of authorizing Armenian deportations, which he exercised without any hesitation. A wartime German document reveals in this connection that General Bronsart sought to extend the deportation measures also to the Greek population. On August 2, 1916, the Ottoman General Headquarters issued a request to General Liman von Sanders, the Commander of the Vth Ottoman Army, which guarded the entire west coast of Asia Minor to Adalia on the Mediterranean inclusive. It concerned the deportation "of Greeks from the coastal zones"; the request was signed by General Bronsart.[47] For a variety of reasons, including political and military considerations, the request was not complied with—for the time being.[48]

Bronsart's protective thrust

The general's decrial of the Armenians was not something common among other high-ranking German officers. Rather, it was peculiar to him and a few other cohorts who seemed to have developed an inveterate urge to be protective of the Turks under most circumstances. In this sense his anti-Armenian posture was in part a function of this pro-Turkish overzealousness. Indeed, General Bronsart had a pathos for Turkey and was equally jealous of its reputation. He went out of his way to challenge the German language daily in Constantinople, *Osmanischer Lloyd,* which was more or less financed by the German Embassy and represented German interests in Turkey. In a letter of protest, addressed to the German Embassy, Bronsart took issue with an editorial in that newspaper in which the theme is developed that "in Europe there is a tendency to ignore Turkey's real needs." The German newspaper evidently picked up that theme from the Turkish daily *Sabah* and, expanding on it, wrote that "despite the fact that thousands of Germans have returned home after three years of service in Turkey, people in Germany have no understanding for the Turkish national soul." Bronsart felt that the German newspaper should "under no circumstances (*keinesfalls*) be permitted" to write such things. Not satisfied with this rebuke, Bronsart raised the issue of another Turkish newspaper article (in *Tercümanı Hakikat*) that evidently was reproduced in the same *Osmanischer Lloyd*. Bronsart urged the embassy to be vigilant about such indiscretions, which he characterized as "political impoliteness" towards the Turkish ally.[49]

Bronsart's compulsion to be protective of the Young Turk Ittihadist leaders attained its climax at the end of World War I when through an elaborate plan he, with the support of Lieutenant General Seeckt (see note 190, Part I), enabled the seven top power-wielders of Ittihad to escape from Istanbul, as by then Turkey, along with Germany, had lost the war. All seven of the escapees were prime suspects with respect to the organization and implementation of the empirewide Armenian deportations and massacres. Consequently, five of them were convicted and condemned to death, in absentia, by the postwar Turkish Military Tribunal investigating the conditions of the World War I anti-Armenian measures. These were War Minister Enver, Marine Minister Cemal, Interior Minister, and since February 1917 also Grand Vizier, Talât, Ittihad's supreme party boss, and the two politician-physicians of Ittihad's supersecret Directorate, Nazım and B. Şakir. This fact is confirmed by several sources but above all by Ittihadist leader Fethi Okyar [who was Interior Minister in the first postwar Ottoman Cabinet. In the ensuing Republic of Turkey he occupied the same post (1923) and thereafter rose to the rank of Prime Minister (1924)]. In his memoirs he states that General Bronsart "organized" (*tertib*) the escape of these leaders[50] whom the Special Turkish Military Tribunal in 1918 branded "fugitives of justice," as it proceeded to divest both Enver and Cemal of their military ranks and to confiscate their properties. It is equally significant that in his memoirs the Secretary-General of the Young Turk Ittihad party disclosed an important fact in this respect: Talât, the architect of the Armenian genocide, who with the others had elected to flee to Berlin, had conceded at the very moment of the collective flight that the flight of these seven men was prompted by the fact of their complicity in the organization of the anti-Armenian measures.[51] A German Naval War Staff officer, a Navy Lieutenant, who administered the elaborate details of the escape, provided an account of these details in a narrative underscoring the extent of stealth used in the entire operation of collective flight.[52] An agent, engaged by the Germans, indicates that General Bronsart needed the help of two other German military officers, Major von Bentheim and Admiral von Rebeur-Paschwitz, in order to mastermind the escape "of these Ittihadist criminals."[53]

The roles and attitudes of other high-ranking German officers

Von der Goltz. Field Marshal

Foremost among these were Marshal von der Goltz and Lieutenants Colonel Feldmann and Boettrich. As described in the section on ideology, Goltz was the original braintrust of the doctrine, spelling a form of ethnic cleansing, which was impressed upon the Turks from the outside; it projected the forcible large-scale evacuation and resettlement of the entire Armenian population of eastern Turkey. This doctrine was a key ingredient of a broader scheme through which Goltz coaxed the Turks to abandon Europe and reorient themselves politically and strategically toward the East, the Orient. He wanted the Turks to mold Asiatic Turkey into a bastion of a resurgent Turkism and Islam, a bulwark against expansionist Tsarist Russia, and a potential springboard for future eastward incursions. But there was an entrenched obstacle, the indigenous Armenian population, which considered eastern Turkey hallowed ancestral territories and large segments of which were seen by the Turks as disloyal people, identified with Russia and its anti-Turkish aspirations. While serving as the principal reformer of the Turkish army and as professor in Istanbul's War College in the 1883–1895 period and subsequently intermittently in various capacities in the 1909–1913 Young Turk period, Goltz acquired a stature and reputation that gave special weight to his advocacy. In fact Goltz had acquired a reputation as being more a Turk than the Turks themselves. Vice Marshal Pomiankowski, the Austrian Military Plenipotentiary to Turkey declared that Goltz was considered by many a "Turkified" (*vertürkt*) German; the vice marshal took issue with this label as "unjust," and as a sign of envy.[54] Before he died from spotted typhus in April 1916, Goltz "Paşa," as he was affectionately called by his Turkish admirers, declared his last wish: he wanted to be wrapped up in a Turkish flag before being buried in a plot in the summer residence of the German Embassy in the Ottoman capital.[55]

In a statement made to Ittihadist leader and at the time Staff Major, Fethi Okyar, Sultan Abdul Hamit let it be known that during one of the audiences he granted Goltz, the latter warned the monarch about the danger of the Turks (the army included) losing their grip of the land; Goltz stated that the non-Muslims were economically as well as demographically in ascendancy.[56] In all his subsequent dealings with the Ittihadists, who had deposed him in 1908, Abdul Hamit tried to drive home his own concordant view that the non-Muslim nationalities of the empire were a serious threat to that empire. It should be pointed out in this connection that the top strata of the Ittihadist leadership held Abdul Hamit, "despite everything," in high esteem, considering him "a great statesman." Talât was observed sobbing at the funeral of the monarch.[57] As a logical consequence of this stance, Abdul Hamit in a secret communication to Interior Minister Talât advised him, Talât, and the Ittihadist leadership, to bide their time and, at an opportune moment, to take the appropriate measures in order to "eradicate" (*kök sökme*) these alien elements.[58] Goltz's involvement in the initiation of anti-Armenian measures was first brought up in a German language Armenian periodical; it essentially confirmed what Talât reportedly had disclosed in his memoirs.[59] According to this periodical, Goltz's involvement was a certainty. "In fact, the plan had been presented to the field marshal, and had been approved by him."[60] When War Minister Enver in the first week of February 1915 appointed Goltz as "Advisor" to him, Goltz received an office in the Ministry of War and, upon Enver's special order, he was made an integral part of the group at the Ottoman General Headquarters. Enver further ordered the German Chief of Staff, General Bronsart, to keep Goltz "apprised" (*unterrichten*) on all matters that concerned [the direction of] the war."[61] It should be noted that the final decision to "deport" the Armenian population of the empire is believed to have been made toward the end of February or early March 1915. Dr. Otto Göppert, German Foreign Office councillor and former Privy Legation Councillor at the German Embassy at Constantinople, saw fit to distinguish between the act of advising and that of consenting (*Zustimmung*). He then stated, "It appears to be true that Enver Paşa showed the order … to Goltz, asking him for his opinion … [Goltz] did, then, think of the evacuation [of the Armenians] as a possibility. Of course we must bear in mind that the Turks would hide behind the utterance of the field marshal."[62] However, in an affidavit signed by three Armenians involved in the construction details of the Baghdad Railway, one of whom was a doctor and the other two were railroad master builders, Goltz, with reference to a particular instance, is depicted as the actual instigator of the deportation of 21,000 Armenians. On his way to Baghdad, Marshal Goltz is described as having come across these Armenians at Osmaniye, a station on the Baghdad Railway line, and "with anger ordered the removal of these 'traitors.' An hour after his departure, the commander of the gendarmerie of Adana, 'Tiger Avni,' assisted by irregular bands (*çetes*), executed the order of Goltz through the use of the latter's bayonets."[63] In this connection it is worth making another reference to the memoirs of Talât in which it is indicated that Goltz in a private letter to Turkish general Pertev Paşa deplored the "insufficiency of our measures" against the Armenians. At the same time, Goltz forecast that the moment the Turks should come around realizing the gravity of the situation, the measures they may adopt "could spell the end of the Armenian race" (*Ermeni ırkın sonu olabilir*).[64]

Unlike General Bronsart, Marshal Goltz unexpectedly became exposed to some of the grievous consequences of the anti-Armenian policy of the Turks. While proceeding with his military retinue, via Aleppo, to the frontline near Mosul, he came across a convoy of Armenians who were being driven to the deserts of Mesopotamia where they were to perish. At the sight of "the boundless misery" (*grenzenloses Elend*) of the Armenian victims, Goltz was apparently shaken. In a letter to his wife on November 22, 1915, he felt constrained to give expression to "the pity" that he experienced "from the bottom of [my] heart" (*in tiefster Seele Mitleid*). He described the entire spectacle as "a terrible national tragedy" (*eine fürchterliche Völkertragödie*).[65]

This episode demonstrates the impact, however furtive or momentary it may have been, of a lived experience upon the mind-set of a person believed to have played a significant role in helping generate that experience in terms of its tragic components. Goltz was afforded a chance, which was denied Bronsart and his cronies, to see for himself the frightful difference between the condition of authorizing from a distance an act, on the one hand, and the condition of personally observing the terrifying results of that act of authorization, on the other. But the more significant question is: How did Goltz respond to this experience? In important aspects of life it is not so much one's experience that counts but one's evaluation of and response to such life experiences. Goltz's first reaction, articulated in the same phrase, was to plead helplessness (*Man konnte doch nicht helfen*). This raises the ancillary question: He couldn't, or he wouldn't? Yet, in another instance, this time involving the deportation of Greeks from Baghdad, which the Turkish deputy governor of Baghdad had ordered, Goltz, perhaps in deference to the German emperor's family ties to the Greek royal family and his sympathy for the Greeks, intervened promptly and energetically and threatened to resign from his post as Commander of the VIth Army in Iraq in a protest telegram to War Minister Enver. In so many words Enver begged him to stay, and through some mutual accommodations the matter was amicably resolved.[66] In his further assessment of the Armenian tragedy, however, Goltz saw fit to blame England as the arch instigator of hostilities that erupted in World War I and avowedly precipitated the destruction of the Ottoman Armenians.[67]

The imperialist impulses in Goltz's Turkophile pathos

Even though there was a significant number of German soldiers and officers who, despite manifold problems, acclimatized themselves to the Turkish milieu and developed some affinities for the Turks, frustration and discontent among most of them was prevalent. Given major cultural differences separating the Germans from the Turks, the Turko-German alliance was inevitably pregnant with elements of friction and conflict. Whether through correspondence with friends and relatives or through personal narrations made during furloughs or after a final return home, these members of the German military on duty in Turkey during the war set out to ventilate their frustrations and allied feelings of ire. The widespread character of these feelings became evident and manifest when General Seeckt, upon his arrival in Turkey as the new Chief of Staff at the Ottoman High Command, was besieged with complaints, mostly directed against the Turks and especially against "the Turkish mentality," a term that was the favorite watchword of the complainants. Seeckt felt constrained to advise the German officers to restrain themselves and instead of complaining to offer solutions. In fact, using the word in an obverse and negative sense, he called these officers "Turkified" (*vertürkte*) Germans.[68] At one level the Turks were disparaged by these Germans as primitive and barbarous folk, so much so that German authorities were forced to forbid explicitly the use of the German word *Banausen,* which these Germans employed for the purpose of disparaging the Turks in that manner.[69] At another level the Turkish military, viewed as a professional establishment and organization, was severely deprecated; it was dismissed, for example, as a useful instrument of warfare in as much as it lacked the requisite facilities of an infrastructure. In one of his ciphers Marshal L. von Sanders makes this point.[70] A similar assessment was made by German ambassador Metternich who in his

December 7, 1915 report to Chancellor Bethmann Hollweg wrote, "We should stop with our base flatteries [intended to please] the Turks. Whatever they are accomplishing, it is the result of our work; it is due to our money, our officers, our canons. Without our help the inflated frog (*der geblähte Frosch*) is bound to collapse. We don't need to be so afraid of the Turks as it wouldn't be so easy for them to swing over to the other side and make peace."[71] (It is significant that this portion too is conveniently deleted from the volume published by Lepsius in 1919.) Even more devastating was the utterance of General Seeckt who ended his long exposure of the shortcomings of the Turkish ally with the words, "*On ne se marie pas avec un cadavre*," thereby castigating severely the German decision to form an alliance with Turkey. In that summary report Seeckt further maintained that "Turkey owed its ability to wage war for four years to Germany" (*deutsches Verdienst*).[72] This view was expounded a year earlier by the Chief of Department of Operations of the German High Command, Lieutenant Colonel Wilhelm Wetzell, who in 1917 categorically declared that "Turkey is dependent upon us."[73] The notion of a "cadavre," a corpse, was expounded four years earlier by General Helmuth von Moltke, the Chief of Staff at the German High Command. In a communication to his Austrian counterpart, General Conrad von Hötzendorff, he declared, "Turkey militarily is a zero" (*Die Türkei ist militärisch eine Null*) … Its army is in a condition that defies description … it has no vitality and is in a state of agony. Our Military Mission resembles a medical faculty watching over the deathbed of a terminally ill patient."[74] These words were uttered in the spring of 1914. All these attitudes and their various manifestations only served to compound the underlying problem due to what German ambassador Count J. Bernstorff called "the mimosaic sensitivity of the Turks" (*die mimosenhafte Empfindlichkeit der Türken*).[75]

It was against this background that Bronsart and Goltz emerged as stout champions of and apologists for Turkey. As such, they became cohorts, if not friends, with Goltz zealously defending Bronsart against attempts to relieve the latter of his post, thereby "preserving" his career.[76] Like Bronsart, Goltz had become highly politicized. He had developed an inveterate urge to identify with the Turks and with Turkish interests—beyond the thresholds of obligations and duties arising from the alliance. The intensity with which he allowed himself to get involved in the pursuit of national Turkish aspirations epitomized his pathos for Turkey. Like Bronsart, Goltz tried to protect the prestige and reputation of Turkey against attempts by fellow German officers and others to belittle Turkey militarily or discredit it otherwise. The incident described below, which caused a new strain in the relationship between the leaders of the two countries, is illustrative of the point. In an April 22, 1915 report marked "top secret" (*streng geheim*), Prince Gottfried Hohenlohe, Austria's ambassador to Germany, apprised his foreign minister in Vienna of a major incident, with serious ramifications for the future of the Turko-German alliance. Before relating it, Hohenlohe pleaded as follows: "I beg you not to avail yourself of this information in such a way that the German Embassy in Constantinople may learn that I supplied this information." It develops that during Goltz's visit at the headquarters of the German High Command some German officers "in the presence of the emperor held the alliance with Turkey of very little value (*sehr gering bewertet*) and actually considered it a burden (*Last*) for Germany." Goltz was "very upset" about these utterances but, upon his return to Constantinople, he "incomprehensibly" complained about them to Enver. This deed produced "a tremendous resentment in the circle of competent Turkish authorities [*eine ungeheuere Verstimmung*]." Hohenlohe added that Turkish Economics Minister Cavid, when in Berlin recently, declared that the people at the German Foreign Office are "very accommodating" but that the circle of military officers are "not appreciative at all" of the Turkish contributions to the war effort and consider the alliance as "completely superfluous." "In the German Foreign Office people are very angry over the blunder, especially over the inopportune talkativeness of the field marshal."[77]

These proactive efforts on behalf of Turkey notwithstanding, Goltz did not hesitate occasionally to express his doubts and even criticism about Turkish society, the Turkish military, and the respective regimes. He decried the methods and scale of corruption he observed in the Abdul Hamit regime and the deleterious effect of that corruption on the morale and martial effectiveness of the Turkish army.[78] Yet, he was instrumental in securing for such German armament firms as Krupp, Loewe, and Mauser, as well as the Schichau Werft (dockyards), contracts costing the Turkish treasury several hundred million francs over a period of about two decades.[79] The unsatisfactory outcome of his plans of military reform, which he tried to institute despite the obstructive inertia erected by Sultan Hamit's functionaries, was amply compensated for, however, through successes attained in the economic domain. German industrial and financial sectors were propelled into high gear on account of the large volume of orders from the Turkish military establishment. When Goltz in 1897 advocated the consolidation of a new rejuvenated Turkey in Asia Minor, he was envisioning the materialization of tremendous economic dividends to accrue to Germany, especially with respect to prospects of exploiting Turkey's vast reserves of raw materials and of creating in Turkey a fecund market for German industrial products.[80] After adducing the main portion of Goltz's doctrine about consolidation in Asiatic Turkey and wholeheartedly subscribing to it, Rohrbach in one of his books declared, "In Asiatic Turkey there is possibly a great potential relative to Germany's future prospects" (*Im türkischen Asien liegt möglicherweise ein grosses Stück deutscher Zukunft*).[81]

It is these attributes of dedication and service to German national interests superseding as they did in value any other activity in Turkey that may be regarded as the core problem in the assessment of the role performance of Goltz. His willingness to help Turkey in any way he could had a major contingency: it had not only to avoid undermining the supreme interests of Imperial Germany but also essentially to aim at buttressing and promoting these interests under all circumstances. Consequently, German prestige and influence grew rapidly in Turkey, and Germany progressively acquired a dominant position in Turkish economic and political life.[82]

In this sense Goltz was not only what Aristotle called "*a zoon politikon*," but apparently he was also a conspirator, capable of intrigue, stealth, bribery and instigation. According to a Turkish source, in an October 16, 1889 letter to General Alfred von Waldersee, the Chief of German General Staff in the 1888–1891 period, Goltz outlined his plan to foment a rebellion in the ranks of certain Turkish troops during the ceremonies of an official parade. He would then proceed to crush the rebellion instigated by him, with the assistance of some Turkish *paşas* who had been receiving bribes from him in connection with orders for weapon procurements. "Many [Turkish] generals are our friends ... They are ready to help us." The idea was to demonstrate to the Sultan that "in face of such a potent rebellion only the German government has the strength to protect him. Exploiting the situation thusly, I may be able to secure his consent for an accord. Our [Turkish] friends will do their part to influence and sway him. I feel also constrained to apprise you of my anticipation that in a fit of suspiciousness Russia is likely to demand from Turkey the payment of the outstanding debts. I can mastermind this operation in a matter of few weeks. I shall immediately dispatch to you the pertinent details. Many generals are our friends and are regularly getting the moneys on which we agreed upon." As is indicated in this correspondence, the ultimate objective was to force the hand of a hesitant Sultan Abdul Hamit and impel him to align himself with Germany, despite the anti-German agitations of Russia and France.[83] It should be noted that Waldersee himself was an advocate of a Turko-German partnership. Like Goltz, and before Goltz like Bismarck, Waldersee believed that a confrontation and future war with Russia was inevitable and that a restructured Turkish army could be a valuable ally of Germany.[84]

What emerges from the constellation of these facts is the profile of a general whose services for Turkey were but an instrument for higher services to his own country, Germany. In this sense, his participation in the scheme to eradicate the Armenian population of Turkey, irrespective of its level and form, may be regarded as a function of projecting and aiming at ulterior German national design and interests. For this reason Goltz had to be a shrewd politician, bent on primarily ingratiating himself with the Turks; he therefore, tried to be pleasing and accommodating in the fulfillment of the tasks with which he believed he was entrusted. Aware of this condition of incongruity, Colonel von Thauvenay, a member of the German Military Mission to Turkey and the Quartermaster in Ottoman General Headquarters, berated Goltz as a dysfunctional military adviser, declaring, "Turkey needed a stern man and not a smiling advisor."[85]

Feldmann. Lieutenant Colonel

The role of Lieutenant Colonel von Feldmann, who was the head of Department I, Operations, at the Ottoman General Headquarters, is less ambiguous as he in 1921 openly declared that he personally was involved in the act of "advising" Turkish authorities on the necessity of "clearing certain regions ... of Armenians." Equally significant is his concomitant admission that other "German officers" were likewise involved.[86] This admission is the more significant as Feldmann, like Bronsart, had accompanied Enver to eastern Turkey and served as staff officer in the 1914–1915 campaign against Russia. According to a German military historian, Bronsart and Feldmann were "the confidants of Enver, and in daily consultations with him had been exchanging views with him in minute detail."[87]

Boettrich. Lieutenant Colonel

The case of Lieutenant Colonel Boettrich, Chief of Railroad Services at Ottoman General Headquarters, is both striking and considerably more revealing than the cases discussed earlier. Like Bronsart, he is another high-ranking German officer who ordered the deportation of the Armenians and *placed his signature on that order*. Involved was the fate of those thousands of Armenians who were working on the Baghdad Railway construction project. Boettrich, discharging his duties, ordered the deportation of these Armenians in two stages and, just as Bronsart, used the words "severe application of the measures" relative to the deportation procedures.[88] The degree of severity of these measures is narrated by an eyewitness of the successive carnages to which the Armenian workmen of the Baghdad Railway in the thousands were subjected for the purpose of extermination. "Like the hundreds of thousands of their brothers before them, they shared the same kind of fate near Viranşehir. They were all dispatched with the knife" (*Mit dem Messer wurden sie alle erledigt*).[89]

There are several points to be made about this document. First, it demonstrates the willingness of a German officer to accommodate the demands of the Turkish ally, irrespective of the costliness of such accommodation to the Turko-German joint war effort. Many of the Armenians in question were skilled laborers, technicians, engineers, and railroad traffic administrators.[90] The speedy completion of the Baghdad Railway project was of the highest strategic importance for that war effort, a compelling necessity for winning the war in the Turkish theater of operations. The German authorities, military and civilian, were fully aware of this. Yet, for reasons of his own, their representative joined the Turks in the decision to deport these craftsmen. Tens of thousands perished as a result, and the project was delayed for several costly months as the authorities found it most difficult to replace those who were disposed of. Historian Ulrich Trumpener indicates that in negotiations with the Ittihadist leaders about the construction, operation, and exploitation of the Baghdad Railway, Goltz and Boettrich cooperated, and that at times the latter sided with the Turks, especially in negotiations with the *Bagdad-Eisenbahn Gesellschaft* (B. E. G.), which was controlled by the *Deutsche Bank*. Boettrich was "disdainful" toward the financial problems of the company, which he accused of ineptness in the matter of promoting the Turkish war effort. The deportation of the Armenian workforce of the railway, which Trumpener describes as the product of "the anti-Armenian mania" of the Turkish leaders, proved disastrous. "… two-thirds of the originally scheduled work had been left undone," causing "significant" revisions in schedules and timetables.[91]

Second, German military and civilian authorities of the highest rank, apparently unaware of General Bronsart's earlier and much more serious blunder, became alarmed and upset when they learned about Boettrich's direct involvement in the issuance of deportation orders. These authorities were alerted by Franz Günther, the Deputy General Director of the Anatolian Railroad Company, who complained that Boettrich was foolish enough to put his signature on this document thereby sanctioning the deportation order, giving it a German imprimatur, and creating a liability for the German state. As he put it,

> Our enemies will some day pay a good price to obtain possession of this document … they will be able to prove that the Germans have not only done nothing to prevent the Armenian persecutions but they even issued certain orders to this effect, as the [Turkish] Military Commander has ecstatically pointed out.[92]

German Foreign Minister von Jagow immediately transmitted the document to Falkenhayn, the chief in the German High Command, for action to be taken against Boettrich.[93] The former refused, however, to dismiss the latter,[94] as recommended by Treutler, German diplomat in the Foreign Office.[95] In commenting on these indiscretions, Count von Lüttichau, the chaplain of the German Embassy, whom German Foreign Minister Kühlmann described as "a symbol of German genius,"[96] declared:

> Indeed German officers consented to the measures of evacuation for military strategic reasons. And, it is possible that … the Turks distorted this consent so as to make it look like a German wish or order. Should it develop that the Turks thrust the German officers to the forefront and the latter allowed themselves to be so pushed without being aware of the political consequences, as I am afraid, might unfortunately be the case, then any attempt of concealment [*Verheimlichung*] will not do because of the existence of written orders, bearing signatures.[97]

Professor Richter, one of the editors of *Allgemeine Missions-Zeitung,* had asserted that German officers had in fact "dispensed advice" (*den Rat gaben*) to the Turks to deport the Armenians.[98]

Guido von Usedom. Admiral

One of the three German admirals engaged by the Turks, Usedom was to help defend the Straits and the coastal fortifications of the area. He first became Inspector General of coastal artillery and mining. Later, he took charge of the High Command for the Defense of the Straits at the Dardanelles and the Bosphorus, for which purpose there was created for him the Special Navy Task Force Admiral von Usedom (*Marine-Sonderkommando Admiral von Usedom).* Usedom embodied many of the Prussian military traditions. Before being assigned to duties in Turkey he served as the German emperor's aide-de-camp, was commander of the latter's yacht *Hohenzollern*, and was made part of the emperor's official retinue.

During a series of exchanges with the German admiral, American ambassador Morgenthau brought up the subject of the deportations just before the outbreak of the war of some 100,000 Greeks from the Asiatic littoral in the Aegean. Usedom admitted that "the Germans had suggested this deportation to the Turks." As to "the Armenian massacres," Morgenthau relates the following, "Usedom ... discussed the whole thing calmly, merely as a military problem, and one would never have guessed from his remarks that the lives of a million human beings had been involved. He simply said that the Armenians were in the way, that they were an obstacle to German success, and that it had, therefore, been necessary to remove them, just like so much useless lumber."[99]

Wilhelm Souchon. Rear Admiral

He was Commander-in-Chief of the Turkish Fleet and the Chief of the Mediterranean Arm of the German Navy (*Mittelmeer Division*), which was spearheaded by the battle cruiser *Goeben* (later renamed *Yavuz* and appropriated by the Turkish Navy), and the light cruiser *Breslau* (renamed *Midilli*). Souchon was the man who directed the naval assault against Russia in October 1914, deliberately triggering the ensuing Russo-Turkish war.

Commenting on the Armenians and their fate in the war, Souchon is quoted as saying, "Turkey is acting against the Armenians with thoroughness and utmost discretion. I hope that this drama will soon come to an end." Four days later, in August 1915, he reportedly added this note in his diary: "It will be salvation for Turkey when it has done away with the last Armenian; it will be rid then of subversive bloodsuckers."[100]

Seeckt. Lieutenant General

Lieutenant General Hans Friedrich Leopold von Seeckt came to Turkey in 1917 following a meteoric rise in the ranks of the German field army, serving as Chief of Staff in the armies commanded by Fieldmarshal F.M. August von Mackensen on the eastern front and subsequently in Serbia where Seeckt played a major role in the German victory. Having succeeded Major General Fritz Bronsart von Schellendorf as Chief of Staff at Ottoman General Headquarters, Seeckt quickly acclimatized himself at his post, establishing a more or less smooth working relationship with War Minister Enver, his superior. With the onset of fluctuations in the fortunes of the war and their inevitable impact upon the cohesiveness of the Turko-German alliance, there began to arise some critical discords that not only threatened to undermine the alliance but also threatened to produce a collision course with the Turks; consequently, the latter were able to preempt the Germans in the common rush to capture and control Baku in the Transcaucasus. In the course of these maneuvers Seeckt was often lied to or circumvented by Enver, his superior. It was in this connection that he acknowledged the duplicitous method of the Turkish leaders in the organization and implementation of the Armenian genocide. When alluding to "the unhappy Armenian question," he called attention to the fact that "formal orders, purporting to reflect official policy, were countermanded by subsequent secret instructions; sometimes these instructions let the recipients know that the formal orders were not to be taken seriously."[101] It is worth noting here parenthetically that this was the standard pattern of the Young Turk Ittihadist leaders relaying to the provinces their orders for "deportation," avowedly for the purpose of a wartime "temporary relocation" of the deported population but secretly informing the provincial authorities that the deported Armenians were to be massacred. This fact was officially acknowledged in one of the postwar sessions of the Ottoman Senate by one of the most distinguished Ottoman statesmen who, as president of the State Council, had come into possession of an Ittihad party document confirming this fact.[102]

These facts notwithstanding, Seeckt favored the cultivation of an east-oriented expansionist Turkish nationalism and was willing to condone the violent removal of the Armenian obstacle. In a letter to an acquaintance, for example, he admitted that he considered it one of his major tasks to divert Turkish aspirations away from Egypt, Palestine, and reluctantly also from Mesopotamia, and redirect them instead "to the Muslim East—to Turanist and Panislamic ends."[103] When Seeckt in January 1918 took up his post in the Ottoman capital, the genocide against the Armenians had all but run its course. Nevertheless, Seeckt not only did not object, let alone condemn, the act of perpetration, but also in a sense he acted as an apologist for the Turks. The militarist credo of a Prussian officer (the belief that the ends of warfare and victory justify practically any and all means available) seemingly blended with his sense of German patriotism to indulge the Turks with respect to their anti-Armenian scheme. In commenting on the wholesale liquidation of the Armenians of the Ottoman Empire, Seeckt is quoted as saying: "The requirements of the war made it necessary that Christian, sentimental considerations ... simply vanish" (... *Rücksicht der Kriegsnotwendigkeit halber verschwinden*). This stance is in tune with the views of the German political priest Naumann with whom Seeckt is known to have corresponded for exchange of ideas.[104] His sense of loyalty to the Turks was strong enough to help implement General Bronsart's plan for the escape from Istanbul at the end of the war of War Minister Enver and his cohort—at the time Grand Vizier—Talât as at that time German help was needed to enable them to flee the country. (see note 190, Part I).

Count Eberhard Wolffskeel von Reichenberg. Major

He arrived in Turkey in January 1915 and was appointed Chief of Staff to the military governor of Syria in February 1915. Four months later he became Chief of Staff of the VIIIth Army Corps with the rank of major of the Ottoman army but remaining a member of the German Military Mission to Turkey.

His involvement in anti-Armenian activity in the April–October 1915 period is significant in two respects. First, it was active participation in military operations in which he played a leading role in obliterating the opposing Armenians. Second, he performed this task by the orders of a Turkish general to whom he was assigned as an adjutant.[105]

The reference is to the suppression of the defensive uprisings of the Armenians at Mussa Dagh, August–September, at which operation Wolffskeel was an observer, and Urfa, September–October 1915, at which he was a decisive participant on the side of the Turks. Faced with imminent deportation and destruction, the Armenians of these two areas decided to sell their lives dear by rising up against the regular units of the Ottoman army. General Fahri, Chief of Staff of the IVth Army Commander Cemal Paşa, and later Commander of the Expeditionary Force in the Hedjaz and defender of Medina, was given the task of supressing and reducing the Armenians who were resisting deportation. When three battalions of the regular standing army and countless irregulars, equipped with two field guns and a howitzer, proved unable to defeat the Armenian defenders of Urfa, Fahri, at the time the commander of the XIIth Army Corps, ordered Major Wolffskeel to bombard and reduce the city's Armenian quarter. In executing that order, the German artillery officer blasted that quarter into the stone age. As Swiss professor put it, "*da kartätschte deutsche Artillerie alles zusammen.*" "Repeatedly" denouncing them as "traitors" *(Verräter),* the major portrayed the Armenians as a source of "trouble" *(Scherereien)* for the Turks, whose methods of dealing with the Armenians he described as a merely "internal Turkish matter" (*innertürkische Angelegenheit*). He concluded that the best solution to the problem would be the wholesale deportation of the Armenians. (Again, it is most significant that in German ambassador Métternich's November 29, 1915 report to Berlin the two references to Wolffskeel with regard to the Urfa episode are crossed out, signaling deletion. Likewise, German Chargé Neurath's extensive paragraphs containing Major Wolffskeel's account of the military operations against the Urfa Armenians are excised in Lepsius's volume in which Neurath's November 20, 1915 communication to German chancellor Bethmann Hollweg is reproduced).

THE POLITICAL INDICATORS OF COMPLICITY

Despite the sway of Prussian militarism in the unfolding German national aspirations, in the months preceding World War I there was sufficient scope for maneuvering politically, rather than militarily, and for calibrating foreign policy in such a way as to attune military to political desiderata and thereby avert the outbreak of the war. The status of William II provided the connecting link between the two spheres of expedients, but he chose to tip the scales in favor of the military, thereby precipitating the war. He was not only the Supreme Ruler of Imperial Germany but also, by entitlement at least, the Supreme War Lord (*Oberster Kriegsherr*), a status proudly acquired and instituted in modern times by Frederick the Great. William II often visited the German Headquarters at Coblenz, Luxembourg, Spa, and Pless. The Chief of the German General Staff daily reported to him. William II was nominally the Commander-in-Chief, as he was also the Head of the State, by virtue of which he did not hesitate to interfere in the conduct of military affairs—for reasons of state.

Equally important is the fact that according to German and Turkish documents William II in 1916 assumed *de jure* supreme authority over the operations and direction of not only the German but also Turkish military units engaged in warfare in and around Turkey. Turkish war minister Enver is described as having offered the Germans in November 1915 the benefit of the subordination of the Turkish High Command to the authority of the German General Staff. "He would like to, and in fact he will, submit completely" (*Er wolle und werde sich völlig unterordnen*). What is even more significant, "long before this arrangement ... Enver acted in tune with the spirit of it," i.e., subordination (*Schon lange vor ... handelte Enver in ihrem Geiste*).[106] The details of the approval by the Ottoman Cabinet Council of this arrangement are put forward by a Turkish author. The resulting agreement contained nine articles concerning "the complete subordination of the Ottoman armies to the supreme command of the German emperor, as far as deployment of troops and direction of operations are concerned." Article 4 emphasized this point. Article 5 stipulated that "the decisions made by the emperor are binding for all the allied states." In addition to the three other Commanders-in-Chief, representing the Triple Alliance, the document was signed by Enver also.[107] Enver's submissiveness to the desiderata of the German High Command is confirmed by General Bronsart in a "top secret" (*streng geheim*) December 15, 1917 memorandum in which Enver is praised for his accommodating stance toward the German General Staff and his Germanophile attitude, "borne by an inner conviction."[108] In his memoirs Ambassador Morgenthau states that in the wake of the signing of the Turko-German pact German ambassador "Wangenheim boasted to me that 'We now control both the Turkish army and navy.' "[109] Historian Wolfram W. Gottlieb for his part maintains that Enver, along with Talât, was completely under the influence of German ambassador Wangenheim,[110] with a Turkish author, a former army officer, maintaining that Enver was beholden to the German secret service.[111]

The role performance of the high ranking German officers, stationed in Turkey during the war, inevitably had political implications, given the terms and thrust of the August 2, 1914 secret Turko-German alliance treaty. Their very presence in Turkey during the war was in itself a foremost political act with subsidiary military implications. Within this perspective, military service in Turkey entailed adaptations to the ancillary political designs of the Turkish ally, including such operations as "ethnic cleansing." In this sense, the attitudes and doctrines of the architects of German foreign policy call for a comment. The chief architect was, of course, the emperor himself who set the stage for casting the foundations of that policy. The formation of the German Military Mission to Turkey (the favorite child of the Prussian Ministry of War) and the staffing of its top echelons through the appointment of several Prussian officers was an extension of this will to chart the course of German wartime alliance policy.

That policy's core element, molded by Emperor William II in the years preceding the war, coincided with and reflected the Goltzian doctrine that Turkey's proper place of dynamic strength and auspicious self-redemption was Asiatic Turkey. In an exchange with the Austrian ambassador the German emperor declared on January 18, 1913, "Turkey should now appreciate the fact that it will have to concentrate its power in Asia; it then might be able to exert some influence in the development of European affairs."[112]

Included in this policy design was the imposition of censorship on the German media with a view to suppressing or withholding information on the unfolding mass murder of the Armenians. Sometimes reticence in this respect is more functional for concealment purposes than joining the campaign of disinformation and denial. The German policy on the Armenian issue essentially was and remained one of studious avoidance of discussion and debate. For this very reason utterances made in this connection on rare occasions do acquire special significance. The following statement, attributed to the German emperor by British Intelligence officials, was reportedly made on the occasion of the emperor's third visit to Turkey (October 15–18, 1917). In a compressed manner it tells of the emperor's attitude toward the destruction of Ottoman Armenians, epitomizing the German policy on that problem. Relying on a "sure source," the Political Intelligence Department at the British Foreign Office, in a memorandum dated May 25, 1918, declared that William II on October 17, 1917, the second day of his visit at the Ottoman capital, told his Turkish hosts that "Armenia ... should be dealt with by the Ottoman government at its discretion."[113] This attitude of permissiveness, bordering on a propensity to sanction the mass murder of Ottoman Armenians, was considered by the Ittihadist leaders risky enough to take extra stringent security measures for the protection of the German monarch. As a result, "a great many (*pek çok*) Armenians were rounded up in Istanbul and were shipped to the nearby islands one day before the arrival of the emperor."[114]

According to the former dean of Columbia University's Pulitzer School of Journalism, a native of Turkey (see Part I, note 146), "Twenty years ago (i.e., 1901), when the Constantinople and Baghdad Railroad was but just planned, the ex-Kaiser told an American university president that some Armenians taught in American colleges *would have to be eliminated* as unruly" (italics added). Continuing on this theme the late Professor Talcott Parsons declared, "Sultan Abdul Hamit alone would never have adventured on the massacres of twenty-five years ago without the backing of Berlin and the adventurers who led Ottoman race and empire to ruin, the triumvirs, Talât, Enver and Djemal, who planned and ordered massacres, had the aid, direction and encouragement of the Kaiser and those about him ... ." When on November 3, 1918 a mutiny broke out in the German fleet, and on November 7–8 a revolution started in Munich, Germany was on the verge of collapse. Consequently, the Kaiser abdicated on November 9 and on the 10th he fled to Amerongen, Holland. Commenting on this, Parsons wrote: "The wretched old man who wanders around Amerongen is the partner and backer of this crime [the Armenian massacres]. In his ears must sound the shrieks of women, the dying sobs of children, and the rattle of German machine-guns playing on throngs of helpless and unarmed men … this continuing crime from which the Armenian nation still suffers and is almost destroyed."[115]

This German permissiveness prefigures in the diplomatic correspondence of German Foreign Minister Jagow. In a March 14, 1914 report sent to a group of German businessmen, he stated that if the Turkish government should continue disregarding German wishes and commercial interests, the German government will become "gravely alienated" (*ernstes Befremden*). As a result, "It will be impossible for us to maintain our friendly policy toward Turkey." He then warned that "unless Turkey undertakes a speedy and fundamental change in her attitude, it won't be able to continue counting on us [in the handling of] such matters as the Armenian and other questions."[116] The Turks yielded, the Germans prevailed, and the alliance was forged in less than five months thereafter.

All these manifestations of acute influence converge in a single knot; they reflect the exertions of a central source of authority, namely, the institutionalized power of the German emperor directing Germany's foreign policy and its war effort. Significant, for example, is his retort to Prince Bernhard von Bülow who had just resigned as chancellor of Germany in June 1909. William II, accepting Bülow's recommendation, had appointed Bethmann Hollweg as Reich's Chancellor, after giving up on General Colmar von der Goltz, the Turkophile Prussian general, who was his first choice. Bülow was praising Hollweg's merits and aptitudes in terms of domestic matters but pointed out what he believed to be Hollweg's ignorance on foreign policy matters. The emperor dismissed this admonition, smugly declaring: "Foreign policy. You can leave it to me."[117] His penchant for autocratic and secret deals in the conduct of the war is epitomized by the manner in which he engineered the creation of the German Military Mission to Turkey in 1913 and undertook to appoint the Prussian general Liman von Sanders as the chief of that mission without the knowledge of the chancellor or the Foreign Affairs Ministry.[118] Whether military officers or diplomatic representatives, German functionaries collaborating with the Turkish leaders in Turkey were in the final analysis the underlings of their emperor; they were the executioners of his policy designs. This fact is clearly evinced in the dispatch of the following "top secret" (*ganz geheim*) order.

> *To the Naval War Staff*
>
> Through the medium of the Foreign Office the following telegram has been sent to Admiral Usedom:
>
>> His majesty the Emperor expects that you, in close conjunction with Admiral Souchon, do submit [*unterordnen*] to the ambassador's political

> views which His Majesty approves. His Majesty considers this as a first condition for a successful performance in Turkey.
>
> In discharge of the Supreme Order
> v. Müller[119]
> (Admiral Georg Alexander v. Müller, head of the German Naval Cabinet)

In such circumstances, it seems inevitable that some military leaders end up becoming ardent politicians, and political leaders, including diplomats, adopt militaristic postures. The discussion in the next section will focus on two such Germans who may be viewed as the outstanding exponents of the idea of laissez-faire regarding the Turkish scheme of liquidation of the Armenian population.

AN AMBASSADOR AND A MARINE ATTACHÉ: THE ISSUE OF PARAMOUNTCY IN COMPLICITY

The formal initiation of an alliance in itself does not ensure its continuity or survival. The pragmatic consummation of the terms of that alliance is a more consequential task, especially in times of war, but more especially when there are religious cleavages and cultural disparities separating the allies from each other. In such situations the alliance needs to be nurtured and cultivated to prevent or obviate the onset of crises threatening to undermine the alliance. In brief, committed watchdogs are needed. One such watchdog was the German ambassador to Turkey.

Ambassador Hans Freiherr von Wangenheim

American ambassador Morgenthau described him as "this perfect embodiment of the Prussian system," even though Wangenheim was a Thuringian and not a Prussian by birth and background. But he had served in the cavalry as a young man and, "like all of his social order, Wangenheim worshipped the Prussian military system; his splendid bearing showed that he had served in the army, and, in true German fashion, he regarded practically every situation in life from a military standpoint." To him the Prussian legacy, "the great land-owning Junker" system, "represented the perfection of mankind" and deserved "to be venerated and worshipped."[120]

Due to political expediency, largely occasioned by military necessity, and William II's wishes, Wangenheim overcame his initial low opinion of the Turkish military potential and in July 1914 recommended to

Berlin that Turkey seriously be considered a candidate for an alliance with Germany. His modus operandi pursuant to the terms of that alliance is a vast subject and reaches beyond the scope of this study. But his method of bullying the Grand Vizier, presumably with the tacit support of Enver, to secure Turkish governmental consent to the German scheme to push Turkey into war with Russia through a foray into Russian territorial waters in the Black Sea, stands out as a monument to his ability to be overbearing and even ruthless in pursuit of higher German national interests. As Wangenheim reported to Berlin, "I told him that the purpose of the foray into the Black Sea was to pursue German interests which on occasion we will be forced to superordinate to the Turkish ones. Though they are at the disposal of Turkey, the ships involved have German identity and, therefore, cannot take direct orders from the Turkish Minister of Marine.... My declarations, which I repeated to other Cabinet ministers, appear to have made an impact."[121] In point of fact, Wangenheim was executing the direct orders of the emperor William II. The order was relayed through Admiral Hugo von Pohl, Chief of the German Naval Staff, later Commander of the German High Sea Fleet.[122] A Turkish author acknowledges Wangenheim's propensity to "even bully Cabinet ministers," adding, "As the typical personification of German militarism, Wangenheim proceeded to intervene in the conduct of the affairs of the Ottoman government. He was the despot of Istanbul."[123]

These details demonstrate the ambassador's aptitude for bellicosity and his readiness to manifest and apply it, when needed. They also demonstrate, however, his uncanny ability to confront the leaders of the Turkish government and with resolve and forcefulness impose upon that government the will of his own government. As noted earlier, he most probably was supported in some of these bold moves by such other leaders as Enver and, to some extent, even Talât and Dr. Nazım, the omnipotent Ittihadist leader operating behind the scenes. But this very fact of support from within the Young Turk Ittihadist power structure evinces the built-in advantages Germany enjoyed in the alliance, affording it a certain measure of preponderance and even some control in the determination of war-related Turkish priorities. Turkey was substantially more dependent upon Germany than the other way. This sense of dependence and an allied appreciation is crisply encapsulated in these words Talât uttered during the war to Colonel Otto von Lossow, at the time the German Military Attaché to Turkey. "Germany is our father, but Austria is just a neighbor" (*L'Allemagne est notre père, L'Autriche, c'est un voisin*).[124] The resulting Turkish vulnerability to German exertions and demands is attested by Talât who in his famous interview with British member of parliament Aubrey Herbert is reported to have declared that "he found himself completely handcuffed by the Germans and said to the Council of Ministers, 'I often wondered why the English wanted to fight the Germans, but now I know.' "[125]

This notwithstanding, Wangenheim studiously avoided interceding on behalf of the Armenians; he had raised that avoidance to a level of firm policy. More than that, whether out of inner conviction or by virtue of constraints imposed upon him by his superiors in Berlin or on account of a combination of both factors, he unhesitatingly sided with the Turks, even when he was receiving harrowing reports from his consuls in the provinces about the unfolding genocide and even when he dutifully was forwarding these reports to Berlin. In this sense his communications to Berlin on this subject are but the formal and official expression of his stance, and indirectly the stance of his government. In April 15, 1915, the month that ushered in the episode of the Armenian genocide, Wangenheim bluntly told Berlin that the situation of the Armenians was more or less hopeless and that higher German interests required that the German government not intervene. The ambassador in that document declared that Germany must be "especially careful not to antagonize the Turkish government. Otherwise we run the risk of jeopardizing more important, and for us more crucial, interests by intervening in a perhaps hopeless matter"(*aussichtslose Sache*).[126]

That characterization of hopelessness was somewhat consistent with his diagnosis of the nature of the general plight of the Armenians in Turkey. In an exchange with the Austrian Military Plenipotentiary to Turkey, Vice Marshal Pomiankowski, which coincided with the then ongoing negotiations on Armenian reforms in 1913, Wangenheim told the latter that the only salvation for the Armenians of Turkey was "conversion to Islam."[127] In the reports on informal conversations with Ambassador Morgenthau, however, a more truculent, if not sinister, picture emerges. As in the case of German General Bronsart, Wangenheim too appears to be opposed to the Armenians, with sentiments ranging from mere antipathy to sheer hatred. Having simply accepted as true Turkish charges and decrials against the Armenians and having adopted their concomitant epithets, Wangenheim told Morgenthau that "the Armenians were simply traitorous vermin."[128]

By a remark he made to Morgenthau, Wangenheim clearly indicated that, if he wanted to, he could help intervene on behalf of any nationality posing problems for Turkey. The Jews, for example, are a case in point. Even though on account of geography and demography they posed much less of a threat, their aspirations for Palestine, harnessed to the Zionist movement, did pose a territorial problem as far as the steadily shrinking Ottoman Empire was concerned. Moreover, Talât harbored an acute dislike of Russian Jews, whose role in the cultivation of designs on Palestine was substantial; in his interview with Aubrey Herbert, mentioned earlier, he described "the majority of the Russian Jews" as "degenerate."[129] Nevertheless, Wangenheim self-confidently reassured Morgenthau that he could intervene. " 'I will help the Zionists' he said, thinking that this remark would be personally pleasing to me, 'But I shall do nothing for the Armenians.' "[130] A document found in Austrian state archives in Vienna reveals that a few weeks after the signing of the secret Turko-German alliance pact, Ambassador Morgenthau (on August 26, 1914) had conveyed to Wangenheim his and British ambassador Sir Louis Mallet's apprehension relative to a danger of impending massacres to be carried out against the Armenians. Wangenheim's brash response represented an effort to interconnect two totally unrelated conditions of the war. It still sounded ominous for the Armenians, however. He is said to have retorted, "As long as England does not attack the Dardanelles, or a Turkish port-city, there is nothing to fear. Otherwise (*im gegenteiligen Falle*), nothing can be guaranteed."[131] Wangenheim then shifted the burden of interceding for the Armenians to the United States. "The U.S. is apparently the only country that takes much interest in the Armenians." Referring to "your people [who] have constituted their guardians," Wangenheim suggested that helping the Armenians was an American responsibility. In a twist of logic, Wangenheim blamed the U.S. government for selling munitions to England and France and the use of shells by the Allies against the Turks at the Dardanelles, adding that "As long as your government maintains that attitude we can do nothing for the Armenians."[132] It is noticeable that throughout these exchanges Wangenheim did not say, or even intimate, that he would like to help the Armenians but that he couldn't in face of insurmountable obstacles erected by the Turks. Instead, he bluntly reiterated the point that he did not wish to. For his part, Marshal Liman von Sanders credited Wangenheim with the ability to know "how to gain his ends in Turkey."[133] Morgenthau was astounded at this display of absurdity by the German ambassador who dared to link American help to the Allies to "Turkey's attacks upon hundreds of thousands of Armenian women and children." He had tried to sensitize Wangenheim to the fact that the issue was not "military necessity, state policy, or else" but simply "a human problem." He appealed to him to consider the fact that at issue was the extirpation mostly of "old men, old women and helpless children. Why can't you, as a human being, see that these people are permitted to live?" Wangenheim was intransigent as he retorted, "I shall not intervene," reciting in English the oft repeated maxim of the militarists: "Our one aim is to win this war."[134]

The stress and strain attending these events apparently damaged the German ambassador's health, afflicting him with some infirmity. According to Morgenthau, who during his exchange, was host to Wangenheim in his office at the American Embassy, upon signaling to Wangenheim that there was no point in carrying on any longer the conversation, "I turned from him in disgust, Wangenheim rose to leave. As he did so he gave a gasp, and his legs suddenly shot from under him. I jumped and caught the man just as he was falling. For a minute he seemed utterly dazed; he looked at me in a bewildered way, then suddenly he collected himself and regained his poise. I took the ambassador by the arm, piloted him down stairs, and put him into his auto… Two days afterward, while sitting at his dinner table, he had a stroke of apoplexy; he was carried upstairs to his bed, but he never regained consciousness." Wangenheim died on October 25, 1915, and, after a huge funeral in the Ottoman capital, he was buried on the grounds of the German summer embassy in Therapia, on the shores of the Bosphorus. As Morgenthau concluded, "He was the one man and his government was the one government, that could have stopped these crimes … the massacre of a nation…."[135]

Some may dispute this judgment, which also implies a verdict, but which appears warranted in the light of the evidence presented in this study. One can only wonder, however, about the irony of a coincidence involved here. Two diplomats, a Russian and a German, a Foreign Minister (Count Lobanof), and an ambassador, vested with enormous powers, deliberately allowed the perpetration in a span of two decades of two instances of mass murders against the Armenians, thereby sharing in a major onus of complicity. They also shared the same experience of illness that culminated in their death as that illness, stroke, proved fatal for both of them. Remarkably, both men were suddenly stricken at the very height of the Abdul Hamit and the Young Turk Ittihadist era massacres—massacres which they adamantly refused to oppose effectively.

Lieutenant Commander of the Navy and Marine Attaché Hans Humann

Of all the German military personnel appointed to posts in wartime Turkey, Humann was the most important in one respect: he was connected to War Minister Enver with abiding bonds of friendship that dated back to the days of Enver's two tours of duty in Berlin where he served as Turkish Military Attaché (1908–1909 and 1909–1912). Antedating this relationship was the heritage of Karl Humann, whose archeological interests had many times brought him to Turkey, where his son Hans was born (Smyrna-Izmir) and where he did much excavation work, with a focus on the memorable edifices of ancient Greek civilization. He eventually became Director of the Oriental Museum of Berlin. His son, Hans Humann, spent a great deal of his childhood in Turkey, developing an affinity for the Turks, which eventually evolved and crystallized itself around a friendship with Enver, first in Berlin and later in Constantinople. Before being assigned to duties in Turkey, Humann had a key position in the intelligence service of the German Navy, which was headed by the powerful Grand Admiral von Tirpitz, whose loyal and admiring protègé Hans Humann was and to whose Pangermanist doctrines he subscribed.

Following the Ittihadist reseizure of power in January 1913, he was appointed commander of *Loreley*, the embassy guard-ship in Constantinople. Subsequently, Humann was appointed Marine Attaché at the embassy. As his friend Ernst Jäckh stated, Humann "became the unofficial German envoy … he had direct access to the Kaiser's entourage over the head of any ambassador. It was an outstanding position of extraordinary influence, to say the least."[136] In this connection Humann is credited with an act that paved the ground for Turkey's intervention in the war. He proposed and pushed through a scheme whereby the German squadron under Rear Admiral Souchon's command and comprising the battle cruiser *Goeben* and the light cruiser *Breslau* in August 1914 escaped the pursuit of British naval forces, entering through the Straits and subsequently joining the Turkish Navy into which it eventually became incorporated only to trigger within weeks the Russo-Turkish war.

His unhampered access to Enver, with whom he communicated in intimate, first-name and German *Du* (i.e., thou) form, enabled him to mediate between such conflicting parties as the head of the German Military Mission, the German ambassador, Enver, and General Bronsart. Yet, he was consorting with those who one way or another supported Enver and his cohorts in the initiation and execution of the wartime anti-Armenian measures, such as Bronsart, Goltz, and Wangenheim. To him, the main challenge consisted in the endeavor to provide optimum accomodation of Turkish needs and demands; everything else was of subsidiary import or not important at all as far as the requirements of the alliance was concerned. In a note to Ambassador Kühlmann, he urged him not to alienate the leaders of Turkey for the sake of "our political interests. We can't afford to alienate them and jeopardize our Near Eastern policies which here in the Orient is always predicated upon personal relations."[137] According to a Turkish author, Humann "persuaded" Enver, the Ittihadist warlord, to get rid of the Armenians who were in the employ of the state and replace them with Turks trained in Germany. They worked out together a program through which promising young men would be selected and sent to Germany for higher education.[138]

In exchanges with American ambassador Morgenthau, he too "discussed the Armenian problem with the utmost frankness and brutality." He declared that based on his intimate knowledge of the Turks and Turkey, "Armenians and Turks cannot live together in this country. One of these races has to go. And I don't blame the Turks for what they are doing to the Armenians. I think that they are entirely justified. The weaker nation must succumb." Morgenthau observed that callous as German ambassador Wangenheim proved to be, he was not as implacable and truculent as Humann, who was "a man of great influence." A German diplomat once told the American ambassador that "Humann was more of a Turk than Enver and Talât."[139] In his refutation of these allegations, Humann in a 12-page report[140] tried to dispute categorically nearly everything said by Morgenthau, thereby raising doubts about the seriousness of his disclaimer. In the process, he parroted the most incredulous charges made by the Turks during the war against the Armenians, such as the claim that "out of 130,000 Turks in Van province, 100,000 were massacred by the Armenians." Moreover, in denying that he was ever involved in consultations about the anti-Armenian measures, he was careful to use the word "official" (*amtlich*), thereby leaving open the possibility that he might have been involved unofficially. Wangenheim himself admitted that he used Humann for consulting and relaying important information to Enver—unofficially. In other words, he avoided official channels when critical issues were involved. It is evident that in this report Humann tried to avail himself of his experience as a veteran Navy intelligence man (*Admiralstab, Marineamt*) to obfuscate issues while trying to dispute charges leveled against him and even to dispense disinformation when deemed necessary.

After examining Morgenthau's allegations against Humann in the official records of the German archives covering the 1914–1915 period, a Swiss author concluded that these records "confirm Morgenthau's perception" of Humann. He cites, for example, Humann's response to the news that the Armenians are being "more or less exterminated"; Humann is quoted as saying, "This is harsh but useful." Two days later (June 17, 1915), Humann added to that statement this note: "… the Turkish government utilizes the time of war and Europe's preoccupation to settle the entire Armenian question by force." According to this author, Humann, like General Bronsart, sustained the tempo of his enmity against the Armenians for many years after the war through the medium of the post-war nationalist German newspaper *Deutsche Allgemeine Zeitung*. He concluded that Humann "welcomed and supported the extermination of the Armenian people in the Ottoman Empire."[141] Ambassador Metternich worked with Humann, observing his contacts, his relationship to Enver, and to other potentates. His judgment on Humann is also a decrial of him, for he characterized Humann as an "arch scoundrel."[142]

TURKISH ASSERTIONS ON GERMAN COMPLICITY

The German government on a number of occasions requested from the Turkish leadership that they publicly deny growing number of reports and hints that the Germans advised the Turks to proceed with the liquidation of the Armenian population. The Turks obliged without hesitation. To underscore such denials they insisted that the wartime treatment of the Armenians by the government was a strictly internal matter and that, therefore, there was no legal basis or justification for any foreign government, including Germany, to intervene in any manner in the decision-making processes of the Turkish government. The picture changed, however, in the aftermath of the war as numerous Turks came forward to implicate Germany in a number of respects. Foremost among these was party boss, Interior Minister, and since February 1917 Grand Vizier Talât (see notes 27, 31, and 125 above).

The views of Turkish publicists

Involved are here assertions and certain declarations which are based on undisclosed sources. During the Armistice, for example, the noted Turkish writer Cenab Şahabeddin, who in 1915 had visited Germany as a member of a delegation of Turkish newspaper men and editors, stated that German military officers were responsible for the initiation of anti-Armenian measures.[143] Another Turkish editor recently likewise asserted that it was the German General Staff that requested that the Armenians be removed in order to make the rear of the Turkish army safe and secure.[144] Still another Turkish editor in the most explicit terms incriminated the Germans, especially "the German orientalists who even before the outbreak of the war had brought up the matter of the deportation of the Armenians within the framework of the analysis of the issues at hand.

A member of the German Military Mission to Turkey had declared that 'the plan to exile the Armenians was a German idea.' "[145] Finally, reference may be made to a monographic study on the German influence in Turkey in which the author maintains that in the face of the outbreak of disorders, Germans influenced Turkish decision making as mentors, operating behind the scenes and pulling the strings (*akıl hocalığı*). It is noteworthy that this author uses the same word "severely" (*şiddetle*) to relate the idea that when the German General Staff urged the Turks to repress the Armenians, they advised severity.[146]

The reported disclosure of a former Turkish Foreign Minister

In the archives of the British Foreign Office lies the record of a protracted correspondence between British and American sources on "the complicity of Berlin in the Armenian massacres." The correspondence revolves around Asım, who in 1911 was Minister of Foreign Affairs of Turkey and subsequently was entrusted by the Young Turk leadership with the task of winning over the Iranians for an alliance with Turkey, for which purpose he was appointed ambassador at Teheran. In one of the pieces of this correspondence there is a cipher telegram stating emphatically that "Assım Bey can afford and has afforded definite information as to instigation and complicity of German Government on Armenian massacres." British sources describe him as having been disappointed with the overall conduct of the Ittihadists, their "scoundrelism," to quote one of these sources, that he is prepared to expose them. Conversant in German and with access to both the ambassadors of Turkey and Germany in Washington, D.C., he reportedly obtained the information on German complicity from the German ambassador.[147] The cipher telegram on "the complicity of Berlin" was sent by Dixon, the editor of the *Christian Science Monitor* in Boston, to G.H. Locock, the British consul general at Boston, but on leave in London at the time.[148] According to A. Harvey Bathurst, the chief of *Christian Science Monitor's* London bureau, the whole episode of willingness to reveal a state secret exploded as a result of a conflict at the Turkish section of the 1915 Panama Pacific Exhibition at San Francisco, whose Armenian director, Vahan Cardashian, was ejected from his post as a result of the intervention of the German ambassador in Washington, D.C. It is not clear, however, how Asım came to be involved in this episode. According to Bathurst, a British source and a lawyer, Asım in the past had some quarrels with Ittihad, was knowledgeable about some of their secrets, and learned more in 1915 through his contacts with the German ambassador.

The latter evidently received the documents in question from the Turkish ambassador. Asım is described as being cognizant of "the inside of the secret plan" against the Armenians and as having communicated "to a few people" his knowledge thereof. Bathurst also indicated that the U.S. government is "none too anxious to add to the feeling on the subject of the Germans here by the disclosures."[149] However, there is no resolution of the issue as far as the correspondence in question is concerned. Beyond the general assertion that a former Turkish Foreign Minister claimed to have documents in his possession regarding German complicity in the destruction of Ottoman Armenians, nothing specific is in fact disclosed or even described. One has to depend upon the perceptions and faith of the British and American sources involved, as well as upon their integrity.

The intimations of two Turkish deputies—before and after the fact

The possibility that some sort of a deal was struck with some German authorities in Germany prior to the war and months before a Turko-German military alliance materialized was hinted at by a member of the Turkish Parliament. In this connection, it may be appropriate to point out here, parenthetically, that attempts at such deals, prior to and during the war, were not lacking. Indeed, in the archives of the German Foreign Office in Bonn there is a document describing the arrival in Berlin in March 1915 of a Turkish delegation, consisting of Young Turk Ittihadist "secret operatives" equipped with a mysterious plan, the nature of which is not revealed or explained in the document. It appears that the Turks had a plan which as judged by the German contacts, had grave political implications and which, when carried out, could have great economic dividends for the Germans. The operatives tried but failed to enlist the support and sponsorship of German potentates interested only on economic matters but shying away from risky political involvements. The extreme caution and the highly camouflaged language with which these initial contacts are described by a certain F. Fröhlich, the preparer of the report, are indicative of a very incriminatory proposal made by the Turks. That proposal involved "a highly political act" (*eine hochpolitische Aktion*) for the consummation of which the Turks were eager to establish "an intimate but unofficial contact between the government in Berlin and that of Istanbul."

Among the names mentioned in the document are Roselius, to whom the report is sent, Reinhard Mannesmann, and Dr. Max Zimmer, as possible suitable candidates to form the requisite committee in order to explore further the proposal of the Turkish "secret committee."[150] In the development of plans to revolutionize the Caucasus, and sabotage and cripple the Baku oil fields, Dr. Zimmer played an important role. Since 1909, he was active in Amasya, Turkey, as the owner of a large farm but in 1914 he was enlisted by the German Embassy in Istanbul for the elaboration of a plan for the Circassians in the Caucasus. Zimmer is described in the document as having boasted of his success in securing "the right threads that lead to Enver."[151]

The significance of this document lies in the emphasis the Turks placed on "informal" and "unofficial" cooptations of the Germans for the execution of their secret schemes. It is also significant in the sense that there were some Germans willing to be coopted, and that Dr. Max Zimmer, a link to the missions of the Turkish Special Organization, was a leader among them (see note 168, Part I for another such operative).

Returning to the hint in question, it came from Deputy Feyzi, representing the province of Diyarbekir. In two successive exchanges with Diyarbekir's British vice consul, who happened to be an Armenian, Feyzi threateningly forecast the demise of the Armenian population of Turkey in the event the Armenian leaders should continue to orient themselves to the British and their allies. In the meeting on August 27, 1914, Feyzi reiterated Turkey's reasons for identifying with Germany and in that vein he disclosed that he was part of a delegation of Turkish deputies who had visited Berlin in the spring of that year. When the Armenian vice consul expressed surprise at the uninhibitedness with which he was uttering such ominous things, the Turkish deputy retorted: "On the basis of what I saw, heard and learned there [in Berlin], I have absolutely reached this conclusion."[152] The vice consul's attributions to Deputy Feyzi are independently confirmed by an Armenian, a Civil Inspector of the First Class, who was spared the fate of his conationals by virtue of his close ties to Ittihad. He confirmed it independently in an affidavit he prepared at the request of the office of the British Commission in Istanbul.[153] This ominous forecast gains added significance by the fact that Deputy Feyzi subsequently proved to be one of the most ferocious organizers of the Armenian genocide in the area of Diyarbekir, his district. According to a British Intelligence report, "Deputy Feyzi was received by the Kaiser and decorated with the Iron Cross."[154]

Another Turkish deputy serving in the new Parliament of the fledgling Kemalist regime is on record as having made a similar intimation about German permissiveness as a factor in the successful execution of the Turkish plan against the Armenians. In the course of a secret session (June 10, 1922) at which the deputies were debating the problem of deporting the Greek population of Pontus in the Trabzon area, Ali Şükrü, the deputy from Trabzon, expressed regrets that the Turkish government failed to tackle this Greek problem during the war when the conditions were so much more favorable. He deplored the reliance in this postwar period on halfhearted and intermittent measures and with a sense of nostalgia invoked the period of the war when "Germany was behind us, complying with every single one of our wishes. But now, we are on our own."[155]

The allusion was, of course, to the drastic methods through which the wartime deportation of the Armenians was successfully enacted to achieve the goal of destruction. Commenting on this end result, Finance Minister Hasan Fehmi, during one of the further stages of the same debate, compared the pending Greek issue with the successful Armenian deportations. He expressed satisfaction that the success was due "to the army being all over the country and the Armenians having no inkling as to what awaited them."[156]

The assertion of a Turkish cabinet minister

Cavid, the Minister of Economy, was in constant touch with the representatives of Germany, negotiating and renegotiating economic and fiscal matters to sustain Turkey amid incremental wartime hardships. He even went to Berlin and had high-level consultations with German officials for the same purpose. In an interview with Folley, the Special Correspondent in the Ottoman capital of the British newspaper *Morning Post*, Cavid in the Armistice period maintained that the Germans are the ones who first brought up the matter of liquidating the Armenian population of Turkey.[157]

A Turkish historian's input

In his multivolume studies on the subject of Turkish struggles for liberation in modern times, Doğan Avcıoğlu appears to be one of the few chroniclers who had, or was allowed to have, access to some of the innermost secrets of the Young Turk Ittihadists. In one of his discussions on the Armenian deportations, he stated that these deportations were of a wide scope, were carried out systematically, and had as their aim "the radical solution of the Armenian question." According to the evidence at his disposal, the plan was championed in the councils of Ittihad by Dr. Şakir and was "endorsed (*onaylandığı*) by the Germans."[158]

These Turkish allegations and assertions are unofficial in character and as such lack the quality of tangible authenticity. But, they do not necessarily lack elements of credibility. Given the nature of the complicity at issue here, one may be hard put to secure any other type of evidence to ascertain definitively any degree of complicitous involvement. As will be discussed in the next section, the German Chief of Staff at the Ottoman General Headquarters removed substantial quantities of files and carried them with him to Berlin upon departure from Turkey at the end of the war. As with the rest of the material relative to the issue of culpability in general, one has to learn to make the best out of what can presently only be circumstantial evidence.

INCIDENTS OF CONCEALMENT AND DISCLOSURE

The conditions of war and preparations for war magnify the need for ordinary secrecy attending the patterns of international diplomacy and related activities of military cooperation. The Turkish plan against the Armenian population was not only part of a war-related secrecy but it was also one of the centerpieces of such secrecy. The German involvement in the genesis and execution of that plan, irrespective of its nature and extent, made German efforts to help the Turks conceal the evidence of the crime, which that plan entailed, an almost compelling necessity. By the same token, such concealment was bound to be even more critical for protecting ancillary German interests insofar as the issue of German involvement was concerned. Apart from German attitudes of indulging the Turks and thereby granting them a laissez-faire license, German intelligence operatives helped the Ittihadists to set up a surveillance bureau within the General Police Directorate in the Ottoman capital. Operating in close association with the Political Section (*Kısmı Siyasi*), which represented one of the three branches of the Police Directorate [the other two were called Administrative (*Idare*) and Legal (*Adli*)], that bureau extended its surveillance to all major centers of Armenian political, social, religious and even charity activity within and without Turkey, including the Armenian Patriarchate in Istanbul, political parties in Egypt, and anti-Ittihadist opponents in Paris.[159] As noted earlier (see note

144, Part I), the purpose was to prepare lists and dossiers on Armenian community leaders to be treated as potential foes of Turkey.[160] In the German state archives there is some correspondence to this effect. Staff Lieutenant Colonel Seyfi, the director of the Department II, Intelligence, at Ottoman General Headquarters, for example, requested from Colonel Lossow, at the time Military Attaché at the German Embassy, the photographs of all the Armenian residents of Bukarest. He had heard that the German consulate at Bukarest had obtained these photographs along with all the pertinent details. Ambassador Metternich knew nothing about such photographs. But the German Embassy at Bukarest informed the German chancellor in Berlin that the Intelligence Department of the German Navy (*Admiralstab der Marine*) through Navy Lieutenant Berg had indeed compiled a list of all Armenians of Bukarest to which were attached the respective photographs.[161] Furthermore, encouraged by the Germans, War Minister Enver reactivated and expanded the residual Special Organization (*Teşkilatı Mahsusa*) as an instrument of wartime agitation, sabotage, and murder, within and without Turkey.[162] According to the candid account of a Turkish author familiar with the operational plans of that organization, one of its missions was the execution of the Armenian "deportations."[163]

The deletions in the main foreign office documentary tome

One of the major targets to which German efforts of concealment were directed was the German public, and even German officialdom. Even though German diplomats (i.e., a succession of German ambassadors to Turkey and a host of German consuls stationed in the interior of Turkey) were inundating the German Foreign Office and the office of the German chancellor in Berlin with details of the mass murder in progress, as will be discussed in detail below, the authorities, including the High Command at the General Headquarters, had issued orders to suppress the evidence by withholding it from the German public. A Protestant missionary historian, Dr. Johannes Lepsius, set out to contest his government by secretly assembling and compiling documentation for the purpose of alerting the public, in the hope that public indignation and a resulting public pressure would induce the government to intervene and stop the carnage. Lepsius was not a novice in the matter of the history of Armenian massacres. In the wake of the Abdul Hamit-era massacres he had undertaken a two-month inspection trip to the sites of the atrocities and published his findings in a book. He undertook a similar trip to Turkey in July 1915; the German authorities relented considerably before issuing a permit to travel. In the course of his visit in Constantinople Lepsius managed to gather secretly incriminating evidence against the Turkish authorities by contact with the American Embassy; the Armenian Patriarchate; German, Swiss, and American missionaries; and some Turkish officials. Included in this activity was a meeting with War Minister Enver, who defiantly told him that he assumed full responsibility for what was happening to the Armenians in the provinces.[164]

With inordinate courage Lepsius prepared *A Special Report* in the form of a 303-page booklet that was printed and secretly mailed to the members of the Reichstag (German Parliament)—the receipt of which was barred by the government—and to 10,000 to 20,000 other Germans, including church leaders, public figures, etc.[165] Many more copies were scheduled for distribution when Ibrahim Hakkı Paşa, Turkish ambassador at Berlin, lodged a vigorous protest in which he invoked the interests of "our common cause" for the sake of "the triumph" of which this "most infamous" piece of propaganda should be suppressed. Within days Foreign Minister Jagow obligingly informed the ambassador that the books in question have been "confiscated."[166] Furthermore, Lepsius was subjected to pressures from all sides, especially the German Foreign Office, to cease and desist; at times these pressures took on the form of intimidation and veiled threats. In Holland, where he was in self-imposed exile, he was subjected to a humiliating treatment by Friedrich Rosen, the German ambassador there, who was demanding that Lepsius refrain from making public statements for the duration of the war.[167] While refusing to remain silent, Lepsius promised not to do or say anything that would undermine German foreign policy and also "offend the sensibilities of the Turkish ally"; he meant to confine himself to charity and relief work to succor the wounds of the survivors.

In the process Lepsius was led, however, to compromise his commitment to presenting the complete truth. He ended up making a deal that constrained him to perform the task of sanitizing to a certain degree official German records whereby Germany could be purged of any guilt or complicity regarding the fate of the Armenians. In this sense, he was impelled to play the role of an apologist for Germany, while emphasizing the fact that Turkey alone was responsible for the crimes attached to that fate. The result was the publication in 1919 of a massive and still most valuable compilation of German Foreign Office documents containing 444 pieces of diplomatic and military correspondence and five pertinent Annexes.[168]

The conditions surrounding the publication of this work betray the symptoms of a profound German concern to exculpate Germany under all circumstances and focus instead on the primacy and magnitude of Turkish culpability and responsibility. As discussed in the Introduction of this book, notes 3–6, the German Foreign Office, through its representative, Dr. Wilhelm Solf, made a deal with Lepsius whereby it would relinquish its plan to publish a White Book on the Armenian deportations and massacres and allow instead Lepsius to have access to its files to produce a substitute volume for which he personally would be responsible. Lepsius accepted, with the stipulation that nothing would be withheld from him and that he would have complete access. The German official who haggled with Lepsius over the need to omit certain documents and delete portions from other documents was Privy Legation Councillor Dr. Otto Göppert.[169] In a mood to accommodate him, Lepsius in his response from Holland to Göppert's June 28, 1919 letter reassured Göppert that "from the very outset I intended to relieve [i.e., exonerate] (*entlasten*) Germany … I believe the book will adequately serve the purpose of dispelling the calumnies against German officials and military officers."[170] When Göppert expressed appreciation for this intent of Lepsius he informed the latter at the same time that he has decided to withhold new material from the files of German consuls that would have been supplementary to the material already supplied. Assembled by former Aleppo Consul Rössler, these new files were deemed to be of no value for the end of serving German interests (*ohne Nutzen für uns*) while capable of "further inculpating the Turks" by injecting into the picture material that "further replenishes the chapter of Turkish atrocities" (*zur Vervollständigung des Kapitels der türkischen Greuel*).[171]

The Lepsius volume is indeed deficient in this respect. Some crucial portions are lifted from certain documents to conceal instances of German attitudes and actions betraying various levels of German consent or involvement, whether direct or indirect; at other places sentences or words are substituted in altered forms. Authors such as Trumpener,[172] Dinkel,[173] and Bihl have noticed these omissions and deletions, with the latter providing a detailed illustration of the method used.[174] A close scrutiny of the condition of the originals of these documents, deposited at the Foreign Office at Bonn, reveals that the deletions were effected by the insertion at chosen spots of faintly penned brackets. While some blame Lepsius for these modifications, the cryptic intervention by someone from the Foreign Office dealing directly with the publisher cannot be ruled out.[175]

The issue of financial liability

Perhaps the most outstanding reason prompting the German authorities to withhold and suppress evidence was revealed by Göppert himself. He expressed his deep concern about the ramifications of the charge of complicity leveled against Germany "in the whole world, and especially America...." He then spelled out the fundamental source of that concern: "This is a heavy charge from which we must free ourselves not least for financial reasons, since otherwise we will be liable for the damages."[176]

The injunctions of German military and civilian censors

As events later were to demonstrate, by explicit and strict orders from the German High Command in Berlin, the multitudes of German officers affiliated with the German Military Mission to Turkey were forbidden to intervene in the process of the extermination of the Armenian population of the empire. This policy of nonintervention was approved at the highest level of the German government and sanctioned by the Kaiser himself. As disclosed on October 2, 1919 in a personal letter by General Bronsart von Schellendorf, the German emperor enjoined a group of high-ranking German officers, who were received in audience by him in the fall of 1913, on the eve of their departure to Turkey as members of the German Military Mission to Turkey, "not to interfere in Turkey's internal affairs." General Bronsart added that this prohibition extended to "the Armenian Question."[177] Furthermore, Maximillian Harden, the noted publisher and editor of the German weekly *Die Zukunft*, leveled a scathing criticism against the Imperial German government for "tolerating and condoning this Turkish affront, this most infamous instance of vileness in history [through which] nearly 1.5 million Armenians were slaughtered." In this connection he made the following disclosure in an editorial: "I personally heard a minion of the Kaiser ... [at a banquet] tell in a low voice the Director of the Bureau of Wartime Press 'I just came from the General Headquarters where I had an audience with His Majesty. In accord with the High Command, it has been decided that nothing will be said in the press about the Armenian issue.' "[178] The same prohibition applied to the thousands of other German officers assisting in the Turkish war effort, whether as commanders in combat or as administrative support personnel. The following account by Ludwig Schraundenbach, the commander of 14th Ottoman Infantry Division, epitomizes the case. It depicts the fate of Armenians who supposedly were being driven to Mesopotamia for purposes of temporary wartime "relocation." The narration belongs to Lieutenant Pfeifer, the commander of a 300-man strong German motorized column, who was a witness to the incidents described. His journal entry on January 28, 1917 reads: "Turkish officers and gendarmes each evening were picking out dozens of Armenian men from the ranks of the deportees and were using them as targets for practice games (*auf sie ein Scheibenschiessen veranstaltete*)."[179] However, the German commander had received specific instructions not to discuss the case of the Armenians. "It was one of the very few instructions ... the Armenian Question was to be treated as *noli me tangere*" (touch me not).[180]

This directive of the German emperor was adopted as a general rule by the Supreme Board of Censorship of the Wartime Press (*Obere Zensur-Stelle des Kriegspresseamtes*), an outfit comprising the representatives of the Foreign Ministry, the General Staff, the High Command, and the Prussian Ministry of Defense. In a press conference on October 7, 1915, the members of the German press were exhorted as follows: "Our friendly relations with Turkey ought not only not to be endangered through an involvement in such administrative matters, but in the present, difficult moment even it ought not to be examined. Therefore, for the time being it is your duty to remain silent."[181] In another conference on December 23, 1915, the same press people were told: "It is better to remain silent over the Armenian Question. The conduct of the Turkish power-wielders in this Question is not particularly praiseworthy."[182] This order was rationalized by twin arguments. First, unconditional support of the Turkish ally for the sake of a common victory in a war in which the issue was survival was to be regarded as a matter that takes precedence over everything else. Second, Germany can ill afford to ignore "Turkish sensitivities" with regard to the Armenian issue.

The removal by the Germans of Ottoman General Staff files

The relevance of these files to the subject matter of this study issues from the critical role the High Command in the Ottoman General Headquarters played in the initiation of the enactment of the Armenian genocide and the extent to which German and Prussian officers controlled that High Command. That control began with the general mobilization. As noted earlier, all Turkish generals, who were reduced to rather subservient roles in the General Headquarters, bitterly complained of the predominance of German officers in the various departments of the General Staff. General Kâzım Karabekir quotes Enver saying that General Bronsart prepared the details of the general mobilization scheme.[183] General Ali Ihsan Sabis likewise declared that General Bronsart was in charge and berates Enver for preoccupying himself with the affairs of the Ittihad party instead of assuming responsibility for military operations.[184] Bronsart was assisted by Colonel Kress von Kressenstein,[185] who at the time was heading Department I in the General Staff and in that capacity performed the task of elaborating the pertinent details of mobilization.

As was explained in another section of this study, Department II in the General Staff at the Ottoman General Headquarters was actively involved in the organization of the logistics and financing of the Special Organization, the principal instrument in the enactment of the Armenian genocide. Even though it simply bore the title Intelligence (*Istihbarat*), Department II was closely identified with the Special Organization[186] as an outfit whose secret missions reached far beyond the thresholds of intelligence, gravitating more to objectives that required the commission of acts of lethal violence, especially mass murder. Given the operative sway in these headquarters of the Germans, especially General Bronsart, who is on record for signing an order for the Armenian deportations, the documentary files of the Ottoman General Staff are bound to contain some evidence of the nature and scope of German involvement in the wartime liquidation of Ottoman Armenians. Indeed the bulk of the material adduced in this study points to the complicity in various ways and degrees of some high-ranking German officers, especially those on duty at Ottoman General Headquarters. This being the case, the records assembled in the archives of that headquarters would be of critical significance. Yet Major General Seeckt, the last German Chief of Staff at that office, whisked away substantial parts of these "secret" records when departing from Turkey at the end of the war. Turkish Cabinet ministers, especially Education Minister Dr. Riza Tevfik and postwar Grand Vizier Izzet Paşa, publicly denounced this move when they became cognizant of it. On November 6, 1918, Grand Vizier Izzet lodged a formal protest to Berlin, accusing Seeckt of a transgression, that is, of carrying with him "*tous les dossiers du Quartier Général Ottoman*," despite Seeckt's formal promise not to take away these pieces "which are the property of the government." Seeckt, on November 24, 1918, promised to return only those files that basically concerned the Turkish military.[187] There is no indication as to the category of the items these files did contain or to the language or languages in which the documents in question were framed. Nor could it be ascertained as to whether these files were in fact returned and, if so, to what extent, when, and to what branch of the Turkish government. This element of uncertainty makes it impossible to probe deeper into the problem and its implications, except to say that it is part of a broad sweep of efforts of concealment.

Thus, taking advantage of the general crisis generated by the outbreak of the war in July 1914, the mobilization in the wake of the signing of the Turko-German alliance, and the state of siege and the corollary martial law, the Turkish authorities proceeded to prepare the ground for the final reckoning with the Armenians while furiously preparing themselves for preemptive war. The ultimate authority that emerged from this process was that of the Central Committee of Ittihad which began to function as a secret and supreme Directorate. What is even more relevant to the generl premise of this study, that Committee, according to the assertion of Turkish general Karabekir, was in part reduced to the level of the Special Organization (*kısmen Teşkilâtı Mahsusa haline getirilerek*).[188] The opportunity for that final reckoning was not only at hand but it was also considerably maximized.

A German document with a revelatory hint

The extraordinary value of this document lies in its rarity. In all the relevant files perused by this author in the archives at Bonn or Potsdam, there is no other official document that approximates the inclination for frankness with which a German intelligence operative in it intimates that there is some truth about the prevalent rumors and allegations on German complicity. The document originates from the office of Otto Günther Wesendonck, a specialist on nationalities in the Political Section of the German Foreign Office and the principal exponent of insurrectionary movements in the border areas of Russia. In a report dated May 4, 1916, he quotes Oswald von Schmidt as declaring that "insightful Turks are contending that the annihilation (*Vertilgung*) of the Armenians was ordered by the Germans" (*auf deutschen Befehl*).[189]

There are several aspects to this caustic remark that deserve special attention. First of all the declaration is accurate when one takes into account the deportation order of General Bronsart (described earlier)—in terms of its consequences. Second, the position of Schmidt renders the declaration more or less reliable insofar as the contacts he had with Turkish and German intelligence operatives involved in special, secret missions are concerned. He was the agent of Count Friedrich Werner von Schulenburg, who, apart from temporary consular services, was involved in the work of organizing and deploying guerillas; the latter's mission was to undermine Russia's war effort through sabotage and insurrectionary acts on its Transcaucasian borders. The umbrella organization coordinating these activities was the Turkish Special Organization. Equally important, Schmidt was associated with two men, a German and a Turk, that is, Humann and Dr. Nazım. Humann's relationship to the developments associated with the Armenian genocide has been examined earlier. The role Dr. Nazım played in the conception, decision making, and organization of that genocide is both paramount and pivotal,[190] and Humann must have known of that role when he wrote a letter of recommendation. Humann was a çareer intelligence officer who knew many of the secrets of Ittihadists through his intimate relationship with Enver. On the occasion of a trip to Berlin, which Schmidt took with Nazım, for example, Humann wrote a letter to Jäckh, the Turkophile German operative enjoying the benefits of the sponsorship of the German Foreign Office, recommending Dr. Nazım. Humann pleaded with Jäckh to "watch over him with a tender loving eye. I don't need to say anything about the foremost importance of this man in the entire political life of Turkey."[191]

The most revealing feature of the document is the adjective Schmidt uses to characterize those Turks who at the time were blaming Germany for "the annihilation" of the Armenians. The adjective he used was the German word "*einsichtig,*" which means "insightful" or "perceptive." There is a total absence of the standard German disclaimer in face of such Turkish assertions, as well as evidence of an urge to praise those making these assertions. These people, who are incriminating the Germans, are not dismissed out of hand but are acknowledged as people with keen minds. As if to punctuate this fact, von Wesendonck is seen in this document as agreeing with Schmidt, if by default; despite his responsible position, he has not chosen to contradict or dispute anywhere in that document Schmidt, who clearly is seen here adopting the Turkish rationale, thereby implicitly concurring with the charge of German complicity. Finally, the same point may be made about Eugen Mittwoch, Professor of Egyptian Studies at the University of Berlin, who had taken charge of the bureau dealing with matters of intelligence and propaganda in the east. His statement, appended to Wesendonck's report in the same document, simply accepts Schmidt's declaration. It is conceivable that this was a confidential piece of communication, intended strictly for in-house use, but was somehow inserted in regular record files.

The involvement of Schmidt in shadowy activities is certified by a number of ancillary German and Turkish sources identified with the secret operations of the Special Organization in the eastern provinces of

Turkey. Foremost among these is Paul Leverkuehn, the adjutant of Dr. Max Erwin von Scheubner Richter who, along with the Ittihadist leader Ömer Naci, was the co-commander of a Special Organization Expedition. Leverkuehn, a sergeant and law student at the time, along with his brother, Karl Gustav, had signed up as a volunteer for this expeditionary foray. In his book, dedicated to the memory of Scheubner Richter, Leverkuehn identifies Schmidt as a member of the German contingent comprising the Expedition Force, at the same time describing him as a Baltic volunteer who had a Ph.D. degree.[192] Equally significant, Leverkuehn identifies the Expeditionary Force as the end result of the preparatory work done in Berlin by the same Count F. von Schulenburg who was mentioned earlier as the organizer of guerrilla and sabotage undertakings in the border region of eastern Turkey. Leverkuehn mentions also the name of Dr. Stoffels, staff physician, who was part of the German personnel of the same Expeditionary Force. Dr. Stoffels' duties were strictly of a medical nature but he was able to observe a particular feature of the Armenian genocide that imparts to it a distinct holocaustal character. In the districts of Muş and Sıırt in eastern Turkey the organizers of the Armenian genocide were particularly fiendish as they used the method of burning alive to exterminate the victim population. Stables, haylofts, and other large storage facilities were used for this purpose. In his account to the Austrian consul, Dr. Kwiatowski, Dr. Stoffels on May 26, 1917 stated that he personally observed the evidence in these two districts of this holocaustal dimension of the Armenian genocide. He was referring to the population of "a large number of formerly Armenian localities" (*eine grosse Anzahl früher armenischer Ortschaften*), the members of which were burned alive "in houses and churches" where he "saw the charred and decomposed remains of women and children" (*Kirchen und Häusern ... verkohlte und verweste Frauen-und-Kinderleichen gesehen*).[193]

A Turkish source closely identified with the Special Organization operational plans in the eastern border zones provides additional details about Schmidt's involvement in the activities of that organization. It develops that Schmidt had the rank of a First Lieutenant and was associated with the Georgian contingent of the Special Organization that was headquartered in Trabzon. "He wore a linen cloth outfit that resembled a military uniform, and his headgear consisted of a fez adorned with military tassels." Evidently, Schmidt participated in some of the Special Organization's onslaughts that were directed against the Russians.[194] The gist of the entire argument is that, given his connections to Dr. Nazım, Humann, and the Turkish operational leaders of the Special Organization, with whom he had intensive contacts, Schmidt was in a position to know, to observe, and to some extent even verify his knowledge about the matter of German complicity. It is neither suggested nor implied that he was complicitous in this respect inasmuch as there is no evidence to that effect. The fact remains that a German official document contains his tacit recognition about the factualness of Turkish assertions of German complicity and that the recognition is not disputed by two officials associated with that document and operating in the German Foreign Office. Assessed against the backdrop of the conditions and facts outlined earlier, the validity of Schmidt's acknowledgment may be considered a piece of evidence that is adequately tested and redeemed. Thus, one more link is obtained in the chain of fragments of evidence that is being explored in this study. (In the section on Turko-German Joint Initiatives in Part I more details are provided on this topic.)

Disclosure through the medium of two veteran Austrian consuls

Dr. Ernst von Kwiatkowski was the Dual Monarchy's consul general at Trabzon and was very active in the gathering of reliable information on the conditions of the Armenian deportations and massacres in the entire province. Of all the Austrian consuls stationed in wartime Turkey he was the most conscientious about this task; his reports to Vienna were both numerous and focused in this respect. In a number of these reports he advised his Foreign Minister, Stephan Baron Burian, that the German consuls at Trabzon and Erzurum, Dr. Heinrich Bergfeld and Dr. Max Erwin von Scheubner Richter, respectively, were being pressured by their government to "tone down" their reports about Turkish massacres.[195] In several other reports Kwiatkowski informed Vienna that the assertion about German complicity is gaining ground in all Turkish circles, including official quarters.[196]

The one particular report that is the principal subject of the present discussion was sent from Trabzon on October 22, 1915; it is marked "confidential" and was addressed to Burian, with a copy to Pallavicini, the Austrian ambassador in the Ottoman capital. In order to appreciate the significance of the provenance of the source (i.e., the port city of Trabzon), the following fact should be taken into account. Trabzon was a central location for the marshaling of the resources, logistics, and the deployment of the guerilla bands of the Special Organization. Several of its leaders on the field, such as Dr. Behaeddin Şakir, Yakub Cemil, Yusuf

Riza, and Yenibahçeli Nail, met and mapped their plans in that city, which thus became a hub for Special Organization–related traffic. Equally significant, German intelligence operatives and agents, one way or another involved in the activities of that organization, converged in Trabzon as the place of rendezvous, including Colonel Stange of the German army, who was in command of a Turkish regiment comprising a contingent of Special Organization guerillas; at one time during the war, both Yusuf Riza and Dr. Şakir were under his command.[197] This is the text of the report of Trabzon's Austrian consul:

> I learned from a German source, which usually is reliable, that the first suggestion for the *Unschädlichmachung* of the Armenians—certainly not in the manner in which it was actually carried out—came from the German camp.[198]

As noted earlier, in German parlance the word *Unschädlichmachung* denotes the idea of rendering the subject incapable of causing any injury; it also connotes the idea of summary liquidation of that subject, as likewise evidenced in the spoken and written words as well as the deeds of the Nazis during World War II. This piece of document is significant on two grounds. It is based on what appears to be a credible German source; its content is in accord with the statement of the German functionary Schmidt discussed earlier. The Austrian consul's effort to protect the identity of that source from his superiors, at least in terms of official records, is also noteworthy.

The other Austrian consul involved is Dr. Arthur Chevalier de Nadamlenzki, on duty at Adrianople (Edirne), in the European part of Turkey. Unlike the case of his colleague at Trabzon, his source is not German but Turkish, namely, "a very influential personality, who has close ties with the Ittihadist clique, and knows all their secrets." Nadamlenzki received the disclosure through one of his confidential informants (*Gewährsmann*), probably a Turkish official, whom he could not persuade to reveal the identity of the source; the informant would merely stress the high profile of that source in such terms as quoted earlier. The disclosure consists in the simple and crude assertion that "Germany wanted the enactment of the anti-Armenian measures." The consul sent this report both to his ambassador and to his foreign minister.[199] The need to exercise some caution, if not suspicion, is warranted in the case of this document, given the vague origin and nature of the source described.

The necessity for exercising such a caveat is indicated by the contents of the report German Embassy chaplain Count von Lüttichau compiled on the entire wartime episode of Armenian deportations and massacres. After describing the many cases where Turks from all walks of life are seen persisting in their eagerness to blame Germany as the arch instigator against the Armenians, Lüttichau focuses on a particular instance. Relying on Turkish sources, who claim to have been present at a meeting Malatya's deputy Haşim is reported to have convened upon his return from the Ottoman capital in the wake of the spring 1916 recess of the Parliament, the chaplain provides the following account. The Turkish deputy reportedly told the notables of Malatya he had gathered together that he personally was present when German ambassador Wangenheim one day [it has to be before his sudden death in October 1915] appeared at the seat of the Ottoman government, the Sublime Porte, in order to "convey his government's congratulations for the comprehensive manner and the crowning glorious success with which the Armenian people were exterminated." Lüttichau in his report, disputing the veracity of the statement attributed to Wangenheim, responds with the retort, "Such shamelessness exceeds all bounds."[200]

THE ANTI-RUSSIAN IDEOLOGY IN THE TURKO-GERMAN PARTNERSHIP AND ITS ANTI-ARMENIAN REPERCUSSIONS

The quest for credible sources is further redeemed by adding to the array of sources used thus far a source that differs from the latter. It involves a source that accurately did forecast the fate of the Armenians six months before the outbreak of World War I. Relying on information, presumably supplied by the agents of the Russian Secret Service, the Russian periodical *Golos Moskoi* in its January 1914 issue directed attention to a "Turko-German scheme to deport the Armenians of the Ottoman provinces to Mesopotamia." According to the editors of the newspaper, this plan was in line with Turkish and German designs to establish homogenous Muslim masses of populations in the east of Turkey, contiguous to those of the Caucasus, thereby enabling these Muslim kinsmen to confront together the Slavic peoples exactly as advocated by Marshal Goltz (see his proposal earlier in this part of the study). Through a reference to this Russian source he made in an editorial on October 17/30, 1918, a former lieutenant of the Turkish security police, an Armenian, who during the war had assisted the Turks in the liquidation of the Armenian notables in the Ottoman capital, confirmed the allegation of a Turko-German scheme to resettle the Armenians in

Mesopotamia. It appears that an Armenian newspaper, *Gohag*, had been punished by the Turkish Court-Martial that, invoking the state of martial law existing at that time, had banned that paper for republishing the Russian forecast; the Armenian newspaper then reappeared under the new name of *Taylaylig*.[201] What is even more significant, *Ikdam*, a Turkish newspaper, that after the war published an open letter to President Wilson admitting the culpabilities of Turkey, in its January 17, 1914 issue took *Golos Moskoi* to task for publishing such "absurdities."[202] It should be noted that *The Okhrana*, the Russian Department of Police, otherwise called the Imperial Russian Secret Police, not only had agents in the Ottoman capital but also had available a number of Turkish sources affiliated one way or another with the Ottoman security system. As if to corroborate indirectly the forecast of *Golos Moskoi*, the *Okhrana,* on January 23, 1914, relayed a secret report through its contacts in the Russian Interior and Foreign Affairs ministries, declaring, "Today, at a secret meeting of panislamists and Ittihadists at Nuri Osmaniye [the party headquarters of Ittihad], several delegates spoke up, lambasting the Russians and the Christians … . At the end of the conclave Talât stated that Turkey is opposed to any type of foreign control in Anatolia [the reference is to the imminent February 8, 1914 Accord on Armenian Reforms in the provinces].[203]

This matter raises the issue of ideology seen as a factor facilitating at another level the growth of a Turko-German partnership under review here; it involves an ideology that is punctuated by anti-Russian elements. A brief commentary may, therefore, be in order. In surveying the whole picture, the Turkish sociologist Ismail Beşikci discerned a Turko-German conspiracy in "the deportation of hundreds of thousands of Armenians which in actuality was a genocide in its truest meaning [*tam anlamıyla bir soykırım*] … it was the result of an undertaking in which German imperialism, in a collision course with Russian imperialism … enabled the Ittihadists to solve the Armenian question by spurring Turkism and panturanism."[204] Moreover, the founder of the ideology of panturanism, the Tatar political leader and journalist from Russia, Yusuf Akçura, espoused the same doctrine. Akçura had joined the Ittihadists after the latter's successful 1908 revolution. He also had founded *Türk Yurdu*, the organ of the panturanists who rallied under the banner of the Turkish Hearth (*Türk Ocağı*). While studying in Paris he had absorbed the racial superiority views of the pangermanists. He too believed that the Germans could help the Turkic peoples of Russia achieve emancipation and freedom from Tsarist rule and oppression. In the first issue of *Türk Yurdu* it was declared that "the rulers of the universe have always been the representatives of only two great nations—Turks and Germans." Akçura in the same issue stated that Russian Turks had great expectations from a new coalition of Turks and Germans.[205] One such expectation involved the removal of Armenians and Armenia from the paths of Ottoman Turks who were gravitating toward their kinsmen in the Caucasus and beyond, that is, to the dreamland of Turan. In a speech on January 29, 1920, delivered at a mass meeting in Istanbul, Akçura stated that the Turkish soldiers sacrificed themselves to secure independence for Azerbaijan. He then declared, "It is necessary to destroy Armenia which the Allies want to erect as a barrier between the two brotherly segments of Turkdom, Anatolia and the Caucasus."[206] In fact Zenkovsky, the noted expert in this field, concluded that "the massacre in 1914–16 of one and a half million Armenians was largely conditioned by the desire of the Young Turks to eliminate the Armenian obstacle" in this respect.[207]

The chief exponent of an alliance of the forces of pangermanism and panturkism was Tekin Alp, who argued that the Slavs were the historical common enemy of both the Turks and the Germans and that, therefore, an alliance between the two nations was "a geographical and historical necessity. The condition of the Germans and Turks vis-à-vis the Slavic peoples has not changed in a millennium of history. They still remain the common enemy of the Slavic power and must, therefore, protect themselves against the Moscowite bear ... panturkism cannot attain a full measure of fruition before the Moscowite monster is overpowered. Russia for her part is impeded in her development by two obstacles: the Germans and the Turks .... So long as there is a Slavic danger, panturkism and pangermanism must remain partners and follow the same path." Completely embracing this ideological blueprint the Young Turk Ittihadists under German tutelage and through the prodding of the German High Command unilaterally intervened in World War I when they precipitated the outbreak of hostilities against Russia.

In a secret circular that was brought to light by Alp himself and, thus far, is to be found nowhere else, the Ittihadists notified their provincial branch offices that it was inevitable for Turkey to get involved in the war for reasons they framed as follows:

> Let us not forget that one of the most important reasons for which we are intervening in the war is related to our national objective which is twofold. On the one hand, we are anxious to destroy the Moscovite enemy in order to create natural borders which allow us to unite with our kinfolk and to incorporate them in our domain. On the other hand, we are driven with a religious zeal to free the Islamic world from the bondage imposed upon them by the infidels and to secure the independence of the Muslim faithful.[208]

This work appeared in German in Weimar with a view to familiarizing the Germans with the tenets of panturkish nationalism and thereby to cement a new mold of Turko-German partnership. The Germans not only adopted the idea of an alliance with Turkey for the purpose of confronting the perceived threat from Russia but also assisted in the initiation of measures that ensured the liquidation of the Ottoman Armenians who were considered to be a subsidiary part of the overall Russian threat. The responses to the outcome of that liquidation by some other representatives of German society, adduced below, may shed further light on this problem.

GERMAN POLITICAL ECONOMISTS AND THE ARMENIAN GENOCIDE

One type of such response involved the manifestation of a sense of affinity with the Turks in terms of a model personality presumed to be embodying certain common character traits. German ambassador Wangenheim had admiringly told Grand Vizier Said Halim, for example, that "Turkey was the Prussia of the Islamic world." When reporting on this ambassadorial tribute, a German economics professor who was also a *Reichstag* deputy and who had just completed a visit to Turkey, proceeded to assess the significance of "the Armenian massacres," which by then had largely run their course. He declared that as the Turkish leaders had through exterminatory massacres eliminated the Armenians, they had enabled "this old master race [*Herrenvolk*]" to achieve a certain level of "a national, or rather a religious cohesiveness" (*eine nationale, oder vielmehr, religiöse Geschlossenheit*).[209] Another economist and a leader of the German Association for Defense (*Wehrverein*) had conducted a five-week inspection tour of Turkey at about the same time as the professor mentioned earlier. In his 26-page report he reproved European attitudes, which, he complained, routinely condemned Turkey for the massacre of the Armenians on the basis of Western standards. As a counterargument, he directed attention to the fact that Turkey was a country where "the political party ruling there willfully can dispose over the possessions and lives of their subjects." In other words, he meant that there was nothing unusual about these massacres. After echoing the Turkish charges of Armenian treason and enmity against Turkey, the author stated that "by February 1916, 1.5 million Armenians were destroyed." Wholeheartedly approving it as "the first step toward the recovery of the [levers of] economic predominance in Turkey," the German author added that "there was 'joy' (*Freude*) in the government circles that the long-desired opportunity (*langgewünschte Gelegenheit*) finally presented itself...." It is noticeable that, while approving of the mass murder he was describing, the author used for that purpose such words as "horrors" (*Greuel*), "butchery" (*Niedermetzelung*), and "extermination" (*Ausrottung*), thereby dispensing with the repetition of the Turkish euphemism "deportation" used by the Turkish authorities to disguise the intended act of genocide.[210] Another German author, likewise examining the economic aspects of the liquidation of the Ottoman Armenians, in 1963 decried, however, the complicity of "the political and military instruments of German imperialism" in the crime of genocide against the Armenians. As he put it, "In order to pave the ground for the turanist invasion of the Caucasus, the Ittihadist leaders proceeded to ruthlessly and completely exterminate the Ottoman Armenians ... By the explicit order of the Turkish government, in the June 1915–March 1916 period more than one million men, women and children were murdered with unprecedented ferocity (*beispiellose Grausamkeit*), and under the pretext that they were being taken to Mesopotamia for the purpose of resettlement."[211]

THE VIEWS OF GERMAN EXPERTS OF CRIMINAL AND INTERNATIONAL LAW ON GERMAN COMPLICITY AS A BY-PRODUCT OF MILITARISM

Perhaps the most common element in the cultivation of the Turko-German partnership was the legacy of militarism dominating many aspects of both German-Prussian and Turkish cultures, which otherwise were quite disparate in many other respects. This convergence, however narrow in scope, was sufficient to afford many high-ranking German officers the latitude to go along with their Turkish counterparts or to spur them on the matter of the elimination of the Armenians as "a military necessity." In some sections of this part of the study this issue has been dealt with at some length. It may be relevant at this point to revisit and reinterpret briefly the legal liability aspect of this factor of militarism that was specifically examined as an ancillary problem earlier.

That relevance issues from the significance of a precedent-setting trial that took place in a district criminal court in Berlin in 1921. It involved the prosecution of a young Armenian who, in broad daylight, had assassinated Talât, the chief architect of the Armenian genocide, on a major boulevard in Berlin and was acquitted after a mere one-hour deliberation by a German jury on grounds of temporary insanity, as provided for in article 51 of the German penal code. German Foreign Office had declined the request of the postwar Ottoman government to have Talât extradited to Turkey for trial as a war criminal; he subsequently was tried in Istanbul in absentia and was sentenced to death. Several aspects of the Armenian genocide came to light during the trial. Foremost among these were the declarations of the defense counsel on the matter of the Turko-German alliance and the issue of German complicity. Dr. Johannes Werthauer, a legal councillor and member of the defense team, rejected the prosecutor's plea to be mindful of the fact that Talât represented a valued ally and was a guest of Germany.[212] He argued instead that Talât and his cronies who had taken refuge in Germany and were "fugitives of justice" were the allies of a government that was "Prussian in make-up, and militaristic." Inveighing against "militarists" as proponents of violence who disdain the notions of right and justice, are eager to wage war, and are prepared to destroy anything and everything under a plea of "military necessity," Werthauer in his closing arguments declared: "We too have men prone to violence, men whom we have sent to Turkey so that they could drill the Turkish military into the art of violence … and it so happens that these men of violence (*Gewaltmenschen*) were the ones who destroyed the Armenian people … the order to deport an entire people is the vilest thought that can ever enter the mind of a militarist … the German people too are being accused of having allowed the issuance of such orders of deportation. Only by way of a total and unreserved repudiation of such principles and a renunciation of such mean-spirited, criminal orders can we regain the respect to which, I believe, we are entitled."[213]

Another member of the defense team was Dr. Niemeyer, Government Privy Councillor and a Professor of Law at the University of Kiel; he was a world-renowned authority on international law. In his closing argument he conceded two points that underscore the relevance of this entire discussion while at the same time accentuating its significance. The Attorney General, Gollnick, had not only tried to defend the reputation of Talât, the murder victim, but had extolled the virtues of the Turko-German alliance that, he said, Talât embodied. Consequently, he said, Talât was catapulted to "the elevated heights of history."[214] Declaring that he feels constrained to respond to this assessment by the Attorney General, Niemeyer stated: "During the war in Turkey military authorities here at home, and over there [in Turkey], maintained silence over and covered up [*verschwiegen und verdeckt*] the Armenian horrors, to an extent which bordered on approval" (*an die Grenze des Zulässigen her-*

anreichenden Weise).[215] Thus, he concurred with Dr. Werthauer, his partner on the defense team, about this aspect of German complicity. Equally important, he submitted for consideration the argument that, in adjudicating a crime under the German penal code, "the generally accepted rules of international law are to be treated as binding integral parts of the law of the German Reich, as provided by Article 4 of the constitution of the empire."[216]

In commenting on these proceedings, the *New York Times* wrote, "The damning German angle to the Turkish war atrocities in Armenia was patent to all present...."[217]

THE SIGNIFICANCE OF EMPEROR WILLIAM II'S SECRET ACTIVITIES

The evaluation of the matter of secrecy and concealment in this study has its most abiding test in the evaluation of the role of Emperor William II. Elsewhere, in this part of the study, his dual status as civilian head of the nation as well as commander-in-chief of the armed forces was briefly sketched. There are indications, however, that he was involved also in activities that border on conspiracy and involve the supervision of plots, authorization of "special missions," and acts of espionage and sabotage outside Germany. One German agent in his memoirs describes, for example, how he was received by William II and performed "secret" missions "for the Kaiser," including one at Constantinople. He provides graphic details of an encounter with William II at the German Foreign Office at Wilhelmstrasse where the emperor personally charged him with a secret mission in Morocco and reportedly added these words: "Outside Count Wedel [Count von Botho Wedel at the time was emperor's Privy Councillor and head of the Secret Service, that was run by the emperor], no one is to know anything of your mission. No one is to know that you are carrying a verbal message from me to the Captain of the warship Panther. Understand?" After inducing the agent to memorize the contents of the slip of paper, William II reportedly asked, "Have you memorized it?" "Yes, Sir." "Then taking the note from me, he at once struck a match and held it under the paper until it was reduced to ashes." With respect to his previous 1905 mission at Constantinople, the same agent states, "I was bidden to keep away from all official German intercourse in Constantinople." This agent also disclosed that William II kept a privy purse to finance these operations. After four months of operations, he returned to Berlin with a report on Abdul Hamit, palace spies, Russian and French gold for bribery, the Young Turk dissidents, and Enver.[218]

The disclosures of another German agent are more pertinent. He performed secret service work in Constantinople on three different occasions, namely, in the latter half of 1908, the first half of 1909, and the closing months of the second Balkan war (i.e., during the spring of 1913.) He had established contact with Enver and was told by his superior in Berlin that the latter was considered a key person for fulfilling German ambitions in Turkey and as a nemesis to Russian ambitions there. He further maintains that German ambassador Wangenheim was "a personal friend" of his. It is against this background that the agent's revelations need to be assessed. In the spring of 1914 Enver undertook "a secret" trip to Germany. "I took him to the station.... He told me he had had a long talk with the emperor, and he seemed particularly cheerful in consequence. More than once I have wondered what bearing that talk had upon subsequent events on the Bosphorus." The agent also states that at the end of June or early July 1914, "William II caused a ciphered message to be forwarded to Enver Pasha, who in obedience thereto hastened to Berlin," spending two days in conference with General Moltke, the Chief of the German General Staff. All this may be better understood in the light of the fact that "Enver Bey had always cherished a grudge against Russia.... He sent secret messengers to Berlin with an offer of service to the Kaiser, declaring to him that the forces of Turkey were at his disposal...." Finally, the author notes that in the fall of 1913, when Ittihad was firmly entrenched in power, large secret funds were remitted to Enver and his Ittihad party.[219]

Some of these assertions are independently verified by other agents or historians. Captain Franz von Rintelen from the German Naval Staff (*Admiralstab*), for example, states that he received a "*Kaiserpass*," an exceptional passport given to people with special missions, entitling the bearer to all manner of assistance from German embassies and legations around the world. Although Bernstorff, German ambassador at Washington, D.C., was kept in the dark about the nature of his mission, which was sabotage, Zimmermann, William II's confidant in the Foreign Office, knew about it.[220] Another German author wrote that the German High Command through the Central Office of Censorship "confidentially" directed the German newspapers not to say anything about Enver's presence in Berlin in April 1917.[221]

THE OFFICIAL FORMULAS OF SUBTERFUGE

The official German posture relative to the Turkish enactment of the genocide had two salient features.

1) Irrespective of the scope and intensity of the process of destruction, the German response was to remain firm and immutable. That response was the expression of a fixed policy that was determined at the highest echelon of German state authority, namely, the Kaiser. Through a series of directives all military and civilian officials operating in Turkey during the war were enjoined not to intervene in the handling by the Turks of the Armenian Question and the Armenians; the matter was to be considered as a purely internal matter. This display of apparent legalistic correctness was not only a form of subterfuge in technicality but also masked the existence of a covert policy that belied the purposes associated with such formal legalism. The Imperial injunction not to intervene was in no way conditional but rather categorical. In other words, no matter what the exigency, the German functionaries were not to get involved. This Imperial command for passivity and inaction, delivered in the vortex of a global war in which the Turks were set to settle scores with the Armenians, predictably functioned as a license for the former to proceed with their plans. One might be willing to concede the rationale of such a posture in a case of impotence, or relative impotence. But the Germans were the stronger partner in the alliance and enjoyed a preponderance of power that had pervaded nearly all the levels of military authority in Turkey. They knew how to exercise and, when necessary, even impose that power upon reluctant or demurring Turkish potentates.

In extending to them optimal latitudes, the German emperor knowingly preconditioned the violent elimination of the Ottoman Armenian population. In fact, he rendered it affordable for the Turks. His March 11, 1915 directive is emblematic in this respect. From his elevated position at the German General Headquarters he exhorted the highest civilian and military authority in Turkey to see to it that "Turkey's trustful attitude toward Germany is preserved" (*vertrauensvolle Stimmung der Türkei*).[222] The date of the directive is most significant, for it signals the time frame in which the deliberations of the Turkish leaders relative to the decision for the Armenian genocide were in full swing and only weeks away from actual initiation of it. 2) Having established the fundamental policy, there emerged the task of defending that policy through a variety of strategies that involved alibis, deflections, and excuses. The Foreign Office was most concerned about the spread of reports on German involvement in the initiation of anti-Armenian measures. As early as August 1915 Ambassador Wangenheim instructed his staff to assemble pertinent material with a view to exculpating Germany in this regard; this was to be the basis of a future White Book.[223]

The compendium was to revolve around three major themes: a) placing the main onus of the blame on the Armenians, b) justifying or explaining away the severity of the Turkish measures while deploring the excesses incidental to the application of these measures, and c) underscoring the fact that Germany did all it could to try to mitigate the suffering of the Armenian people by offering friendly advice to the Turks and by delivering occasional protest notes. In a lengthy memorandum Undersecretary Zimmermann in October 1915 developed these themes, which subsequently became policy guidelines for all German officials involved. He was prompted by Dr. Faber, a German publicist, who after listening to a lecture by Lepsius—it was for the representatives of the Berlin press and was not meant for the public—wrote a "confidential" report and urged Zimmermann to deal with the problem of exoneration of Germany.[224] Zimmermann in his memorandum claimed that the Armenians allowed themselves to be agitated by the Russians and resorted to espionage, sabotage, and rebellion. The Turkish response was "a measure that was militarily understandable" (*militärisch verständliche Massregel*). He ended his brief stating that "our sons and brothers are closer to us than the Armenians" and the Turko-German alliance cannot be fractured because Turkish military help is needed for the Germans fighting on other fronts.[225] What is missing in this rhetorical artifice is any sign of deploring the *prima facie* evidence of a gigantic mass murder in progress, of the indisputable underlying intent to eliminate the bulk of a nation from its ancestral territories through lethal means. It involved the kind of elimination about which Zimmermann's protégé and confident, Ambassador Wangenheim, and his deputies had reported to Berlin in the preceding months through a succession of cipher telegrams, emphasizing in them the exterminatory intent of the perpetrators.

About a year after Zimmermann prepared this brief the Political Section in the Reserve General Staff of the same Foreign Office issued another policy declaration: The anti-Armenian measures of the Turkish government are, as a matter of principle, to be recognized as justified measures of self-defense by the state (*als staatliche Notwehr gerechtfertig anzuerkennen*). Germany could not exert too much pressure on Turkey lest it illicitly (*unstatthaft*) intervene in the internal affairs of Turkey.[226] This declaration was prompted by an article in the January 4, 1917 issue of *Kölnische Zeitung*, a renowned German newspaper that, under the title "Dedications to Mr. Wilson" (*Widmungen*), denounced attempts in the enemy camp to blame the Germans for the tragic fate of the Armenians. By quoting "simple" as well as "educated Turks," these enemy sources were depicting the Germans as "the instigators of the atrocities against the Armenians" (*die Anstifter dieser Greuel*). Among these quotations is one attributed to the chief of the Turkish deportation office, probably Şükrü Kaya, who reportedly justified the anti-Armenian measures by stating, "We Turks want only Turks, exactly as Germany would only want Germans to live in Germany." The tone of the entire article was reflective of the instructions the German Foreign Office in cooperation with the Reserve General Staff (*stellvertretender Generalstab*) replayed to the German press to defend German national interests. In fact, attached to the document containing the above-mentioned latter policy declaration were directives for the use of the members of the German press.[227] (Additional details on this topic on pp. 81–88).

A TRENCHANT REJOINDER FROM A GERMAN NEWSPAPER EDITOR

The introduction here of a composite picture of observations, recitation of facts and judgments on the matter of German responsibility in the annihilation of the Ottoman Armenian population by the wartime correspondent of the same renowned German newspaper *Kölnische Zeitung* may fittingly serve the purpose of an exposure that is free from the constraints of diplomacy. During his 1915-1916 tour of duty in Turkey he conducted investigative journalism on the fate of the Armenians to the extent he could. That picture emanates from a man who underlines two important facts. First, he went to Turkey "with a good deal of friendly feeling toward the Turk. I was even quite well disposed toward the Young Turks. ..."[228] Second, he proceeded to investigate "this drama of massacre and death ... without my having any particular sympathy for the Armenians, for it was not till much later that I got to know them and their high intellectual qualities through personal intercourse."[229] "... I must hold the German government as equally responsible with the Turks for the atrocities they allowed them to commit"[230] *(... ich muss die deutsche Regierung mitverantwortlich machen für die Schandtaten, die sie den Türken zu begehen erlaubte)!*

* * *

"They [the Turks] suddenly and miraculously discovered a universal conspiracy among the Armenians of the empire. It was only by a trick of this kind that they could succeed in carrying out their system of exterminating the entire Armenian race. The Turkish government skillfully influenced public opinion throughout the whole world and then discovered, nay, arranged for, local conspiracies. They then falsified all the details so that they might go on for months in peace and quiet with their campaign of extermination[231] (*... entdeckte eine allgemeine Verschwörung unter den Armeniern des Reiches. Nur durch eine solche cynische Fälschung konnte sie ans Ziel gelangen, ihr wohldurchdachtes System der Ausrottung der gesamten armenischen Rasse durchführen. Mit bewusster Täuschung der öffentlichen Meinung der ganzen Welt erfand, ja bestellte die türkische Regierung lokale Verschwörungen, fälschte alle Zusammenhänge, um ganz ruhig ihre Ausrottungscampagne durch Monate hindurch betreiben zu können*).

* * *

"... the meanest, the lowest, the most cynical, most criminal act of race-fanaticism that the history of mankind has to show ... it was committed with the cowardly consent of the German government which was in full knowledge of the facts"[232] (*die gemeinste, zynischste, verlogenste, verbrecherischste Tat von Rassenfanatismus ist, welche die Geschichte der Menschheit zu verzeichnen hat* ... The balance of the quotation adduced here is deleted from the English text: *und begangen mit feiger Zustimmung der deutschen Regierung in voller Kenntnis der Tatsachen!*).

* * *

"I thought of the conversations I had had about the Armenian question with members of the German Embassy in Constantinople and, of a very different kind, with Mr. Morgenthau, the American ambassador. ... I had never felt fully convinced by the protestations of the German Embassy that they had done their utmost to put a check on the murderous attacks on harmless Armenians far from the theater of war, who from their whole surroundings and their social class could not be in a position to take an active part in politics, and on the cold-blooded neglect and starvation of women and children apparently deported for no other reason than to die. The attitude of the German government toward the Armenian Question had impressed me as a mixture of cowardice and lack of conscience on the one hand and the most shortsighted stupidity on the other"[233] (*Ich entsann mich der Unterhaltungen, die ich mit den Herren von der Deutschen Botschaft in Konstantinopel und auch mit dem amerikan-*

ischen Botschafter Morgenthau wiederholt über die Armenierfrage gehabt hatte. Ich hatte mich niemals überzeugt gefühlt von den Versicherungen der deutschen Botschaft, sie sei bisan die Grenze des Nöglichen gegangen, um dem mörderischen Treiben gegen harmlose Armenier weit vom Kriegsschauplatz, die nach ihrem ganzen Milieu, nach ihrer sozialen Klasse gar nicht in der Lage sein konnten, sich an der Politik aktiv zu beteiligen, sowie dem kaltblütigen Dahinsterbenlassen eigens zu diesem Zwecke deportierter Frauen und Kinder Einhalt zu gebieten. Ich hatte im Gegenteil vom Verhalten der deutschen Regierung in der Armenierfrage den Eindruck zurückbehalten von einem Gemisch von Feigheit und Gewissenlosigkeit einerseits, von kurzsichtiger Dummheit anderseits).

* * *

"The attitude of Germany was, in the first place, as I have said, one of boundless cowardice. For we had the Turkish government firmly enough in hand, from the military as well as the financial and political point of view, to insist upon the observance of the simplest principles of humanity if we wanted to"[234] (*Das Verhalten Deutschlands war zunächst eine bodenlose Feigheit, sagte ich. Denn wir hatten die türkische Regierung wahrlich militärisch, finanziell und politisch fest genug in der Hand, um wenigstens die Beachtung der allereinfachsten Grundsätze der Menschlichkeit durchzusetzen, wenn wir nur wollten*).

* * *

"Turks themselves have found cynical enjoyment in this measureless cowardice of ours ... Our attitude was characterized, secondly, by lack of conscience. To look on while life and property, the well-being and culture of thousands, are sacrificed, and to content oneself with weak formal protests when one is in a position to take most energetic command of the situation, is nothing but the most criminal lack of conscience, and I cannot get rid of the suspicion that, in spite of the fine official phrases one was so often treated to in the German Embassy on the subject of the 'Armenian problem,' our diplomats were very little concerned with the preservation of this people"[235] (*Türken selbst haben uns wegen dieser masslosen Feigheit zynisch ausgelacht ... Eine Gewissenlosigkeit, zweitens, war unser Verhalten. Zusehen, wie Leben und Besitz, Wohlbefinden und Kultur von Hunderttausenden geopfert wurden, und sich mit schwachen formellen Protesten begnügen, wo man in der Lage gewesen wäre, höchst energisch aufzutreten, ist nichts als verbrecherische Gewissenlosigkeit, und ich kann mich des Verdachts nicht erwehren, dass trotz der schönen offiziellen Phrasen, die einem im deutschen Botschafts-*

gebäude über das «Armenierproblem» oft zuteil wurden, unseren Herren Diplomaten im Grunde an der Erhaltung dieses Volkes herzlich wenig lag).

* * *

"And cases have actually been proved to have occurred, from the testimony of German doctors and Red Cross nurses returned home from the Interior, ..."[236] (*Und die Fälle sind ja auch ... erwiesen, ... durch Aussagen von aus dem tiefen Innern zurückgekehrten deutschen Ärzten und Schwestern vom Roten Kreuz erhärtet).*

* * *

"To answer the Armenian Question in the way I have done here, one does not necessarily need to have the slightest liking or the least sympathy for them as a race. (I have, however, intimated that they deserve at least that much because of their high intellectual and social abilities.) One only must have a feeling for humanity to abhor the way in which hundreds of thousands of these unfortunate people were disposed of ... one only must open one's eyes and look at the facts dispassionately to deny utterly and absolutely what the Turks have tried to make the world believe about the Armenians, in order that they might go on with their work of extermination in peace and quiet; one only must have a slight feeling of one's dignity as a German to refuse to condone the pitiful cowardice of our government over the Armenian question."

"The mixture of cowardice, lack of conscience, and lack of foresight of which our government has been guilty in Armenian affairs is quite enough to undermine completely the political loyalty of any thinking person who has any regard for humanity and civilization. Every German cannot be expected to bear as lightheartedly as the diplomats of Pera the shame of having history point to the fact that the annihilation, with every refinement of cruelty, of a people of high social development, numbering over one and a half million, was contemporaneous with Germany's greatest power in Turkey"[237] (*Um die Armenierfrage in ganz demselben Sinne zu beantworten, wie ich es hier tue, braucht man nicht die geringste Vorliebe, ja nicht einmal irgendwelche Sympathie für diese Rasse zu empfinden. (Ich habe angedeutet, dass sie mindestens durch ihre hohen geistigen und kulturellen Fähigkeiten solche durchaus verdient). Man braucht nur ein Gefühl für Menschlichkeit zu haben, um niemals die Art und Weise hinzunehmen, wie mit Hunderttausenden aus diesem unglücklichen Volke verfahren wurde ... man braucht nur die Augen aufzumachen und die Tatsachen zu sehen und sich als wahrhaft gebildeter*

Mensch von Idiosynkrasie gegen eine Rasse freizuhalten, um niemals das zu glauben, was die Türken der Welt über die Armenier weismachen wollen, um sie dann in aller Ruhe ausrotten zu können; und man braucht nur als Deutscher ein leises Gefühl von Würde zu empfinden, um die erbärmliche Feigheit unserer Regierung in der Armenierfrage nicht ohne Schamröte hinzunehmen. Das Gemisch von Gewissenlosigkeit, Feigheit und Kurzsichtigkeit aber, dessen unsere Regierung sich in der Sache der Armenier schuldig gemacht hat, kann allein schon genügen, um die politische Loyalität eines denkenden Menschen, dem an Menschlichkeit und Zivilisation etwas liegt, vollständig zu untergraben. Es ist eben nicht jedes Deutschen Sache, so leichten Herzens wie jene Herren Diplomaten von Pera [Istanbul] die Schande zu ertragen, dass die Weltgeschichte die Tatsache verzeichnen wird, dass die raffiniert grausame Vernichtung eines kulturell wertvollen Volks von anderthalb Millionen mit dem Zeitpunkt der stärksten deutschen Macht in der Türkei zusammenfiel).

* * *

These utterances carry considerable weight in several respects. First of all there is the statement that the author came to Turkey with marked sympathies for the new Young Turk Ittihadist regime which had begun its career with conjurations for constitutionalism and the ideals of equality, freedom and justice for all. In the same vein, the author states that he had no such positive or Armenophile sentiments inasmuch as he knew very little about the Armenians. Thus, the favorable prejudices he entertained about the new leaders of Turkey, proved untenable. As a result, the prejudices are not only discarded but they are supplanted by denunciations of that regime. Such a drastic shift in attitude is indicative of the gravity of the disappointment involved and of the magnitude of the regime's abuses associated with that disappointment.

As a rule prejudices are resistant to change and even to modification; it takes the experience of considerable letdown, pique, or shame for someone to forsake them. In his account of the string of disappointments that shocked him, Dr. Stürmer emphasizes the broad spectrum of people, including diplomats and German military officers stationed in Turkey during the war, whom he interviewed in order to grasp the reasons for the ongoing deportations and massacres of the Armenians. As far as it is known, no other newspaperman, foreign or local, conducted this type of investigative journalism pertaining to that grim and in many respects treacherous subject in wartime Turkey. In this sense, his report has the attribute of some kind of empirical research that is as daring as revealing.

In order to appreciate this fact one has to be mindful of the many other journalists, especially those from Germany, who either avoided the subject or conveniently relied on official Turkish accounts, denials or outright falsehoods.

But even the most seasoned and astute journalist at times may confront situations where a keen appetite for factual reporting cannot be kept free from the emotions of ire and outrage; here, morality and factuality become inextricably intertwined. In the case under review here, the editor of the distinguished German newspaper, *die Kölnische Zeitung,* confronted a situation which defied the norms of pure objectivity in reporting; the infernal character of that situation, in fact, became a defining moment for him and resulted in his eventual resignation from his post and in his subsequent retirement to Switzerland. Because of its critical import for the understanding of Stürmer as a maverick German journalist, the episode in question is detailed below in his own words.

> One day in the summer of 1916 my wife went out alone about midday to buy something in the *Grand Rue de Péra*. We lived a few steps from Galata-Seraï and had plenty of opportunity from our balcony of seeing the bands of Armenian deportees arriving at the police-station under the escort of gendarmes. Familiarity with such sights finally dulled our sympathies, and we began to think of them not as episodes affecting human individuals, but rather as political events.
>
> On this particular day, however, my wife came back to the house trembling all over. She had not been able to go on her errand. As she passed the *karakol,* she had heard through the open hall door the agonising groans of a tortured being, a dull wailing like the sound of an animal being tormented to death. "An Armenian," she was informed by the people standing at the door. The crowd was then dispersed by a policeman.
>
> "If such scenes occur in broad daylight in the busiest part of the European town of Pera, I should like to know what is done to Armenians in the uncivilised Interior," my wife asked me. "If the Turks act like wild beasts here in the capital, so that a woman going through the main streets gets a shock like that to her nerves, then I can't live in this frightful country." And then she burst into a fit of sobbing and let loose all her pent-up passion against what she and I had had to witness for more than a year every time we set a foot out of doors.
>
> "You are brutes, you Germans, miserable brutes, that you tolerate this from the Turks when you still have the country absolutely in your hands. You are cowardly brutes, and I will never set foot in your horrible country again. God, how I hate Germany!"

It was then, when my own wife, trembling and sobbing, in grief, rage, and disgust at such cowardliness, flung this denunciation of my country in my teeth that I finally and absolutely broke with Germany. Unfortunately I had known only too long that it had to come.[238]

An einem Sommertag 1916 gegen Mittag ging meine Frau, um etwas einzukaufen, allein in die Grand' Rue de Péra. *Wir wohnten ein paar Schritte von Galata-Seraï und hatten täglich vom Balkon aus genügend Gelegenheit, die Gruppen unglücklicher armenischer Deportierter unter Gendarmerieeskorte die Polizeiwache betreten zu sehen. Man wird schliesslich auch gegen solche traurigen Anblicke abgestumpft und sieht zuletzt darin kaum mehr das menschliche Einzelschicksal, sondern fast nur noch das Politische. Dieses Mal aber kam nach wenigen Minuten meine junge Frau am ganzen Körper zitternd wieder zurück in die Wohnung. Sie hatte ihren Weg nicht fortsetzen können. Am* Karakol *vorbeigehend, hörte sie aus dem offenen Vestibül die klagenden Töne eines Gefolterten, dumpfes Stöhnen wie von einem halb schon zu Tode gequälten agonisierenden Tiere. "Ein Armenier," gab einer von dem am Eingang Stehenden meiner Frau zur Auskunft. Dann wurde die Menge von einem Polizisten weggejagt. "Wenn solche Szenen am hellen Mittag am belebtesten Punkt der Europäerstadt Pera vorkommen, dann möchte ich wissen, was man mit den armen Armeniern im unzivilisierten Innern treibt," frug mich meine Frau. "Wenn die Türken sich hier in der Hauptstadt wie wilde Tiere benehmen, so dass eine Frau, die durch die Hauptstrasse geht, einen Nervenchok bekommt, dann kann ich nicht leben in diesem furchtbaren Lande!" Und dann brach sie, laut schluchzend, in ihrer furchtbaren Empörung los, die sie angesammelt über alles das, was sie seit mehr als einem Jahre, so oft sie auch nur den Fuss auf die Strasse setzte, mit mir zusammen hatte ansehen müssen: "Ihr seid Schweine, ihr Deutschen, erbärmliche Schweine seid ihr, dass ihr das bei den Türken duldet, wo ihr das Land doch vollständig in der Hand habt, feige Schweine seid ihr, und nie will ich jemals wieder den Fuss in euer verfluchtes Land setzen. O Gott, wie ich Deutschland hasse!" In diesem Augenblick, wo meine eigene Frau, vor Schmerz, Empörung und Ekel über so viel Feigheit laut schluchzend und zitternd, mir den nationalen Fluch ins Gesicht schleuderte, habe ich mit Deutschland innerlich gebrochen. Gewusst hatte ich ja leider schon seit lange genug!*

When predicated on faulty understanding, however, moralistic indignation is not only useless but can also be quite misleading. Indeed, unless the underlying elements of such "immoral" conduct are adequately assessed, the act of condemnation is reduced to a preoccupation with mere symptoms; the result is that the quest for remedies becomes misdirected and the malaise persists. In condemning his government and its civilian and military representatives in wartime Turkey, Stürmer emphasized and even overemphasized the idea of cowardice. This is a misdiagnosis of the core of the problem as it fails to recognize the essence of German motivation and confounds it with its deceptive appearance. As noted earlier, the cumulative evidence developed in this study points to the existence of a firm German policy, forged at the highest levels of the government, to allow and, whenever required, to assist, as unobtrusively as possible, in the implementation of a Turkish scheme to eliminate the Armenians in Turkey by way of exploiting the opportunities afforded by World War I. The Zimmermann-Wangenheim political combination on the one hand, and the cooperation of the German High Command with the Ottoman General Headquarters, on the other, were the main factors which helped carry out that policy, with General Bronsart, Navy Lieutenant Commander Humann, and Marshal von der Goltz acting as principal facilitators.

A FINAL COMMENTARY ON THE ISSUE OF GERMAN RESPONSIBILITY

By any definition, a crime, resulting from an act of conspiracy of one kind or another, does not easily lend itself to probing and, consequently, to the establishment of probative evidence; uncertainties and ambiguities often surround the crime. In fact these are part of the makeup of the act of conspiracy itself; often they are deliberately created and structured so as to avoid or encumber detection and apprehension or to deflect them. Furthermore, one is dealing here with sets of records that are quintessential state secrets; they have the potential to prove highly compromising, if not inculpatory, as far as the reputations of the governments of both Turkey and Germany are concerned. The wartime destruction of the Ottoman Armenian population clearly involved a secret scheme. Despite the incidence of certain ambiguities, the realities of a Turko-German political and military alliance are significant and illuminating enough to overcome measurably the problem these ambiguities tend to create. To be considered in this respect are: the condition of the secrecy of the genesis of that alliance; the close cooperation at the Ottoman General Headquarters between Turkish officers, especially War Minister Enver on the one hand and high-ranking German officers on the other; and the evidence that the deportation of the victim population was the result of the pressures and initiatives of these military leaders. These are paramount considerations. They favor the acceptance of the view that German authorities cannot entirely be seen as divorced from a degree of involvement in the decision-making processes relating to the deportations and massacres. This view becomes even more plausible when one brings to bear upon the inquiry a historical perspective focusing on the distinct and aberrant conduct of German authorities in the face of and, particularly, in the aftermath of the 1894–1896 Abdul Hamit-era Armenian massacres. Oblivious to the revulsion and ire of the rest of Europe, William II chose to indulge the Sultan and his regime; the empirewide, organized bloodbaths failed to make a dent on the direction of his pro-Turkish policy. In the fall of 1898 he was boastfully reiterating this fact, declaring, "… I am the only one who still sticks by the Sultan."[239] Nor was he devoid of any rationale he needed to justify such callous behavior. He considered it as useful to be serpentine in his dealings with people as he equally considered it virtuous to be as harmless as doves. Quoting from the Bible, he equated such serpentine behavior with an exercise of wisdom.[240] This resort to a studied indulgence of "the Red Sultan" served its intended purpose. It brought the two monarchs even closer to each other as German prestige in Turkey began to gain ascendancy; attendant economic dividends, accruing to German industry, began to proliferate in the markets of the empire ruled by Abdul Hamit. The latter was more than happy to reward the German emperor for "his benevolent attitude" (*wohlwollende Haltung*) during the massacres for which attitude the Sultan "once more expresses his gratitude. The entire Turkish nation shares this sentiment." The Turkish monarch had sent General Şakir, his Aide-de-Camp, to Saurma, the German ambassador to Turkey, to convey this feeling of gratefulness.[241] This "benevolent attitude" of the Kaiser became once more manifest a few years later. Malakia Ormanian, the Patriarch of the Armenians of Turkey, had pleaded with the German ambassador to induce the German monarch "to bring his powerful influence to bear upon the Sultan for the benefit of the suffering [Armenian] population." In rebuffing, the Kaiser wrote this marginalia on the report of Ambassador Marschal, "Doesn't concern me" (*Geht mich nichts an*).[242] As if to demonstrate the inexorableness of this stance the Kaiser during the apex of the Adana massacre in April 1909, questioned the necessity of sending German cruisers to deter the Turkish perpetrators. In the mistaken belief that the lives of Germans were in danger, he had approved the dispatch of two cruisers. Upon learning, however, that there was no such danger for the Germans, he became irritated at the false report and exclaimed, "why send then two cruisers. The Armenians [being killed] are of no concern to us" (*die Armenier gehen uns nichts an!*)[243]

The ambiguities alluded to earlier are further dissipated at two other levels of consideration; they refer to concrete German attempts at concealing any role the German military might have played in the deportation of the Armenians. The case of Lieutenant Colonel Boettrich's indiscretion and the ensuing panicky reaction of the German Foreign Office has been examined earlier. The vehemence of that reaction did not so much attach to the cooperation of Boettrich with his Turkish colleagues at the headquarters on the authorization of the deportation of a particular segment of the Armenian population but rather to his foolishness to reveal his active role by placing his signature on the respective order. The postwar efforts by German authorities to remove or withhold pertinent files and documents or alter or modify portions of documents have also been examined earlier. The significance of these attempts and efforts is twofold. First, they contradict the spirit and the letter of the series of protests the German government dutifully lodged with the Turkish government, thereby exposing the pro-forma character (and the allied intent to create a basis for postwar alibis) of these diplomatic remonstrances and protests. Second, they betray certain anxieties that imply a sense of fear of discovery of complicity, if not genuine guilt. In the absence of such anxieties, the procedure warranting credibility is to let the records speak for themselves—without any interference and resort to a variety of methods to "handle" them.

The condition of the relevant records in terms of their complete accessibility was and is a factor that continues to pose a problem at another level. That level refers to the formidable obstructions resulting from the Turkish denial syndrome. The persistence with which the Turks continue to deny the historical fact of the Armenian genocide has served the intended purpose to reduce the genocide to a controversy and in the process to obfuscate the central issues of that Armenian genocide, including the issue of German involvement through the complicity of certain German officials. No party can afford to confirm the possession of any pertinent records on a crime whose very occurrence it sees fit to negate. Hence, the issue of German complicity is reduced to irrelevance as far as the Turks are concerned, even though they may concede that there is complicity only at the level of the problem of deportations, as distinct from a deliberate act of genocide. This conditional concession is as specious and untenable, however, as the undergirding argument that the anti-Armenian measures merely involved deportations for the sole purpose of wartime temporary relocations. As reiterated throughout this study, however, the real purpose of an undertaking is best gauged by the actual outcome of that undertaking and not by the label appended to that undertaking in order to mask its purpose. The label "deportation" was meant to mask the intended destruction of the victim population ostensibly being merely deported and relocated.

For reasons described earlier the issue of German complicity has ultimately to be resolved in relation to the position of William II as the supreme instance of German authority. He was vested with requisite powers to prescribe or proscribe, to allow or to disallow, to exercise control or to relax control over certain of the patterns of the behavior of his representatives—patterns that could have consequences for the fate of a minority facing annihilation by a close ally of Germany. In other words, he was not only responsible for his own conduct but also for the conduct of his subalterns. As far as these subalterns are concerned, the available evidence on the matter of directly ordering the deportation of the Armenians is such as to overshadow the issue of mere complicity and directly inculpate two high ranking German military officers, namely, General Major Bronsart and Lieutenant Colonel Boettrich, as actual or first-degree perpetrators (see earlier in this Part II of the study.) Those German officers who one way or another participated in consultations or deliberations leading up to the decision to deport the Armenians are liable to the charge of co-conspirators, especially Marshal von der Goltz and Lieutenant Colonel Feldmann.

These are but the known cases where the evidence is direct, authentic, and verifiable, as far as the deportations are concerned. The web of indirect evidence, however, is no less significant. As underscored throughout this study, the nature of the crime warrants a degree of reliance on indirect evidence or, in legal-technical language, circumstantial evidence. Criminal law and justice has always allowed the marshaling of such evidence in the presence of unusual conditions such as the gravity of a crime and the quality of the ensemble of the pieces of circumstantial evidence. The wealth of fragments of testimony by American ambassador Morgenthau on admirals Usedom, Souchon, Navy Lieutenant Commander Humann, and on Ambassador Wangenheim, committed to writing through daily entries in his diary, may in some quarters be subject to dispute. But the string of ciphers he sent to Washington at the time the events were unfolding and the array of corroborative evidence from a host of diverse and independent sources, including Trabzon's Austrian consul Kwiatkowski and German intelligence operative Oswald von Schmidt, is too compelling to doubt the veracity of Morgenthau's accounts or to discount the relevance and significance of the corpus of circumstantial evidence or to question its reliability. One is faced here with a configuration of bids of evidence, from sources that are as diverse as they are independent from each other, including an incriminating statement attributed by British Intelligence to the emperor. In all this material the quantity of diverse sources and data tends to acquire qualitative value, thereby rendering the sources even more credible and compelling.

What stands out in that evidence is a central feature of German complicity, namely, the willingness of a number of German officials, civilian and military, to aid and abet the Turks in their drive to liquidate the Armenians. They thus qualify to be regarded as co-perpetrators and "accessories to the crime," the bearers of the onus of what the Germans call "*Mitschuld*" (i.e., complicity). Subsumed in this general category of inculpation are those German officers who actually signed deportation orders and as such are in fact co-perpetrators; additionally to be considered are, however, the two major variants depicting the twin modalities of German involvement. One is described as "suggestion" (*Anregung*); the involvement here is active as the actor is seen taking the initiative to sensitize or incite the Turks against the Armenians. The other is in the form of consent (*Zusage*); the actor is in a passive role as he merely is responding, albeit positively, to the scheme presented to him by the Turks. This notwithstanding, the difference is such as to subside into insignificance, if not irrelevance, when one considers the oneness of the consequence resulting from the underlying indistinguishability of both types of roles, namely, the role of unscrupulous abettors in the Turkish enactment of the genocide against the Armenians.

Still in bondage to the shackles of obdurate atavism and still profiting from the fruits of the negative reward (i.e., the impunity accruing to it), Turkey may continue for a while to deny any and all culpability. The expectations from Germany in this respect are rightly of a different order for it has demonstrated a capacity for redemption, a large measure of which it attained with respect to the cataclysm of the Holocaust. Such a capacity cannot be separated, however, from another level of consideration. It concerns the underlying commitment to the quest for unmitigated truth, extending to and, at the same time, punctuating the tragic fate of another but less potent and influential victim nation. Perhaps the historians and perhaps even the statesmen of Germany will find it pertinent and seemly to reconsider the central issue raised here. In the final analysis what is at stake here is the triumph of the forces of civilization over a legacy of barbarism that almost succeeded in bringing about the extirpation of an ancient nation.[244]

Notes to Part II

1. *Russian Imperial Archives* (St. Petersburg). Ministerstvo Inostranikh Del. Spornik diplomaticheskikh dokumentof. Reformee v Armenyee, 26 noiabria 1912 goda—10 maia 1914 goda. (*The Orange Book*). Collection of Diplomatic Documents. The Reform in Armenia. November 26, 1912 to May 10, 1914. (Hereafter cited as *DAR*). (1915). Docs. No. 8, 22, 32.
2. André Mandelstam, *Le sort de L'Empire Ottoman* (Lausanne, 1917), 236, 243.
3. Carl Mühlmann, "Deutschland und die Türkei 1913–1914." *Politische Wissenschaft* 7 (1929): 70–80.
4. *Ibid.*, 39–43; A. A. Türkei 142/40, A21135, Wangenheim to the Foreign Office, September 8, 1914; *ibid.*, A25509, his October 6, 1914 report.
5. Joseph Pomiankowski, *Der Zusammenbruch des Ottomanischen Reiches* (Graz, 1969), 54–55; A. A. Türkei, No. 139/39, (Überlassung) report No. 123, January 29, 1916. According to a report sent to Berlin on November 2, 1914, by Hans Humann, Navy Lieutenant Commander and Marine Attaché at the German Embassy in the Ottoman capital, the Russians sustained the following losses resulting from this incursion into the Black Sea by the combined Turko-German fleet. The German battle cruiser *Goeben* bombarded the docks at Sevastapol causing a considerable number of fires. It also sank the mine-layer *Pruth* with 700 mines and 250 men aboard. The German light cruiser *Breslau,* and *Berk* bombarded Novorossisk while the Turkish *Hamidiye* bombarded Theodosia, after issuing an unsuccessful ultimatum to the Russians demanding the surrender of all serviceable ships intended for military purposes. The *Breslau* and *Nilufer*, and the *Samsun* also laid mines in several places. And the *Nilufer* brought in 121 prisoners. A total of 21 ships were destroyed and 55 oil tanks and many grain warehouses shot up in flames. All ships of the attacking combined naval armada returned safely. Jackh, *The Rising Crescent* [n. 136], 117–118. The role of these two German warships, the *Goeben* and *Breslau*, in the intensification and prolongation of the war, including the launching of the Armenian genocide, which coincided with the failure of the Allied naval armada to force the Straits and destroy these warships, was substantial. In commenting on it Winston Churchill observed that their entering the Dardanelles caused "more slaughter, more misery and more ruin than has ever before been borne within the compass of a ship." Winston Churchill, *The Aftermath.* vol. 4, *The World Crisis* (New York, 1929), 271.
6. Şevket Süreyya Aydemir, *Makedonyadan Ortaasya'ya Enver Paşa* (Enver Paşa. From Macedonia to Central Asia) vol. 2 (Istanbul, 1971). On pp. 531–35, the author describes a scene of such deliberate pampering. It seems that the Emperor wanted to inflate Enver's ego through a public display of preferential treatment at a banquet he had staged for that purpose. He had seated Enver at the head of the table, which was reserved for the principal guest of the evening, and offered the following rationale to the other attachés present: "You have higher ranks than Enver, but he will soon be catapulted into the position of head of a great empire. That is why I accorded him the honor of principal guest." Following the banquet, William II picked him out, locked arms, and nudging him into an adjoining room, declared, "Enver, I will furnish you all the assistance you may ask after you take charge." Burhan Oğuz, *Yüzyıllar Boyunca Alman Gerçeği Ve Türkler* (The German Reality Throughout Centuries) (Istanbul, 1983) 265.
7. Ali Ihsan Sabis, *Harb Hatıralarım* (My War Memoirs), vol. 1 (Istanbul, 1943) 130–32; idem, vol. 2 (Ankara, 1951), 68, 101; Kâzım Karabekir, *Istiklâl Harbimizde Enver Paşa ve Ittihat Terakki Erkânı* (Enver Paşa and the Leadership of Ittihad ve Terakki During the Independence War) (Istanbul, 1967), 139.
8. Kâzım Karabekir, *Istiklâl Harbimizin Esasları* (The Essentials of Our Independence War) (Istanbul, 1933–1951), 23–24.
9. Ahmet Izzet Paşa, *Feryadım* (My Lamentation) vol. 1 (Istanbul, 1992), 94.
10. Şevket Süreyya Aydemir, *Ikinci Adam* (Second Man) vol. 1, 3rd ed. (Istanbul, 1973), 86.
11. Alptekin Müderrisoğlu, *Sarıkamış Dramı* (The Drama of Sarıkamış) vol. 1 (Istanbul, 1988), 193.

12. Kâzım Karabekir, *Birinci Cihan Harbine Nasıl Girdik?* (How Did We Enter World War I) vol. 2 (Istanbul, 1994), 159; Sabis, *Harb* [n. 7], vol. 2, 114–15.
13. *Sabah*, December 12, 1919; Fuat Balkan, "Beş Albaylar" (Five Colonels) *Yakın Tarihimiz* 2 (1926): 297; Mehmed Zeki, *Raubmörder als Gäste der deutschen Republik* (Berlin, 1920), 35.
14. Vahakn N. Dadrian, "The Secret Young-Turk Ittihadist Conference and the Decision for the World War I Genocide of the Armenians" *Holocaust and Genocide Studies* 7, 2 (Fall 1993): 173–201.
15. Jehuda L. Wallach, *Anatomie einer Militärhilfe. Die preussisch-deutschen Militärmissionen in der Türkei 1835–1919* (Düsseldorf, 1976), 268.
16. The reference to deportations for France and Belgium is in Fritz Fischer, *Griff nach der Weltmacht* (Düsseldorf, 1967), 99.
17. Grand Admiral von Tirpitz, *My Memoirs.* vol. 2 (New York, 1919), 329.
18. *German Foreign Ministry Archives.* (*Die Diplomatischen Akten des Auswärtigen Amtes*) Die Grosse Politik der Europäischen Kabinette 1871–1914 (Hereafter cited as *DAG*) vol. 12 (2), Doc. No. 3339, "Confidential" report No. 57, p. 562. March 5, 1898.
19. C. Freiherrn von der Goltz, "Stärke und Schwäche des türkischen Reiches" (The Strength and Weakness of the Turkish Empire) *Deutsche Rundschau.* XXIV, 1 (October 1897): 104, 106, 109, 110, 118.
20. Goltz, *Denkwürdigkeiten* [n. 61], 111–12.
21. René Pinon, *La Suppression des Arméniens. Méthode allemande-travail turc* (Paris, 1916), 12–3.
22. Henry Morgenthau, *Ambassador Morgenthau's Story* (Garden City, N. Y., 1918), 366–67. The article was written by Max Hoschiller, and appeared in the March 29, 1916, issue of the French newspaper.
23. Zaven Archbishop, *Badriarkagan Housherus. Vaverakirner yev Vugayutiunner* (My Patriarchal Memoirs. Documents and Testimonies) (Cairo, 1947), 104. *See also* A. S. Baronigian, *Blicke ins Märtyrerland* (Lössnitzgrund i. Sachsen, 1921), 3, 4, 6.
24. A. A. Türkei 183/39, A28384, enclosure No. 2, August 5, 1915.
25. Rev. Krikoris Balakian, *Hai Koghkotan. Trouakner Hai Mardirosakroutiunen. Berlinen Tebee Zor 1914–1920* (The Armenian Golgotha. Episodes from the Armenian Martyrilogy. From Berlin to Zor 1914–1920) vol. 1 (Vienna, 1922), 32–3. The author was a Berlin-educated Armenian priest, a survivor of the genocide, who subsequently became the Primate of the Armenian Diocese of Manchester and later Marseille, France. Upon the outbreak of the war he returned to Constantinople and was among those Armenian leaders who on April 24, 1915 were arrested and deported to be destroyed. But through the assistance of a German major he escaped and survived.
26. "Dzerougee Hishadagneru 1915–1918" (The Memoirs of Dzeroug 1915–1918). *Djagadamard* (namesake of *Azadamard,* organ of the Dashnak party, a daily in Istanbul, which often was closed down by the Turkish authorities and reappeared temporarily under new names) March 2, 1919 issue.
27. Cemal Kutay, *Talât Paşanın Gurbet Hatıraları* (The Memoirs of Talât Paşa in Exile) vol. 3 (Istanbul, 1983), 1197.
28. *Talât Paşanın Hatıraları* (The Memoirs of Talât Paşa), E. Bolayır, ed. (Istanbul, 1946), 63–64.
29. Cemal Kutay, *Osmanlıdan Cumhuriyete. Yüzyılımızda Bir Insanımız* (From the Ottoman to the Republic Era. Our Man of the Century). *Hüseyin Rauf Orbay (1881–1964).* vol. 4 (Istanbul, 1992), 317.
30. *Ibid.,* vol. 3, p. 610.
31. Aubrey Herbert, "Talât Pasha" *Blackwood's Magazine.* CCXIII (April, 1923): 426, 436. *See also* idem, *Ben Kendim. A Record of Eastern Travel.* 2d. ed. (London, 1924), 309.
32. Zaven, *Badriarkagan* [n. 23], 98.
33. FO 371/9158/E5523, folios 106–7, British High Commissioner Nevile Henderson's May 22, 1923 dispatch.

34. In the orders issued during the Abdul Hamit era massacres the same word *şedide* was used to convey the sense of massacre being inflicted upon the victims as a method of exterminatory terror. J. Lepsius, *Armenien und Europa* (Berlin, 1897), 125.
35. Dr. Salahi Sonyel, *Displacement of the Armenians. Documents* (pamphlet) (Ankara, 1978), 1 (A reprint from *Belleten*, a Turkish Historical Society Publication. No other detail is provided).
36. *Austrian Foreign Ministry Archives*. Vienna. PA 12. Karton 380, Zl.21, folio 209. May 26, 1917 report of Austrian Consul General Kwiatkowski.
37. A. A. Türkei 183/44, A24663, enclosure No. 3. The English translation of portions of this report is in *Germany, Turkey and Armenia* (A selection of documentary evidence relating to the Armenian atrocities from German and other sources) (London, 1917), 80–85.
38. *Ibid.*, 183/38, A28019, K. No. 90/B. No. 1950, enclosure No. 1.
39. Rafael de Nogales, *Four Years Beneath the Crescent* Muna Lee, trans. (New York, 1926), 141, 150.
40. Morgenthau, *Ambassador* [n. 22], 303–04.
41. A. A. Türkei 142/41, A27535. Report No. 241. October 16, 1914.
42. *See* note 35.
43. Liman von Sanders, *Five Years in Turkey* (Annapolis, 1927), 2, 3.
44. A. A. Bonn. Göppert Papers (*Nachlass*) vol. VI, file 5 (files 1–8), p. 4, February 10, 1919.
45. *German Federal Military Archive* (Freiburg at Breisgau) BA. MA. MSg, 1/2039, from his diary. Cited in Christoph Dinkel, "German Officers and the Armenian Genocide" *Armenian Review* 44, 1/173 (Spring 1991): 103.
46. Morgenthau, *Ambassador* [n. 22], 148.
47. A. A. Türkei 168/15. August 3, 1916, report of General L. v. Sanders.
48. General Sanders' and German ambassador Metternich's, August 3 and 4, 1916, negative responses are in *ibid.*
49. A. A. *Botschaft Konstantinopel.* 434, I 5255/17. Grosses Hauptquartier No. 15994. October 5, 1917.
50. Fethi Okyar, *Üç Devirde Bir Adam* (A Man Across Three Eras) C. Kutay, ed. (Istanbul, 1980), 251.
51. Mithat Şükrü Bleda, *Imparatorluğun Çöküşü* (The Collapse of the Empire) (Istanbul, 1979), 124.
52. Kapitänleutnant a. D. Baltzer, "Das romantische Ende der drei grossen Türken der Kriegszeit, Talaat, Enver und Dschemal Pascha. Eine Erinnerung an den 1. November 1918" *Orient-Rundschau* (November 10, 1933), 121–22.
53. Mehmed Zeki, *Raubmörder als Gäste der deutschen Republik.* Part I (Berlin-Wilmersdorf, 1920), 24.
54. Pomiankowski, *Der Zusammenbruch* [n. 5], 216–17.
55. Cemal Kutay, *Siyasi Mahkûmlar Adası: Malta* (Malta: The Island for the Politically Condemned People) (Istanbul, 1963), 228.
56. Okyar, *Üç Devirde* [n. 50], 93–4.
57. This assessment comes from one of the top secret service agents of the fledgeling Turkish Republic with close ties to a surviving Special organization administrative director, Hüsameddin Ertürk. Galib Vardar, *Ittihad ve Terakki Içinde Dönenler* (The Inside Story of Ittihad ve Terakki Party) S. N. Tansu, ed. (Istanbul, 1960), 275–76.
58. *Ibid.*, 120–122. It appears that Talât had sent to the ex-monarch a list of questions which Fethi Okyar had taken to Saloniki where the former was being kept in a villa, in a sort of house arrest, with Okyar serving as the commander of the special guard detail. Upon completing his responses and Okyar taking them back to Istanbul, Talât invited a small group of his Ittihadist cronies, including Secretary-General Mithat Şükrü, the two doctors Nazım and B. Şakir, Enver, Ömer Naci and Yenibahçeli Nail, to his home where the reponses were read out for the purpose of a general discussion. In this sense Dr. Nazım's reaction is noteworthy. He expressed his rage at the fact that "he is supplying a prescription for our woes and we are not daring to ask him why he himself didn't solve the problem during his rule of 30 years or so." p. 121.

59. *See* note 27.
60. Dinkel, "German Officers" [n. 45], 79.
61. Colmar Freiherr von der Goltz, *Denkwürdigkeiten* (Memoirs) Friedrich v. d. Goltz, W. Foerster eds. (Berlin, 1929), 393, n. 1; Sanders [n. 43], 49, 133.
62. Dinkel, "German Officers" [n. 45], 80–01.
63. The affidavit is typed in French and comprises 11 pp. and an Annex of 4 pp; it also lists the names of the perpetrators of that mass murder, their residence and their positions and ranks. It was prepared on December 20, 1918 in Aleppo and was sent to the Armenian Patriarchate in Istanbul. The authors are M.D. Ph. Hovnanian, and railroad master builders Vartivar Kabayan and Garabed Gueukdjeian. Nubar Library Archive (Paris). Archives du Patriarcat de Constantinople (APC), Documents Officiels et Rapports (DOR), 4/3. file No. 5 on Amanos. The quotation is from pp. 3–4.
64. Kutay, *Talât* [n. 27], 120.
65. Goltz, *Denkwürdigkeiten* [n. 61], 428.
66. *Ibid.*, 444–45, n.1.
67. *Ibid.*, 428.
68. Wallach, *Anatomie* [n. 15], 233.
69. *Ibid.*, 228.
70. A. A. *Grosses Hauptquarier*, vol. 191, 41/6, Registry No. 1405, June 22, 1918. *See also* the scathing criticism of Navy Lieutenant Commander Büchsel, who in 37 typed pages dissects and evaluates the shortcomings and defects of Turkish society as problems spilling over into the Turkish military. *Bundesarchiv-Militärarchiv*, (hereafter B. M.) Bestand RM 5/V.1571. Berlin, June 30, 1916.
71. A. A. Türkei, 183/40, A36184. Registry No. 711, p. 3 of the report..
72. B. M. [n. 70], N247/202 c. November 4, 1918.
73. Wallach, *Anatomie* [n. 15], 228.
74. *Ibid.,* 150.
75. A. A. Türkei, 158/18, A 36878. November 3, 1917.
76. Frank G. Weber, *Eagles on the Crescent—Germany, Austria, and the Diplomacy of the Turkish Alliance 1914–1918* (Ithaca, 1970), 112.
77. *Austrian Foreign Ministry Archives*. Vienna. (Hereafter cited as *DAA*) P. A. 1. Karton Rot. 947 (f). Secret report No. 5139, cipher No. 189.
78. Wallach, *Anatomie* [n. 15], 46, 48, 54.
79. *Ibid.,* 105.
80. Burhan Oğuz, *Yüzyıllar Boyunca Alman Gerçeği ve Türkler* [n. 6], 90; Walter Goerlitz, *History of the German General Staff*, B. Battershaw, trans. (New York, 1953), 87, 88, 90.
81. Paul Rohrbach, *Vom Kaukasus zum Mittelmeer. Eine Hochzeits—und Studienrise durch Armenien* (Berlin, 1903), 51–52.
82. Ilber Ortaylı, *Osmanlı Imparatoluğunda Alman Nüfuzu* (The German Influence in the Ottoman Empire) (Istanbul, 1983), 55, 79, 80.
83. *Ibid., 78–9.* The Turkish author notes that the Ottoman authorities somehow got hold of this very incriminating letter which, according to the author, is presently deposited at *Başbakanlık Arşivi.* Yıldız Section. file 15. folios 74–81.
84. Count Alfred von Waldersee, *Denkwürdigkeiten,* H. O. Meisner, ed. vol. 1 (1923), 222, 232. Quoted in Wilhelm von Kampen, *Studien zur Deutschen Türkeipolitik in der Zeit Wilhelm II.* (Kiel, 1968, Ph. dissertation), 18.
85. Wallach, *Anatomie* [n. 15], 172.
86. *Allgemeine Missions-Zeitschrift* (monthly, published by Professor Julius Richter and J. Warneck) (June 30, 1921), quoted in Dinkel, "German Officers" [n. 45], 26.
87. Carl Mühlmann, *Das deutsch-türkische Waffenbündnis im Weltkriege* (Leipzig, 1940), 292.
88. Boettrich's order is in A. A. *Grosses Hauptquartier*, vol. 194, Türkei 41/I, A32610, registry No. 6882, enclosure No. 3, October 3, 1915, folios 137, 138. *See also* A. A. Botschaft Konstantinopel, K 171, v. 24.

89. The description of this slaughter of the Armenian workers of the Baghdad Railway is provided by the Swiss pharmacist of the area, Jakob Künzler, *Im Lande des Blutes und der Tränen. Erlebnisse in Mesopotamien während des Weltkrieges* (Potsdam-Berlin, 1921), 76. *See also* the following German official reports involving similar atrocities in areas transited by the Baghdad Railway. A. A. 183/38, A23991; 183/38, A28019; 183/44, A24663.
90. Weber, *Eagles on the Crescent* [n. 76], 145.
91. Ulrich Trumpener, *Germany and the Ottoman Empire 1914–1918* (Princeton, 1968), 285, 299, 306.
92. The document, dated October 3, 1915, was discovered by the officials of the British High Commissioner in Istanbul during the Armistice and was promptly sent to London with a translated version. FO 371/5265/E7556, July 22, 1920. The Günther's letter itself is dated October 28, 1915.
93. A. A. *Grosses Hauptquartier*, [n. 88], Registry No. 209, folio 136, November 13, 1916.
94. *Ibid.,* folios 139–40, November 19, 1915. Trumpener, *Germany* [n. 91], 299.
95. *Ibid.,* folio 140, Treutler's communication.
96. Richard von Kühlmann, *Erinnerungen* (Memoirs) (Heidelberg, 1948), 467.
97. A. A. Türkei 183/55, A4156, February 6, 1919 in Dr. Karl Axenfeld's report to General B. v. Schellendorf. *See also* Lüttichau's own report. *Ibid.*, 183/54. A44066, p. 8, of 20 pp. report, Summer 1918.
98. *Allgemeine Missions-Zeitschrift* (February 1919): 36.
99. Morgenthau, *Ambassador* [n. 22], 49, 365, 395.
100. Dinkel, "German Officers" [n. 45], 116.
101. General von Seeckt "Die Gründe des Zusammenbruchs der Türkei" in Wallach, *Anatomie* [n. 15], 260.
102. The Statesman was Reşit Akif Paşa who at the time was serving as Senator; he made the disclosure during the November 21, 1918 sitting of the Upper House of the Ottoman Parliament. Vahakn N. Dadrian, *The Armneian Genocide in Official Turkish Records.* Special Issue of *Journal of Political and Military Sociology.* Reprint (Spring 1995), 81. It originally appeared in vol. 22, No. 1, (Summer 1994), 8. *See also* idem., "The Naim-Andonian Documents on the World War I Destruction of Ottoman Armenians: The Anatomy of a Genocide," *International Journal of Middle East Studies* 18 (1986): 339, 355, n. 104.
103. Mühlmann, *Das Deutsch-Türkische* [n. 87], 273–74. These notions of panturanism and panturkism did not originate with Seeckt or the other contemporaries of his such as Tekin Alp. As far as it is known, it was first expounded by the first Prussian officer sent to Turkey to reform its army, namely, then colonel, Count Helmuth von Moltke, who as early as in 1842 urged the Turks to shift their attention from Europe to Asia where millions of their kinsmen were languishing under foreign domination and needed to be liberated and integrated in a vast Turkish empire. Anticipating Goltz by several decades (or Goltz echoing him), Moltke even suggested that they relocate the Ottoman capital in Konya, or further east, consolidating themselves in Anatolia—as a condition for their rejuvenation. Zarevand, *United and Independent Turania. Aims and Designs of the Turks.* V. N. Dadrian, trans. (Leiden, 1971), 20. Four decades later the Orientalist, Arminius Vambery, "the father of Panturkism," who for a while tutored young prince Abdul Hamit, and subsequently became one of the rarest confidants of the sultan, in his *Travels in Central Asia* advocated a similar eastern expansion, as a prerequisite for the erection of a viable and mighty Ottoman Empire, encompassing an array of more or less homogenous ethnic elements. The colossus which might rise up out of this integrative process, Vambery stated, could well measure itself against the other colossus in the North, i.e., Russia. *Ibid.,* 20–21. It should be noted that Goltz himself relied a great deal on a series of articles Vambery had published in *Cosmopolis* in the March, April and May 1897 isues, i.e., a few months before Goltz himself published his own in *Deutsche Rundschau*, as cited in note 19. Furthermore, Marschall von Bieberstein, German Foreign Minister (1890–96), and ambassador to Turkey (1897–1912), had forged the doctrine that

Turkey's future lie in Asiatic Turkey where German and Turksih national and economic interests converged and as such were to be treated by Germany as unaissalable, and as untouchable. Wangenheim, Marschall's successor in Istanbul, subscribed to and adopted the same doctrine.

104. Hans Meier-Welcker, *Seeckt* (Frankfurt am Main, 1967), 154, 622.
105. While serving in Turkey in the March-October, 1915 period, Major Wolffskeel wrote a number of letters to his family, especially to his wife and father. His suggestion on the need for the wholesale deportation of the Armenians is excerpted from his September 15, and the other on "internal Turkish matter" is excerpted from his October 16, 1915 letter. *German Federal Military Archive* [n. 119], Papers (*Nachlass*) Wolffskeel N138/2, N138/6. His remark on Armenians as being "traitors" was repeatedly made in the presence of a German eyewitness of the Urfa bloodbath. Bruno Eckart, *Meine Erlebnisse in Urfa* (Berlin-Potsdam, 1922), 27. Another eyewitness was the Swiss medic-pharmacist who observed the arrival in Urfa of Wolffskeel along with General Fahri, whose "German Adjutant" he was. Ida Alamuddin, *Papa Kuenzler and the Armenians* (London, 1970), 67. *See also* the work of another Swiss author who underscores the fact that Wolffskeel was in charge of "the Turkish battery that roared for days on end." Karl Meyer, *Armenien und die Schweiz* (Bern, 1974), 95. Still another Swiss author, a professor, who had investigated the matter by interviewing Swiss engineers associated with the Baghdad Railway construction work, described Wolffskeel's devastating role through German canons. His graphic description in the German original is cited in the text. A. A. Türkei 183/54, A38243, registry No. 2228, September 7, 1919 report of the lecture which was given by Prof. Ragaz. Finally reference may be made to a British subject who was interned in Urfa during the war as an enemy alien. He witnessed the carnage and in his report to the British Foreign Office he made repeated references to "the bombardments" directed against the Armenians and the role of "a German officer" in this onslaught. F0608/78/2610, February 10, 1919 report, folios 152–154.
106. Mühlmann, *Das Deutsch-Türkische* [n. 87], 251.
107. Dr. Veli Yılmaz, *1ci Dünya Harbinde Türk-Alman Ittifakı ve Askeri Yardımlar* (The World War I Turko-German Alliance and the Range of Military Assistnace) (Istanbul, 1993), 154–58.
108. Ernst Werner, "Ökonomishce und Militärische Aspekte der Türkei-Politik Österreich-Ungarns 1915 bis 1918" *Jahrbuch für Geschichte* 10 (1974): 396.
109. Morgenthau, *Ambassador* [n. 22], 102.
110. Wolfram W. Gottlieb, *Studies in Secret Diplomacy during the First World War* (London, 1957), 44.
111. Hasan Amca, *Doğmayan Hürriyet. Bir Devrin Iç Yüzü 1908–1918* (Freedom Unborn, The Inside Story of an Era 1908–1918) (Istanbul, 1958), 123, 155, 180.
112. A. A. Orientalia Generalia No. 5. secr. vol. 17, quoted in Kampen [n. 84], 348.
113. FO 371/4363. Confidential. Foreign Office Political Intelligence Department. May 25, 1918. Memorandum on the Present State of Mind in Turkey. The P. I. D. is particularly indebted to Sir H. Rumbolds' weekly reports and to another "sure source" for preparing this memo.
114. Yusuf Hikmet Bayur, *Türk Inkilâbı Tarihi* (History of the Turkish Revolution) vol. 3, part 4, (Ankara, 1983), 344.
115. Talcott Parsons, *Turkey. A Wold Problem of To-day* (Garden City, N.Y.), 196, 278, 301.
116. A. A. Türkei 158/13, A5135, cipher No. 72.
117. Fürst Bernhard von Bülow, *Denkwürdigkeiten*. vol. 2 (Berlin, 1930), 512.
118. Erich Eyck, *Das persönliche Regiment Wilhelms II: Politische Geschichte des deutschen Kaiserreiches von 1890 bis 1914* (Zürich, 1948), 682–83.
119. *German Federal Military Archive*. Bundesarchiv Militärarchiv. Kaiserliche Marine-Kabinets Archiv der Marine. RM 2/V. 1115, 4995/14. August 22, 1914.
120. Morgenthau, *Ambassador* [n. 22], 5, 6, 383. Two studies have at length discussed many of these areas. *See* Ulrich Trumpener, *Germany and the Ottoman Empire 1914–1918* (Princeton, 1968) and F. Weber *Eagles on the Crescent* (Ithaca, 1970).

121. *Grosses Hauptquartier*. vol. 185, Türkei 18, Registry No. 505, September 21, 1914, Wangenheim to Undersecretary Zimmermann.
122. *Ibid.*, 18/1, Registry No. 93. September 12, 1914. These details are more or less confirmed by Grand Vizier Said Halim who was being detained at Malta by the British for later trial on charges of complicity on crimes associated with the Armenian deportations and massacres. In his letter of protest from Malta Said Halim referred to "the treacherous staging by the Germans of the Black Sea incident which irretrievably compromised the neutrality of Turkey." FO 371/4174/127758, folios 408–09. The 8-page letter of protest was written on August 12, 1919 in Malta and was addressed to the British Prime Minister Lloyd George.
123. Ilber Ortaylı, *Osmanlı Imparatorluğunda Alman Nüfuzu* [n. 82], 137, and 137 n. 13.
124. A. A. Türkei 158/15, A14133, folio 126. April 25, 1916.
125. Herbert, "Talât Pasha" [n. 31], 430; idem, *Ben Kendim* [n. 31], 314.
126. A. A. Türkei, 183/36, No. 228, April 15, 1915 report. The portion cited in this note is deleted from the volume compiled by Lepsius, *Deutschland und Armenien* (Potsdam-Berlin, 1919), Doc. No. 26, p. 49.
127. Pomiankowski, *Der Zusammenbruch* [n. 5], 163.
128. Morgenthau, *Ambassador* [n. 22], 370.
129. Herbert, "Talât Pasha" [n. 31], 435; idem., *Ben Kendim* [n. 31] 321.
130. Morgenthau, *Ambassador* [n. 22], 370.
131. DAA [n. 77], P. A. XII, Karton 207, cipher No. 494. Austrian Ambassador Pallavicini's telegram to the Austrian Foreign Ministry, August 26, 1914.
132. Morgenthau, *Ambassador* [n. 22], 371.
133. Liman von Sanders, *Five Years in Turkey* (Annapolis, 1927), 14.
134. Morgenthau, *Ambassador* [n. 22], 381, 382.
135. *Ibid.*, 383.
136. Ernst Jäckh, *The Rising Crescent*, (New York, 1944), 119.
137. A. A. Botschaft Konstantinopel. vol. 137, Doc. No. 240. February 22, 1917. Deutsches Militär in der Türkei.
138. Oğuz, *Yüzyıllar* [n. 6], 382.
139. Morgenthau, *Ambassador* [n. 22], 375–76.
140. For this report of denial *see* A. A. Türkei 183/55, A11259.
141. Dinkel, "German Officers" [n. 45], 110, 113, 115.
142. Ulrich Trumpener, *Germany and the Ottoman Empire 1914–1918* [n. 91], 127.
143. *Hadisat*, November 7, 1918.
144. Çetin Altan, *Sabah*, January 20, 1992.
145. Dilek Zabıtcıoğlu, *Cumhuriyet*, April 20, 1993.
146. Ilber Ortaylı, *Osmanlı Imparatorluğunda Alman Nüfuzu* [n.82], 122.
147. FO 371/2488/161837 Nov. 1, 1915; *ibid.*, /171151, November 15, 1915.
148. *Ibid.*, /148432, October 12, 1915.
149. *Ibid.*, /161837, November 1, 1915; *ibid.*, /171151, November 15, 1915.
150. A. A. Weltkrieg 11° geheim, 545/7 Türkei. March 6,1915.
151. *Ibid.*,11 d. secr., vol. 3. Ambassador Wangnenheim's 374 No. report to Chancellor Bethmann Hollweg. January 20, 1915.
152. Tovmas Mugurditchian, *Deekranagerdee Nahankin Tcharteru Yev Kiurderou Kazanioutounneru* (The Massacres in Diyarbekir Province and the Savageries of the Kurds) (Cairo, 1919), 22–26. The slightly abridged version of this book in English is to be found in U.S. National Archives. R.G.59. 876.4016/417.58 pp.
153. F0371/6500, folios 77–81/344–48. The Armenian civil inspector in question was Mihran Boyadjian.
154. F0371/4142/24597, No. 63490, folio 304.
155. *T. B. M. M. Gizli Celse Zabıtları* (The Transcripts of the Secret Sessions of the Grand National Assembly of Turkey) vol. 3, (Ankara, 1985), 377.
156. *Ibid.*, 394.

157. The content of the interview was published in instalments in the Turkish newspaper *Tanin*. The excerpt is from the issue of September 8, 1945.
158. Doğan Avcıoğlu, *Milli Kurtuluş Tarihi* (History of the National Liberation) vol. 3 (Istanbul, 1974), 1135.
159. This highly sensitive information was revealed in the post-war memoirs of an Armenian police lieutenant who early in February 1915 was recruited by the Turkish Security and Intelligence Bureau (*Emniyeti Umumiye*) to help round up the members of the Armenian intelligentsia of Turkey by way of compiling the requisite lists; he later assisted the Turkish police in tracking down those who had managed to evade it and who were in hiding. Haroutiun Mugurditchian, "Kaghdniknerou Gudzigu" (The Thread of the Secrets) *Hairenik* (an Armenian daily published by the author during the Armistice for a very short period in Istanbul). Instalments Nos. 1 and 2, October 28/November 10, and October 30/November 12, 1918, issues.
160. Special attention was paid to the members of the Ottoman Chamber of Deputies, some of whom reportedly were observed of having visited the Russian Embassy in Istanbul in connection with the revival of the Armenian Reforms issue. Fethi Okyar, *Üç Devirde Bir Adam* (A Man Across Three Eras), C. Kutay, ed. (Istanbul, 1980), 106, n. 1; Cemal Kutay, *Talât Paşanın Gurbet Hatıraları* (The Memoirs of Talât Paşa in Exile) vol. 2 (Istanbul, 1983), 523, 906–07.
161. Seyfi's request is in A. A. Türkei 183/42, A 10003, No. 22571. April 4, 1916; Ambassador Metternich's reply is in *ibid.,* No. 166. April 12, 1916; the answer from the German embassy at Bukarest is in *ibid.*, A11337, No. 186. April 27, 1916.
162. Doğan Avcıoğlu, *Milli Kurtulş Tarihi* (History of the National Liberation) vol. 3 (Istanbul, 1974), 1135; Ilber Ortaylı, *Osmanlı Imparatorluğunda Alman Nüfuzu* [n.82], 122; Ziya Şakir, 1914–1918 *Cihan Harbini Nasıl Idare Ettik* (How Did We Direct the 1914–1918 World War) vol. 1 (Istanbul, 1944), 49–54.
163. Ihsan Birinci, "Cemiyet ve Çeteler" (The Party and the Irregulars [Brigands mostly]) *Hayat* 2 (October 1, 1971): 33. For similar Turkish views acknowledging the involvement of the Special Organization in the liquidation of Ottoman Armenians *see* Vahakn N. Dadrian, "The Role of the Special Organization in the Armenian Genocide during the First World War" in *Minorities in Wartime*. P. Panayi, ed. (Oxford, 1993).
164. Dr. Johannes Lepsius, "Mein Besuch in Konstantinopel Juli/August 1915" *Der Orient* (monthly) 1/3 (1919): 25; *see also Todesgang* [n. 168], v–xxix.
165. A missionary monthly put the number 10,000. *See* Dinkel [n. 45], 40; but in Richard Schäfer, *Persönliche Erinnerungen an Johannes Lepsius* (Potsdam, 1935), 12, and p. xxvii, *Todesgang* [n. 168] the 20,000 number is given. 191 Reichstag deputies were barred from receiving the *Bericht. Der Orient* [n. 164]: 129.
166. A. A. Türkei 183/44, A24404, September 9, 1916, *ibid.*, September 15, 1916. The piece involved is *Bericht über die Lage des Armenischen Volkes in der Türkei* (Potsdam, Berlin, 1916).
167. A. A. Türkei 183/45, A31131, November 16, 1916; A34247, November 28, 1916, November 30, 1916, December 2, 1916; A32822, December 2, 1916; 183/47, A178182, May 18, 1917. The order to confiscate Lepsius booklets is in *ibid.*, 183/44, A24404 September 15, 1916.
168. Johannes Lepsius, *Deutschland und Armenien 1914–198. Sammlung diplomatischer Aktenstücke* (Berlin-Potsdam, 1919). Some eleven years later, and four years after his death, an enlarged version of his wartime *Bericht* was published post-humously under the new title, *Der Todesgang des Armenischen Volkes* (Berlin-Potsdam, 1930).
169. Göppert Papers [n. 44], February 13, 1919, vol. VI, file 1, p. 2.
170. A. A. Türkei 183/56, A20906. The Haag. July 13, 1919.
171. *Ibid.*, July 26, 1919.
172. Trumpener, *Germany* [n.91], 206, n. 15; an example of the case is a quotation from Undersecretary Zimmermann on p. 219, the second part of which is deleted in the Lepsius volume, p. 136, without Trumpener indicating the deletion.
173. Dinkel, "German Officers" [n. 45], 86.

174. Wolfdieter Bihl, *Die Kaukasus-Politik der Mittelmächte* Part I. (Vienna, 1975), 176, n. 402.
175. In the production of the volume were involved, beside Lepsius, Dr. Solf, Dr. Göppert and Dr. W. Rössler from the German Ministry of Foreign Affairs. While doing research in Berlin in 1978, this author raised the question of omissions and deletions with Ms. Gitta Lepsius, one of Lepsius' daughters who at the time had served as his secretary, typing the entire manuscript for him. She categorically denied receiving any instructions from anyone regarding omissions or deletions about which, she asserted, she was hearing for the first time. In other words, she maintained she didn't even know about their incidence.
176. Dinkel, "German Officers" [n. 45], 82.
177. A. A. Göppert Papers, VI/1, p. 3 of the General's 7-page letter to Dr. Karl Axenfeld, a leader in the German missionary movement.
178. Maximillian Harden. "Zwischen 0st und West. Armenien in Moabit" *Die Zukunft*, 29, 37 (11 June, 1921): 300, 301.
179. Ludwig Schraudenbach, *Muharebe* (War) (Berlin, 1924), 315. This form of atrocity was confirmed by a Turkish grocer who after the war had migrated and settled in Portland, Maine, U.S.A. As recounted to his Irish-American friend, this is what he personally experienced during the World War I Armenian genocide. "As a young soldier in the Turkish army he was part of a unit escorting a large group of Armenians into the countryside where they were to be left to die of starvation. At a pause in the march, he told me, an officer in his company walked over to him and told him and his companions to go into the group and bayonet some of them for practice, since they were going to die anyway. 'God help me', he said almost in tears, 'I did.' " William J. McLaughlin, *Boston Globe,* 18 September, 1987. Schraudenbach's book of recollections is full of narrations of similar acts of atrocities which evoked in him images of "Dante's Inferno," he said (p. 345). Referring to Salihzeki, the governor of the district of Der Zor in the desert, who "greeted us very politely and was wearing elegant European clothes," the author states that "shocking atrocities" (*haarsträubende Greuel*) were perpetrated in that region, including "the tying of the Armenian children between wooden boards and setting them on fire" (pp. 351–52).
180. Ibid., 147
181. Kurt Mühsam, *Wie wir belogen wurden. Die amtliche Irreführung des deutschen Volkes* (How we Were Deceived. The Official Acts of Misleading the German People) (Münich, 1918), 76. The practice of this censorship was evidently extended to foreign journalists as well. In his memoirs the War Correspondent of the Associated press in Constantinople describes how the German Embassy refused to help him relay his wartime report on the Armenian massacres to his bureau chief in Berlin. George A. Shriner, *From Berlin to Baghdad* (New York, 1918), 333.
182. *Ibid.,* (Mühsam), 13, 79.
183. Karabekir, *Birinci Cihan Harbine* [n. 12], 158; vol. 1, 69.
184. Sabis, *Harb Hatıralarım* [n. 7], 111, 118.
185. Bayur, *Türk Inkilâbı Tarihi* [n. 114], vol. 3, part 1 (1953), 476; Ziya Şakir *1914–1918 Cihan Harbini Nasıl Idare Ettik?* (How Did We Direct the 1914–1918 World War?) (Istanbul, 1944), 36.
186. Oğuz, *Yüzyıllar Boyunca* [n. 80], 299.
187. A. A. Türkei 158/21, A48179, folios 158–59, 175; Tevfik, Çavdar, *Talât Paşa* (Ankara, 1984), 435–37.
188. Karabekir, *Birinci Cihan Harbine* [n. 12], 279.
189. A. A. Türkei 183/42, A11715.
190. For a discussion of Dr. Nazım's role *see* Vahakn N. Dadrian, "The Role of Turkish Physiciaans in the World War I Genocide of the Armenians" *Holocaust and Genocide Studies* 1, 2 (1986): 169–174.
191. A. A. Türkei 158/16, A31746, folios 095–96. Humann's November 15, 1916 report.
192. Paul Leverkuehn, *Posten auf ewiger Wache. Aus dem abenteuerreichen Leben des Max von Scheubner-Richter* (Essen, 1938), 48.
193. *Austrian Foreign Ministry Archives.* XII. Türkei/380, folio 909.

194. A. Mil, "Umumi Harpte Teşkilâtı Mahsusa" *Vakit,* installment No. 4, November 5, 1933; instal. No. 28, November 30, 1933; instal. No. 34, December 6, 1933. The quotation is from instal. No. 4. (A. Mil is most probably a fictitious name disguising the identity of a well-informed and guerrilla-wise very active Special Organization leader working with the two prominent architects of the Armenian genocide in eastern Turkey, namely Dr. Şakir and Filibeli Hilmi).
195. Bihl, *Die Kaukasus-Politik* [n. 174], 334, n. 405.
196. *DAA* [n. 77], XXXVIII/368 No. Zl. 54/P. September 4, 1915; *ibid.*, XII/380, No. 84/P., December 17, 1915.
197. Sanders, *Five Years* [n. 43], 106; Bihl, *Die Kaukasus-Politik* [n.174], 351, n. 24; Sabis, *Harp Hatıralarım* [n. 7] vol. 2, 191; A. A. Botschaft Konstantinopel, vol. 23, I5845, Military Mission. October 27, 1917.
198. *DAA* [n. 77], XII/463, No. 70/P. Trabzon, October 22, 1915.
199. *Ibid.*, PA. XII/209, Z. 100/P, and No. 96/P. C. November 10, and 17, 1915, cipher telegrams, respectively. Nos. 20 and 23.
200. A. A. Türkei, 183/54, A44066, pp. 8, 9 of the reports October 18, 1918.
201. *Hairenik* (Istanbul Armistice Newspaper) October 17/30, 1918.
202. *Houshartzan Abril Dasnumegi* (In Memoriam of April 24) (Istanbul, 1919), 96.
203. *The Hoover Institution on War, Revolution and Peace.* Stanford. Interior Ministry. Foreign Affairs Department of the Secret Service of the Police. Section 4. Doc. No. 16609. January 23, 1914.
204. Ismail Beşikci, *Kürdistan Üzerinde Emperyalist Bölüşüm Mücadelesi: 1915–1925* (The Fight over Kurdistan's Imperialist Partition 1915–1925) vol. 1 (Ankara, 1992), 88–101.
205. S. A. Zenkovsky, *Pan-Turkism and Islam in Russia* (Cambridge, MA, 1967), 110–11.
206. Quoted in René Pinon, "L'Offensive de l'Asie" *Revue des deux Mondes* (April 15, 1920): 810–11.
207. S. A. Zenkovsky, *Pan-Turkism and Islam in Russia* [n. 205], 111.
208. Tekin Alp, *Türkismus und Pantürkismus* (Weimar, 1915), 46–7, 50, 53. Following the defeat of the Turks at the first Balkan war the author, who was originally from Saloniki, settled in Istanbul in 1912. He was a strong advocate of the need for "the Turks [to pursue their] economic independence in their own land," and for "the economic lifting" (*Hebung*) of Turkey through Turkish nationalism, to be applied by ministers adhering to the ideology of Turkism, pp. 38, 39, 43, 45.
209. *German Foreign Ministry Archives.* A. A. Türkei 134/35, A8212, pp. 9 and 10 of the "confidential" report. The author, Prof. Dr. von Schulze Gaevernitz, who had visited Turkey in March 1916 and conducted "detailed interviews" with "leading Turkish statesmen," among others, was Privy Councillor of the Treasury Department.
210. A. A. Türkei, 134/35, A18613, pp. 1, 2, 3, 4. The report, titled "Volkswirtschaftliche Studien in der Türkei" (Political Economic Studies in Turkey), was anonymously written on July 2, 1916 and submitted to the Foreign Office on July 14, 1916.
211. Lothar Rathmann, *Stossrichtung Nahost 1914–1918. Zur Expansionspolitik des deutschen Imperialismus im ersten Weltkrieg* (Berlin, 1963), 138.
212. *Der Prozess Talaat Pascha.* Stenographic account of the trial. (Berlin, 1921), 84.
213. *Ibid.*, 109, 112, 113, 123.
214. *Ibid.*, 84.
215. *Ibid.*, 125.
216. *Ibid.*, 118.
217. *The New York Times*, June 3, 1921.
218. Dr. Armgaard Karl Graves, *The Secrets of the German War Office* (with the collaboration of E. L. Fox) 4th ed. (New York, 1914), 56, 73, 118–19, 121.
219. **** (n.a.), *The Near East From Within* (New York, n. d., probably winter 1914–15), 51, 59, 83–84, 235.
220. Captain von Rintelen, *The Dark Invader. Wartime Reminiscences of a German Naval Intelligence Officer* (New York, 1933), 74, 81, 83, 84.
221. Mühsam, *Wie wir belogen wurden* [n. 181], 149.

222. A. A. Türkei142/45, A8918. The order was sent through the office of Admiral G. A. von Miller, head of the German Naval Cabinet. It was forwarded to Marshal L. V. Sanders, Ambassador Wangenheim, Colonel Leipzig, the Military Attaché, to Foreign Office diplomat Treutler, and to the Chief of the General Staff.
223. *Ibid.,* 183/37, A22101. No. 590. August 4, 1915.
224. *Ibid.,* 183/39, A29675. October 7, 1915.
225. *Ibid.,* 183/44, A24118.
226. *Ibid.,* 183/46, A3267. No. III a 1358. January 28, 1917.
227. *Kölnische Zeitung*. January 4, 1917. filed in ibid.
228. Dr. Harry Stuermer, *Two War Years in Constantinople. Sketches of German and Young Turkish Ethics and Politics* E. Allen, trans. (New York, 1917), 35. Expanding further on this point, the author states that he had read the Turkophile French man-of-letters Pierre Lofi and was influenced by him. "I was determined to extend to the Turkish government the strong sympathy I already felt for the Turkish people—and let me here emphasize it, still feel. To undermine that sympathy, to make me lose my confidence in this race, things would have to go badly indeed. They went worse than I ever thought was possible." (p. 36). "I investigated everything, even right at the beginning of my stay in Turkey, and always from a thoroughly pro-Turkish point of view. That did not prevent me, however, from coming to my present point of view." (p. 50).
229. *Ibid., 50–51.*
230. *Ibid.,* 42. The German original is in *Zwei Kriegsjahre in Konstantinopel. Skizzen Deutsch-Jungtürkischer Moral und Politik* (Lausanne, 1917), 36.
231. *Ibid.,* 49; the German version, *ibid.,* 42–43.
232. *Ibid.,* 51; the German version, *ibid.,* 44–45.
233. *Ibid.,* 63–64; the German version, *ibid.,* 55–56.
234. *Ibid.,* 65; the German version, *ibid.,* 56–57.
235. *Ibid.,* 66–67; the German version, *ibid.,* 58.
236. *Ibid.,* 68; the German version, *ibid.,* 59.
237. *Ibid.,* 72–73; the German version, *ibid.,* 63–64.
238. *Ibid.,* 62–63; the German version, *ibid.,* 54–55. Such practice of torture was amply in evidence during the preceding regime of Abdul Hamit. In alluding to it the British author George Young relates an incident very similar to that described by Stürmer's wife. He mentions "the testimony of an officer who was driven away from his guardhouse by the shrieks of Armenians who were being interrogated in a nearby building in connection with the plot to assassinate the Sultan in 1905." George Young, *Constantinople. Depuis les origines jusqu'a nos jours,* (Paris, 1934), 281. For a comprehensive study of this type of torture as a legacy of Turkish political culture sustained to this day in modern Turkey *see* Taner Akçam, *Siyasi Kültürümüzde Zulüm ve Işkence* (Atrocity and Torture in Our Political Culture) (Istanbul, 1992).
239. Isaiah Friedman, *Germany, Turkey, and Zionism 1897–1918* (Oxford, 1977), 76.
240. *Ibid.,* 66. Friedman quotes him as saying, "Be ye wise as serpents and harmless as doves." The full wording in the Bible is, however, as follows: "Behold, I send you forth as sheep in the midst of wolves; be ye therefore wise as serpents and harmless as doves." Matthew 10:16.
241. A. A. Orientalia Generalia No. 5, vol. 40. The visit to Ambassador Saurma took place on March 3, 1897 and was reported to Berlin the next day.
242. A.A. Türkei 183/24, Ambassador Marschal's report to Hohenlohe. September 14, 1899. Quoted in Saupp, N. *Das Deutsche Reich und die Armenische Frage* (The German Empire and the Armenian Question) doctoral thesis at the University of Köln (Cologne, 1990), 163.
243. *Ibid.*, 134/22, Marschal's telegram No. 152, April 19, 1909. Quoted in Saupp, *ibid.*, 184
244. It is a historical fact that under certain sets of circumstances almost any nation is capable of committing acts of barbarism, including mass murder. In this sense scholarly efforts may benefit from undertakings that are descriptive or analytical, or both, without being unduly sanctimonious. The following two comments on Turkish proneness to bar-

barism are significant in two respects. First they emanate from two key diplomats whose knowledge of the horrors of the Armenian genocide did not prevent them from persisting in their Turkophile attitudes. Here the affirmation of genocidal behavior is separated from any consideration of condemnation and punishment. Second, they are identified with two nation-states whose governments are manifestly on record, however, for publicly registering their sense of contrition for past instances of mass murder of one kind or another, and for concomitantly instituting prodigious packages of indemnities. Naturally, the issue of indemnity is of subsidiary significance in the context of the present discussion. Barbarism perpetrated on a sweeping scale cannot be meaningfully remedied by any measure of material compensation but it may be atoned by the test of genuine remorse. But atonement presupposes acknowledgment of guilt. The Turkish refusal in this respect is not only categorical and persistent but it is punctuated by a defiant truculence. This raises the question whether the perpetration of the Armenian genocide was a lapse into barbarism or something other than a mere lapse. Here are the two comments alluded to above. In a long and intimate letter to a "dear friend" at the German Foreign Office Ambassador Wangenheim on December 30, 1914, i.e., a few months before the launching of the genocide, referred to the eruption of "Turkish fury the extent of which cannot always be predicted given the barbarous condition of the population." A. A. Türkei, 139/34, A46. In the Armistice period when Kemalist insurgents were resuming the massacres against the remnants of the Armenian population in the interior of the country, their principal champion in the Ottoman capital, Admiral Bristol, the U.S. High Commissioner, felt constrained to advise Washington as follows, "It is known that the Turks will rob, pillage, deport and murder Christians whenever the opportunity is favorable from their point of view… It is my opinion that, knowing the character of the Moslem Turks,… if you arouse the brutal instincts of the Turks, together with his fanatical tendencies, he will attack the Christian races if he is not restrained by absolute force." *U.S. National Archives.* Record Group (RG) 59. 867.00/1361. Bristol's October 23, 1920 report to Washington, pp. 1 and 2. For details of these massacres by the Kemalists see the two reports of C. von Engert, an official attached to Admiral Bristol's U.S. High Commissioner's Office in the Ottoman capital. He made reference to the massacre of "several thousand Armenians" whom he described as victims of the same "insolent spirit" that had run amuck during World War I and had imperiled the Ottoman Armenians. For the February 28, 1920 cable *see ibid.* 867.00/1127; for the March 15, 1920 cable, likewise dispatched from Beirut, see *ibid.* 867.00/1165.

APPENDIX-A

THE TRANSITION OF PROMINENT GERMAN OFFICIALS FROM SERVICE IN TURKEY TO SERVICE IN NAZI GERMANY

Not all of these officials had become fervent Nazis in the new regime; nor were they all necessarily silent opponents of Hitler and his clique. Rather, some of them were adaptive state functionaries, or bland bureaucrats; they could, therefore, be coopted by the protagonists as well as the antagonists of the Nazis. But their experience in Turkey, and with the Turks, was a mark of distinction, and in some respects an asset. That experience included their first-hand knowledge of the state-organized liquidation of a victim population, the Armenians. In this sense their involvement, especially the involvement of those who had become committed Nazis, in the destructive machinery of the Nazi state, acquires particular significance. Three such officials were prominent in the Nazi Foreign Service. Franz von Papen helped the Nazis seize power when he was Chancellor in postwar Germany (June 1932). He was Chief of General Staff of the IVth Turkish army in World War I. In the January 30, 1933–June 1934 period Papen served as Hitler's Vice Chancellor and as President of Prussia. In 1934 he became Special Ambassador to Austria where he paved the ground for the 1938 *Anschluss,* the annexation of Austria to the Nazi Reich. When the funds of the Nazi party ran out, Papen arranged the delivery of financial help from the big industrialists of the Rhine and Ruhr regions. Prior to his engagement in the Turkish army in World War I, he was military attaché at Washington D.C., but upon the discovery of some espionage activities in which he was implicated, he was expelled from the U.S.A. in 1915.[1] Konstantin Freiherr von Neurath, a *Junker* from Swabia, and of aristocratic lineage, occupied the post of Foreign Minister in Papen's cabinet and continued on in that post when Hitler became Chancellor, thus imparting respectability to Hitler's regime. Following the occupation of Czechoslovakia by the German army, he became Protector of Bohemia and Moravia where he had to give cover to the terror of Reinhard Heydrich who eventually replaced him. In World War I Neurath served as Councillor at the German Embassy in Constantinople 1915–16, and was instructed by Chancellor Hollweg to monitor the operations against the Armenians.[2] Count F.W. von der Schulenburg, an army captain, had a long career in German Foreign Service before becoming ambassador to Russia (1934–1941), serving as Minister to Iran and Minister to Rumania. He was executed by the Nazis in connection with the July 20, 1944, assassination attempt against Adolf Hitler. In World War I he was Interim Consul at Erzurum, Turkey, August 1915–February 1916, and at the same time was involved in the organization of guerrilla operations in Eastern Turkey and the Caucasus.

During the war, there were two other German officials who from Berlin directed German policy in Turkey and Turko-German insurgency actions against Russia, but who, after the war, became diplomats, both serving as ambassadors to Turkey. Privy State Councillor Frederic Hans von Rosenberg was the head of the Eastern Department at the German Foreign Office, and Rudolf Nadolny, an army captain, was in charge of the Political Section in the Reserve General Staff (*Stellvertretender Generalstab*) conducting intelligence and sabotage undertakings against Russia from Turkish bases.[3]

Preceding these men in a transition from service in World War I to post-World War I diplomatic service in Germany was Wilhelm Solf, Real Privy Councillor and Minister of Colonial Affairs (*Reichskolonialamt*). In October 1918 he became Foreign Minister of Germany. During World War II Solf served as ambassador to Japan. On two occasions he became involved in developments surrounding the World War I Armenian massacres. In the spring of 1916 Chancellor Hollweg sent him to Constantinople to investigate the Turkish complaints against Ambassador Metternich who repeatedly had been remonstrating against the atrocities which were then being committed against the Armenians. In fact, it was Solf who, together with Albert Ballin had tried and succeeded in getting Metternich appointed to the post of German ambassador to Turkey in October 1915. The Turkish authorities were demanding the recall of the ambassador. Solf recommended against it, and his friend Metternich stayed-for a while at least. During his tenure as Foreign Minister Solf adamantly refused to extradite Talât who in the Fall of 1918 had fled to Germany and whose surrender was being demanded by postwar Turkish authorities. His rationale was that Talât was a loyal friend of Imperial Germany and in the absence of valid legal documents he could not be extradited.[4]

There were a host of high-ranking military officers who, having served in wartime Turkey, likewise stand out as connecting links between the German army of World War I and the subsequently emerging Wehrmacht as well as the SS military formations. Foremost among these was Lieutenant General Hans von Seeckt, whose record as a brilliant staff officer was matched by his reputation as an ideal Prussian military leader imbued with the ethics of duty and service to the state. In the last year of the war he served as Chief of Staff at Ottoman General Headquarters. But upon his return to Germany at the end of the war he set out to prevent the dissolution of the German army and proceeded to rebuild it instead. In the 1919-1926 period he laid the ground-work for the emergence of the Wehrmacht through a carefully crafted restructuring of the Reichswehr, the 100,000 German army allowed by the Versailles Treaty. Even though Seeckt initially had some misgivings about Hitler, after his second meeting with him in 1931, he expressed his approval of the Nazis as "saviors" of a Germany which was beset by crises. He believed in "the task of German policy" which must be "to prepare for the next war."[5] Utilizing his ties with former War Minister Enver, who at that time was, like Talât, a fugitive in Berlin, Seeckt secured Enver's mediation for reaching a secret agreement with Russia to procure weapons for the projected buildup of the German army.[6] When he died in 1936, Hitler honored him by ordering a state funeral which he attended.

General Seeckt was to a great degree politically identified with the Ittihadist top leaders; at the end of the war, he offered them German naval units to effect their escape from Turkey.[7] That help was extended to Enver in 1920 again when through the intervention of Seeckt the intelligence department of the residual German High Command arranged for his escape by plane from a prison at Kaunas, Lithuania and, subsequently, for his trip to Russia.[8] Moreover, Seeckt was well informed of the wartime fate of the Armenians of Turkey but consistent with his ideals of Prussian militarism, he in so many words justified the calamity by invoking the principle of "military necessity."

Two other German generals who were Seeckt's colleagues in wartime Turkey were key players in the emergence of Bavaria as a center of anti-Berlin insurrectionary movements which eventually paved the ground for the rise of National Socialism. As the city of Munich, the capital of Bavaria, became a center of gravitation for rightist nationalists (including a number of high-ranking Prussian officers) in the aftermath of the March 1920 abortive Kapp *Putsch,* Hitler's relationship with Bavaria's civilian and military authorities became a test case for the future of the Nazi movement. These developments adversely affected the authority of General Seeckt who was in charge of the *Reichswehr.* One of them was Major General Otto von Lossow who during the war was Military Attaché to Turkey. During the insurrectionary turmoils in Bavaria he was the commander of the XIIth district and was in charge of the district's XIIth infantry division. The other was Major General Kress von Kressenstein who at one time during the war was Chief of Operations at Ottoman General Headquarters and later served as Chief of Staff of the IVth Turkish Army and finally as Commander-in-Chief of the VIIIth

Turkish Army. During Hitler's troubles in Munich in 1923, Kressenstein was the artillery commander of the military district in Munich. Both generals had conducted extensive correspondence with Berlin on the Armenian genocide.[9]

Some of the highest ranking military officers serving Hitler and Nazi Germany, but with a background of military services in the Armed Forces of wartime Turkey, deserve special attention. Foremost among them was Karl Dönitz, Grand Admiral and Supreme Commander of the German Navy. In his Last Will and Testament Hitler elevated Dönitz to the rank of President of the Reich and Supreme Commander of the German Armed Forces. At the start of World War I Dönitz was an ensign on duty on board of the light cruiser *Breslau* (later assigned the Turkish name *Midilli*). In a 1917 pamphlet on *Die Fahrten der Breslau*, Dönitz describes the combined Turko-German preemptive naval assault against Russian ships and coastal installations in the Black Sea (October 28–29, 1914) that served to precipitate the intended Russo-Turkish war a few days later. At the end of the war Dönitz was promoted to the rank of captain. Moreover, General Alfred Jodl, Hitler's chief of Wehrmacht operations, Chief of Staff of the High Command, was assigned to a tour of duty (1934–1937) in Turkey as part of a military exchange program. Likewise to be mentioned is Pfeffer von Wildenbruch, who was a first lieutenant in wartime Turkey but in World War II he had become SS Obergruppenfuhrer (General) and the military governor of Budapest.[10] World War II general, Alexander von Falkenhausen, also served in Turkey in the 1916–18 period and in the 1940–44 period was military governor in Belgium. Finally, reference may be made to Rudolf Höss, the Commandant of the Auschwitz extermination camp 1940–43 and Deputy Inspector of concentration camps at SS Headquarters 1944–45. After running away from a home, dominated by his authoritarian father, in 1916 he joined the German forces serving in Turkey when he was only 16, and after the war he joined the Freikorps. These were private armies in postwar Germany, consisting of ex-soldiers, and led by former regular officers, with Munich becoming a refuge for them.[11]

Of these officials and officers in Nazi Germany, who were tried at Nuremberg, General Jodl was sentenced to death and was executed on the gallows in the wee hours of October 16, 1946. Neurath was sentenced to fifteen years but in 1954 was released for health reasons. Dönitz was sentenced to ten years in prison and finished his term in 1956. Von Papen was acquitted but in January 1947 he was retried by a German de-Nazification court and on February 1, 1947, was sentenced to eight years' hard labor; he was released in 1949. Höss was convicted and hanged by the Poles at Auschwitz camp in 1947.

Notes to Appendix-A

1. Franz von Papen, *Der Wahrheit eine Gasse* (Münich, 1952).
2. A.A.Türkei 183/39, A33278; 183/40, A33705.
3. Rudolf Nadolny, *Mein Beitrag* (Wiesbaden, 1955).
4. For Solf's correspondence with Metternich, *see* E. von Vietsch ed,, *Cegen die Unvernunft. Der Briefwechsel zwrischen Paul Graf Wolff Metternich und Wilhelm Solf 1915-1918* (Bremen, 1964), 7, 42. On the matter of extradition, see Vahakn N. Dadrian, *The History of the Armenian Genocide. Ethnic Conflict from the Balkans to Anatolia to the Caucasus* (Providence/Oxford, 1995) Ch. 22, n. 6, p. 391.
5. Walter Goerlitz, *History of the German General Staff l657-1945*, B. Battershaw, trans. (New York, 1953), 174, 260.
6. *Ibid.,* 231; Ulrich Trumpener, *Germany and the Ottoman Empire 1914-1918* (Prince ton, 1968), 362 63.
7. *Ibid.,* 359, n. 17; Frank G. Weber, *Eagles on the Crescent* (Ithaca, 1970), 253.
8. Şevket S. Aydemir, *Makedonyadan Orta Asya 'ya Enver Pąsa* (Enver Paşa. From Macedonia to Central Asia) vol. 3 (Istanbul, 1972), 545.
9. For excerpts from their reports to Berlin on the extermination of the Armenians see Vahakn N. Dadrian, "Documentation of the Armenian genocide in German and Austrian Sources" in *The Widening Circle of Genocide. Genocide: A Critical Bibliographic Review.* vol. 3, Israel W. Charny ed. (New Brunswick, N.J., 1994), 123-24.
10. Some of the data about these officers were culled from Werner Haupt, "Deutsche unter dem Halbmond:" *Deutsches Soldatenjahrbuch* (1967), 216, 217.
11. Gerald Reitlinger, *The SS. Alibi of a Nation. 1922–1945* (New York, 1957), 283, 468.

APPENDIX-B

THE INDIGNITY OF DECORATING THE ARCH PERPETRATORS

The intensity of any war is often commensurate with the intensity of a pathos for hero worship on the part of the populations identified with the warring parties. Apart from satisfying the common need for creating legends and thereby enhancing national self-images, the identification and honoring of wartime heroes has additionally the function of boosting the morale of the combatants and of stimulating the drive for heroic acts among them. In the process, some combatants are often unduly lionized, others are deprecated or underestimated, and still others are glossed over or discounted. Barring some exceptions, many an act of hero recognition is more often than not due to a blend of fortuitous circumstance, luck, and an untainted relationship with superiors recommending the conferral of decorations of one kind or another. Moreover, the quality of such acts of recognition, generally speaking, has an inverse relationship to the quantity of these acts; the greater the multitude of distinguished heroes, the lesser the value of the act of distinction itself. To mitigate this problem, the principle of gradations has been introduced whereby heroes have been assigned to categories that have a hierarchical character and reflect the recognition of different degrees of heroism. Notwithstanding, the profusion of decorations at middle and lower levels in modern times has been a common problem among nation-states locked in progressively optimal warfares requiring reliance on a multitude of combatants. As a result, the attribute of rarity in the act of recognizing heroic deeds and related heroes has been diluted. Instead, there has emerged a trend whereby governments are inclined to redefine heroism and merit on the basis of political pragmatism disguised as a higher form of patriotism. In other words, the principle of merit recognition has been reduced to an instrument of state policy, confounding simple duty performance with meritorious role performance and substituting political expediency for the need to be discriminating in recognizing and rewarding merit and distinction.

The conduct of German authorities in Berlin and Istanbul in showering a host of Turkish military and civilian officials in wartime Turkey with a variety of Prussian and German decorations epitomizes this trend. But, it is more than that, for most of these officials were incriminated in the organization and implementation of the Armenian genocide. Thus, they were not just recognized as meritorious allies of Germany but, in complete disregard of their complicity in what the British historian Toynbee called "this gigantic crime,"[1] they were thus, indirectly, and perhaps even directly, rewarded given their involvement in that crime. The significance of this act of rewarding arch perpetrators may be measured by considering the scale and magnitude of the crime itself. Since the specifics of such a consideration fall outside the purview of this appendant discussion, the adducing here of the explicit, unequivocal, and succinct conclusions of three principal historians may be in order. With considerable detachment all three of them have immersed themselves in the examination of the disastrous fate of the Armenians in World War I, with two of them undertaking that examination in the context of the World War I Turko-German alliance. Of these, Ulrich Trumpener used the words "the Armenian holocaust" when explaining interim German ambassador Hohenlohe's abortive efforts to "stop" that "holocaust" about which he had communicated to German chancellor Bethmann Hollweg.[2] For his part, Frank G. Weber, likewise dealing with the fate of the Armenians in the context of the Turko-German alliance, used exactly the same word "holocaust" as he described the protests against it of Ambassador Metternich, Hohenlohe's successor.[3] Consistent with his wartime diagnosis of the nature and scope of the same mass murder, Toynbee, a half century later, used the current designation "genocide" to identify and characterize that mass murder. In his autobiographical work he referred to "the largely successful attempt to exterminate [the Armenians] during the First World War in 1915 … [This] genocide was carried out under the cloak of legality by cold-blooded governmental action."[4] Before he joined the camp of the advocates of "the Turkish point of view" and the allied revisionists, noted authority Bernard Lewis in his major work on modern Turkey had likewise concluded that the Armenians suffered "the terrible holocaust" of the World War I, in consequence of which "a million and half Armenians perished."[5]

In the statements of Trumpener and Weber the evidence of two German ambassadors endeavoring to mitigate and even stop the unfolding "holocaust" of the Armenians is once more cast into the foreground. As observed throughout this study, however, their endeavors proved entirely ineffective; they were ignored not only by the Turkish authorities but even by their own German superiors. The treatment in 1916 by Berlin of Ambassador Metternich aptly illustrates the order of German priorities in this respect. Metternich had been clashing with the Young Turk Ittihadist leaders on account of the latter's exterminatory policy against the Armenians; his relationships with these leaders steadily deteriorated.

Berlin sent Field Marshal August von Mackensen, as Emperor William II's personal emissary, on a damage control mission to Istanbul. He brought with him a bejeweled marshal's baton to be bestowed upon the reigning Turkish Sultan. The German marshal took the occasion to publicly praise the wisdom of the Ittihadist leaders' overall policies in an effort to placate the latter. In every speech he delivered he emphasized Germany's appreciation of the services of the Turkish ally while avoiding, as much as he could, any contact with Ambassador Metternich. When Metternich tried to modify Marshal Mackensen's exaggerated statements, "he found the army telegraph station closed to the transmission of his dispatches." Upon the prompting of the German General Staff Metternich's reports were censored before transmission to Berlin following the departure of Marshal Mackensen from the Ottoman capital.[6] The ultimate demise of the ambassador was not late in coming; upon the insistence of both Ittihadist bosses, War Minister Enver and Interior Minister Talât, he was relieved of his post in September 1916 when other matters of contention compounded the brewing antagonism between the ambassador and the Turkish leadership.[7]

Two aspects of this incident deserve special attention as they bear upon the German propensity to rather profusely conferring a variety of wartime decorations on an array of Turkish perpetrators. 1) The dominant position of the German military, especially the German General Staff at the General Headquarters in relation to the German Foreign Office, 2) The concordance in this regard of Emperor William II, as the Supreme War Lord and the Supreme Ruler of Imperial Germany, with the dispositions of the German High Command. In fact, any discussion on the German system of dispensing wartime decorations must take into account the critical import of the authority of the emperor. Practically all World War I decorations, in order to be actually conferred on any individual, could materialize only if the initiators went through the chain of command which meant the ultimate approval of the emperor. This chain of command, in the case of candidates from Turkey, involved the High Command at General Headquarters to which recommendations were directed initially from the German Military Mission to Turkey. The Mission was the collection point or receptacle of formal applications for individual decorations. As a rule, the German Embassy in Istanbul was consulted about any objections or reservations (*Bedenken*) to the act of decorating a particular individual. Barring such objection or reservation, the application was then forwarded to the emperor for his approval and through the agency of the Chief of the Military Cabinet, the Military Inspector, or General Quartermaster at the General Headquarters, the candidate was informed of the impending decoration; the office of the chancellor was often kept abreast of these outcomes.

Basically there were four avenues for initiating requests for individual decorations. The first involved adherence to the principle of near-automatic reciprocity. If members of a German delegation, as a ceremonial matter, were honored by their Turkish hosts through the random distribution of medals, the Turks expected a reciprocal gesture. A second avenue was the unilateral approach. Turkish potentates subtly, and often not so subtly, would let it be known that they desire or deserve a certain decoration or, for that matter, any German decoration; jealousy and rivalry among them were often a driving force in this connection. Far more significant, and for the present discussion most relevant, however, are the other two avenues, for they involved strictly German motivations and German initiatives. One of these served the purpose of enticing, inducing, or encouraging certain Turkish officials to assist in or facilitate the execution of certain tasks with which different Germans were entrusted; this was an indirect form of bribery. The most blatant and, from the vantage point of the theme of the present discussion, most compromising for the integrity of the German system of military decorations, was the fourth avenue. A number of German civilian and military officials on their own volition took the initiative to have a coterie of "notorious exterminators" (to use the language used in a related British Foreign Office document), decorated with a variety of German insignias and Orders intended for honoring and rewarding war heroes. What follows is a list of select Turkish officials belonging to this category and the decorations they received.

The Honorees and their Medals

Among the provincial governors-general (*vali*) seven stand out.

1. *Hüseyin Azmi. Vali* of Konya province and subsequently of Beirut. Even though Ludwig von Mutius, German consul general at Beirut, refused to support a proposal to honor him with a medal on the ground that he had rendered no particular service to Germany,[8] he was eventually decorated with the Iron Cross.[9] Azmi was appointed to the post of chief of police of Istanbul following the Ittihadist overthrow of the Itilafist Kâmil Paşa Cabinet on January 23, 1913. He subsequently assisted Dr. Nazım in organizing clandestine activities against Armenian political leaders within and without Turkey on the eve of World War I. His assistant was Sudi, subsequently Lazistan deputy in the Ottoman Lower House and one of the principal organizers of the massacre of the Armenians of Erzurum province. Azmi was one of the

seven top Ittihadist leaders who on the night of November 1/2, 1918 escaped from Istanbul on board a German torpedo boat; most of them took refuge in Germany. He barely escaped assassination when two Armenian "justice commandos," on April 17, 1922, shot to death his two Ittihadist cohorts and principal architects of the Armenian genocide (Dr. B. Şakir and Trabzon *vali* Cemal Azmi) who had just taken leave of him after a family visit to his home in Berlin.

2. *Atıf.* Interim *vali* of Angora (Ankara), and *vali* of Kastamonu. The proposal to decorate him with the Iron Cross 2nd class came from Marshal Liman von Sanders, the chief of the German Military Mission.[10] Only in his twenties, Atıf proved to be one of the most ferocious exterminators of the Armenians, especially of those in Angora. Not satisfied with that result he succeeded to have the benign and decent *vali* of Kastamonu province relieved only to end up replacing him in that post. Consequently, the Armenian population of the province was promptly deported as well. In an affidavit prepared by a Turkish notable of Angora at the request of the Military Tribunal's Inquiry Commission Atıf is quoted as saying that he "received orders from his superior [Talât]" to destroy the Armenians (*Amirimden emir aldım. Ermeniler yaşamayacaktır*).[11]

3. *Haci Adil (Arda). Vali* of Adrianople (Edirne). At the time, i.e., 1916, he was being recommended for the conferral on him of the Order of the Red Eagle 1st class (*Roter Adler Orden I. Klasse*), and which recommendation was approved by the emperor, he was president of the Chamber of Deputies.[12] He was an ardent Ittihadist; in 1910 he served as secretary general of Ittihad party. In the 1911–1912 period he held twice the post of interior minister. According to a British document he "took lead in the policy of exterminating the Armenians in 1915."[13]

4. *Mustafa Abdulhalik (Renda). Vali* of Bitlis and subsequently Aleppo province. His candidacy for decoration was proposed by Major Grovenstein, commander of the communication zone, attached to the German Military Mission, and on duty in the Aleppo district. In a letter to his superior, the German ambassador in the Ottoman capital, German consul Rössler points out that Abdulhalik is being proposed not so much for any meritorious services to Germany but rather in the hope that he will be more disposed to cooperate with the German military units in the area.[14] The complicity of this governor is substantial as it involves the organization of the extermination of not only the largest Armenian population of the province of Bitlis but also of the multitudes of emaciated and exhausted other Armenians who had

miraculously survived the long and decimating treks of deportation from the interior of Turkey. They were subjected to a new round of massacres in the deserts of Mesopotamia under the supervision of this governor.[15]

5. *Ahmed Muammer. Vali* of Sıvas and Konya provinces. His candidacy for Iron Cross 2nd class came from the German camp (*Es ist von deutscher Seite angeregt worden*). The intent was to bring about a situation whereby he becomes "favorably disposed for the promotion of German interests" (*für deutsch-militärische Interessen günstig zu stimmen*). The request from the German General Headquarters states that unless the German Embassy has reservations, the request of the German Military Mission will be submitted for Kaiser's approval and signature.[16] Muammer, according to the testimony of Dr. G. White, the American president of Anatolia College in Merzifun, Sıvas province, "was responsible for the deportation of over 100,000 Armenians … he is an absolutely heartless villain … it is recommended very strongly that he should be hanged for his misdeeds." In the same British archive file there is a document stating that Muammer was observed accompanying in a carriage and "in brigand (*çete*) uniform" a convoy of Armenian male deportees "tied together in fours." The carriage contained also Abdul Gani, Ittihad party's responsible secretary for Sıvas (who was convicted by the Turkish Court-Martial for his part in the deportation and massacres of that province. *Takvimi Vekâyi* No. 3772, p.5), and Colonel Pertev, the acting commander of Xth Army Corps at Sıvas. The men of the convoy were never seen again.[17]

6. *Mehmed Memduh.* Governor *(mutasarrıf)* of Erzincan and *vali* of Bitlis and later Mosul. It is most significant that his candidacy for decoration came from Dr. Colley, Red Cross German staff surgeon at Erzincan.[18] A German author describes the surgeon as a physician whose Turkophile attitudes were matched by his inordinate callousness. In the midst of the exterminatory massacres enveloping the Armenian population of the entire district of Erzincan Colley is reported to have declared that he will not lift a finger as "he had to protect higher interests" (*in der Sache keinen Finger rühren zu wollen, er habe höhere Interessen zu wahren*).[19] The evidence against Memduh as a ferocious massacrer is not only ample but reflects a pattern of sustained extermination of Armenians in all the regions in which he served as governor. American nurse Grisell M. McLaren, who was serving in the Erzincan hospital and knew Turkish, states that Memduh "was proud of the fact that he had cleaned out" the

Armenian population of Erzincan.[20] An Armenian civil inspector, who was spared elimination on account of his strong ties to Ittihad, in his affidavit prepared at the request of British authorities, stated that after liquidating the Armenians of Erzincan, Memduh continued his exterminatory policy in his subsequent posts as *vali,* namely, Bitlis and Mosul, especially targeting the surviving Armenian soldiers engaged in labor battalions. In Bitlis which was about to fall to the Russians, he ordered a Turkish physician to kill all Armenian women and children serving in the American Mission. His most fiendish act was the burying alive in July 1915 of some 1,500 Armenian children at a location in Kemakh, 10 km southwest of Erzincan, in a large pit which Armenian laborers were forced to dig.[21]

7. *Tahir Cevdet. Vali* of Van and subsequently of Adana. The request for decoration of this governor came from the German Chief of Staff of the area's (Syria and Palestine) IVth Army. In supporting that request, Adana's general consul Büge furnishes important insights in the criteria by which such decorations are dispensed. Turkish civilian and military officials, he avers, expect to be rewarded through medals, when they are engaged for services benefiting a foreign state—without actually achieving any particular distinction. Moreover, continues Büge, the Turks will fail to understand and even be offended, when told that the conferring of medals is contingent on particular services to the German cause, and that not all *valis* can be automatically decorated. Finally, Büge repeats the German Chief of Staff's observation that Cevdet is the brother-in-law of War Minister Enver (as the preceding *vali* Memduh was Cevdet's brother-in-law, both men having married the respective sisters), and consequently, "many a problem can be overcome through a decoration" (*manche Schwierigkeit durch eine Dekorierung ... aus dem Wege geschafft werden könnte*).[22] Joseph Pomiankowski, vice marshal and Austrian military plenipotentiary to Turkey, characterized Cevdet a "real panther in human form" (*ein wahres Ungeheuer in Menschengestalt*) who distinguished himself through a bloodthirstiness with which he organized the massacres of Van Armenians" (*durch besondere Blutgier ausgezeichnet*).[23] (For more details see Part I on Van uprising, especially notes 76 and 81).

It is significant also that like his cohort, Muammer, the *vali* of Sıvas, Cevdet too was observed in the uniform of a brigand (*çete*) in connection with a massacre operation in Bitlis involving a group of Armenian men "who were killed with axes."[24]

From the National Security Office (*Emniyeti Umumiye*) of the Interior Ministry three prominent men received German decorations also.

1. *Tevfik Hadi*. Director of Political Section of the General Directorate of Police (*Kısmı Siyasi*) with the rank of lieutenant colonel of Gendarmery. Previously, he was director of the one of the other two sections, namely, the Legal (*Kısmı Adli*). Even though subject to the jurisdiction of the Interior Ministry, the Directorate of Police in the Ottoman capital had sufficient authority and power to function just like a Cabinet Ministry. He was recommended for the Prussian Order of the Royal Crown 2nd class.[25] According to a document from the archives of the Jerusalem Armenian Patriarchate, Hadi was a member of a special Council of Terror headed by Talât. The Council's mission consisted of terrorizing, reducing and decimating "the internal foes" of Turkey by resort to exile, confiscations and murder, including the organization of the mass arrests in the Ottoman capital on the night of April 23/24, 1915 of the hundreds of Armenian community and political leaders, teachers, priests and professionals, and the subsequent liquidation of most of them.[26]

2. *Ismail Canbolat.* He was director of National Security at the outbreak of World War I with the rank of Captain of Gendarmery, and in 1915 became *vali* and prefect of Istanbul. In the months preceding the war, he was director of Intelligence in the Interior Ministry. Thereafter, he became undersecretary in the Interior Ministry and Interior minister in 1918. In the document cited above, in connection with the case of T. Hadi he is described as a member of the Council of Terror which took its orders from the Central Committee of Ittihad party.[27] He worked hand in hand with Talât in using the provincial gendarmery that was subject to the jurisdiction of the Interior Ministry, as an instrument of deportation and massacre and with Istanbul Police Chief Bedri to whom he was related by matrimonial ties.[28] The request to decorate Canbolat came from Turkish authorities. He had joined Halil, the Turkish Foreign Minister to Berlin to denounce and unilaterally abrogate a number of treaties, including the Treaties of Paris (1856) and Berlin (1878) and on that occasion had visited the German General Headquarters. As if to reward this act of annulling the treaties Emperor William II readily complied with the Turkish request[29] and bestowed the Prussian Order of the Royal Crown 2nd class on Canbolat who at the time was undersecretary in the Interior Ministry. Upon receipt of the decoration, Canbolat in a letter thanked profusely the German authorities, especially the emperor "for the favor he

granted me. I shall always remain grateful for the good wishes attached to the Prussian insignia." Addressing his words to the German ambassador, he wrote, "In anticipation of the pleasure I will have in shaking your hands … ."[30] Canbolat was arrested by postwar Turkish authorities on January 30, 1919 and subsequently was deported to Malta by the British for trial before an international court "on account of his complicity in deportations etc. of Armenians … ."[31] According to other German documents Canbolat was decorated also with the Order of the Red Eagle 2nd class with star.[32]

3. *Osman Bedri*. He occupied the post of Istanbul Police Chief which, as noted earlier, was equivalent to the post of Minister of Police. Associated Press War Correspondent George Schreiner, who knew him well, called Bedri "the very embodiment of terror," especially with respect to the Armenians "who fear massacre …"[33] Turkish Historian Ismail Danişmend describes him as "Ittihad's instrument of terror" (*tedhiş âleti*).[34] Two Turkish chroniclers of Ittihadist eras state that Bedri received his orders from the Central Committee of Ittihad,[35] and that every night, he went to the headquarters of the party to keep Kara Kemal, one of the chief operators of the party, apprised of the day's happenings.[36] When discussing Turkish methods of torture being inflicted on Armenian leaders, who were suspected of conspiracy or seditiousness, American ambassador Morgenthau relates an encounter with Bedri:

> One day I was discussing these proceedings with Bedri Bey, the Constantinople Prefect of Police. With a disgusting relish Bedri described the tortures inflicted. He made no secret of the fact that the Government had instigated them, and, like all Turks of the official classes, he enthusiastically approved this treatment of the detested race. Bedri told me that all these details were matters of nightly discussion at the headquarters of the Union and Progress Committee. Each new method of inflicting pain was hailed as a splendid discovery, and the regular attendants were constantly ransacking their brains in the effort to devise some new torment. Bedri told me that they even delved into the records of the Spanish Inquisition and other historic institutions of torture, and adopted all the suggestions found there. Bedri did not tell me who carried off the prize in this gruesome competition, but common reputation throughout Armenia gave a pre-eminent infamy to Djevdet Bey, the vali of Van, whose activities in that section I have already described. All through this country Djevdet now becomes known as the "marshal blacksmith of Bashkale," for this connoisseur in torture had

invented what was perhaps the masterpiece of all—that of nailing horseshoes to the feet of his Armenian victims.

Yet these happenings did not constitute what the newspapers of the time commonly referred to as the Armenian atrocities; they were merely the preparatory steps in the destruction of a race. The Young Turks displayed greater ingenuity than their predecessor, Abdul Hamit.[37]

Bedri, like his colleague Canbolat, was decorated with the Order of the Red Eagle 2nd class with star.[38]

Two military officers and one civilian official who played a pivotal role in the organization and employment for massacre duty of the cadres of the Special Organization, the actual killer bands, were likewise honored with German decorations.

1. *Colonel Behiç (Erkin).* He was deputy director of the Supply Department (*Ikmal Şubesi*) of the Operations Section of the Ministry of War. Appearing before the Ottoman Parliament he strongly urged that legislative body to approve the pending bill which would legalize the release of convicts from the prisons of the empire. In doing so, he concealed the fact that these felons were intended to be enrolled in the ranks of the murderous Special Organization. Instead, he pretended that they were needed for the Ottoman regular army. When challenged by a senator that convicts do not belong in the army, he reluctantly conceded the plan to incorporate them in the ranks of the Special Organization.[39] Behiç received two medals. On July 28, 1915 the emperor approved the conferral on him of the Iron Cross 2nd class,[40] and August 3, 1917 the Prussian Order of Royal Crown 2nd class with swords.[41]

2. *Colonel Seyfi.* Chief of Department II (Intelligence), a post jointly held at the Ministry of War and at General Headquarters. Seyfi may rightly be called *the principal Ittihadist military officer* who masterminded the military aspects of the Armenian deportations and massacres.[42] He was decorated with the Iron Cross 2nd class.[43]

3. *Yusuf Kemal (Tengirşenk).* Undersecretary in the Ministry of Justice. He too was instrumental in pushing through the Ottoman Senate the bill authorizing the release of convicts from the prisons of the Ottoman Empire for enrollment in the ranks of the Special Organization. In fact, he urged the legislative body to consider the approval of the bill a patriotic mandate. He succeeded. It was approved as an "emergency bill" (*müstaceliyet*).[44] He was decorated with the Prussian Order of Red Eagle 2nd class.[45]

In addition, the decoration of two foremost military commanders deserves special attention for both of them had a substantial share in the extermination of the large concentration of Armenians in their ancestral territories in eastern and central-eastern Turkey.

1. *Mahmud Kâmil Paşa.* Major-General and Commander-in-Chief of the Ottoman IIIrd Army (February 1915–February 1916). The command zone of this army encompassed the six provinces, often described as part of historic Armenia, and the province of Trabzon. As has been described in detail in Part I of this study, General Kâmil stands out in the organization of the destruction of Ottoman Armenians as a principal character. His close ties with the top leaders of Ittihad's Directorate, his identification with the secret designs of that party, his key position as Commander of the IIIrd Army, and his working relationship with the Special Organization, which was likewise headquartered in Erzurum, were the operative ingredients of this major role he played. Beyond the documentation adduced in Part I, two more examples may be introduced here to underscore the decisiveness of this role in the obliteration of the Armenian population of Turkey. According to the former Grand Vizier, Minister of War, and Army Commander, Ahmet Izzet Paşa, it was General Mahmud Kâmil who first urged the Ottoman High Command at General Headquarters to effect the massive deportation of the Armenians.[46] A commander of the Special Organization, actually one of the right hand men of Behaeddin Şakir, the chief of that organization, in his memoirs reveals that General Kâmil authorized the formation of the Special Organization cadres in his command zone by designating them as "milice" forces.[47] (For the wide ranging involvement of this Turkish general in the enactment of the Armenian genocide see Part I, section on The Role of the IIIrd Army High Command. It's Commander-in-Chief, and Pre-Designed Wholesale Massacres, notes 92–107). General Kâmil was decorated twice. In August 1915 he received the Iron Cross 2nd class.[48] In July 1917 he was decorated once more (the available German document does not specify the medal).[49]

2. *Halil (Kut).* General and Commander-in-Chief of the Ottoman VIth Army, and subsequently of Army Groups East. By his own admission, he had killed at least 300,000 Armenians who resided in his command zones. Moreover, he also saw to it that all Armenian soldiers and officers, found in his army formations, were executed by fellow Turkish military men.[50] Halil too was decorated twice. About a month before his death (he succumbed to spotted typhus), Field Marshal von

der Goltz recommended to Emperor William II that Halil be decorated with Iron Cross Ist class.[51] Less than a year later the emperor decorated him again, this time with the Prussian Order of the Royal Crown 1st class with swords.[52]

The Decorations Given to Dr. Behaeddin Şakir and Talât Paşa

The German spree of honoring through medals Turkish potentates during World War I reached its apogee of ignominy when such honor was heedlessly extended to the two foremost architects of the Armenian genocide, Dr. Behaeddin Şakir and Ittihad party boss, Interior Minister, and ultimately (February 1917) Grand Vizier, Talât Paşa. As in practically all other cases enumerated and described within the framework of this Appendix, in the case of these two men too the German authorities were fully informed of the paramount role they played. In a report marked "secret" Colonel Stange had sent a detailed account to Istanbul on the unfolding mass murder of the Armenians which he characterized as "a long before established plan" (*einen lang gehegten Plan*). In it he singled out Dr. B. Şakir as one of the Ittihadist party leaders who masterminded the conception and decisionmaking for "the deportation and destruction of the Armenians" (*die Austreibung und Vernichtung der Armenier*).[53] (For more details on the contents of Stange's report see Part I, notes 184 and 185). The German Foreign Office was deluged with ambassadorial and consular reports on the cardinal role Talât played in the conception, decisionmaking, organization, supervision and implementation of the genocide. In his December 7, 1915 report Ambassador Metternich informed Berlin that Talât was "the soul of the Armenian persecutions" (*die Seele der Armenierverfolgungen*).[54] As Trumpener put it, "Talât's leading role in the Armenian persecutions ... was patently obvious to anyone who knew what was going on ..."[55] But in the clash between higher national interests, on the one hand, and awareness of loathsome facts operating at a disjointed level, on the other, politicians and nationalist leaders almost always placed a higher premium on the promotion of the former. "Cognitive dissonance" under these circumstances rarely disturbed these men sufficiently to change course. The refusal of the German government to extradite Talât to Turkey in 1918 and 1919 was consistent with this stance. Germany refused to surrender Talât Paşa, who as Grand Vizier was the de facto head of the Ottoman state when he fled to Germany at the end of the war. German Foreign Minister Solf invoked paragraph 2 of article 5 of the 1917 Turko-German Extradition Treaty which permitted extradition under three conditions: an arrest order, a verdict against the person whose extradition is being sought, or the submission of related judicial documents. As the Court-Martial in Istanbul had not yet taken place, there was no judicial documentation of a verdict. At any rate, added Solf, "Talât stuck with us faithfully, and our country remains open to him."[56] Notwithstanding, Talât was court-martialed in absentia as a "fugitive of justice," was convicted, and was sentenced to death on July 5, 1919 as an arch perpetrator.[57] Likewise, Dr. Behaeddin Şakir was tried in absentia (he too had fled to Germany with Talât), convicted and sentenced to death as an arch perpetrator in the enactment of the extermination of the Armenians.[58]

According to a communication of the German Military Mission (November 12, 1917), Marshal Liman von Sanders, the Chef of the Mission, on September 14, 1917 has conferred on Dr. Şakir the Iron Cross 2nd class.[59] As to Talât, throughout the war he was literally inundated with all sorts of decorations, to such an extent that on March 8, 1921 he offered to give as security deposit all his decorations for a personal loan from an acquaintance.[60] Among the many decorations Talât received was the Iron Cross 1st class,[61] and the Prussian Order of Red Eagle1st class. But one of the most significant ones was the Prussian Order of Black Eagle.[62] This is one of the highest German decorations and is seldom conferred on non-Germans. When Ambassador Kühlmann applied to Berlin on behalf of Talât a week earlier he had stated that he wouldn't dare to formally request the granting of the Black Eagle Order since the emperor was likely to object. He then added, "In view of the fact, however, that Talât is by far the most important personality in entire Turkey, I urgently recommend that he be decorated with the highest medal possible under present conditions."[63]

There should be a measure of understanding, if not appreciation, for the episodes described above. After all alliances do provide latitudes for generating good will and mutual appreciation among the partners indulging in the practice of exchanging medals and other insignias. The system of conferring decorations cannot, therefore, be treated as an isolated occurrence; it is more or less an extension of the explicit and implicit terms of a military alliance. But are there no boundaries to the principle of understanding? Is a military alliance intrinsically so sacrosanct that it is accorded a degree of permissiveness by which it becomes "untouchable" and from which may issue a license for complicitous behavior? The recurrent German theme, articulated in a series of diplomatic Notes, that 1. Turkey was an indispensable ally, and that, therefore, 2. Germany could not afford to alienate, much less lose it, Turkey, is belied by concrete German wartime initiatives in relation to that Turkish ally. They may be described briefly.

When Turkey was wavering about intervening in the war following the entry into the Dardanelles of the two German cruisers, German Ambassador Wangenheim proudly reported to Berlin that he stormed into the office of the Turkish Grand Vizier and in so many words told him that Germany's will shall prevail and that Turkey must submit to that will and let these cruisers proceed to the Black Sea and provoke hostilities with Russia. They did proceed, and within days Turkey's hand was forced as Russia, as well as England and France, promptly declared war against Turkey. The proclivity of Ambassador Wangenheim to bully the Turks when needed was legend in the political circles in Istanbul; it was attested to by Marshal Liman von Sanders [64] and by the Turks themselves, who called him "the despot of Istanbul." [65] Moreover, in all his conversations with American Ambassador Morgenthau Ambassador Wangenheim reiterated the point that he doesn't want to help the Armenians. As far as it is known, he never excused himself saying that he is handicapped, he just couldn't; rather, he emphasized that he wouldn't "I shall do nothing whatever for the Armenians" he declared. [66] Why would an ambassador be so adamant and implacable in face of an unfolding mass murder? The answer may lie in the assertion of German historian Fritz Fischer that Wangenheim executed the policies of Emperor William II as represented by Zimmermann, the Undersecretary in the Foreign Office. [67]

The contention that Turkey for Germany was an indispensable ally is belied even more patently. Indeed, despite treaty obligations and despite so many pledges made orally and in writing to the Turks, German diplomats in 1916 proceeded to make secret deals with Japan whereby Russia would be allowed to retain not only "Turkish-Armenia" but the other adjacent territories it had occupied in the course of the war. One of the conditions under which Turkey had agreed to yield to German pressures and to sign the August 2, 1914 secret political and military alliance with Turkey was a German commitment to help Turkey recover the provinces it had lost to the Russians in the 1877–78 Turko-Russian war. Now, with the full knowledge of the Kaiser, German diplomates, in quest for a separate peace with Russia, were willing not only to renege on their commitment but go even so far as to cause its ally Turkey to sustain additional territorial losses. [68] How is this deed, if not misdeed, in any way congruous with the claim of the indispensability of an ally? How can a government proceed to secretly betray an ally and then, at another level, pretend being careful not to offend or alienate that ally? Herein lies the main rationale of branding as an indignity the German track record of decorating the arch perpetrators.

Notes to Appendix-B

1. Arnold Toynbee (compiler and commentator) *The Treatment of Armenians in the Ottoman Empire 1915–1916.* Documents Presented to Viscount Grey of Fallodon. Viscount Bryce, ed. (London, 1916. Miscellaneous No. 31, official publication of British Foreign Office), 653. For the relative accuracy of the documents contained in this massive volume and, therefore, authenticity of the volume itself *see* the lengthy discussion in note 3 of chapter 14 of Vahakn N. Dadrian, *History of the Armenian Genocide. Ethnic Conflict from the Balkans to Anatolia to the Caucasus* (Providence/Oxford, 1995), 228–29.
2. Ulrich Trumpener, *Germany and the Ottoman Empire 1914–1918* (Princeton, 1968), 219.
3. Frank G. Weber, *Eagles on the Crescent—Germany, Austria, and the Diplomacy of the Turkish Alliance 1914–1918* (Ithaca, 1970), 190.
4. Arnold Toynbee, *Experineces* (Oxford, 1969), 241, 341.
5. Bernard Lewis, *The Emergence of Modern Turkey* (London/New York, 1961, reprinted 1962), 350. When Lewis was challenged by a group pf scholars, artists, civil rights advocates and writers in France on his new revisionist stance, he tried to defend himself on the basis of his claim that he had come across new research evidence. That claim was implicitly made in his submission of October 21, 1994 to the 17th Court at the Palace of Justice (*17 éme Chambre du Tribunal Correctionnel de Paris*) where the lawsuit against him was being adjudicated. However, he failed to respond to the December 27, 1994 request of Prof. Israel Charny from Hebrew University in Jerusalem and the director of the Institute on the Holocaust and Genocide, "to send me, as soon as possible, a compilation of researches on which you base your statement to the court that the evidence about the massacres of the Armenians has changed in the direction of disproving any organized and operational program of extermination. P.S. For your information, I would like to publish and circulate your reply when I receive it along with a copy of this letter." *Internet on the Holocaust and Genocide.* Special Tenth Anniversary Issue. 1985–1995. Nos. 54/55/56. April 1995. p. C–10.
6. Weber, *Eagles on the Crescent* [n. 3], 191.
7. *Ibid.*, 163–65, 202; Trumpener, *Germany and the Ottoman Empire* [n. 2], 96–7, 126–28.
8. A. A. Botschaft Konstantinopel, K 22, I 113/17, folio 19.
9. *Zhamanag* (Istanbul Armenian newspaper), March 27/April 9, 1918.
10. A. A., K 23. Doc. No. 1304. Military Mission Registry. November 17, 1917. I/6154.
11. Text of affidavit in *Jerusalem Armenian Patriarchate Archive.* Dossier 21. File M, No. 252.
12. A. A., K 20. I 1648, folio 30; A. A. Grosses Hauptquartier 203. Dekor. 7/1+2. No. 137, January 22, 1917.
13. FO 371/7814/E6954, folio 126.
14. A. A., K 22. Doc. No. 3424. I 113/17. December 27, 1916; *ibid.*, folio 19.
15. For details on this subject see Vahakn N. Dadrian, "The Naim-Andonian Documents on the World War I Destruction of Ottoman Armenians: The Anatomy of a Genocide" *Interntional Journal of Middle East Studies* 18, 3 (August 1986): 336–38.
16. A. A., K 26. 1012 No. "Secret" (*geheim*) Document. June 5, 1918.
17. FO 371/6500, folio 429/63.
18. A. A., K 12. No. 8810, folio 28. October 16, 1915.
19. Dr. Ernst Sommer, *Die Wahrheit über die Leiden des armenischen Volks in der Türkei während des Weltkriegs* (Frankfurt a. Main, 1919), 16.
20. Grace H. Knapp, *The Tragedy of Bitlis* (Narrative of Grisell M. McLaren) (New York, 1919), 131.
21. FO 371/6500, folio 443/179, 446/182, 447/183.
22. A. A., K 22. J. No. 892. I 113/17, folios 12–13, December 6, 1916.
23. J. Pomiankowski, *Der Zusammenbruch des Ottomanischen Reiches* (Graz, Austria, 1969), 160, 200–201.
24. *Djagadamard*, No. 45 (1859), January 8, 1919.

25. A. A., K 45. Ottoman Foreign Ministry letter-head. I 5648/19. 1917.
26. *Jerusalem Armenian Patriarchate Archive*, Dossier 22. File Hee, No. 204. Individual dossier No. 31, sheet No. 1.
27. *Ibid.*
28. FO 371/6500, folio 392/125. Malta island internee No. 2692.
29. A. A. Grosses Hauptquartier 203, Dekor. 7/1+2. No. 1252. October 11,1916.
30. A. A., K 18, I 4428. December 22, 1916.
31. British Military Attaché Brigadier General W. H. Deeds report. FO 371/6500, folio 388/121.
32. A.A., K 22, I 4713/17, folio 86.
33. George A. Schreiner, *From Berlin to Bagdad. Behind the Scenes in the Near East* (New York 1918), 39.
34. Ismail Hami Danişmend, *Izahlı Osmanlı Tarihi Kronolojisi.* vol. 4 (Istanbul, 1961), 451.
35. Hüsameddin Ertürk, *Iki Devrin Perde Arkası*, S. Tansu, ed. (Istanbul, 1957), 142.
36. Mustafa R. Esatlı, *Ittihad ve Terakki Tarihinde Esrar Perdesi* (Istanbul, 1975), 517.
37. Ambassador Henry Morgenthau, *Secrets of the Bosphorus* (London, 1918), 202. It is noteworthy that in the American edition (p. 307) the name Bedri is substituted by the words "a responsible Turkish official."
38. *See* note 32.
39. Vahakn N. Dadrian, "The Documentation of the World War I Armenian Massacres in the Proceedings of the Turkish Military Tribunal," *International Journal of Middle East Studies* 23, 4 (November 1991): 565.
40. A. A., K 11, No. I 18996. folio 165. 1915.
41. *Ibid.*, K 26, I 22562/119229. folio 69. August 24, 1917.
42. Dadrian, *History of the Armenian Genocide* [n. 1], 219–20, 226–27 note 1, 229 notes 5 and 6.
43. *See* note 40.
44. *See* note 39.
45. A. A., K 22.
46. Ahmet Izzet Paşa, *Feryadım*, vol. 1 (Istanbul, 1992), 201.
47. A. Mil, "Umumi Harpte Teşkilâtı Mahsusa" November 15, 1933 issue of *Vakit*, instalment No. 13.
48. A. A., K 11, No. 7044. folio 174.
49. *Ibid.*, K 22, No. I 20118/105305. I 3850. July 27, 1915.
50. For the details of Halil's complicity *see* Dadrian, *History of the Armenian Genocide* [n. 1], 352–53, 354–55 note 20.
51. A. A., K 14, No. 200, cipher No. 3123, folio 81, March 16, 1916.
52. *Ibid.*, K 20, No. I 3501/21247. I 702, February 9, 1917.
53. A. A., K 170. Report No. 3841. August 23, 1915. For a fuller discussion of the respective role of B. Şakir *see* Dadrian, "The Naim-Andonian Documents" [n.15], 329–31; idem. "The Role of Turkish Physicians in the World War I Genocide of Ottoman Armenians" *Holocaust and Genocide Studies* 1, 2 (1986): 169–174, 184; *idem.* "The Role of the Special Organization in the Armenian Genocide during the First World War" in *Minorities in Wartime* P. Panayi, ed. (Oxford, 1993), 15–18.
54. A. A. Türkei 183/40, A36184.
55. Trumpener, *Germany and the Ottoman Empire* [n. 2], 245–46.
56. A. A. Türkei 183/54 A45718; *Takvimi Vekâyi* (Ottoman government's legal publication covering the Court-Martial trials) No. 3407. For the protracted exchange on this subject between the German Foreign Office and the Ottoman Foreign Ministry, *see* FO 371/4173/82190, 371/4174/98910, 371/5173/E6949, 618/113/1941, folio 404–15; *see also* Y. Bayur, *Türk Inkilâbı Tarihi,* 3,Part 4 (Ankara, 1983), 782.
57. *Takvimi Vekâyi* No. 3604, p. 220.
58. *Ibid.*, No. 3771, p. 2.
59. A. A., K 23. No. 302M.17. I 6042.

60. *Journal D'Orient*. March 19, 1921. A week after his letter of soliciting a loan, i.e., on March 15, 1921, he was assassinated in Berlin by an Armenian student acting as an "avenger" of the murder of his family in Turkey.
61. A. A., K 22. I 4713/17. folio 86.
62. *Ibid.*, Türkie 158/17. A 9661m. March 22, 1917.
63. *Ibid.*, K 19. No. 339. I 1113. folio 96. March 14, 1917.
64. Liman von Sanders, *Five Years in Turkey* (Annapolis, 1927), 14.
65. Ilber Ortaylı, *Osmanlı Imparatorluğunda Alman Nüfuzu* (Istanbul, 1983), 137.
66. Henry Morgenthau, *Ambassador Morgenthau's Story* (Garden City, N. Y., 1918), 370.
67. Fritz Fischer, *Griff nach der Weltmacht* (Düsseldorf, 1967), 112.
68. *Ibid.*, 195–96.

APPENDIX-C

THE DIFFERENTIAL TREATMENT OF THE GREEKS AND THE JEWS (AGAINST THE BACKGROUND OF THE ARMENIAN GENOCIDE)

The Ottoman Doctrine of Domination and the Legacy of Nationality Conflicts—A Historical Perspective

One may never be able to grasp in full measure the reasons for the perpetration of the Armenian genocide. But by further probing the matter within a limited comparative framework new insights may be gained in this respect.

The first question that poses itself here is: what is the relationship of the anti-Armenian genocide policy of the Ittihadists to the overall problem of nationality conflicts in the Ottoman Empire? Secondly, why did the conflict with the Armenians entail the latter's destruction but similar conflict with the Greeks and Jews did not result in wartime exterminatory massacres? What was the role of the Germans in averting the total expulsion of the Greeks from Anatolia up until when Greece in 1917 decided to join up with the Entente Powers and became a belligerent party against Turkey? Likewise, what was that role in containing the conflict with Jewish Zionists about Palestine? The discussion below will address this series of questions.

One of the major premises of this study is the view that the World War I genocide against the Armenians was essentially a form of problem-solving behavior. It was aimed at resolving the protracted and festering Turko-Armenian conflict. But that conflict itself was part of a much larger conflict besetting the latter stages in the career of the Ottoman Empire. Subsumed under the heading of "nationality conflicts," this constituted a problem that was in large part endemic to the theocratic organization of the Ottoman state. There developed a set-up trough which the non-Muslim subject nationalities of the empire were thrust into a precarious position that was pregnant with conflict with the dominant Muslim element of that empire. No amount of contemporary scholarship, partisan of otherwise, can detract from the pervasive reality of this condition, which was both structural, and as far as Ottoman theological doctrines were concerned, immutable. The theocratic dogma, mandating the imposition of a permanently fixed inferior status upon the empire's non-

Muslim subjects, was indeed a factor pregnant with manifold elements of conflict. As the empire weakened progressively, lapsing into many forms of decrepitude, the condition of inferior status, which for a long time had been endured by the non-Muslims through some relief they obtained from the workings of a symbiotic relationship with their Muslim overlords, deteriorated dramatically. The more the scope of inevitable inequities expanded and their tempo intensified, the more the latent character of nationality tensions became energized to transform into acute nationality conflicts. Through the mechanism of escalation, the incidence of nationality conflicts was no longer a mere liability for the maintenance of the empire, but during the Ittihadist regime these conflicts became the Achilles Heel of the empire—as far as its survival was concerned.

Current attempts to mostly gloss over, minimize the significance of, or altogether discount this cardinal fact and its intimate connection with the ultimate demise of the Ottoman Empire by a growing number of contemporary Ottomanists is patently evident. These attempts appear to be intended to avoid disturbing the paths of more or less state-directed Turkish historiography, bent on downplaying the significance of nationality conflicts, and thereby to avoid displeasing those Turkish authorities on whose good-will they may be counting for one reason or another. This dependency-avoidance syndrome is inhibiting many historians committed to examining the root causes of the collapse of the Ottoman Empire.[1] The Armenian genocide epitomizes the corrosive nature of the problem of nationality conflicts that precipitated the disintegration of the Ottoman Empire. The standard references to benevolence, tolerance and pluralism held out as the signal attributes of that empire's social system are by and large partisan avowals that are belied by the historical record—a record that is punctuated by recurrent episodes of sanguinary clashes with and exterminatory massacres against subject nationalities. In commenting on Ottoman state's legacy of lethal violence against its own subjects, a Turkish military commander and historian not only deplored the suborning of the Ottoman military to achieve the ends of such lethal violence but he also prognosticated the grim and fatal outcome of this legacy. The allusion is to Turkish general (*Birici Ferik*) and Commander of Cavalry *(Süvari Kumandanı)* Izzet Fuad Paşa.He was the grandson of the famous Ottoman statesman Keçecizade Fuad Paşa who in the 1863–1866 period twice served as Grand Vizier, and in the 1856–1860 period likewise twice served as Ottoman Foreign Minister. General Izzet Fuad had received his military training in France and in the Abdul Hamit-era had served as ambassador to Spain. In 1908 in Paris he published a volume analyzing the 1877–1878 Russo-Turkish war and the errors and missed opportunities associated with that war. This is what he wrote in the preface of that book:

> But why these wars against our own subjects or vassals? … The imperial Government employed brutal force against peaceful and weak people, who were ventilating their grievances, by mobilizing against them entire armies in order to prevent them from seeking from God, the protector of the oppressed, deliverance from their miseries. And God heard the non-Muslim populations. What was the end result of the engagement of these combative permanent armies: the loss of the most beautiful provinces of the Empire, the material and moral ruination of the Turks. Fatal mistakes, irreparable mistakes.

Here is the fuller and original French text:

> Puisqu'il y avait des insurrections, il fallait bien y affecter des troupes; mais pourquoi ces guerres contre nos propres sujets ou vassaux? Pour quel motif notre chère armée perdrait-elle son noble et précieux sang en combattant ses frères?
>
> Pour réparer les torts de notre administration!
>
> Cette armée devenait ainsi une gendarmerie puissante, pour réparer les abus des gendarmes qui étaient bien plus habiles et prompts à les engendrer que capables d'agir pour calmer les crises nationales qu'ils faisaient naître.
>
> Le bien-être national, la fraternité si nécessaire entre les élèments qui composent l'Empire, l'amour du même drapeau, la convergence indispensable des intérêts, au lieu d'être assurés et obtenus par des moyens normaux et paternels, avaient pour ennemis acharnés nos coupables et féodaux administrateurs, nos valys, nos mutessarifs, nos caïmacams, nos alaÿs beys et nos defterdars, qui agissaient de manière à opprimer par las force brutale les paisibles et les faibles et qui obligeaient le gouvernement impérial à faire marcher des armées entières contre des mécontents, pour les empêcher de demander au Dieu protecteur des opprimés la fin de leurs misérers.
>
> Et Dieu écouta les populations non musulmanes!
>
> Et quel fut le résultat de ces armées permanentes qui combattaient les idés des uns et les revendications des autres: la perte des plus belles provinces de l'Empire, et la ruine matérialle et morale des Turcs!
>
> Erreurs fatales, erreurs irréparables![2]

The Young Turk Ittihadist leadership was neither cognizant of the source of these errors, nor appreciative of the need of ascertaining and rectifying them. As accurately predicted by General Izzet Fuad, this double failure proved not only disastrous for the Ittihadist regime, but, more important, it proved fatal for the empire. In their pertinent statements three foremost representatives of that leadership unwittingly supplied material that typically substantiates this argument, not to speak of a vast array of other such evidentiary material. In August 1910 Ittihadist party chief Talât conceded in a speech he delivered to a secret conclave of Ittihadist leaders that given the tenets of "the *Şeriat* (Sacred laws of Islam), our whole past history, and the sentiments of hundreds of thousands of Mussulmans ..." equality with non-Muslim elements of the empire was impossible.[3] Hüseyin Cahid (Yalçın), the prominent Ittihadist editor and publicist, categorically declared that irrespective of the outcome of the ongoing nationality conflicts in Ottoman Turkey "the Turkish nation is and will remain the ruling nation" (*milleti hâkime*).[4] Ziya Gökalp, the pillar of panturanist ideology and a powerful member of the Central Committee of Ittihad party, was likewise categorical in rejecting the liberal ideals of 19th century *Tanzimat* to which he counterpoised his notion that "Islam mandates domination," and that non-Muslims can co-exist only as subordinate subjects.[5] For all practical purposes then, it is preordained, according to this dogma, that these subjects, can live, labor and thrive as individuals or as communities only at the sufferance of their Muslim-Turkish overlords. The conflict of the Armenians, like the conflict of most other nationalities with the dominant Turks, was a consequence of the institutionalization of this dogma.

It was inevitable that the effects of lingering conflicts between the Ottoman state and a host of disaffected, discordant, or territorially or demographically covetous nationalities in Ottoman Turkey, would carry over into the caldron of wartime tensions and hostilities. In fact, the emergencies and exigencies intrinsic to the war would supply a rare opportunity to the Ittihadist power-wielders to resolve these conflicts by resort to drastic means. But two major considerations impelled the Turks to exercise caution and restraint. One involved the matter of priorities. The general thrust of most of the conflicts with non-Muslim nationalities involved problems associated with inequality and resulting inequities, on the one hand, and the surge of reactive and contentious ethnocentrism, on the other. However, the specifics of these conflicts were quite divergent as far as their history, intensity and channels of expression were concerned. In order to deal with them, the Turkish leaders had to assess them in terms of their own priorities against which the significance of these conflicts was gauged. Their sense of threat to national interests, as defined by them, and the degree of animosity with which they were anxious to settle old scores, were part and parcel of this agenda of priorities.

The second consideration was related to practicality and feasibility. The main question was: which of the discordant nationalities could be dealt with with minimum risk and cost, and which might be a potential source of serious trouble if dealt with in the same manner? The result of these considerations in the present case was containment at one level and selective targeting at another—through the cooptation of the top echelons of the German civilian and military cadres stationed in wartime Turkey.

The Case of the Greeks

Until June 1917 when the Greek king Constantine I abdicated in favor of his son, Alexander, and the Greek government, led by Premier Venizelos, entered the war on the side of the Allied Entente Powers, Turkish antagonism toward the Greek population of Turkey was restrained and measured. It found expression mainly in forcible expulsions (and attendant confiscations) of large clusters of Greek populations inhabiting various coastal and border regions; but it did not reach the level of large-scale exterminatory massacres. Even after the Greeks severed their relations with the Central Powers, including Turkey, the Ittihadists did not want to exacerbate the situation lest the condition of severance deteriorated into one of active warfare with the Greeks. In commenting on this fact Austrian chargé Karl Count zu Trautmannsdorff—Weinsberg told his foreign minister in Vienna that at the time the Turks were exterminating the Armenians, i.e., 18 months ago, they were infused with greater animosity against the Greeks than the Armenians. He went on to say that they would have acted against the former "in a much nastier manner" *(in noch ärgerer Weise*) than they acted against the Armenians—had they actually tried to ventilate these animosities.[6] Two years earlier, Austrian ambassador Johann Markgraf Pallavicini had informed the then Foreign Minister Stephan Baron Burian in Vienna that a top Ittihadist leader had confided to "a credible middleman" that the fate befalling the Armenians awaits the Greeks also. As soon as they were done with the former, they would proceed against the latter (*Nach den Armeniern sollen die Griechen folgen*).[7] On April 8, 1916 the same ambassador repeated the assertion that the Ittihadists would like very much to extend the "inhuman" measures they were applying against the Armenians to the Greeks also but that they were recoiling because of foreign policy considerations.[8] In fact, Ali Şükrü, a deputy in the new Parliament of the fledgling Kemalist regime, in a way confirmed this information. In the course of one of the secret sessions, he expressed regret that the wartime Turkish leaders had failed to take advantage of the war to radically resolve the Greek problem as it related to the conflict about Pontus on the Black See coast.[9]

The conflict with the Greeks, from a Turkish point of view, had both historical and contemporary implications. Greek aspirations against the territories of the Ottoman Empire were particularly energized at the end of the first Balkan War in 1912 when the redoubtable Turkish army was effectively trounced by the Greek army and as a result large populations of European Turkey were appropriated and annexed to Greece.This victory and the subsequent further decline of Turkish Empire served to stimulate among the Greeks of Turkey an irredentism with twin variations, namely, Byzantinist and Greek-Hellenist. The former involved a pathos for a reversion to the conditions of the ancient Byzantine Empire; the latter was a drive for the creation of a Greater Greece with expanded territories bestriding Europe and western Anatolia, especially the Aegean littoral, as well as the Pontus region on the Black Sea. Factors of demography and economy considerably influenced the rise and growth of this irredentist trend and Turkish response to it. The series of Turkish military defeats in the first Balkan war had produced hundreds of thousands of Muslim refugees fleeing before the onslaught of Greek, Bulgarian and Serbian armies and streaming into Istanbul. Terror-stricken, emaciated and destitute to the extreme, these refugees not only became filled with hatred against Christians but transmitted to the rest of the Turkish population a burning desire for revenge that became contagious and in no small way contributed to the wartime initiation of ferocious acts of vendetta against large clusters of non-Muslim populations. This forced exodus continued in 1914 and 1915 when "53,718 Turkish refugees from the territories annexed by Greece" arrived in Istanbul.[10] Turkish reprisals against much more numerous West Anatolian Greeks were not long in coming; they were initiated and in stages in 1916, 1917, and 1918 were expanded to encompass the entire Greek population of the empire.

Though initially these expulsions were organized within the framework of an exchange of Greek and Muslim populations, for which purpose Venizelos, the Greek Premier, in April and May 1914 had negotiated,[11] they actually were "administered" in large part by the secret operatives of the Special Organization. Eşref Kuşcubaşı, the head of the organization, revealed in his postwar accounts that the party and the army, through the cooperation of War Minister Enver and party boss Talât, secretly synchronized their plans to mastermind the undertaking. To these Ittihadist leaders, the underlying, but central problem involved the demographic factor which, as far as they were concerned touched the very heart of national security and survival. Smyrna (Izmir) was dubbed by the Turks *Gâvur* Izmir to emphasize the reality of the overall, but especially economic, control of that city, and of the entire region, by "infidel" non-Muslims, Greeks in particular. In his accounts Kuşcubaşı reveals further that secret conferences were organized at the War Ministry in the months of May, June and August 1914 to which were invited young staff officers who had been appointed by War Minister Enver as Chief of Staff at a number of Army Corps.

They came to Istanbul "under false pretenses" (*birer vesile ile*), and even some Cabinet ministers were kept in the dark about these deliberations. The purpose of these meetings was the need to come up with a plan to "liquidate these densely formed non-Muslim population clusters" (*gayrı-Türk yığınakların tasfiyesi*). Entrusted with this task, Kuşcubaşı undertook an exploratory trip to the region. To conceal the purpose of his mission he was to avoid contact with Turkish officials and to wear garbs that disguised his identity. His closest collaborator in this enterprise was Celal Bayar, at the time the youngest Responsible Secretary of Ittihad party, whose innocuous sounding party title, responsible secretary, belied the enormous power with which he and all other provincial responsible secretaries were vested.[12] In describing the "terrorism" and its "systematic" application to the thousands of Greeks who were thus being expelled in 1914, Toynbee confirms the employment of the *Çetes,* the brigand cadres of the Special Organization, which included "the Rumeli refugees" from the Balkans.[13] Subsequent developments in warfare, such as the occupation in the spring of 1916 of the three vitally strategic Greek islands of Mitylini-Lesbos (*Midilli*), Chios (*Sakız*), and Samos (*Sisam*), by the naval forces of the Entente Powers, and the advent of Venizelos' pro-Entente government, were considered by the Turks critical enough to prompt them to broaden the scope of the deportations.

In all these proceedings one condition stands out as being most noteworthy—insofar as the subject of the Armenian genocide is concerned. As Toynbee underscored, throughout the application of these measures against the Greeks, whether Ottoman Greeks or so-called Hellenic Greeks, i.e., Greeks who were citizens of Greece but dwelled in Turkey, no large scale exterminatory massacres took place.[14] A brief inquiry into the reasons of this condition may shed more light on the circumstances of the Armenian genocide and the matter of German responsibility in that respect.

In his memoirs American ambassador Morgenthau not only confirms Toynbee's assessment about the absence of large scale exterminatory massacres in the deportation of the Greeks, but offers an explanation also. "These caravans suffered great privations, but they were not submitted to general massacre as were the Armenians. ... The Turks showed them this greater consideration not from any motive of pity. The Greeks, unlike the Armenians, had a government which was vitally interested in their welfare. ... It was only a matter of state policy, therefore, that saved these Greek subjects of Turkey from all the horrors that befell the Armenians."[15] That expression of Greek state policy was brought to bear upon Turkish state policy by way of restraining it to some extent. Two months after Turkey intervened in the war, and the Special Organization project to evict and expropriate large segments of the Greek population of the Aegean Sea Littoral was activated, Greek Premier Venizelos sent a warning to the Ittihadist rulers. Unless they relented in their drive to persecute the Greeks, the Greek government "might be obliged to resort to strong measures ..." i.e., reprisals against the Turkish subjects of Greece. To put emphasis to this warning, the Austrian and German ambassadors in Athens were apprised of it; they were expected to urge upon the Turks the exercise of a measure of moderation. The British document containing this information states that the warning more or less served its purpose.[16]

But there was another factor that served to deter the Turks from escalating their level of victimization of the Greeks to a level of genocide applied to the Armenians. That was the German factor. Until the time when he abdicated, June 1917, Greek king Constantin I was known for his pro-German orientation; his wife, Sophia of Prussia, was the sister of German emperor William II. Even though German generals, especially Bronsart and Sanders, at one time or another favored the deportation of certain clusters of Greek populations from certain zones as a matter of "military necessity,"[17] the overarching German attitude in this respect was cautious protectiveness.

Without being confrontational, a number of high ranking German military and civilian officials tried to dissuade those Turkish potentates who were authorizing draconian measures. In December 1917, for example, Marshal Liman von Sanders alerted the German ambassador Bernstorff about an order by War Minister Enver who wanted "the deportation of virtually all Greeks of the coast to inland areas. ..." Enver had prepared a list of five categories for the deportation order. Sanders "had personally intervened and had succeeded *because he had threatened to resign*." The German Foreign Office supported the efforts of Sanders and Ambassador Bernstorff, and let it be known that it "advised strongly against the deportations."[18] A similar *threat of resignation* by Marshal von der Goltz materialized when the Turkish deputy governor of Baghdad in 1916 ordered the wholesale deportation of the Greek residents of that city. As

Commander-in-Chief of the VIth Ottoman Army in Iraq (Sanders commanded the Vth Army) Goltz energetically and swiftly protested against the order and War Minister Enver had to be accommodative in order to avert his actual resignation.[19] All the while, however, "the plundering and burning down of a large number of Greek villages … and the forcible relocation in the interior of Turkey of 70,000 Greeks from the Littoral, stretching from Bafra to Tirebolu [on the Black Sea] continued; many of the victims in all likelihood died due to the privations they incurred."[20]

To demonstrate his solidarity with the deported Greeks, German emperor William II authorized the allocation of 10,000 Deutsche Marks to be used as relief money for the needs of these deported Greeks. Chancellor Bethmann Hollweg instructed German consul Dr. Bergfeld, who was taking care of the needs of the consulates of Trabzon and Erzurum (at that time it was located in Sıvas) to monitor the condition of these deportees and assist those in need with monetary disbursements. In relaying this information to his ambassador in the Ottoman capital, Austrian Consul Kwiatkowski stated: "This instruction of the Chancellor reflects, according to sources in local German circles, the acute interest which His Majesty, the German Emperor, brings to bear on all Greek matters (*entspringt dem hohen Interesse … allen griechischen Angelegenheiten entgegenbringt*).[21]

Many of the constraints dissipated, of course, following the new Greek government's decision in the summer of 1917 to enter the war on the side of the Allies. But by then the military setbacks of the Turkish army and the near collapse of the eastern front in face of the steady Russian onslaughts there had sufficiently demoralized the Ittihadist leadership which consequently recoiled before new initiatives of exterminatory massacres to be enacted against a new victim population, the Greeks. Nevertheless, by Turkish resort to methods other than outright massacre the bulk of the Greek population of Turkey for all practical purposes was eventually eliminated also. This process of elimination was attended by a protracted guerrilla campaign the Greeks waged against the Turks, especially in the Black Sea Littoral area, during and in the wake of World War I when the Greco-Turkish war ended in 1922 with the victory of the insurgent Kemalists.

The Case of the Jews

Compared to the Armenian and Greek cases, the case of the Jews stands out in several respects, especially so in one respect. Unlike the Greeks and the Armenians, the Jews were spared the level of persecution and destruction that was inflicted upon the former—when one disregards a few incidents of forced deportations and "evacuations" of Jews in Smyrna, Syria, Iraq and Palestine. This, despite the fact that, like in the case of the Armenians and Greeks, so in the case of the Jews certain groups of individuals chose to join the Allied armies as volunteers to fight against the Turks, and some other individuals among them engaged in espionage for the benefit of the Entente Powers, particularly England. A number of factors combined to induce, if not impel, the Turks to accord the Jews this differential and, for practical purposes, indulgent treatment. Foremost among these was the German factor. Indeed, active and effective intervention on behalf of threatened Jews in wartime Turkey, Palestine, Iraq, and Syria in particular, was more or less a by-product of interventionist German policy that was practiced throughout the war. The German Foreign Office in Berlin and successive German ambassadors in Istanbul, especially Wangenheim, often went out of their way to come to the rescue of imperiled Jews; they clearly had the support of Kaiser Wilhelm II. This is the more significant when one considers the recurrent German argument that the Turkish treatment of Ottoman Armenians was an internal Turkish affair and as such it precluded, legally and otherwise, German intervention. Even more significant is the fact that German and Austrian diplomats, when reporting to their foreign offices about the unfolding Armenian genocide, occasionally complained that the Turks were using the alliance with Germany and Austria as a "prop" (*Stütze*), as a "shield" (*Schutz*), to "proceed in the severest manner" against the Armenians,[22] and to "resolve the Armenian question," as a result of which they caused "the ruination (*Untergang*) of hecatombs of innocent people."[23] There is a paradox in this phenomenon of shifting roles and postures concerning the enactment of the Armenian genocide and the proffered alternative rationales associated with these roles and postures. On the one hand the alliance is used by the victimizers as a prop to decimate a victim population, and on the other hand, it is also used by Turkey's allies as a prop to deter and consequently avert the victimization, perhaps on a much lesser scale, of another potential victim population. Such are the leeways of the uses and misuses of power.

The Factor of Jewish Dispersion and Demography

The complexities of this phenomenon require, however, a broader and more detailed discussion through which more light may be shed on the intentions and motives of German officials who elected to abet, directly or indirectly, the Turkish genocide against the Armenians, and concomitantly elected to protect the Jewish population from the perils of massive deportations. In comparing the treatment accorded to the Jews with the more calamitous fate of the Armenians and Greeks one has to be cognizant first of all of the critical importance of twin factors through the examination of which that differential treatment may lend itself to a greater understanding. The reference is to the factors of history and demography. Whereas the relationships of the Greeks and Armenians with the Turks were critically strained by the tensions stemming from the lingering Turko-Greek and Turko-Armenian conflicts, the Jews by and large were free from the burdens of such a legacy. On the contrary, Turko-Jewish relations for centuries were in the main punctuated by elements of concordance and harmony rather than discord and conflict. Given the adversities they have been experiencing in Europe, including Russia, in terms of discriminatory practices which at times escalated to active forms of persecution, including pogroms, the Jews found in Ottoman Turkey a refuge which served for them as a safe haven from such persecution. This type of treatment of the Jews by Ottoman authorities is highlighted by a major historical event: the benevolent hospitality the latter extended to the Jewish exiles who were expelled from Spain at the end of the fifteenth and the beginning of the sixteenth centuries. This large scale exodus had followed similar but lesser expulsions in the preceding two centuries, namely, from England in 1290, and France in 1329, and was itself followed by an expulsion from Portugal in 1497. Like the Armenians and the Greeks, these Jewish refugees subsequently could organize themselves and function under the Ottoman *millet* system which allowed for a measure of autonomy in religious and civil matters. Moreover, given the religious underpinnings of this system, the Chief Rabbi (*Khahambaşı*) was given broad scope in the administration of this autonomous system; he functioned more or less as the head of the Jewish community, with the commensurate authority having been vested in him by the Ottoman state. This condition was most noteworthy on two accounts. It provided a special impetus to, and thereby accented, the religious ingredients of the Jewish sense of national identity. Equally significant, it contrasted sharply with the ill-treatment of Jews in Christian Europe, even though elsewhere, where Islam dominated, Jewish experience began with massacre and expulsion, such as in the northern part of the Arabian peninsula, in North Africa (the Jews of Almohade), and Yemen in the twelfth and thirteenth centuries.

But these elements of history were not a *sui generis* phenomenon; they were inextricably interwoven with a companion phenomenon in which history and demography converged to impart to the Jews in the Ottoman state system a status and a significance that was dramatically at variance with those of the Armenians and Greeks. The allusion is to the history of Jewish exile that was triggered by the destruction of the ancestral Jewish state on the part of the Romans. The resulting worldwide dispersion of the Jews and the formation of an array of separate diasporas led not only to the geographic fragmentation of the Jewish people but also precluded the emergence within the Ottoman domain, such as in Palestine, of a territorially cohesive Jewish population. Consequently, Turkey was free from the type of troubles which were besetting it as a result of the nationality conflicts involving the Greeks and the Armenians. Eager to emancipate themselves from Turkish domination and misrule, they sought not only foreign intervention but also the support of their co-nationals inhabiting in territories which were contiguous to Ottoman Turkey. These external ties, the geography, the density and size of the Greek and Armenian population clusters were factors which combined to thrust the Turko-Armenian and Turko-Greek conflicts to the forefront of Turkish national concerns; radical designs of conflict resolution followed the inevitable radicalization of the conflict as afforded by the opportunities and exigencies of the war. In accounting for the main motive of the perpetrators of the Armenian genocide, for example, a prominent Turkish publicist and Ittihadist, who had received his Ph.D. training as a sociologist at Columbia University, underscored the threat the Armenians posed to Turkey by virtue of their geographic concentration near the Russian border, and their density of population. While in detention in the British island of Malta for later trial, he was able to learn a great deal from some of the most notorious organizers of the Armenian genocide who were likewise being detained there by the British. According to him, the rationale of "Those who put forward the policy of general extermination" was as follows: "A dense Armenian population, in the Eastern Provinces, has proved to be danger to the very existence of Turkey. We are acting as instruments to remove this danger. We know that successful or not successful, we shall be universally despised and condemned."[24] Another Ittihadist, who later became a lifelong confidant of the founder of the Republic of Turkey, Mustafa Kemal (Atatürk), likewise wrote about one of these organizers of the genocide. "Şakir was bent on eliminating the Armenian nation in order to prevent the formation of a future Armenia. … Had the Armenians remained concentrated in the East, there is no doubt that in 1918 at the time of the Armistice they undoubtedly immediately would have created an Armenia. … Genocide is one of the gravest crimes against humanity. …"[25] In brief, the Jews of Turkey were not burdened with the perilous ballast of the factors of history and demography animating on the one hand the Greeks and the Armenians, and on the other, the Turks, who were resolved to divest themselves of that ballast at the first opportunity.

One has to inject here, however, a caveat lest the inference is made that traditional Turkish liberality and tolerance towards the Jews was pure benevolence and magnanimity. Rather, there were conditions circumscribing this attitude. They were the same conditions which reduced the Armenians and Greeks to the status of subordinate "infidels," relegating them to an inferior status; they could live and even prosper only at the sufferance of their Muslim overlords. The precepts of the *Koran,* the restrictions and proscriptions of the *Şeriat*, the canon law of Islam, and the theocratic structure of the Ottoman state system were such as to disallow any other alternative. Even the so-called "privileges," often held out as symbols of Ottoman benevolence toward non-Muslim subject, had an ambivalent purpose. While they offered broad scope for religious freedom, at the same time, however, they provided mechanisms for the segregation and exclusion of the very subjects who ostensibly were being accorded privileges. Indeed, Article 11 of the 1876 Ottoman Constitution, which granted such "religious privileges" to the subject non-Muslim nationalities, declares at the same time categorically that "Islamism is the religion of the State." And Islam does not allow equality for people who are not Muslims. It is precisely for this reason that Tekin Alp, one of the high priests of modern Turkish nationalism, rejected the validity of the claim of "privileges". Instead, he defined Article 11 as "the high separation wall" between dominant Muslims and subordinate non-Muslims.[26] The prominent French expert of international law Ed Engelhardt, likewise maintained that "privilege" meant "separation" involving "religious antagonism" and "state reason."[27] That antagonism was nurtured and sustained through a degree of contempt, bordering on sheer hatred, that many Muslims, especially those identified with the Ottoman religious establishment, such as the majority of *softas, mollas, ulemas, kadis* and *müftis*, harbored toward non-Muslims, including the Jews. That the Jews endured abuses in this connection was acknowledged by one of the German Jewish pioneers of Zionism who tirelessly labored to protect the interests of the Jews in Palestine during World War I and was reasonably successful in checking the passions of some Ittihadist leaders who were bent on enacting large scale Jewish deportations. In his memoirs Richard Lichtheim declared, "Like the Armenians and the Greeks, the Jews of Turkey owned up to their nationality and religion. Assimilation was out of the question. But in Europe there had spread the myth that all was well with the Jews of Turkey. One could not forget the persecution (*Verfolgung*) inflicted upon the Jews by earlier sultans, and with the emergence of the Young Turk Ittihadists the relationships between the Turkish overlords *(Herrenvolk)* and the non-Turkish nationalities perceptibly intensified."[28]

The Rudiments of Zionism and the Ottoman Stonewalling

The beginnings of that intensification, as far as the Jews were concerned, coincide with the advent of Zionism in the arena of international politics, and the initiatives of Theodor Herzl, espousing, advocating and promoting that Zionism. Indeed, with the stirrings of new Jewish national sentiment in Europe, especially Germany and Russia, in the second half of the nineteenth century, and the channeling of that sentiment into the vistas of a new movement that envisaged salvation for Jewry only in Ingathering, i.e., the recreation of the Palestinian homeland, there developed in diplomacy and politics a new focus on the Jews and Jewry as an international problem. The core of that new national sentiment was formed by the general perception that anti-Semitism will continue to haunt and trouble the Jews everywhere in the global diaspora and that assimilation even when accepted by host countries, was not and could not be a panacea against that affliction. The transition from reactive to self—assertive nationalism opened up a new era of confrontation for the pillars of the new Zionist movement concentrating on the task of launching a large scale immigration project; the goal was to create extensive and accelerated Jewish settlements in Palestine by a variety of means, including acquisition of tracts of land, property, and the establishment of agricultural colonies.

But Palestine was part of the Ottoman Empire and Turkey in the latter half of the nineteenth century was in progressive decline on account of several factors but primarily on account of a series of corrosive nationality conflicts resulting from structural inequities and attendant chronic misrule. These conflicts, and the Ottoman-Turkish method of resolving them through sanguinary repression had provoked the Powers to intervene, thereby further aggravating the overall problem of nationality conflicts. Herzl's unrelenting efforts for the realization of his central objective must be assessed against this cardinal fact. His ability to engage first the attention of the German emperor, his success in securing an audience with him (September 2, 1898) to plead his cause, followed by his ultimate failure when three months later the same Kaiser refused to receive him, are part of the vicissitudes of the struggle that was to be waged in face of an apprehensive and obdurate sultan. While he claimed to be "interested" in and even "sympathetic" to the "fundamental idea of Zionism," William II let it be known that he would be glad to get rid of the Jews whom he derisively called "*the Mauschels*," adding "Let them go to Palestine, the sooner they move off the better." One reason for this attitude was the perception that the Jews tended to concentrate in large cities, did become adherents of the Social Democratic party, and thus constituted a "real political danger" to Germany and to the monarchy. In his first and, as far as it is known, last effort to intercede with Sultan Abdul Hamit on behalf of the Zionists, William II again used disparaging words about the Jews while ostensibly trying to assist them in their cause. During the banquet honoring his second October 1898 visit to Constantinople, a way-station for his main trip to Damascus and Jerusalem, he is said to have declared to his host, the Sultan, "… everywhere the Jews are a nuisance … one should like to get rid of them." The result was that "the Sultan rejected the Kaiser's suggestion so brusquely that it was not possible to pursue the matter further."[29]

Undaunted, Herzl pursued the matter independently. His main effort was directed to the goal of personally persuading the Sultan that it was in Ottoman-Turkish interest to allow the creation in Palestine of a Jewish homeland, and that the Ottoman state could expect to be amply rewarded for its assent. In fact the 1897 Basle program was predicated upon a simple condition: "Zionism strives to create for the Jewish people a home in Palestine, secured by public law" (*Der Zionismus erstrebt für das jüdische Volk die Schaffung einer öffentlich-rechtlich gesicherten Heimstätte in Palästina*). The Charter Herzl sought to obtain for this purpose was denied to him, despite his personal meeting with the Sultan (May 18, 1901) and four additional trips to the Palace in the May 1901 – July 1902 period. Herzl's difficulties were compounded by resistance to him and his movement from a variety of sources in the Jewish diaspora. Jewish communities in the Ottoman domain were afraid of Turkish backlash. Many German-Jewish groups, including rabbinical groups, denounced Zionism as offensive to their sense of German citizenship and even patriotism, and to the religious tenets of Judaism. The bulk of Jewish financiers and industrialists in Western Europe initially refused to offer financial help. But, in the final analysis, the failure was bound up with Turkish intransigence, the core elements of which call for a brief review.

An important ingredient of the nationality conflicts in the Ottoman Empire involved the system of capitulations affording growing numbers of non-Turks the excuse to claim protection from foreign Powers while evading the clutches of a corrupt and venal court system. That system of capitulations not only derogated the principle of sovereign jurisdiction but ushered in a companion system of foreign interventions. The majority of the Jews, especially the Ashkenazim from Europe, and subsequently Jews from Russia, who were able to migrate to Palestine, refused, or indefinitely delayed, their naturalization through the adoption of Ottoman citizenship. To forestall the deterioration of this trend, the Ottoman authorities introduced a new regulation whereby the immigrants' permits to enter and stay in Palestine had to be countersigned by Turkish authorities. Other restrictions on residence, economic activity and taxation followed; the new Law of Nationality in 1869 had already severely restricted the practice of claiming a right to foreign protection. But the main Turkish concern, bordering on paranoia, related to the demographic implications of the Jewish scheme of Ingathering. The formation of a new concentric Jewish population within the borders of the Ottoman realm portended to the Turks problems and perils they could readily conjure up and identify with against the backdrop of their history of nationality conflicts throughout the empire.

The Armenian Angle in the Struggle of Zionism

This is precisely the reason why both parties, Herzl on the one hand, and the Ottoman authorities on the other, injected into the picture the example of the case of Ottoman Armenians as a yardstick for evaluating and extrapolating the ramifications of the Zionist plan of immigration and settlements in Palestine. The three aspects of this use of the Armenian angle are worth noting.

1. Apart from availing himself of the assistance certain Armenian functionaries at the Palace and the Ottoman Foreign Office readily offered him,[30] Herzl tried to accommodate the Sultan in his bid to win the latter's favors for the Zionist cause. He offered to play the role of a conciliating intermediary between the beleaguered Sultan and the Armenian revolutionaries militantly challenging the latter to implement the reforms he had undertaken to carry out (October 1895) under the pressure of the six European Powers. The Sultan let Herzl know, through

the mediation of Philip Michael de Newlinski, a Polish-Austrian journalist, an agent and apparently one of the rare confidants of the Sultan, that he might grant an audience, which Herzl was so eagerly seeking, if he would see to it that the foreign press in London, Paris, Berlin and Vienna treated the Armenian question in a pro-Turkish fashion, and if he were to influence the Armenian leaders to the effect that in exchange for the concessions the Sultan was prepared to make to them they would submit to his authority.[31] The suggestion was actually Newlinski's who impressed upon Herzl the idea that by inducing the Armenians to accept a truce, or to delay their assault against the Sultan, he could promote the Jewish cause by telling the Sultan that "It was Jewish power that rendered him this service" (*dass die Judenmacht ihm diesen Dienst geleistet habe*). The task then was "to grab and make use of the Armenian affair" (*die Armenische Sache nützlich verschleppen*).[32] When the Armenian Dashnak revolutionaries struck on August 14/26, 1896, in their raid against Bank Ottoman, the nerve center of European, and indirectly Ottoman, Finance, and captured it, three days later Herzl entered in his diary the remark that "the moment was very favorable to negotiate a deal" with the Sultan.[33] As author Norman Kotker observed in this connection, "Though Herzl was not insensitive to the horrors of the Armenian situation, he was not averse to trading on the misery of the Armenians for his own benefit."[34] In the end, however, he was outmaneuvered by the crafty monarch whose final *coup de grace* involved using Herzl's offer to consolidate the huge Ottoman Public Debt against the granting of concession for his plan of Jewish colonization; the Sultan was thus able to induce the French to outbid Herzl for the same purpose of debt consolidation.[35]

2. When Herzl's proposal was being rejected on February 4, 1898, the critical issue was whether the legal foundation of the concept of "a home in Palestine," that was launched at the Basle Congress of the Zionists, were to be anchored on Ottoman public law, or international law, in which case, European Powers could intervene in terms of binding engagements. At that time Turkish Foreign Minister Ahmed Tevfik Paşa told Herzl that Jewish immigrants were welcome to Turkey but no specific territory could be set aside for them; nor could there be any question of autonomy. When informing Tevfik that such an arrangement was unacceptable to Herzl, it was understood that the latter had likened that arrangement to a "settlement of new Armenians in Turkey."[36]

3. The intensity of Turkish intransigence against a plan of Jewish home in Palestine was matched by the ferocity of spirit underlying it. That ferocity came to the fore when the same Tevfik Paşa is reported to have declared at the time that " ... the Turks had settled their accounts with the Armenians in three days; with the Zionists it would take only three hours."[37]

The Young Turks and the Palestine Issue

The banner of liberalism under which the Ittihadists in 1908 had launched their revolution and deposed Abdul Hamit, the autocratic monarch, had inspired great hopes among the non-Muslim nationalities of the Ottoman Empire. Those Jews, identified with Zionism, were particularly hopeful as regards their prospects of a homeland in Zion. There were some grounds for such optimism. The most vibrant center of the Ittihadist revolution was Saloniki where, out of a total population of 173,000, some 80,000 were Jews. Most of them were the progeny of the multitudes who had escaped from Spain and Inquisition. A number of them had converted to Islam and were labeled *dönmes,*[38] which meant that their assimilation into the culture of Islam was not complete as they were believed to be harboring covertly a residual sense of Jewish identity.[39] Nor was their conversion always accepted by the Muslims surrounding them. A quasi-sectarian subculture developed as a result. Furthermore, many of the leaders of the Jewish community of that city, including the Chief Rabbi, the mayor, and the editor of the prominent newspaper, *L'Epoca*, were sympathetic to Zionism. Most important, some influential members of Ittihad party were *dönmes*, such as the Parliament deputies Emmanuel Carasso, Nesim Masliyah, and Nesim Russo, who was also Director of the Special Secretariat (*Hususi Kalem*) in the Ministry of Finances. In December 1908 they declared their intention to join the Zionist Organization and found an Ottoman branch with the proviso that Zionism would disavow any autonomist or separatist goals. A few months later Carasso proposed to found an Ottoman Immigration Company for Palestine, and "Turkey in general." This group of deputies was joined by Avram (*Chaim*) Nahum, who soon after his promotion from the rank of Deputy to Chief Rabbi of Turkey expressed solidarity with Zionism by sending a congratulatory telegram to a group of Zionists who had convened in Odessa.

All these manifestations of cautious ardor for the cause of Zionism received a signal boost from a source that was as authentic as powerful. One of the foremost leaders of the Young Turk Ittihad party was Dr.

Nazım, likewise from Saloniki, who in an interview spoke favorably about Zionism;[40] he advocated the immigration into Turkey of six to eight million Jews whom he considered to be the "most reliable element." In this sense he approved Saloniki deputy Carasso's plan of Jewish immigration into Turkey.[41] There were some specific reasons for this proactive stance which Nazım assumed. He was eager to promote the complete integration of Saloniki *dönmes* into the mainstream of Turkish national life. According to Turkish author and chronicler Doğan Avcıoğlu, the Ittiahdists had been cultivating close ties with Saloniki *dönmes* and Jews who belonged to certain Masonic lodges, lodges of which these Ittihadists had become members also.[42] This objective was given great publicity when the Central Committee of Ittihad decided to "appropriate" the marriage of Turkish publicist Zekeriya Sertel with a *dönme* girl. As described by Sertel, this is what happened: "Dr. Nazım summoned me and after congratulating me asked me whether I was aware of the import of what I was doing. 'You may not know it but you are opening up a path for the blending of two communities who look at each other disdainfully. You are delivering the death-blow to the cast of the *dönmes.* We should capitalize on this event and celebrate it as an occasion for the union of the Turks with the *dönmes.* It is necessary to define this as a national and historical event. We ourselves shall perform your wedding and publicize it in the newspapers; we shall take it out of its purview as a family affair and treat it instead as a national event.'" The wedding took place with great pomp and circumstance. Party boss Talât and prominent Ittihadist Tevfik Rüşdü (later in the Turkish Republic era, Foreign Minister) acted as "best man," with the party underwriting the expenses of the entire wedding.[43]

Another significant reason involved the Ittihadist perception of the other nationalities of the empire which was negative in essence and thrust. To that perception was being counterpoised that of the Jews as the "most reliable element," to quote Nazım again.[44] As Nahum, at the time Deputy Chief Rabbi of Turkey, declared succinctly, the Turks needed "an alliance with the Jews in order to counter the influence of the Greeks and the Armenians."[45] During the economic boycott the Ittihadists launched in the pre-war years against Austria, Italy, and particularly Greece, "the Jews and *dönmes* in pursuit of profits, supported the Ittihadist nationalist drive that was being energized through the scheme of a 'national economy' and at the expense of the Greeks, who were more identified with England and France, on account of their commerce with them."[46] In explaining his rationale Nazım further averred that the antagonism of the Arab deputies from Syria to the Ittihadist regime "would weigh strongly in the Zionists' favor."[47]

But Nazım's support of Zionism was neither unconditional nor entirely independent from the desiderata from his Ittihadist cohorts situated in the top echelons of the party. Already at the time he was patronizing Carasso's plan of immigration into Palestine he had stipulated a condition. "He would allow no more than two to four million Jews to come; settlement in excess of this number would constitute 'a danger'."[48] As underscored a number of times in this discussion that danger spelled: demography and the pitfall of centrifugal tendencies of separatist autonomy. Dr. Alfred Nossig, who at one time was very active in the Zionist movement in Germany and in 1909 had established the General Jewish Colonization Organization (*Allgemeine Jüdische Kolonisations-Organisation*), with ambitions to blend in his endeavors the roles of Herzl and of Baron Edmond Rothschild,[49] had personally known Dr. Nazım and described him as "the most powerful man" (*der stärkste Mann des Komitees*) of Ittihad party. But he also pointed out in his book that despite appearances, Ittihad operated on the basis of collective decisionmaking produced by a small clique.[50] The subsequent debates within the inner circle of Ittihad not only confirmed this fact but also indicated the anti-Zionist drift of that clique—as far as the plans of a Palestinian homeland were concerned.

In order to understand the reasons for the constancy of this posture of the party through the years of World War I, the circumstances of its formal initiation and consolidation may be detailed briefly. The March 31/April 13, 1909 counter-revolution against Ittihad, and its bloody repression by the pro-Ittihad Turkish army, had ushered in a period of mutual recriminations within the higher strata of party leadership. Diatribes and invectives dominated some of the ensuing discussions. One of the areas of cleavage was caused by the contention of some dissidents challenging the leadership that was in control that the twin influences of Zionism and freemasonry were making inroads into the politics of some top party leaders and that there was a danger of these influences growing and permeating the entire party apparatus. In the process an alarm was sounded about the presumed perils threatening the eventual loss of Jerusalem and Palestine. The controversy was activated for the first time by Colonel Sadık, one of the original co-founders of the party. Prior to the convening in Saloniki of the 1909 annual party convention, he prepared a memorandum in which he detailed his observations about what he considered to be Zionist and Masonic inroads into Turkish political life through the instrumentality of some prominent Ittihadists. In the process he inveighed against what he called "Jewish-Masonic domination of world economy and world press. They are twisting and channeling world public opinion in any direction they want. They are finding ways and means to win over and for their benefit to catapult into the high offices and the parliaments of every nation those people who are after high positions, fame, profit and glory—thanks to the help provided by freemasonry and other organizations. They have permeated also the universities. We did not embark upon a revolution to free ourselves from the yoke of Abdul Hamit only to see the emergence of these upstarts and to be enslaved by them. The Zionists are dreaming today of the collapse of the Ottoman state; they are at least dreaming of the breakout of Jerusalem and Palestine and the establishment of a Jewish government."[51]

Given the inflammatory character of the contents of this memorandum and its focus on the sensitive problem of nationalities, it was not included in the formal agenda of the party since the congress participants comprised many representatives of different religions and nationalities. But it was read and discussed in a special party conclave to which were invited only those members who had joined the party prior to the outbreak of the July 1908 revolution, and the members of the Central Committee of the party; there were former and currently active masons in both groups. The two foremost leaders of the party, Talât and Dr. Nazım, categorically rejected the allegations and denunciations of Colonel Sadık. Nazım defended the *dönmes,* especially, Cavid, the party's expert on economics, by arguing that among those who enriched Turkish history and brought glory to it, there were many who belonged to different religions and to different races. Colonel Sadık, he said, is trying to become instantly the leader of "the party and with the intent to proceed to becoming a high executive of government. Therefore, he is restless" (*bihuzurdur*).[52]

Despite this recourse to rebuttal in the meeting, however, the party leaders launched a series of arrangements and measures to curb the perceived influences of Zionism and freemasonry. They decided to strengthen, for example, the Islamic education of the general public and the school population. Moreover, the Central Committee of the party "speeded up the fight against Zionism and freemasonry and for this purpose created in the Directorate of Police a special bureau."[53] The episode ultimately culminated in "a historical decision which the party's Central Committee reached on January 16, 1910." (old style) After acknowledging the usefulness of "the negotiations with our brother, Colonel Sadık, the Central Committee unanimously (*ittifakla*) decided:

the party cannot favor (*iltizam*) the immigration of the Jews into the Ottoman realm under the standard of Zionism." In the same vein it rejected the efforts of deputies Carasso and Nesim Russo to have a memorandum about Jewish immigration debated in the Chamber of Deputies; therefore, the decision went on to say, "it should be completely quashed" (*külliyen iptal*).[54] Notwithstanding, the bitter feuds did not abate as factionalism and personal animosities and rivalries among the leaders of Ittihad and between these and the leaders of other parties, continued to fuel these feuds. On February 16, 1910 (old style), or March 1, 1911 (new style) these feuds found expression in a bitter confrontation between Ismail Hakkı, deputy of Gümülcine, a former Ittihadist and at the time president of the rival *Ahali* party, and Interior Minister and at the same time Edirne deputy, Talât. The former accused some Ittihadist leaders of consorting with the Zionists of Berlin, of having allowed broad scope to the latter to project new settlements in Palestine. In response, Talât denied having made any deals with the Zionists, at the same time declaring that the Jewish proposal of settlements in Turkey was "categorically (*kesinlikle*) rejected by the government." Ibrahim Hakkı, the president of the Chamber (later Grand Vizier), joined Talât in casting aspersions on the veracity of Ismail's charges.[55] During the same debate Greek deputy Kossimidi accused Cavid, who often served as Ittihadist Minister of Finances, of favoring Jewish interests at the expense of the Ottoman State. Deputy Ismail Hakkı, on the other hand, saw in Cavid's negotiations with British and French financiers "a finger of Zionism" which was an "evil creed bent on erecting a Jewish state" in Palestine through the help of highly placed Jews in Turkey.[56] British sources played some role in the dissemination of such allegations with special emphasis on the role of freemasons as instrumental props.[57]

Thus, the bitter lessons of history, and inability to grasp the root causes of these bitter experiences, were factors which impelled the Ittihadists to prevent by all means the Zionists from realizing their ideal of Jewish Ingathering in Palestine—up to World War I. The specter of a new and perilous configuration of demography was disconcerting enough for the Turks to resist and reject all Jewish overtures for a deal-making in this connection.

Anti-Turkish Jewish Military Operations and Espionage and the Factor of Jewish Vulnerability in Wartime Turkey

The abortiveness of the Zionist scheme to create a Jewish homeland in Palestine was only in part due to the failure of the Jewish diasporas to forge a common front for the realization of the scheme. In large part, and perhaps decisively, it was due to the intractability of Ottoman-Turkish authorities opposing that scheme, be they those of the Abdul Hamit-era or the young Turk Ittihadist regime. Herzl and his colleagues could not enlist the firm support of the Powers, especially England and Germany, because the reluctance of these Powers to antagonize the Turks on this score.

The outbreak or World War I and the delayed intervention in that war by Turkey (October-November 1914), were dramatic enough events to usher in a set of circumstances that were pregnant with both opportunities and pitfalls for Zionism and its goals. Aware of this condition of ambivalence, the leadership of that movement had decided to assume a neutral stance.[58] And for this reason, the main focus of interest and attention during that war, at least until the middle of 1917, was the welfare of the Jews in Turkey in general, and in Palestine in particulars, as far as relations with the Young Turk Ittiahdists were concerned. The situation was less clear, however, with the positions of the Powers which were now divided into two enemy camps: The Allies of the Entente Powers (Great Britain, France and Russia), on the one hand, and the Central Powers (Germany, Austria, and Turkey, mainly), on the other. Consequently the Jews (whether Zionists or non-Zionists) in these countries felt certain pressures to identify with the political interests of their host countries; the more assimilated or assimilation-prone ones did not need such pressures. When describing such Jewish leaders in Germany, for example, Chaim Weizman derisively calls them "obsequious, super-patriotic," who are "eagerly anticipating the wishes and plans of the masters of Germany … the usual type of *Kaiser-Juden*."[59] In this sense the Jews, Zionists included, were considered by the respective governments a useful capital to be exploited in the pursuit of tactical as well as strategic goals. The resulting clashes of interest found their reflection in the feuds and dissensions besetting geographically separated various Jewish communities in Europe, and ultimately in Palestine. Typical in this respect was the controversy about the language of instruction at Haifa *Technikum*, a technical college established by some pioneers of the Zionist movement from Germany and Russia. The German government through the active intervention of Zimmermann, the undersecretary in the Foreign Office, had obtained the permission from the Turkish government for the purchase of the land and the erection of the building shortly before the outbreak of the war. He insisted on the use of German as the language of instruction but the Jewish teachers and other members of the Board of the *Hilfsverein der Deutschen Juden*, which administered the *Technikum,* insisted on Hebrew. When the latter prevailed and the German Jews withdrew their financial support, the Zionists, who also had insisted on Hebrew, took charge of the school. For its part, however, the pro-Entente *Alliance Israelite Universelle* of Paris continued the use of French in its system of Jewish schools in Palestine. Weizman observed similar trends among many leaders of the Jewish community in Great Britain whose identification with British interests caused them to place the highest premium on loyalty to these interests and concomitantly to deprecate and even crusade against Zionism. He called them "the assimilationists" and "the obstructionist Jews."[60]

While the efforts of Weizman and other leaders of Zionism were essentially projective, i.e., aimed at the future of Jewry (efforts which in November 1917 would culminate in the issuance of the Balfour Declaration), the efforts of other Zionists as well as non-Zionist Jews were directed at the protection of the 85,000 Jews living in wartime Palestine. Such protection was needed for several reasons. First of all the emergencies and exigencies of the war provided an opportunity to the Turkish authorities to intensify their unfriendly, if not hostile, attitude toward the non-Muslim populations through scapegoating and other devices; the level of the vulnerability of the latter was considerably heightened. Moreover, the proclamation of *cihad*, holy war, against "the infidels" punctuated the dangers hanging over these populations. These facts served to further compound the vulnerability of a particular and large segment of Palestine Jews on account of their citizenship status. For reasons of expediency and even personal safety many immigrant Jews, European as well as Russian, refused to adopt Ottoman citizenship, or indefinitely postponed the initiation of the requisite naturalization procedures, as noted above. They thus had become enemy aliens. The Turkish authorities in this respect had gained the type of leverage over this Jewish population which was transformed by a number of Turkish potentates, serving in and around wartime Palestine, into a license for willful anti-Jewish persecution. A parallel danger emerged for all Jews living in Palestine when in 1917 the area became a primary theatre of military operations and deportations on a large scale were being initiated by the local Turkish authorities.

But the gravest danger for all Jews living in the Ottoman domain during the war sprang up when on two fronts Jews intervened on the side of the Entente Powers to oppose the Turks and to cripple the Turkish military effort in Palestine. One of these involved the formation of Jewish military units and their engagement in combat operations directed against the Turks. In March 1915 the Zion Mule Corps, consisting of transport troops, participated in the abortive Gallipoli campaign. It was put together by Joseph Trumpeldor, a Russian Jew, and a former officer in the Tsarist army, who recruited several hundred young Jews in Alexandria, Egypt whither they were exiled from Palestine in December 1914 as alien Jews. The idea had originated from British General Maxwell; the resulting formation served under the command of Lieutenant Colonel Henry J. Patterson and sustained heavy casualties.[61] But that was not the end of Jewish military involvement against the Turks. Vladimir Jabotinsky, another Russian Jew, a journalist, a polyglot orator, and a capable organizer, was eager to form "several Jewish regiments." The purpose of these efforts was "to lay the basis for political demands [on behalf of the Zionists] at the peace conference."[62] In the end, however, there was created in February 1917 in England only the Jewish Regiment, sometimes called the Jewish Legion, which in 1918 joined the forces of British general Sir Edmund Allenby and rendered "valuable services … in the conquest of Palestine."[63] In order to avoid provoking the ire of the Turks, at least for the time being, the regiment, which contained some 120 survivors of the Gallipoli Expedition, was called The Royal Fusiliers.

From the Turkish point of view, the Jewish support of the Allied war effort on another front was no less severe in terms of its ramifications. That support was carried out through espionage at the Palestine front. A young Zionist by the name of Aaron Aaronson who belonged to a well-to-do Jewish family in Jaffa, decided to assist the British in their drive to what Aaronson and his group of Zionists considered to be an act of liberating Palestine and his people from the yoke of the Turks. His hatred against the latter was matched by the intrepidity with which he set out to collect and transmit to the British War Office and Intelligence in Egypt valuable military information. His sister, the 27-year old Sarah, who shared her brother's ideals and his sentiments against the Turks, was in a sense the leader of the brain-trust of the espionage ring *Nili* (an acronym for a biblical phrase meaning "The Eternal of Israel will not fail us"). Jaffa fell to the British on November 17, 1917, and twenty-two days later Jerusalem surrendered. Sarah was captured, however, by the Turkish military police and was subjected to harrowing tortures, but she would not reveal the identity of her cohorts, including that of her brother. When the Turks apprehended a member of the espionage ring who was trying to cross the Egyptian frontier, they learned of the role of Sarah. For three days she was tortured before the eyes of her old father in her own house when, in a moment of unguardedness, she ended all that by killing herself with a hidden revolver. Having learned of the conditions of the death of his sister, Aaron reportedly "borrowed a machine gun from his British army acquaintances ... he landed at Jaffa ... located a few of his friends and they went Turk hunting ... there was an Old Testament flavor of vengeance he sought for his sister ... Aaronson and his hastily recruited squad of irregulars shot Turks till their ammunition had been exhausted, stragglers and prisoners, sick and wounded—the Ottoman uniform was all the target they looked for."[64]

Turkish sources confirm the existence and operation of such espionage and sabotage activities. Military historian General Fahri Belen states that "Some Jews who were part of the Zionist movement were bent on breaking the Ottoman rule (*ihlâl*) through a secret organization. Following investigations it was established through captured documents that this organization had its own postal service, court of law and flag; and much other evidence directly pointed [to endeavors imperiling] the authority of the state."[65]

Before examining the Turkish response to them, the Armenian angle to these Jewish undertakings may be briefly explained by way of a minor digression. The example of the Turkish treatment of the Armenians, its genocidal dimensions with all its horrors, had made a deep and sobering impact upon the members of the Aaronson family. One of the mechanisms of that genocide was the disarming of the victim population as a warrant for the relatively smooth enactment of the mass murder. When in the spring of 1915 the Turkish authorities demanded "the surrender of whatever firearms or weapons ... our people ... had in their possession ...," wrote Dr. Alexander Aaronson, the brother of Aaron, "our people were in a state of great excitement ... we knew that similar measures had been taken before the terrible Armenian massacres, and we felt that some such fate might be in preparation for our people."[66] The sentiments of Sarah, the sister of the two brothers, were even more pronounced in this respect. She had personally witnessed scenes of atrocities which overwhelmed her with shock and a sense of singular tragedy. But upon reflection, she became also apprehensive. Will the Jews be next? The question preoccupied her intensely. In the face of the impunity with which a government could in cold blood exterminate a subject nationality, could her own people be safe? She decided to inform her brothers and other leaders in Palestine of the mass murder against the Armenians and sensitize them to the portents of that crime for the Jews upon her return to Palestine. Here is an excerpt from her report culled from a 1916 British Foreign Office document; given the dangers existing for her and her family at the time when she composed the report (December 1915), the British authorities concealed her identity as a matter of precaution. "... the bodies of hundreds of Armenian men, women and children lying on both sides of the railway. Sometimes Turkish women were seen searching the corpses for anything that might be of value; at other times dogs were observed feeding on the bodies. There were hundreds of bleached skeletons. At either Gulek or Osmanieh [on the Baghdad Railway] I saw thousands of starving and fever-stricken Armenians. ... They were lying about the station on the sidings, and some on the track itself. Some were jostled on the line when the train arrived, and the engine ran over them to the joy of the engine driver, who shouted to his friends, 'Did you see how I smashed about fifty of these Armenian swine?' [I] fainted at the sight, and on recovery two Turkish officers, speaking French, remonstrated with [me] on [my] lack of patriotism since the Armenians were enemies."[67]

However gruesome this portrayal of Armenian martyrdom, the apprehensions of the Aaronson family regarding the possibility of a similar fate befalling the Jews proved unfounded. The Turks were not unanimous in the consideration of the need to retaliate and punish collectively the Jews under their control. Nor did they assign the same degree of magnitude to any threat the Jews might be posing to the empire at that time as they were prone to assign to the threat they perceived coming from the camp of the Armenians. Most important, however, was this consideration: unlike the Armenians, the Jews could rely on an array of external sources of deterrence as well as protection. The specifics of this phenomenon are discussed in the next section.

The Constraints of Realpolitik and Turko-German Solicitousness Toward the Jews

As indicated earlier, similar acts of isolated incidents of espionage and the intervention of contingents of volunteers, fighting alongside the Allies against Turkish armed forces, proved very costly to the Armenians. These acts were so embellished, were so inflated by the Ittihadists that they ultimately served as subterfuge to which the Turks resorted for the wholesale destruction of the bulk of the Armenian population of Turkey. In the absence of countervailing forces to deter or to check such purposive amplifications of relatively inconsequential incidents, a perpetrator group with the advantages of concentrated power can resort to any radical means in order to prevail in a conflict situation it chooses to define as "perilous." Even though the scales of the conflict with the Jews were not commensurate with those involving the Armenians, and the demographic factor was far less weighty in the case of the Jews, the

Turks nevertheless could, if they wanted to, exaggerate the import of the partisan and anti-state activities of some segments of the Jewish population to target the entire population for deportation and elimination. This would be quite consonant with the Ittihadist motto, which was: "Turkey for the Turks" and which they set out to implement in the vortex of the myriad opportunities afforded by the war.[68] But, they studiously refrained from doing such a thing. Whatever was done to the Jews in terms of preventive or retributive measures was distinctly limited on two accounts. 1. It encompassed mainly, but not exclusively, the Jews in Palestine. 2. The measures were not ordered by the central, but rather by the regional authorities, often in defiance of, or without the knowledge of, the former. Consequently, at times, these central authorities had to intervene to restrain the local potentates, or to have their orders rescinded. Occasionally some local governors, who were involved in anti-Jewish activities, were relieved of their posts or were transferred to other jobs. A brief description of these happenings by way of illustration may be in order.

In December 1914, military authorities in Palestine ordered, in compliance with the instructions of IVth Army Commander and "Viceroy" of Syria and Palestine, Cemal Paşa, the immediate deportation to Egypt of all Jews holding Russian citizenship. There were some 5,000 Russian Jews who for a long time had put off their naturalization and thus remained enemy aliens; together with their families they constituted a population comprising 15-20,000 Jews. But through prompt German intervention, the order was rescinded, and only some 600 could be deported on the very first day of the proclamation of the order, i.e. December 17, 1914. The victims were simply rounded up in the streets of Jaffa and Tel Aviv and were pushed into the ship.[69] In the area of the port city of Smyrna (Izmir) on the Aegean Sea some hundred Jews, Allied subjects, were likewise deported to Nymphio, eight hours distant from the port city. "Some were seized in their houses at five a.m. and were not given time to put on their shoes. … They were locked in dirty prisons, without food, were beaten and were threatened that if they did not raise large sums of money they would be sent on foot to Sıvas—a sentence equivalent to a lingering and painful death."[70] In October 1915 the deputy governor-general of Baghdad province, Şefik Bey, expelled 1,800 Jews from Bakuba, Sahraban and Deltava and continued to oppress all non-Muslim subjects of Baghdad. The religious heads of the respective communities, including the Chief Rabbi, pleaded with the Austrian consul there to intercede as Şefik in November ordered the arrest of 70 community leaders, Christian and Jewish.[71] With the opening of the British offensive in 1917, Cemal Paşa in March ordered the evacuation of all Jews from the cities of Jaffa and Tel Aviv and the adjoining areas. Thousands of families plunged into destitution and despair as a result of the ensuing forceful dislocations. The Allies tried to exploit the situation by charging that "the Turks were preparing a repetition of the Armenian Massacres."[72] In fact a few months earlier, Cemal Paşa was reported to have declared that "because of Zionism, Palestine might become a second Armenia."[73] Once more, German intervention, reinforced by the support which the American Embassy offered, obviated the anti-Jewish campaign of the regional authorities.

There were several factors which converged in the determination of the policy the Ittihadist leadership ended up pursuing vis a vis the Zionists and indirectly the Jews in general who were living in the Ottoman domain during World War I. But the overarching factor involved a line of behavior which in diplomatic parlance passes as *Realpolitik.* It was the kind of politics which not only served the interests of the Turko-German alliance but separately the interests of Germany and Turkey also. The thrust of that politics was the inclination to exercise restraint in the treatment of the Jews identified with Zionism and, by the same token, to even be willing to indulge, to the extent possible, those pro-Entente activities of some of these Zionists which were directed against the Turkish war effort. *Realpolitik* here simply becomes adaptive politics. Long-term ideological goals are suspended for the sake of emerging exigencies that require modification of behavior. These exigencies included mainly two principal elements. 1. The cost factor relative to any scheme that provided for the institution of any kind of comprehensive anti-Jewish measure; Turkey could expect to pay a huge price for instituting such measures, and was, therefore, inhibited. 2. The German factor. Unlike in the case of the Armenians, in the case of the Jews the Germans in Berlin and Istanbul rarely hesitated to intercede on behalf of them; in fact the resolve they displayed in this regard in their dealings with the Ittihadist leaders proved a weighty factor in their drive to prevail and to impel, if not compel, the latter. As a demonstration of this will to be of help to the Zionists the German Foreign Office took an unusual step. In December 1914 it allowed Lichtheim, the young Zionist operative in Turkey, to avail himself of the German diplomatic courier service and its cipher code system in his communications with the Zionist leaders in Berlin and Jaffa. As a result "hundreds of telegrams and thousands of letters were rapidly and safely transmitted in the system of communication that was established by the Zionist Organization in the Berlin-Istanbul-Jaffa tri-city link-up."[74]

The above arguments call for specification and illustration. As early as summer 1914 Wangenheim reassured Lichtheim that he needed instructions from Berlin to actively support Zionism "for which I always had a sympathy;" but he promised to do so "unofficially."[75] The December 1914 deportations of Russian Jews in Palestine were stopped by the prompt and effective intervention of German ambassador Wangenheim who personally sought Talât and was able to persuade him to rescind the order "after consultations with Cemal Paşa."[76] Moreover, Wangenheim was instrumental in the removal of the two Turkish officials, Behaeddin, the county executive (*Kaymakam*), and Hasan, the military commandant of Jaffa, "the tormentors of the Jewish population." In denouncing them with manifest anger, Wangenheim had shouted, "These two guys, these scoundrels (*Halunken*), must go; I can no longer put up with the mess (*Schweinerei*)."[77] Furthermore, Lichtheim after protracted negotiations in Berlin and Istanbul, in January 1916, managed to have Berlin issue to the embassy in Istanbul formal instructions (*Anweisungen*) to the effect that German consuls in Palestine were authorized to use their influence, in an unofficial manner, for the protection of the Jewish population there. The instructions, though approved by Chancellor Hollweg, avoided using the words "Zionism" or "Palestine," but instead referred to the immigration and settlement of Jews in "Turkey." They were not to be publicized. It was hoped that the instructions would implicitly impress upon Turkish authorities the reality of Germany's support for Zionism.[78] On December 20, 1915, a Turkish court-martial in Jerusalem summoned five officials of the Palestine Office (*Palästinaamt*), who were accused of "high treason" on grounds that the Jewish National Fund stamps they were using bore the images of Herzl, or Max Nordau, the close collaborator of Herzl; for lack of court-martial evidence the case was later transferred to the Criminal Court that tried common crimes. The new indictment absurdly charged the defendants with the crime of "forging" Ottoman stamps, whereas the military court had charged them "with separatist aspirations."[79] Responding to the pleas of the Zionist leaders in Berlin and Istanbul, the German authorities, civilian and military, intervened again. Since Wangenheim had died, Metternich, the new ambassador, authorized Embassy Councillor von Neurath to handle the matter. Instead of interceding directly with Cemal Paşa, Neurath in December 1915 asked Colonel Kress von Kressenstein, the latter's Chief of Staff at the IVth Ottoman Army, to do so. Cemal not only rejected the intervention but berated the embassy for meddling in internal Turkish affairs when, on instructions from Neurath, in January 1916, Colonel von Kressenstein, again asked Cemal to stop the trials, which he described as senseless. Neurath tried one more time. Upon his instructions, Jerusalem's German consul Edmund Schmidt pressed the matter with a sense of urgency, at the same time denouncing the trial as a senseless act. Cemal yielded and the trial ended with the prompt acquittal of the defendants ("the Imperial seal was not engraved on the stamps"). Lichtheim's comment on this episode has a direct bearing upon this entire discussion. "This event confirmed again a reality that I often experienced, namely, that the Turkish potentates first act out with an air of rage but eventually yield when they come face to face with the firm resolve of the German Embassy" (... *aber schliesslich doch zurückwichen, wenn sie sich dem festen Willen der deutschen Botschaft gegenübersahen*).[80]

A similar pattern is observable in the March 1917 confrontation between Cemal and the Germans intervening on behalf of the Jews in Palestine. Even though the British attack in Gaza had failed, claiming "military necessity" the district governor (*mutasarrıf*) of Jerusalem, Izzet, sought to evict the Jewish population of Jaffa and its environs. Those without the means to relocate themselves would be transported (deported) to the Syrian hinterland and be cared for by the government. As Friedman put it, "With the memory of the Armenian atrocities fresh in their minds, the Jews feared the worst."[81] Karl Freiherr von Schabinger, the newly appointed German consul at Jaffa, suspected that "the only objective of the Turks was to annihilate the Jews, irrespective of citizenship."[82] After two failed attempts to dissuade the Turkish district governor, Schabinger on his third attempt appealed to him by underscoring the loyalty and devotion to Turkey of German Jews. The terse response was: "*Ça ne me regard pas*!" Schabinger then threatened to accompany the Jews subject to evacuation. Cemal, upon learning of these efforts by the German consul of Jaffa, summoned to his office Heinrich Brode, the German consul at Jerusalem and issued "a stern warning against unwarranted interference in Ottoman internal affairs." The Zionist leaders and their German guardians were convinced that Cemal was testing the waters for larger undertakings aiming at the ultimate removal of all Jews from Jerusalem. Consul Brode anticipated the extension of the order for evacuation to Jerusalem. Before anything could be done, 9,000 Jews were deported and Tel Aviv, Jaffa's Jewish quarter that was created in 1909 by the original Jewish colonists, became "a dead city." The records of the evacuation contain such lamentations as "We shall never forget this gruesome spectacle, nor shall we forgive ... this was the hardest blow we have ever experienced." No transport facilities were provided; the evacuees had to travel on foot. Theft, plunder and extortions by the officials were rampant. "About 6,000 of the evacuees concentrated in the neighborhood of Petach-Tikva, others moved northward to Samaria and Galilee." Consul Brode's forecast materialized. Ten days after Jaffa's evacuation Cemal announced to the consuls that he had to evacuate Jerusalem's civilian population within twenty-four hours.[83]

But before the Jerusalem tragedy could unfold, the Germans once more came to the rescue of the Jews. The potentiality of that tragedy is described by General Kressenstein in his memoirs as follows: "Dislocation of so large a population would have led to unimaginable consequences. The terrible incidents of the Armenian exodus would have been repeated. ... Thousands would have died of starvation ... and epidemics. ... Thank God the danger was averted in good time."[84] Several German civilian and military officials, using their chains of command, intervened, such as Jerusalem Consul General Brode, Colonel Kress, the military attaché at Istanbul embassy, Zimmermann, who at that time was promoted to the post of Foreign Affairs Minister, and the German High Command. The key and decisive role was played, however, by Zimmermann. He knew the limitations of the leverage of diplomats and decided, therefore, to seek the intervention of the German High Command and of the military authorities running it. "... on their explicit instructions Enver Pasha [the Turkish Was Minister] ordered Djemal to cancel the evacuation." In commenting on the significance of this effective intervention, Friedman wrote: "... it cannot be denied that it was chiefly owing to Germany's forceful intervention that the danger which hovered over the Palestinian Jews in 1917 was averted. The chief credit for this must go to Zimmermann. Had it not been for his singular determination nothing would have stopped Djemal Pasha from delivering a crippling blow to the Yishuv [The 'Old Settlement' whose foundation was laid by the Ashkenazim, the Central and East European Jewry and their offsprings]."[85]

The consistency with which German authorities in Berlin and Istanbul intervened on behalf of the Jews, especially those in Palestine, indicated, if not demonstrated the existence of a relatively firm policy in this regard, determined at the highest level of government. This became evident in the handling of the Nili espionage case involving mainly the Aaronson family. The Turks preferred that General Erich von Falkenhayn, who in September 1917 was placed in command of the Palestinian front after the Yıldırım plan to recapture Baghdad from the British was relinquished, conduct the investigation. At the same time Count Johann Heinrich von Bernstorff, the German ambassador, approached the Grand Vizier for as mild a treatment of the Jews (*für tunlichst milde Behand-*

lung) as was practicable under the circumstances. Talât responded by giving "unequivocal assurances," declaring, "We have done much harm to the Armenians but we shall do nothing to the Jews." The Turks wanted to avoid being forced into a situation where they would have to take drastic measures against the Jews. As Foreign Minister Nesimi confided, the Ittihadists wanted "to share the responsibility" in this matter with the Germans. The Zionist leader Ruppin excused the Jewish colonists at large by decrying those involved in the espionage web as "adventurous" people and as "irresponsible individuals."[86] The clue to the existence of a policy to be as much protective as possible toward the Jews in Turkey is provided by the revelation made by Ambassador Bernstorff in a November 9, 1917 report. It develops that before leaving for his trip to Turkey, General Falkenahyn was summoned by Kaiser William II and "instructed to prevail upon Djemal Pasha to treat the Jews considerately."[87] The central authorities in Istanbul issued orders and all Jews who were arrested and incarcerated unlawfully were released. Talât in the same vein sharply condemned the anti-Jewish measures of the regional and local officials and threatened to dismiss or to punish those who would dare to disobey his orders.[88] The same Talât gave German ambassador Bernstorff "the most binding assurances that there would be no repercussions of the espionage affair."[89]

The Turkish response to the role of the Zion Mule Corps in the Dardanelles campaign was along the same lines. As Egmont Zechlin stated, that role "had no effect upon the attitude of the Turks."[90] In describing the significance of the Nili espionage ring from a military point of view, Turkish general and military historian Belen attributes to the workings of "German influence" (*Almanların tesiri*) the fact that the treatment of alien Jews, identified with Zionism, was rather mild.[91] It should be noted in this connection that Talât's solicitousness toward the Jews was not entirely free from underhanded duplicitousness.[92] He especially played the Arab card, covertly and almost perfidiously. In an exchange with Ambassador Bernstorff he stated, "I will gladly establish a national home for the Jews to please you, but mark my words, the Arabs will destroy the Jews."[93] As if to help bring about such a development, Talât was inflaming the passions of the Arabs and agitating them against the Jews[94] as he was campaigning against the Balfour plan, which he belittled as "a hoax" (*une blague*).[95] According to a secret report by Sir Mark Sykes, the Middle East expert of the British Foreign Office, this policy of inflaming the Arabs against the Jews, continued in the months following the end of the war. On January 6, 1919, Sykes sent a cipher telegram from Aleppo apprising the Foreign Office of "anti-Jewish propaganda among Arabs."

He believed this agitation to be "ultimately of C.U.P. [Ittihadist] origin" and to be "making considerable strides in Syria." Sykes in the same cipher stated that "Turkish agents are making great efforts to provoke hostility between Arabs and Armenians and Arabs and Jews. I am doing my best to counter and am well supported but would urge Sokolow and Weizman to give all assistance on their side."[96]

Another dimension of the *Realpolitik* under review here involved a degree of political sensitivity in which German and Turkish attitudes converged and which had primarily a single focus. The reference is to the American factor with a focus on the importance of the Jewish component of it. As early as January 1915, in the wake of his successful December 1914 intervention on behalf of the Russian Jews, Zimmermann expressed to Lichtheim the wish that "we give due publicity in America to the fact that the German Embassy supports … and protects us by all means at its disposal."[97] Moreover, according to Weltmann, the Germans hoped to use the Zionists for their own aims of foreign policy after the war and, therefore, were eager to "win the sympathy of public opinion," in the U.S.A. "by actively protecting the Jewish community in Palestine."[98] These expectations were corroborated by the assessments of Sir Cecil Spring-Rice, British ambassador at Washington D.C. In November 1914, he wrote to Sir Edward Grey, British Foreign Affairs Minister, that "the New York German Jewish bankers who were getting hold of the principal New York papers and bringing them over as much as they dare to the German side and toiling in a solid "phalanx to compass our destruction."[99]

The Turkish orientation toward favorable public opinion in the U.S.A.

The Turkish motivation for a desire to favorably impress the Jews of America had similar but not identical ingredients; financial needs and hopes for American assistance in this regard were major considerations also. This was made clear when in February 1917 Finance Minister Cavid in a speech in the Ottoman Parliament acknowledged the dire economic and financial needs of Turkey. He was anxious, he said, "to enter into commercial intercourse with all countries, especially the richest one in the world." A day earlier, Cavid had invited Abram Elkus, the new American ambassador, to be present to listen to his speech. "Both Djavid and Talaat courted Elkus assiduously, in the apparent hope that they might secure America's backing in case of emergency."[100] About a year and a half later Talât told Victor Jacobson, the Zionist leader: "*Les Juifs sonts une force, je ne veux pas qu'ils soient contre l'Empire.*"[101]

In conclusion it may be argued that whereas in the Greek case the existence of a state capable of a measure of retaliation, served to temporarily restrain the Turks, in the case of the Jews it was a vigilant and potent diaspora, reinforced by a vibrant Zionist movement, that served to deter the Turks from any attempt to purge these regions of its Jewish population, at the same time playing the religious card.

Of all the authorities on the subject of Zionism, especially in terms of its struggle in wartime Turkey, it was Richard Lichtheim, one of the most astute leaders of Zionism operating in Berlin and Istanbul, who attached particular significance to that struggle by assessing it against the background of a concomitant event, the Armenian Genocide. In fact, he argued that without "visualizing" the horrors of that mass murder, one could not adequately appreciate the gravity of the risk the Zionist struggle faced. He believed that the enkindling of the Jewish question by IVth Army Commander Cemal Paşa "very easily" could have led to the victimization of the Jews by way of a replication of the treatment accorded the Armenians and other minorities. "The emphatic support we sought and received from the German and American embassies warded off this danger (*wandte diese Gefahr ab*). ..." Lichtheim's account of the genocide against the Armenians focuses on the exigencies of "the World War I" which afforded the Turks "a good opportunity to finally solve the troublesome nationality question." The victimization of the Armenians represents "the first case in recent history" of a systematic liquidation of a race, and "resembles the first phase of the Hitlerite enactment of the destruction of the Jews in the 1940–1942 period." As if to confirm the central thesis of this study, Lichtheim declares that the German representations made to the Turkish authorities on behalf of the Armenians "were not too energetic" as "the German General Staff had given the word that Germany's alliance policy could not be imperiled by intervening in Turkey's internal affairs." Lichtheim then offers an explanation for the differential treatment of the Jews. "The intervention of the German government on behalf of the Jews of Palestine constituted indeed the only exception to this rule." When accounting for this act of making an exception Lichtheim indicated that due consideration was given to "the strong influence of the Jews on the public opinion in America and in other neutral states (*den starken Einfluss der Juden auf die öffentliche Meinung Amerikas und der anderen neutralen Staaten*). ..." In brief, Lichtheim maintained that one should keep in mind the fate of the Armenians in order to "adjudge rightly the difficulties of the politics of Zionism and the extent of its success" (*die Schwierigkeiten der zionischten Politik und das Maß ihres Erfolges richtig zu beurteilen*).[102]

Notes to Appendix-C

1. In an essay dealing with this issue, the late Terrence des Pres deplored the subversivness of a growing number of academics to the lures and rewards of "power," at the expense of "the integrity of knowledge." He wondered whether the deliberate misuse of the maximum that "there are two sides to every issue" has not reduced it to "a gimmick" to undermine and distort, rather than to "foster truth." He went on to state: "We are told no genocide took place but only a vague unfortunate mishap determined by imponderables like time and change, the hazards of war, uncertain demographics. There is a commonsense sound to the Turkish proposal. ... [However,] Turkey's denial of the Armenian disaster is backed by something larger than mere doubt. ..." Terrence des Pres, "On Governing Narratives: The Turkish-Armenian Case," *The Yale Review*, 75 (October 1986): 518–19. In a subsequent essay, he scorned the "increasing attempts to suborn the academy. ... The issue, then, is whether or not we wish to be menials, for at the very least scholars who spend their resources defending the honor of nation-states serve something other than truth." Idem, "Introduction. Remembering Armenia," in Richard G. Hovannisian, ed., *The Armenian Genocide in Perspective* (New Brunswick, NJ, 1987), 15.
2. Général Izzet-Fuad, *Autres Occasions Perdues ... Critique Stratégique de la Campagne d'Asie Mineure 1877–1878* (Paris, 1908), Préface, xi–xii. The disparity between the author's diagnosis of a major problem with which the Ottoman Empire was afflicted, and Ittihadist party chief Talât's following statement, ignoring the root causes of that problem, is most significant; in fact, it goes a long way to explain the ultimate demise of that empire. The statement was made to American ambassador Morgenthau who recounted it thusly in his postwar memoirs: "Talaat explained his national policy: these different *blocs* in the Turkish Empire, he said, had always conspired against Turkey; because of the hostility of these native populations, Turkey had lost province after province—Greece, Serbia, Rumania, Bulgaria, Bosnia, Herzegovina, Egypt, and Tripoli. In this way the Turkish Empire had dwindled almost to the vanishing point. If what was left of Turkey was to survive, added Talaat, he must get rid of these alien peoples. 'Turkey for the Turks' was now Talaat's controlling idea." Henry Morgenthau, *Ambassador Morgenthau's Story* (Garden City, N. Y., 1918), 51.
3. Vahakn N. Dadrian, *The History of the Armenian Genocide. Ethnic Conflict from the Balkans to Anatolia to the Caucasus* (Providence/Oxford, 1995), 180.
4. *Ibid.*, 5.
5. *Ibid.*, 180–181.
6. *Austrian Foreign Ministry Archives.* Vienna, (Hereafter cited as DAA) PAI, Karton 463, No. 75/P.D, September 15, 1917 report to Ottokar Count Czernin.
7. *Ibid.*, XII/463, No. 92/P.C. November 2, 1915.
8. *Ibid.*, XII/210, No. 28/P.A. "Very Confidential" report to Austrian Foreign Minister Burian.
9. *See* Part II, Note 155 for further details.
10. Arnold J. Toynbee, *The Western Question in Greece and Turkey (*Boston, 1922), 138–39, 145.
11. Yusuf Hikmet Bayur, *Türk Inkilâbı Tarihi* (History of the Turkish Revolution) vol. 2, Part 4 (Ankara, 1983), 260–62.
12. Celal Bayar, *Ben de Yazdım. Milli Mücadeleye Giriş* (I Too Have Written. The Start of the National Struggle) vol. 5 (Istanbul, 1967), 1572–1582. The quotation about liquidation is from p. 1573.
13. Toynbee, *The Western Question* [n.10], 145.
14. *Ibid.*,143.
15. Morgenthau, *Ambassador* [n. 2], 325.
16. *British Foreign Office Archives.* FO371/2480/2622. "Confidential" Doc. No. 281, folio 252. Sent to British Foreign Secretary Sir Edward Grey from the British Embassy, Athens.
17. *The Military Archives of the German Federal Republic.* (Freiburg i. Breisgau) BA. MA. Msg, 1/2309, from the diary of German General Bronsart von Schellendorf. Quoted in

Christoph Dinkel "German Officers and the Armenian Genocide" *Armenian Review* 44, 1/173 (Spring 1991): 87–92.

18. *Ibid.*,88–89.
19. *See* Part II, note 66.
20. DAA [n. 6], XII/380, Zl. 17/pol., folio 219. Consul Kwiatkowski's March 13, 1918 report, issued from Samsun.
21. *Ibid.*, XII/369. February 6, 1917.
22. DAA [n. 6], XII/210, N. 28/P.A. Austrian ambassador Pallavicini's "very confidential" April 8, 1916 report.
23. A.A. Türkei 183/38, A 23991. Aleppo's German Consul Rössler's July 27, 1915 "confidential report to Chancellor Hollweg.
24. Ahmed Emin (Yalman), *Turkey in the World War* (New Haven, CT. 1930), 220.
25. Falih Rıfkı (Atay) *Dünya,* December 17, 1967. Atay's weekly column Pazar Konuşması (Sunday talk). Writing on the formation and missions of the Special Organization, the top-secret wartime Ittihadist outfit in charge of the killing fields in the interior of Turkey, an American author for his part singled out one of those missions, which was, to "thwart any Russian-Armenian plans for an independent Armenia carved out of Ottoman Turkey." Philip H. Stoddard, *The Ottoman Government and the Arabs, 1911 to 1918: A Preliminary Study of the Teskilâtı Mahsusa.* (An Arbor, MI, 1963), 56.
26. Dadrian, *The History of the Armenian Genocide.* [n. 3], 29.
27. *Ibid.,*
28. Richard Lichtheim, *Rückkehr. Lebenserinnerungen aus der Frühzeit des deutschen Zionismus* (Stuttgart, 1970), 217–18.
29. Isaiah Friedman, *Germany, Turkey, and Zionism. 1897–1918.* (Oxford, 1977), 59, 65, 67, 77. As early as July 28, 1890, the same sultan had categorically rejected the Zionist plan of settlements in Palestine on account of "the probability of the formation of a Jewish government" there. He added that "such a development is not right at all" (*hiç de caiz değildir*) while the state is "confronting the Armenian problem of seditiousness (*fesad*)." Kemal Öke, *II. Abdülhamid, Siyonistler ve Filistin Meselesi* (Abdülhamid II. The Zionists and the Palestine Problem) (Istanbul, 1918), 97
30. *See* Part I, note 21.
31. *Theodor Herzl's Tagebücher 1895–1904.* 3 vols. vol. 1 (Berlin, 1922); vol. 2 and 3 (Berlin, 1923). vol. 1, 444–45, 447.
32. *Ibid.,* 396.
33. *Ibid.,* 528.
34. Norman Kotker, *Herzl the King* (New York, 1972), 275. Herzl's other declarations confirming this brand of opportunism are examined in Marwan R. Buheiry, "Theodor Herzl and the Armenian Question" *Journal of Palastine Studies* (February 1977): 87, 96–97.
35. Friedman, *Germany* [n. 29], 101–102; *Theodor Herzl's Tagebücher* [n. 31], vol. 3, pp. 242–45.
36. Quoted in *Ibid.,* (Friedman), 95.
37. *Ibid.,* 80. Alive of to the danger of such Turkish reactions, the Chief Rabbi in Constantinople at the time, Moses Halevi, issued a warning to the Chief Rabbi of Jerusalem, Elyashar, "to keep clear of Herzl. Ottoman Jewry should not get mixed up with a movement to which the Sultan objected."
38. Dr. Abdurrahman Küçük, *Dönmeler ve Dönmelik Tarihi* (The Dönmes and the History of the Practice of Becoming *Dönmes*) (Istanbul, 1979?). These converts had become members of a sect that was ostensibly Muslim in form and appearance but had a Jewish origin. They were the followers of Shabbetai Zwi, who proclaimed himself Messiah in the seventeenth century, converted to Islam, and thereby set an example for these members who likewise converted.
39. M. Zekeriya Sertel, *Hatırladıklarım. 1905–1950* (The Things I Remember) (Istanbul, 1968), 59. Focusing on this condition of marginality, Sertel describes how it continued even in the new era of the Turkish Republic where many of these *dönmes* established their own quarters of residence and schools thereby sustaining a form of semi-segregated life. 59–60.

40. Lichtheim, *Rückkehr* [n. 28], 189.
41. Friedman, *Germany* [n. 29], 144–45.
42. Doğar Avcıoğlu, *Milli Kurtuluş Tarihi 1830 den 1995e* (The History of National Liberation. From 1838 to 1995) vol. 3 (Istanbul, 1974), 1112, footnote. According to a British Foreign Office document, Dr. Nazım himself was believed to be a *dönme.* FO 424/250. Turkey. Annual Report 1910. Printed in April 1911, February 14. p. 3 of the report, folio 34.
43. Sertel, *Hatırladıklarım* [n. 39], 61–62.
44. Friedman, *Germany* [n. 29], 145.
45. *Ibid.,* 141.
46. Avcıoğlu, *Milli Kurtuluş* [n. 42], 1112.
47. Friedman, *Germany* [n. 29], 145.
48. *Ibid.*
49. Lichtheim, *Rückkehr* [n. 28], 119.
50. Dr. Alfred Nossig, *Die Neue Türkei und Ihre Führer* (Halle, 1917), 71–72.
51. Topçu Ihsan (Former Minister of Navy), "Ittihad ve Farmasonlik" *Resimli Tarih Mecmuası* 2, 18 (June 1951): 780.
52. *Ibid.,* 782.
53. *Ibid.*
54. Feridum Kandemir, "Ittihat-Terakki" *Yakın Tarihimiz* 2 (1962): 243.
55. Ali Necat Ölçen, *Osmanlı Meclisi Mebusanında Kuvvetler Ayırımı ve Siyasal Işkenceler* (The Debate in the Ottoman Chamber of Deputies on Separation of Powers and Politically Inspired Tortures) (Ankara, 1982), 49, 58. *See also* Prof. Dr. Hikmet Tanyu, *Tarih Boyunca Yahudiler ve Türkler* (Jews and Turks in the course of History) vol. 1, 2nd expanded ed. (Ankara, 1977), 455–57. On p. 351 the author maintains that Zekeriya Sertel himself was a *dönme,* not just his bride, as stated in the text.
56. Friedman, *Germany* [n. 29], 152.
57. To be noted in this respect are first of all 1. G. H. Fitzmaurice, the first Dragoman of the British Embassy at Istanbul, and a "rabid Catholic" whose contempt for the Freemasons and Jews at the time was exceeded only by his hatred of them. 2. British ambassador Sir Gerard Lowther whose ideas were largely a reflection of those of Fitzmaurice. *See* in this connection Elie Kedourie, "Young Turks, Freemasons and Jews" with an Appendix on Lowther, in *Middle Eastern Studies* 7, 1 (January 1971): 89–94; Appendix, 94–104. *See also* Ernest E. Ramsaur, *The Young Turks. Prelude to the Revolution of 1908* (Beirut, 1965), 103–108. According to a Turksih author, Freemasonry rapidly spread in Turkey after the 1908 Young Turk revolution as most prominent Ittihadists, including Talât, Midhat, Şükrü, Cemal Paşa, Ismail Canbolat, Said Halim Paşa, Cavid, and even Şeyülislam Musa Kâzım, became members of this or that lodge. Ilhami Soysal, *Dünya ve Türkiyede Masonlar ve Masonluk* (Freemasons and Freemasonry in the World and in Turkey) (Istanbul, 1980), 197, 208, 417–18.
58. Saadia E. Weltmann, "Germany, Turkey , and the Zionist Movement, 1914–1918" *The Review of Politics* 23, 1 (January 1961): 251, 256; Lichtheim, *Rückkehr* [n. 28], 306.
59. Chaim Weizman, *Trial and Error. Autobiography.* 3rd ed. (London, 1949), 184.
60. *Ibid.*, 255, 261. On p. 194 Weizman states that in a meeting with Lloyd George, who at the time was Chancellor of the Exchequer, he told him, "the rich and powerful Jews were for the most part against us [Zionists];" he included in his list of such antagonists to the cause of Zionism the Rt. Hon. Edwin Montagu, an M. P., and later Secretary of State for India. p. 194. ("one of our bitterest opponents"), and pp. 197, 227, 255, 257, 259.
61. Lichtheim, *Rückkehr* [n. 28], 274 n. 2.
62. Weltmann, "Germany" [n. 58], 253.
63. Philip Paneth, *Turkey-Decadence and Rebirth* (London, 1943), 82n. 2.
64. Lichtheim, *Rückkehr* [n. 28], 377–78; Friedman, *Germany* [n. 29], 354; Richard W. Rowan, *The Story of Secret Service* (New York, 1937), 536–37; for a brief and general statement on anti-Turkish activities of Jews *see* Colonel W. Nicolai, *Geheime Mächte. Internationale Spionage und ihre Bekämpfung im Weltkrieg und heute.* (Leipzig, 1923), 93. In World War I, the author was Chief of Intelligence in the German High Command.

65. General Fahri Belen,*Birinci Cihan Harbinde Türk Harbi. 1916 Yılı Harekatleri* (The Turkish War in World War I. The Actions of 1916) vol. 4 (Ankara, 1965), 181. Among the less serious and more demagogical works on this subject are Cemal Kutay, *Birinci Dünya Harbinde Teşkilâtı Mahsusa* (The Special Organization in World War I) (Istanbul, 1962), 168–171; Cevat R. Atilhan, *Filistin Cephesinde Yahudi Casuslar* (Jewish Spies in the Palastine Front) (Istanbul, 1947); idem. *Meşhur Yahudi Casusu Suzi Liberman'ın Hatıra Defteri* (The Diary of Famous Jewish Spy Suzi Liberman) (Istanbul, 1961).
66. Friedman, *Germany* [n.29], 198–99.
67. FO 371/2781/253852, Appendix A, p. 9, December 13, 1915, report, relayed through Colonel Mark Sykes. *See also* I. Cowen and I. Gunther, *A Spy for Freedom: The Story of Sarah Aaronson* (New York, 1984).
68. Lichtheim, *Rückkehr* [n. 28], 263.
69. *Ibid.,* 278–286, 291, 308; Weltmann, "Germany" [n. 58] who on p. 255 offers the 800 number for the deported Jews.
70. George Horton, *Recollections Grave and Gay* (Indianapolis, 1927), 223–24. Horton was American Consul General at Smyrna 1911–1917.
71. DAA [n. 6], PA XII/463, No. 93/P.B. Consul's November 7, 1915 report.
72. Weltmann, "Germany" [n. 58], 255.
73. *Ibid.,* footnote 25.
74. Lichtheim, *Rückkehr* [n. 28], 283–85.
75. *Ibid.,* 245.
76. *Ibid.,* 277–78.
77. *Ibid.,* 289, 295.
78. *Ibid.,* 320–28, 333–34; Weltmann, "Germany" [n. 58], 259.
79. *Ibid. (Weltmann), 272; (Lichtheim), 339.*
80. Lichtheim, *Rückkehr* [n. 28], 339–40.
81. Friedman, *Germany* [n. 29], 348.
82. *Ibid.*
83. *Ibid.,* 350–51.
84. Friedrich Freiherr Kress von Kressenstein, *Mit den Türken zum Suezkanal* (Berlin, 1938), 248–50. Quoted in *ibid.,* 352.
85. Friedman, *Germany* [n. 29], 347, 353.
86. *Ibid.,* 370.
87. *Ibid.,* 371.
88. *Ibid.*
89. Count Bernstorff, *Memoirs of* (New York, 1936), 206.
90. Egmont Zechlin, *Die deutsche Politik und die Juden im ersten Weltkrieg* (Göttingen, 1969), 347.
91. Belen, *Birinci Cihan Harbinde* [n. 65], 181
92. Some such incidents are described in Friedman, *Germany* [n.29], 410–12; Lichtheim, *Rückkehr* [n. 28], 222–23.
93. Bernstorff, *Memoirs* [n. 89], 205.
94. *U.S. National Archives.* R.G. 59.76372/13450. Doc. No. 17, p. 3 of American Intelligence Officer at Cairo, William Yale's report No. 17.
95. Weltmann, "Germany" [n. 58], 265.
96. FO371/4141/4885. cipher No. 65. Private for Oliphant and Ormsby Gore. The cipher ends with the request: "Please paraphrase and destroy original."97. Friedman, *Germany* [n. 29], 215–16.
97. Friedman, *Germany* [n. 29], 215–16.
98. Weltmann, "Germany" [n. 58], 260.
99. William Yale, *The Near East. A Modern History* (new ed., revised and enlarged) (Ann Arbor, 1968), 268.
100. Friedman, *Germany* [n. 29], 287.
101. *Ibid.,* 404.
102. Lichtheim, *Rückkehr* [n. 28], 340, 341, 342.

APPENDIX-D

THE IMPASSIONED APPEAL OF GERMAN WRITER ARMIN T. WEGNER, AN EYEWITNESS TO THE GENOCIDE

AN OPEN LETTER TO PRESIDENT WILSON (Excerpts)

Berlin, January 1919

Mr. PRESIDENT,

In your message to Congress of January 8, 1918, you made a demand for the liberation of all non-Turkish peoples in the Ottoman Empire. One of these peoples is the Armenian nation. It is on behalf of the Armenian nation that I am addressing you.

As one of the few Europeans who have been eyewitnesses of the dreadful destruction of the Armenian people from its beginning in the fruitful fields of Anatolia up to the wiping out of the mournful remnants of the race on the banks of the Euphrates, I venture to claim the right of setting before you these pictures of misery and terror which passed before my eyes during nearly two years, and which will never be obliterated from my mind. I appeal to you at the moment when the Governments allied to you are carrying on peace negotiations in Paris, which will determine the fate of the world for many decades. But the Armenian people is only a small one among several others; and the future of greater States more prominent in the world's eye is hanging in the balance. And so there is reason to fear that the significance of a small and extremely enfeebled nation may be obscured by the influential and selfish aims of the great European states, and that with regard to Armenia there will be a repetition of the old game of neglect and oblivion of which she has so often been the victim in the course of her history.

But this would be most lamentable, for no people in the world has suffered such wrongs as the Armenian nation. The Armenian Question is a question for Christendom, for the whole human race.

The Armenian people ... were victims of this War. When the Turkish Government, in the Spring of 1915, set about the execution of its monstrous project of exterminating the Armenians, all the nations of Europe were unhappily bleeding to exhaustion, owing to the tragic blindness of their mutual misunderstanding, and there was no one to hinder the lurid tyrants of Turkey from carrying on to the bitter end those revolting atrocities which can only be likened to the acts of a criminal lunatic …

The men were struck down in batches, bound together with chains and ropes, and thrown into the river or rolled down the mountain with fettered limbs. The women and children were put on sale in the public market; the old men and boys driven with deadly bastonados to forced labor. Nor was this sufficient; in order to render indelible the stain on their criminal hands, the captors drove the people, after depriving them of their leaders and spokesmen, out of the towns at all hours of the day and night, half-naked, straight out of their beds; plundered their houses, burnt the villages, destroyed the churches or turned them into mosques, carried off the cattle, seized all the vehicles, snatched the bread out of the mouths of their victims, tore the clothes from off their backs, the gold from their hair and mouth. Officials—military officers, soldiers, shepherds—vied with one another in their wild orgy of blood, dragging out of the schools delicate orphan girls to serve their bestial lusts, beat with cudgels dying women or women close on childbirth who could scarcely drag themselves along, until the women fell down on the road and died, changing the dust beneath them into bloodstained mire … Here they died—slain by Kurds, robbed by gendarmes, shot, hanged, poisoned, stabbed, strangled, mown down by epidemics, drowned, frozen, parched with thirst, starved—their bodies left to putrefy or to be devoured by jackals.

Children wept themselves to death, men dashed themselves against the rocks, mothers threw their babes into the brooks, women with child flung themselves, singing, into the Euphrates. They died all the deaths on the earth, the deaths of all the ages. …

The voice of conscience and humanity will never be silenced in me, and therefore I address these words to you …

This document is a testament. It is the tongues of a thousand dead that speak in it.

Mr. President, the wrong suffered by this people is immeasurable. I have read everything that has been written about the war. I have carefully made myself acquainted with the horrors in every country on this earth, the fearful slaughters in every battle, the ships sunk by torpedoes, the bombs thrown down on the towns by aircraft, the heartrending slaughters in Belgium, the misery of the French refugees, the fearful sickness and epidemics in Roumania. But here is wrong to be righted such as none of these peoples has suffered—neither the French nation, nor the Belgian, nor the English, nor the Russian, nor the Serbian, nor the Roumanian, nor even the German nation, which has had to suffer so much in this war. The barbarous peoples of ancient times may possibly have endured a similar fate. But here we have a highly civilized nation, with a great and glorious past, which has rendered services that can never be forgotten to art, literature and learning; a nation which has produced many remarkable and intellectual men … acquainted with all the languages of the world, men whose wives and daughters have been accustomed to sit in comfortable chairs at a table covered with a clean white cloth, not to crouch in a cave in the wilderness. Sagacious merchants, distinguished doctors, scholars, artists, honest prosperous peasants who made the land fruitful, and whose only fault was that they were defenseless and spoke a different language from that of their persecutors, and were born into a different faith.

Every one who knows the events of this war in Anatolia, who has followed the fortunes of this nation with open eyes, knows that all those accusations which were brought, with great cunning and much diligence, against the Armenian race, are nothing but loathsome slanders fabricated by their unscrupulous tyrants, in order to shield themselves from the consequences of their own mad and brutal acts, and to hide their own incapacity for reconciliation with the spirit of sincerity and humanity.

But even if all these accusations were based on the truth, they would never justify these cruel deeds committed against hundreds of thousands of innocent people.

I am making no accusation against Islam. The spirit of every great religion is noble, and the conduct of many a Mohammedan has made us blush for the deeds of Europe.

I do not accuse the simple people of Turkey, whose souls are full of goodness; but I do not think that the members of the ruling class will ever, in the course of history, be capable of making their country happy, for they have destroyed our belief in their capacity for civilization.

Turkey has forfeited for all time the right to govern itself.

Mr. President, you will believe in my impartiality if I speak to you on this subject, as a German, one of a nation which was linked with Turkey in bonds of close friendship …

In the Berlin Treaty of July 1878, all the six European Great Powers gave the most solemn guarantees that they would guard the tranquillity and security of the Armenian people. But has this promise ever been kept? Even Abdul Hamit's massacres failed to bring it to remembrance, and in blind greed the nations pursued selfish aims, not one putting itself forward as the champion of an oppressed people.

In the Armistice between Turkey and your Allies, which the Armenians all over the world awaited with feverish anxiety, the Armenian question is scarcely mentioned. Shall this unworthy game be repeated a second time, and must the Armenians be once more disillusioned?

The future of this small nation must not be relegated to obscurity behind the selfish schemes and plans of the great states. Mr. President, save the honor of Europe. …

It is not enough, Mr. President, that you should know the sufferings of these people. It is not enough that you should give them a state in which the houses are destroyed, the fields laid waste, the citizens murdered. The exhaustion of this country is such that by its own strength it cannot rise again. Its trade is ruined; its handicrafts and industries have collapsed. The asset of its annihilated population can never be restored. The incalculable riches of the victims, which the cruel power-wielders of this land, animated with an insatiable greed, have piled up, constitute only a small pawn.

Many thousands of Armenians were converted to Islam by force, thousands of children and girls kidnapped, and thousands of women carried away and made slaves in Turkish harems. [To all these must be given perfect assurance of their return to freedom.] All victims of persecution who are returning to their homes after spending two years and more in the desert must be indemnified for the wealth and goods that they have lost, all orphans must bc cared for. What these people need is love, of which they have so long been deprived. This is, for all of us, a confession of guilt.

Mr. President, pride prevents me from pleading for my own people (the Germans). I have no doubt that, out of the plenitude of its sorrow, it will gain power by sacrifice to cooperate in the future redemption of the world. But, on behalf of the Armenian nation, which has suffered such terrible tyranny, I venture to intervene; for if, after this war, it is not given reparation for its fearful sufferings, it will be lost for ever.

With the ardor of one who has experienced unspeakable, humiliating sorrows in his own tortured soul, I utter the voice of those unhappy ones, whose despairing cries I had to hear without being able to still them, whose cruel deaths I could only helplessly mourn, whose bones bestrew the deserts of the Euphrates, and whose limbs once more become alive in my heart and admonish me to speak.

Once already have I knocked at the door of the American people when I brought the petition of the deportees from their camps at Meskene and Aleppo to your Embassy at Constantinople, and I know that this has not been in vain …

If you, Mr. President, have indeed made the sublime idea of championing oppressed nations the guiding principle of your policy, you will not fail to perceive that even in these words a mighty voice speaks, the only voice that has the right to be heard at all times—the voice of humanity.

Armin T. Wegner

Published in the German newspaper *Berliner Tageblatt*, No. 86. February 23, 1919 with the title *Ein Vermächtnis in der Wüste* (A Testament in the Desert). *See also* A. A. Türkei 183/55, A5773. The complete English translation is provided as an Appendix in *The Memoirs of Naim Bey. The Genocide of the Armenians by the Turks* (Newton Square, Pennsylvania, 1964. First published in 1920), 72–84. Below are adduced excerpts from the text of this translation.

* * *

Berlin, Januar 1919.

Herr Präsident! (*Auszüge*)

[Verschließen Sie Ihre Ohren nicht, weil ein Unbekannter zu Ihnen redet.] In Ihrer Botschaft an den Kongreß vom achten Januar des vergangenen Jahres haben Sie die Forderung der Befreiung aller nichttürkischen Völker des osmanischen Reiches aufgestellt. Zu diesen Völkern gehört ohne Zweifel auch das armenische. Diese Nation ist es, für die ich rede.

Als einer der wenigen Europäer, die ihren furchtbaren Untergang von seinem ersten Beginn in den glücklichen Städten, auf den fruchtbaren Äckern Anatoliens bis zu der Vernichtung ihrer kläglichen Reste an den Ufern des Euphrats, in den Steinöden der mesopotamischen Wüste mit eigenen Augen erlebt hat, erkenne ich mir das Recht zu, diese Bilder der Not und des Entsetzens vor Ihnen heraufzurufen, die fast durch zwei Jahre an meinen Blicken vorübergingen und die mich nie mehr verlassen werden. Ich tue dies in dem Augenblick, da die Ihnen verbündeten Regierungen sich bereiten, die Friedensverhandlungen in Paris zu beginnen, die über das Schicksal der Welt für viele Jahrzehnte entscheiden werden. Aber das armenische Volk ist nur ein geringes unter vielen; die Zukunft größerer und ruhmreicherer Staaten steht zur Verhandlung. Da liegt es nahe, daß die Bedeutung einer kleinen, so auf das äußerste geschwächten Nation von den gewaltsamen und selbstsüchtigen Zielen der großen europäischen Staaten zurückgedrängt oder beiseite geschoben wird, daß sich so für Armenien das gleiche Spiel der Nichtachtung und des Vergessens wiederholt, das ihm im Laufe der Geschichte so oft widerfuhr. Dies aber wäre auf das tiefste zu beklagen; denn keinem Volke der Erde ist je ein Unrecht geschehen wie dem armenischen. Es ist eine Frage des Christentums, es ist eine Frage der ganzen Menschheit.

Das armenische Volk … war ein Opfer dieses Krieges. Als die türkische Regierung im Frühjahr 1915 an die Ausführung ihres unfaßbaren Planes ging, … [die] Armenier vom Erdboden auszurotten, da waren die Hände ihrer europäischen Brüder Frankreichs, Englands und Deutschlands vom eigenen unseligen Blute feucht, das sie in der traurigen Blindheit ihres Mißverständnisses in Strömen vergossen, und niemand hinderte die finsteren Machthaber der Türkei, ihre qualvollen Folterungen zu beenden, deren Ausführung man in der Tat nur der Handlung eines wahnsinnigen Verbrechers vergleichen kann. … metzelte die Scharen ihrer Männer in Massen nieder, stürzte sie, mit Ketten und Seilen aneinandergefesselt, in den Fluß, rollte sie mit gebundenen Gliedern die Berge hinab, verkaufte ihre Frauen und Kinder auf den öffentlichen Märkten oder hetzte Greise und Knaben unter tödlichen Bastonaden auf die Straßen zur Zwangsarbeit. Nicht genug damit, seine verbrecherischen Hände so für alle Zeiten beschmutzt zu haben, jagte man das Volk, seiner Häupter und Wortführer beraubt, aus den Städten, zu jeder Stunde des Tages und der Nacht halb nackt aus den Betten, plünderte seine Häuser, verbrannte die Dörfer, zerstörte die Kirchen oder verwandelte sie in Moscheen, raubte sein Vieh, nahm ihnen Esel und Wagen, riß ihnen das Brot aus den Händen, die Kleider von den Gliedern, das Gold aus den Haaren und aus dem Mund. Beamte, Offiziere, Soldaten, Hirten wetteiferten in ihrem wilden Delirium des Blutes, schleppten die zarten Gestalten der Waisenmädchen zu ihrem tierischen Vergnügen aus den Schulen, schlugen mit den Knüppeln auf hochschwangere Weiber oder Sterbende ein, die sich nicht weiter schleppten, bis die Frau auf der Landstraße niederkommt und verendet, und der Staub sich unter ihr in einen blutigen Schlamm verwandelt. … Hier starben sie, von Kurden erschlagen, von Gendarmen beraubt, erschossen, erhängt, vergiftet, erdolcht, erdrosselt, von Seuchen verzehrt, ertränkt, erfroren, verdurstet, verhungert, verfault, von Schakalen angefressen. Kinder weinten sich in den Tod, Männer zerschmetterten sich an den Felsen, Mütter warfen ihre Kleinen in die Brunnen, Schwangere stürzten sich mit Gesang in den Euphrat. Alle Tode der Erde, die Tode aller Jahrhunderte starben sie. …

… Die Stimme des Gewissens und der Menschlichkeit wird niemals schweigen in mir, und darum spreche ich diese Worte zu Ihnen. Dieses Schreiben ist ein Vermächtnis. Es ist der Mund von tausend Toten, der aus mir redet.

Herr Präsident, das Unrecht dieses Volkes ist maßlos gewesen. Ich habe alles gelesen, was über diesen Krieg geschrieben wurde, ich habe die Greuel aller Länder dieser Erde verfolgt, die furchtbaren Metzeleien aller Schlachten, die von den Torpedos zerrissenen Schiffe, die von den Flugzeugen auf die Städte herabgeworfenen Bomben, die abscheulichen Ermordungen in Belgien, das Elend der französischen Flüchtlinge, die entsetzliche Not der verschleppten Deutschen und Gefangenen in Sibirien, die grauenvollen Krankheiten und Seuchen in Rumänien. Hier aber gilt es, ein Unrecht wieder gutzumachen, wie es keines dieser Völker erlitt, nicht das französische, nicht das belgische, nicht das englische, nicht das russische, nicht das serbische, nicht das rumänische und auch nicht das deutsche, das doch so viel in diesem Kriege erdulden mußte. Nur die wilden Völker des Altertums haben vielleicht annähernd ein ähnliches Schicksal ertragen. Hier aber handelte es sich um eine Nation von hoher Kultur, von reicher und ruhmvoller Vergangenheit, von unvergeßlichen Verdiensten um die Werke der Kunst, Literatur, Wissenschaft, mit zahlreichen bedeutenden und geistvollen Männern, … und die alle Sprachen der Erde kannten; dessen Frauen und Töchter wohl eher gewöhnt waren, in einem Schaukelstuhl oder vor einem reinlich gedeckten Tische zu sitzen, als um ein Erdloch in der Wüste zu kauern, kluge Kaufleute, Ärzte, Gelehrte, Künstler, aufrechte und glückliche Bauern, die das Land fruchtbar machten, und deren einzige Schuld es war, wehrlos zu sein, eine andere Sprache zu sprechen, und als die Kinder eines anderen Glaubens geboren zu sein. Jeder, der die Vorgänge dieses Krieges in Anatolien kennt, der das Schicksal dieses Volkes mit offenen Augen verfolgt hat, weiß, daß alle jene Beschuldigungen, die man mit Weisheit und vieler Mühe gegen die armenische Rasse erhob, nichts sind als eine Abscheu erregende Verleumdung ihrer gewissenlosen Machthaber, die sie zum Schutze ihrer rasenden und brutalen Gewalt erfanden, die sich mit dem Geist der Wahrhaftigkeit und des Menschentums niemals vereinen lassen. Aber selbst wenn alle diese Vorwürfe auf Wahrheit beruhen sollten, würden sie niemals jene grauenhaften Taten rechtfertigen, die man gegen Hunderttausende Unschuldiger begangen hat. Ich klage nicht den Islam an. Der Geist jeder großen Religion ist edel, und die Handlung manchen Mohammedaners hat uns die Augen vor den Taten Europas niederschlagen lassen. Ich klage nicht das einfache Volk dieses Landes an, dessen Seele von tiefer

Sittlichkeit erfüllt ist. Aber ich glaube nicht, daß die Kreise seiner führenden Herrenkaste jemals im Laufe der Geschichte fähig sein werden, es glücklich zu machen, nachdem sie unseren Glauben an ihre Kulturfähigkeit so tief zerstörten, und die Türkei scheinbar das Recht, sich selbst zu lenken, für alle Zeiten verwirkt hat.

Herr Präsident, Sie werden mir die Unparteilichkeit meiner Stimme glauben, wenn ich als Deutscher zu Ihnen darüber rede, als der Angehörige eines Volkes, das auf das tiefste mit der Türkei befreundet war … . Im Berliner Vertrage vom Juli 1878 hat ganz Europa die heiligsten Garantien übernommen, die Ruhe und Sicherheit des armenischen Volkes zu schützen. Aber hat es jemals dieses Versprechen eingelöst? Selbst die Massenmorde Abdul Hamids haben es nicht zur Besinnung gebracht, und in blinder Begierde verfolgte es die Ziele seines Eigennutzes, nicht gewillt, sich zum Beschützer eines bedrohten Volkes zu machen. In den Waffenstillstandsbedingungen zwischen der Türkei und den ihnen verbündeten Völkern, die von den Armeniern der ganzen Erde mit fieberhafter Spannung erwartet wurden, ist die armenische Frage nur kurz berührt worden. Soll sich dieses unwürdige Spiel ein zweites Mal wiederholen, und sollen die Armenier von neuem die enttäuschenden Lehren aus der Vergangenheit ziehen? Die Zukunft dieses kleinen Volkes darf nicht zurücktreten hinter den selbstsüchtigen Plänen und Ansprüchen der großen Staaten. Herr Präsident, retten Sie die Ehre Europas!

… Es genügt nicht, Herr Präsident, daß Sie das Elend dieses Volkes kennen. Es genügt nicht, daß Sie ihm einen Staat geben, dessen Häuser zerstört, dessen Felder verwüstet, dessen Bürger ermordet sind. Die Erschöpfung dieses Landes ist so groß, daß es sich aus eigener Kraft nicht wieder emporraffen kann. Der Handel ist niedergebrochen, das Handwerk, die Industrie ohne Arbeit. Das Kapital, das an Menschen vernichtet wurde, kann niemals ersetzt werden. Die unermeßlichen Reichtümer, die die grausamen Machthaber dieses Landes in ihrer unersättlichen Gier aus den Schätzen der Vertriebenen angehäuft haben, sind nur ein geringes Pfand. Viele Tausende von Armeniern wurden mit Gewalt zum Islam bekehrt, Tausende von Kindern sind verschleppt und Tausende von Frauen geraubt und in türkischen Harems zu Sklavinnen gemacht worden. Ihnen allen muß die unverbrüchliche Versicherung ihrer Rückkehr in die Freiheit gegeben werden. Alle Opfer der Verfolgung, die ihre Heimat betreten, die zwei Jahre und mehr in der Wüste gelebt haben, müssen an Reichtümern und Gütern, die sie verloren, entschädigt, alle Waisen erzogen werden. Wessen dieses Volk bedarf, das ist die Liebe, die es so lange entbehrt hat. Das ist die Erkenntnis der Schuld unserer aller.

Herr Präsident, für mein eigenes Volk zu bitten, verbietet mir der Stolz. Ich zweifle nicht, daß es aus der Fülle seines Schmerzes die Kraft gewinnen wird, sich opfernd mitzuwirken an der künftigen Erlösung der Welt. Für die armenische Nation aber, die so furchtbar gedemütigt wurde, drängt es mich, einzutreten; denn wenn sie auch nach diesem Kriege nicht die Genugtuung ihrer furchtbaren Leiden erfahren sollte, wird sie für immer verloren sein. Mit der Inbrunst dessen, der die unausdenkbare Schmach ihrer Leiden an der eigenen gefolterten Seele erfuhr, erhebe ich die Stimme jener Elenden, deren verzweifelte Klagen ich hilflos hören, deren grauenvollen Tod ich ohnmächtig beweinen mußte, deren Knochen die Wüsten des Euphrats bedecken und deren Beine noch einmal Fleisch werden in meinem Herzen und mich mahnen, zu Ihnen zu reden. Schon einmal habe ich an die Tür des amerikanischen Volkes geklopft, als ich die Bittbriefe der Vertriebenen aus den Flüchtlingslagern von Meskene und Aleppo auf Ihre Botschaft nach Konstantinopel brachte, und Ich weiß, daß dies nicht vergeblich gewesen ist … wenn Sie, Herr Präsident, die erhabene Idee, den unterworfenen Völkern Hilfe zu bringen, in der Tat zur Richtschnur Ihrer Politik gemacht haben, so werden Sie nicht verkennen, daß auch aus diesen Worten eine machtvolle Stimme spricht, die einzige, die das Recht hat, zu allen Zeiten gehört zu werden: die Stimme der Menschlichkeit.

Armin T. Wegner

Commander Rafael de Nogales

Henry Morgenthau, American ambassador to Turkey

Ambassador Morgenthau with his grandsons and daughters of the Swedish Minister to Turkey standing on the terrace of American Embassy in Constantinople

Marshal Colmar von der Goltz

Marshal Liman von Sanders

General Fritz Bronsart
von Schellendorf

General Kress
von Kressenstein

General von Falkenhayn inspecting Turkish troops

Baron von Wangenheim,
German ambassador to Turkey

The funeral of Baron von Wangenheim, Istanbul

Dr. Arthur Zimmermann

Dr. Bethmann Hollweg

Enver Paşa and General von Seeckt

The Grand Vizier Talât Paşa

Kaiser William II in Constantinopel in 1917

Kaiser William II inspecting Turkish Troops

Enver Paşa

Cemal Paşa

Battle Cruiser Goeben *(Yavuz)*

Admiral Souchon

German and Turkish Navy officers on board the Goeben

General Seeckt and Hitler attending the maneuvers of the German army at Illehausen

General Seeckt reviewing his regiment on parade

BIBLIOGRAPHY

PRIMARY SOURCES. STATE AND NATIONAL ARCHIVES. OFFICIAL DOCUMENTS

I. AUSTRIA

Österreichisches Staatsarchiv. *Die Akten des k. u. k. Ministeriums des Äussern, 1848–1918* (Foreign Ministry Archives of Austria, in Vienna) Abteilung XII: Türkei, Kartons (files) 462,463; XL. Interna, File 272; Konsulate 38, file 303; Karton Rot 947.

III. GERMANY

Federal Republic of Germany, *Akten des Auswärtigen Amtes 1867–1920* (West Germany's Foreign Office Archives, Bonn) Abteilung IA (Political Dept.)

Orientalia Generalia. No. 5. vol. 30. (1896).

Türkei, file numbers 158 and 183, with sets of volumes (Band), and corresponding entry numbers, preceded by letter A, attached to them.

Botschaft Konstantinopel (K) Consular files.

Grosses Hauptquartier, vols. 185, 187, 194.

German Military Archives (Bundesarchiv-Militärarchiv), i.e., BA/MA. (Freiburg i. Breisgau)

Deutschland und Armenien, 1914–1918: Sammlung diplomatischer

Aktenstücke. J. Lepsius ed., 1919. (German Foreign Office archive documents dealing almost entirely with the World War I Armenian deportations and massacres).

The German Documents on the Outbreak of the War 1914. (*Die deutschen Dokumente zum Kriegsausbruch 1914*), compiled by K. Kautsky, Max Graf von Montgelas, and Walter Schückling, eds., 2nd expanded ed, vol. 1. Berlin, 1922.

The Talât Paşa Trial (*Der Prozess Talaat Pascha*) Stenographic Records. Berlin, 1921.

A. A. Bonn. Göppert Papers (*Nachlass*) vol. VI, file 5 (files 1–8).

IV. FRANCE

Archives du Ministère des Affaires Étrangères. Quai d'Orsay, Paris (Foreign Ministry Archives).

Archives du Patriarcat de Constantinople (APC). Documents Officiels et Rapports (DOR), Paris (Nubar Library).

Nouvelle Série: *Correspondance politique et commerçiale 1897*: *Turquie. Politique intérieure. Dossier General,* vols. 7 and 8. Jeunes Turcs.

Guerre 1914–1918: vols. I, II, III. *Turquie*. 887–889 Arménie. August 1914–December 1915, January 1916–March 1917, April 1917–May 1918.

Les Grandes Puissances, L'Empire Ottoman et les Arméniens dans les archives françaises (1914–1918). (A. Beylerian, ed. 1983). (French Foreign, War, and General Headquarters Office documents dealing with the Armenian genocide).

V. GREAT BRITAIN

Foreign Office (FO) *Archives.* Public Record Office, London and Kew.

Class 371 Files. Political: *General Correspondence, 1915–1920.* (persecution, deportation, massacres of Armenians in Turkey)

Class 608 Files. *Paris Peace Conference Records, 1919–1920*

WO 106. *War Office Directorate of Military Operations and Intelligence.*

Great Britain, Parliament. *The Treatment of the Armenians in the Ottoman Empire: Documents Presented to Viscount Grey of Fallodon, Secretary of State for Foreign Affairs.* (Compiled by A. Toynbee, Miscellaneous No. 31, 1916). (A massive collection of accounts on the Armenian genocide up to summer 1916 by European and American observers in wartime Turkey.)

Armenia. Parliamentary Debates, House of Lords. (November 13, 1918); House of Commons (October 23, 24, 30, 31, November 6, 7, 12, 14, 18, 1918) A. Raffi, ed. London, 1918.

British Documents on the Origins of the War 1889–1914. Part I, vol. 9. Gooch and Temperley, eds. London, 1926.

Documents on British Foreign Policy 1919–1939, vol. 4. First Series, W. Woodward and R. Butler, eds. London, 1952.

VI. TURKEY (OTTOMAN EMPIRE AND THE TURKISH REPUBLIC)

Corps de Droit Ottoman, Code de Procédure Pénale (Treatise of Ottoman Law, Code of Criminal Procedure) G. Young, vol. 7. Oxford, 1906.

Türkiye Büyük Millet Meclisi Gizli Celse Zabıtları (The Transcripts of the Secret Sessions of the Grand National Assembly of Turkey) (Türkiye Iş Banka Cultural Series, Publ. No. 267). vol. 3 (March 6, 1922–February 27, 1923), and vol. 4. (March 2, 1923–Oct. 25, 1934) Ankara, 1985.

Takvimi Vekâyi issues (Ottoman government's official gazette whose supplements *[ilâve]* served as judicial journal, recording the proceedings of the Turkish Military Tribunal that tried the authors of the Armenian genocide Istanbul, 1919–20).

Meclisi Mebusan Zabıt Ceridesi (Transcripts of the Proceedings of the Chamber of Deputies) Third Election Period. Fifth Session. 1918.

Meclisi Âyan Zabıt Ceridesi (Transcripts of the Proceedings of the Senate) Third Election Period. Fifth Session. 1918.

Harb Kabinelerinin Isticvabı (War Cabinet Ministers' Hearings) by Ottoman Chamber of Deputies Fifth Committee. November–December, 1918 (1334). (This is an abbreviated version of the transcripts of the hearings which the Istanbul Turkish daily *Vakit* in 1933 published in the form of a Special Supplement. The complete version of the transcripts was published by the Fifth Committee itself under the title Meclisi Mebusan Zabıtları [Records of the Proceedings of the Chamber of Deputies] Third Parliament, 5th session, No. 521) Istanbul, 1918.

Nutuk. Kemal Atatürk (Speech, K. Atatürk), vol. 3, 7th ed. Istanbul, n.d.

Tarihi Muhakeme (Historical Trial [of the authors of the Armenian genocide]) (Kit. Sudi ed.) Istanbul, 1919 (This volume contains the transcripts of the first two sessions of the Cabinet Ministers' trials described under V1, Takvimi Vekâyi).

K. Karabekir, *Istiklâl Harbimiz* (Our War of Independence). Istanbul, 1st ed. 1960; 2d ed. 1969. (A massive compilation of official documents covering mainly the political and military correspondence between the fledgling Ankara government and the Commander in Chief of Ankara's Eastern Front Army 1919–20).

The Imperial Ottoman Penal Code. J. Bucknill and H. Utidjian trans. Oxford, 1913.

Documents. (purporting to demonstrate Armenian guilt and the relative innocence of the Ittihad government), vol. I. Compiled by The Office of Press and Information, Directorate General, Prime Ministry. Ankara, 1982.

Sonyel, Dr. Salahi, *Displacement of the Armenians. Documents* (pamphlet in English, French and Turkish) Ankara, 1978.

VII. UNITED NATIONS

Escor Comm. on Human Rights, Sub-Comm. on Prevention of Discrimination and Protection of Minorities.

U.N. ESCOR Comm. on Human Rights, Sub-Comm. on Prevention of Discrimination and Protection of Minorities (38th sess.) (Item 57) 7, U.N: Doc. E/CN.4/Sub.2/1985/SR.36 (1985) (summary record of 36th meeting, Aug. 29, 1985).

Agenda Item 4, Prevention and Punishment of the Crime of Genocide (1985) (the Whitaker report reviewing the historical antecedents of genocide).

Summary Record of the 36th Meeting of Sub-Comm. (1985) (the Sub-Commission's favorable response to the Whitaker report defining the World War I massacre against the Armenians as genocide). *Revised and updated report on the question of the prevention and punishment of the crime of genocide,* 38 U.N. ESCOR Comm. on Human Rights, Subcomm. on Prevention of Discrimination and Protection of Minorities, (Agenda Item 4), 8–9, U.N. Doc. E/CN.4/Sub.2/1985/6 (1985).

The United Nations War Crimes Commission, History of the United Nations War Crimes Commission and the Development of the Laws of War. London, 1948.

VIII. UNITED STATES

United States, Dept. of State, National Archives, Record Groups, i.e., R.G. 59 Relating to the:

Internal Affairs of Turkey 1910–1929 R.G. 59. 867.4016, Race Problems (persecution, deportation, massacres and expulsion from Turkey of the Armenians).
The American Commission to Negotiate Peace at the Paris Peace Conference. R.G. 256. 867.00. Turkey (political affairs).
United States, Dept. of State. *Papers Relating to the Foreign Relations of the United States. 1915 Supplement. The World War.* Washington, 1928.
United States, Dept. of State. *Papers Relating to the Foreign Relations of the United States. The Lansing Papers. 1914–1920.* (L.) (In two volumes) vol. 1. Washington, D.C., 1939.
132 Cong. Rec. (1986) (Statements by a host of U.S. Senators noting the Armenian genocide in their arguments in support of the U.S. ratification of the U.N. Convention on Genocide).
The Hoover Institution on War, Revolution and Peace. Stanford. Imperial Russian Interior Ministry. Foreign Affairs Department of the Secret Service of the Police.

SECONDARY SOURCES

Turkish

Akçam, T. *Siyasi Kültürümüzde Zulüm ve Işkence* (Atrocity and Torture in Our Political Culture). Istanbul, 1992.
Amca, H. *Doğmayan Hürriyet. Bir Devrin Iç Yüzü 1908–1918* (Freedom Unborn, The Inside Story of an Era 1908–1918). Istanbul, 1958.
Atilhan, C. R. *Filistin Cephesinde Yahudi Casuslar* (Jewish Spies in the Palastine Front). Istanbul, 1947.
______. *Meşhur Yahudi Casusu Suzi Liberman'ın Hatıra Defteri* (The Diary of Famous Jewish Spy Suzi Liberman). Istanbul, 1961.
Avcıoğlu, D. *Milli Kurtuluş Tarihi.* (History of the National Liberation), vol. 3. Istanbul, 1974.
Aydemir, Ş.S. *Makedonyadan Ortaasya'ya Enver Paşa* (Enver Paşa. From Macedonia to Central Asia), vol. 2. Istanbul, 1971; vol. 3. Istanbul, 1972.
Aydemir, S¸.S. *Ikinci Adam* (Second Man) vol. 1, 3rd ed. Istanbul, 1973.
Bayar, C. *Ben de Yazdım. Milli Mücadeleye Giriş* (I Too Have Written. The Start of the National Struggle) vol. 5. Istanbul, 1967.
Bayur, Y. H. *Türk Inkilâbı Tarihi* (The History of the Turkish Revolution), vol. 2. Part 4. Ankara, 1952; vol. 3. Part 1. 1953; vol. 3. Part 3. 1957; vol. 3. Part 4. 1983.
Beşikci, I. *Kürdistan Üzerinde Emperyalist Bölüşüm Mücadelesi: 1915–1925* (The Fight over Kurdistan's Imperialist Partition 1915–1925), vol. 1. Ankara, 1992.
Bleda, M. *Imparatorluğun Çöküşü* (The Collapse of the Empire), Istanbul, 1979.
Belen,Gen. F. *Birinci Cihan Harbinde Türk Harbi. 1916 Yılı Hareketleri* (The Turkish War in World War I. The Actions of 1916) vol. 4. Ankara, 1965.
Çavdar, T. *Talât Paşa.* Ankara, 1984.
Esatlı, M.R. *Ittihad ve Terakki Tarihinde Esrar Perdesi* (The Curtain of Secrecy in the History of Ittihad). Istanbul, 1975.
Izzet, P.A. *Feryadım* (My Lamentation), vol. 1. Istanbul, 1992.
Karabekir, K. *Istiklâl Harbimiz* (Our War of Independence), lst ed. Istanbul, 1960, 2d ed. Istanbul, 1969.
______. *Birinci Cihan Harbine Nasıl Girdik?* (How Did We Enter World War I) vol. 2. Istanbul, 1994.
Kutay, C. *Talât Paşanın Gurbet Hatıraları* (The Memoirs of Talât Paşa in Exile), 3 vols., vols. 2 and 3. Istanbul, 1983.
______. *Osmanlıdan Cumhuriyete. Yüzyılımızda Bir Insanımız* (From the Ottoman to the Republic Era. Our Man of the Century). *Hüseyin Rauf Orbay (1881–1964).* vol. 4. Istanbul, 1992.
______. *Siyasi Mahkûmlar Adası: Malta* (Malta: The Island for the Politically Condemned People). Istanbul, 1963.
______. *Birinci Dünya Harbinde Teşkilâtı Mahsusa* (The Special Organization in World War I) Istanbul, 1962.

Küçük, Dr. A. *Dönmeler ve Dönmelik Tarihi* (The Dönmes and the History of the Practice of Becoming *Dönmes*. Istanbul, 1979?

Müderrisoğlu, A. *Sarıkamış Dramı* (The Drama of Sarıkamış), vol. 1. Istanbul, 1988.

Oğuz, B. *Yüzyıllar Boyunca Alman Gerçeği ve Türkler* (The German Reality in the Course of Centuries and the Turks). Istanbul, 1983.

Öke, Dr. K. *Ermeni Meselesi 1914–1923* (The Armenian Question), Istanbul, 1986.

______. *II. Abdülhamid, Siyonistler ve Filistin Meselesi* (Abdülhamid II. The Zionists and the Palestine Problem) Istanbul, 1981.

Okyar, F. *Üç Devirde Bir Adam* (A Man of Three Eras). C. Kutay, ed. Istanbul, 1980.

Ölçen, A. N. *Osmanlı Meclisi Mebusanında Kuvvetler Ayırımı ve Siyasal Işkenceler* (The Debate in the Ottoman Chamber of Deputies on Separation of Powers and Politically Inspired Tortures) Ankara, 1982.

Ortaylı, I. *Osmanlı Imparatorluğunda Alman Nüfuzu* (The German Influence in the history of the Ottoman Empire). Istanbul, 1983.

Refik, A. (Altınay), *Iki Komite Iki Kıtal* (Two Committees and Two Massacres) Ottoman Script. Istanbul, 1919.

Sabis, A.I. *Harb Hatıralarım* (My War Memoirs), vol. 1. Istanbul, 1943;*i*dem, vol. 2. Ankara, 1951.

Şakir, Z. 1914–1918 *Cihan Harbini Nasıl Idare Ettik* (How Did We Direct the 1914–1918 World War). Istanbul, 1944.

Samih, A. *Büyük Harpte Kafkas Cephesi* (The Caucasus Front in the Great War). Ankara, 1934.

Tahsin, P. *Abdülhamit Yıldız Hatıraları* (Abdul Hamit's *Yıldız* [Palace] Memoirs). Istanbul, 1931.

Sertel, M. Z. *Hatırladıklarım. 1905–1950 (*The Things I Remember). Istanbul, 1968.

Soysal, I. *Dünya ve Türkiyede Masonlar ve Masonluk* (Freemasons and Freemasonry in the World and in Turkey) Istnbul, 1980.

Talât Paşanın Hatıraları. (The Memoirs of Talât Paşa). E. Bolayir, ed., Istanbul, 1946.

Tunaya, T. Z. *Türkiyede Siyasal Partiler* (The Political Parties in Turkey), 3 vols., 2d enl. ed. Istanbul, 1984.

Tanyu, Dr. H. *Tarih Boyunca Yahudiler ve Türkler* (Jews and Turks in the course of History) vol. 1, 2nd expanded ed. Ankara, 1977.

Türkgeldi, A.F. *Görüp Işittiklerim* (The Things I Witnessed and Heard). 2d ed. Ankara, 1951.

Vardar, G. *Ittihad ve Terakki Içinde Dönenler* (The Inside Story of Ittihad ve Terakki Party). S.H. Tansu, ed. Istanbul, 1960.

Yılmaz, V. *1ci Dünya Harbinde Türk-Alman Ittifakı ve Askeri Yardımlar* (The World War I Turko-German Alliance and the Range of Military Assistnace). Istanbul, 1993.

English

Alamuddin, Ida. *Papa Kuenzler and the Armenians,* London, 1970.

Barrows, J. O. *In the Land of Ararat.* New York, 1916.

Bassiouni, M.C. *Crimes Against Humanity in International Law*. Boston, 1992.

Count Bernstorff, *Memoirs of.* New York, 1936.

Bryce, J. *The Treatment of Armenians in the Ottoman Empire 1915–16*. Compiled by A. Toynbee. London, 1916.

Carnegie Endowment for the International Peace, *Violations of the Laws and Customs of War: Report of the Majority and Dissenting Reports of the American and Japanese Members of the Commission on Responsiblities at the Conference of Paris, 1919*, Pamphlet No. 32, Oxford, 1919.

Churchill, Winston. *The Aftermath,* vol. 4, *The World Crisis*. New York, 1929.

Dadrian, V.N. *The History of the Armenian Genocide. Ethnic Conflict from the Balkans to Anatolia to the Caucasus*. Providence/Oxford, 1995.

Emin (Yalman), A. *Turkey in the World War.* New Haven, CT. 1930.

Friedman, I. *Germany, Turkey, and Zionism. 1897–1918.* Oxford, 1977.

Goerlitz, W. *History of the German General Staff 1657–1945*, B. Battershaw, trans. New York, 1953.

Gottlieb, W.W. *Studies in Secret Diplomacy during the First World War*. London, 1957.

Graves, Dr. A.K. T*he Secrets of the German War Office* (with the collaboration of E. L. Fox) 4th ed. New York, 1914.
Herbert, A. *Ben Kendim. A Record of Eastern Travel*, 2nd. ed. London, 1924.
Horton, G. *Recollections Grave and Gay*. Indianapolis, 1927.
Jäckh, E. *The Rising Crescent*. New York, 1944.
Knapp, G.H. *The Tragedy of Bitlis*. New York, 1919.
Kotker, N. *Herzl the King*. New York, 1972.
Lewis, Bernard. *The Emergence of Modern Turkey*. London/New York, 1961, reprinted 1962,
Morgenthau, H. *Ambassador Morgenthau's Story*. New York, 1918.
______. *Secrets of the Bosphorus*. London, 1918.
n.a. *The Near East From Within*. New York, n. d. (probably winter 1914–15).
de Nogales, R. *Four Years Beneath the Crescent*. M. Lee, trans. New York, 1926.
Paneth, P. *Turkey—Decadence and Rebirth*. London, 1943.
Ramsaur, E.E. *The Young Turks. Prelude to the Revolution of 1908*. Beirut, 1965.
Reitlinger, *G.The SS. Alibi of a Nation. 1922–1945*. New York, 1957.
von Rintelen, Captain. *The Dark Invader. Wartime Reminiscences of a German Naval Intelligence Officer*. New York, 1933.
Rowan, R. W. *The Story of Secret Service*. New York, 1937.
von Sanders, L. *Five Years in Turkey*. Annapolis, Maryland, 1927.
Schreiner, George A. *From Berlin to Bagdad. Behind the Scenes in the Near East*. New York, 1918.
Stoddard, P. *The Ottoman Government and the Arabs, 1911 to 1918: A Preliminary Study of the Teşkilatı-Mahsusa* (Special Organization). Univ. Microfilms. Ann Arbor, Mich., 1963.
Stürmer, H. *Two Years in Constantinople*. E. Allen, trans. New York, 1917.
Tirpitz, A. *My Memoirs*, vol. 2. New York, 1919.
Toynbee, A. J. *The Western Question in Greece and Turkey*.Boston, 1922.
Trumpener, U. *Germany and the Ottoman Empire 1914–1918*. Princeton, 1968.
Ussher, C. *An American Physician in Turkey*. Boston, 1917.
Weber, F.G. *Eagles on the Crescent*. Ithaca, NY, 1970.
Weizman, C. *Trial and Error. Autobiography*. 3rd ed. London, 1949.
Yale, W. *The Near East. A Modern History* (new ed., revised and enlarged). Ann Arbor, 1968.
Zarevand, *United and Independent Turania. Aims and Designs of the Turks*. V.N. Dadrian trans. Leiden, 1971.
Zenkovsky, S. *Pan-Turkism and Islam in Russia*. Cambridge, Mass., 1967.

German

Alp, T. *Türkismus und Pantürkismus*. Weimar, 1915.
Baronigian, A.S. *Blicke ins Märtyrerland*. Lössnitzgrund i. Sachsen, 1921.
Bihl, W. *Die Kaukasus-Politik der Mittelmächte*. Part I. Vienna, 1975.
von Bülow, F.B. *Denkwürdigkeiten*, vol. 2. Berlin, 1930.
Eckart, B. *Meine Erlebnisse in Urfa*. Berlin-Potsdam, 1922.
Ehrhold, K. *Flucht in die Heimat* (Flight into the Homeland). Dresden-Leipzig, 1937.
Eyck, E. *Das persönliche Regiment Wilhelms II: Politische Geschichte des deutschen Kaiserreiches von 1890 bis 1914*. Zürich, 1948.
Fischer, F. *Griff nach der Weltmacht*. Düsseldorf, 1967.
von der Goltz, C.F. *Denkwürdigkeiten* (Memoirs). Friedrich v. d. Goltz, W. Foerster eds. Berlin, 1929.
Guse, F. *Die Kaukasusfront im Weltkrieg*. Leipzig, 1940.
Gust, Wolfgang, *Der Völkermord an den Armeniern. Die Tragödie des ältesten Christenvolkes der Welt*, Ulm, 1993. (The Genocide of the Armenians. The Tragedy of the World's Oldest Christian People.
Guttmann, B. *Schattenriss einer Generation* (The Silhouette of a Generation). Stuttgart, 1950.
Theodor Herzl's Tagebücher 1895–1904. 3 vols. vol. 1, 1922; vols. 2 and 3, 1923, Berlin.
Hohenlohe-Schillingshurst, C. *Denkwürdigkeiten der Reichskanzlerzeit* (Memoirs from the Time of Service as Chancellor). Stuttgart, 1931.
Jäckh, E. *Der Goldene Pflug* (The Golden Ploughshare). Stuttgart, 1954.

von Kampen, W. *Studien zur Deutschen Türkeipolitik in der Zeit Wilhelms II* (Studies on Germany's Policy on Turkey in William II's Time). (doctoral thesis at the University of Kiel), 1968.

von Kressenstein, Kress Friedrich *Mit den Türken zum Suezkanal.* Berlin, 1938.

von Kühlmann, R. *Erinnerungen* (Memoirs). Heidelberg, 1948.

Künzler, Jacob. *Im Lande des Blutes und der Tränen. Erlebnisse in Mesopotamien während des Krieges.* Potsdam-Berlin, 1921.

Lepsius, J. *Armenien und Europa.* Berlin-Westend, 1897.

______. *Deutschland und Armenien 1914–1918. Sammlung diplomatischer Aktenstücke* Berlin-Potsdam, 1919.

Leverkuehn, P. *Posten auf Ewiger Wache. Aus dem abenteuerreichen Leben des Max von Scheubner-Richter.* Essen, 1938.

Lichtheim, R. *Rückkehr. Lebenserinnerungen aus der Frühzeit des deutschen Zionismus.* Stuttgart, 1970.

Ludwig, E. *Wilhelm der Zweite.* Berlin, 1926.

Meier-Welcker, H. *Seeckt.* Frankfurt am Main, 1967.

Meyer, Karl. *Armenien und die Schweiz.* Bern, 1974.

Mühlmann, C. *Das deutsch-türkische Waffenbündnis im Weltkriege.* Leipzig, 1940.

Mühsam, Kurt. *Wie wir belogen wurden.* Munich, 1918.

von Müller, G.A. *Der Kaiser ... Aufzeichnungen des Chefs des Marinekabinetts Admiral G. A. V. Müller über die Ära Wilhelms II.* (Navy Cabinet Chef Admiral Müller's Notes on William II's Era of Rule) W. Göllitz ed. Göttingen, 1965.

Nadolny, R. *Mein Beitrag.* Wiesbaden, 1955.

Naumann, F. *Asia.* Berlin-Schoneberg, 1911.

Nicolai, Col. W. *Geheime Mächte. Internationale Spionage und ihre Bekämpfung im Weltkrieg und heute.* Leipzig, 1923.

de Nogales, R. *Vier Jahre unter dem Halbmond.* Berlin, 1925. A major feature of this edition, which by one year preceded the English edition of the original Spanish text is the magnitude of deletions of portions which depict the Turks, especially War Minister Enver, in unsavory situations.

Nossig, Dr. A. *Die Neue Türkei und Ihre Führer.* Halle, 1917.

von Papen, F. *Der Wahrheit eine Gasse.* Münich, 1952.

Pomiankowski, J. *Der Zusammenbruch des Ottomanischen Reiches.* Original Edition 1928, Vienna. Reprint, Graz, 1969.

Rathmann, L. *Stossrichtung des deutschen Imperialismus im ersten Weltkrieg.* Berlin, 1963.

Rohrbach, P. *Vom Kaukasus zum Mittelmeer. Eine Hochzeits—und Studienreise durch Armenien.* Berlin, 1903.

Saupp, N. *Das Deutsche Reich und die Armenische Frage* (The German Empire and the Armenian Question) Cologne or Köln, (doctoral thesis at the University of Köln), 1990.

Schäfer, R. *Persönliche Erinnerungen an Johannes Lepsius.* Berlin-Potsdam, 1935.

Schraudenbach, L. *Muharebe.* (War) Berlin, 1924.

Sommer, Dr. Ernst, *Die Wahrheit über die Leiden des armenischen Volks in der Türkei Während des Weltkriegs.* Frankfurt a. Main, 1919.

Ular A. and Insabato, E. *Der Erlöschende Halbmond. Türkische Enthüllungen.* Frankfurt A.M. 1909.

von Vietsch, ed., E. *Cegen die Unvernunft. Der Briefwechsel zwischen Paul Graf Wolff Metternich und Wilhelm Solf 1915-1918.* Bremen, 1964.

Wallach, J.L. *Anatomie einer Militärhilfe. Die preussisch-deutschen Militärmissionen in der Türkei 1835–1919.* Düsseldorf, 1976.

von Waldersee, A.G. *Denkwürdigkeiten* (Memoirs), vol. 1. H.O. Meisner, ed. Stuttgart, 1923.

Zechlin, E. *Die deutsche Politik und die Juden im ersten Weltkreig.* Göttingen, 1969.

Zeki, M. *Raubmörder als Gäste der deutschen Republik.* Berlin, 1920.

French

Bérard, V. *La politique du Sultan.* Paris, 1897

Izzet-Fuad, G. *Autres Occasions Perdues ... Critique Stratégique de la Campagne d'Asie Mineure 1877–1878.* Paris, 1908.

Kevorkian, R. H. and Paul B. Paboudjian. Les Arméniens dans l'Empire Ottoman à la veilee du génocide. Paris, 1992.
Mandelstam, A. *Le Sort de L'Empire Ottomane*. Lausanne, 1917.
Pinon, R. *La Suppression des Arméniens. Méthode allemande-travail turc*. Paris, 1916.
Young, G. *Constantinople. Depuis les origines jusqu'a nos jours*. Paris, 1934.

Armenian

Andonian, A. *Medz Vodjiru* (The Great Crime). Boston, 1921.
Balakian, Rev. K. *Hai Koghkotan. Trouakner Hai Mardirosakroutiunen. Berlinen Tebee Zor 1914–1920* (The Armenian Golgotha. Episodes from the Armenian Martyrilogy. From Berlin to Zor 1914–1920), vol. 1. Vienna, 1922.
Houshartzan Abril Dasnumegi (In Memoriam of April 24, 1915). Istanbul, 1919.
Mugurditchian, T. *Dikranagerdee Nahankin Tcharteru Yev Kiurderou Kazanioutounneru* (The Massacres in Diyarbekir Province and the Savageries of the Kurds). Cairo, 1919.
Zaven Arkyebiskobos. *Badriarkagan Housherus. Vaverakirner yev Vugayoutiunner* (Patriarch Zaven's Memoirs. Documents and Testimonies), vol. 1. Cairo, 1947.

ARTICLES

Turkish

Arvas, I. "Tarihi Hakikatler, Eski Van Mebusu Ibrahim Arvasın Hatıraları," (Historical Facts.The Memoirs of Former Van Deputy Ibrahim Arvas) *Yeni Istiklâl*, April 21, 1965, No. 193.
Balkan, F. "Beş Albaylar" (Five Colonels). *Yakın Tarihimiz* 2 (1962).
Birinci, I. "Cemiyet ve Çeteler" (Ittihad party and the Brigands), *Hayat* 2 (October 1, 1971).
Ihsan T. (Former Minister of Navy). "Ittihad ve Farmasonlik." *Resimli Tarih Mecmuası* 2, 18 (June 1951).
Kandemir, F. "Ittihat-Terakki." *Yakın Tarihimiz* 2 (1962).
Rıfkı (Atay), F. *Dünya*, December 17, 1967. Atay's weekly column *Pazar Konuşması* (Sunday talk).

English

Buheiry, M. R. "Theodor Herzl and the Armenian Question." *Journal of Palastine Studies* (February 1977).
Charny, Israel. "A Letter from Professor Lewis," *Internet on the Holocaust and Genocide*. Special Tenth Anniversary Issue. 1985–1995. Nos. 54/55/56 (April 1995).
Dadrian, V.N. "The Anticipation and Prevention of Genocide in International Conflicts." *International Journal of Group Tensions* 18, 3 (1988).
______. "The Convergent Aspects of the Armenian and Jewish Cases of Genocide. A Reinterpretation of the Concept of Holocaust." *Holocaust and Genocide Studies* 3, 2 (1988).
______. "Genocide as a Problem of National and International Law: The World War I Armenian Case and Its Contemporary Legal Ramifications" *Yale Journal of International Law* 14, 2.
______. "The Naim-Andonian Documents on the World War I Destruction of Ottoman Armenians—The Anatomy of a Genocide." *International Journal of Middle East Studies* 18, 3 (1986).
______. "The Role of Turkish Physicians in the World War I Genocide of the Armenians." *Holocaust and Genocide Studies* 1, 2 (1986).
______. "The Role of the Turkish Military in the Destruction of Ottoman Armenians: A Study in Historical Continuities," *Journal of Political and Military Sociology* 20 (Winter, 1992).
______. "The Role of the Special Organization in the Armenian Genocide during the First World War" in *Minorities in Wartime*, P. Panayi, ed. Oxford, 1993.
______. "The Secret Young-Turk Ittihadist Conference and the Decision for the World War I Genocide of the Armenians," *Holocaust and Genocide Studies* 7, 2 (Fall, 1993).
______. "Documentation of the Armenian Genocide in German and Austrian Sources" in *The Widening Circle of Genocide* I. Charny, ed. New Brunswick, N.J., 1994.

______. *The Armenian Genocide in Official Turkish Sources*. Collected Essays. Special Issue of *Journal of Political and Military Sociology*, Roger Smith, guest ed., vol. 22, 1 (Summer, 1994).

______. "The Comparative Aspects of the Armenian and Jewish Cases of Genocide: A Socio-Historical Perspective," in Rosenbaum, Alan, ed., *Is the Holocaust Unique?* Boulder, CO: Westview Press, 101–135 (1966).

Dinkel, C. "German Officers and the Armenian Genocide," *Armenian Review* 44, 1/173 (Spring, 1991).

Haley, C. D. "The Desperate Ottoman: Enver Pasha and the German Empire" *Middle East History* 30, 1 (January 1944) and 30,2 (April 1994).

Herbert, A. "Talât Pasha," *Blackwood's Magazine* CCXIII (April, 1923).

Kedourie, E. "Young Turks, Freemasons and Jews." *Middle Eastern Studies* 7, 1 (January 1971).

des Pres, T. "On Governing Narratives: The Turkish-Armenian Case." *The Yale Review*, 75 (October 1986).

______. "Introduction. Remembering Armenia." in *The Armenian Genocide in Perspective* R. G. Hovannisian, ed. New Brunswick, NJ, 1987.

Sonyel, S. "Armenian Deportations: A Reappraisal in the Light of New Documents." *Belletin* (January 1972).

Weltmann, A. E. "Germany, Turkey , and the Zionist Movement, 1914–1918." *The Review of Politics* 23, 1 (January 1961).

German

Baltzer, K.a.D. "Das romantische Ende der drei grossen Türken der Kriegszeit, Talaat, Enver und Dschemal Pascha. Eine Erinnerung an den 1. November 1918" *Orient-Rundschau* (November 10, 1933).

von der Goltz, Colmar "Stärke und Schwäche des türkischen Reiches" (The Strength and Weakness of the Turkish Empire) *Deutsche Rundschau* XXIV, (October 1, 1897).

von der Goltz, Freiherr (baron), Retired Colonel, "Die Spionage in der Türkei" *Die Weltkriegs-Spionage*, Major-General Lettow-Vorbeck, ed., Munich, 1931.

Guse, F. "Der Armenieraufstand 1915 und seine Folgen" *Wissen und Wehr* vol. 6 (1925).

Haupt, W. "Deutsche unter dem Halbmond." *Deutsches Soldatenjahrbuch* (1967).

Harden, M. "Zwischen Ost und West. Armenien in Moabit," *Die Zukunft*, 29, 37 (June 11, 1921).

Hartmann, M. "Der Krieg und der Orient" *Deutsche-Levante Zeitung* 18/19 (October 1, 1914).

Klinghardt, Dr. K. "Frau Koch-v. Winckler aus Aleppo zum Gedächtnis" *Orient Rundschau* XVI,9 (September 10, 1934).

Lepsius, J. "Mein Besuch in Konstantinopel Juli/August 1915" *Der Orient* (monthly) No. 1/3 (1919).

Mühlmann, C. "Deutschland und die Türkei 1913–1914." *Politische Wissenschaft* 7 (1929).

Paraquin, E. "Politik im Orient," *Berliner Tageblatt* (January 24, 28, 1920 installments). A synopsis of the series is filed in the German Foreign Ministry Archives. A.A. Türkei 158/24, A1373.

Treue, W. "Max Freiherr von Oppenheim—Der Archäologe und die Politik" *Historische Zeitschrift* 209 (1969).

Werner, E. "Ökonomishce und Militärische Aspekte der Türkei-Politik Österreich-Ungarns 1915 bis 1918," *Jahrbuch für Geschichte* 10 (1974).

French

Pinon, R. "L'Offensive de l'Asie" *Revue des deux Mondes* (April 15, 1920).

Armenian

Khoren S. "Hishoghutiunner" (Memories), In Teotig, *Amenoun Daretzouytzu* (Everyone's Almanac), 10–14: 132–36. (1916–1920).

Mesrob, K. "Turkahayern u Turkeru (1914–1918). Andeeb u Bashdonagan Pastatoughter" (Turkish Armenians and the Turks 1914–1918. Unpublished and Official Ducuments) *Haygashen Almanac*. vol. 1 (1922).

Mugurditchian, H. "Kaghdniknerou Gudzigu" (The Thread of the Secrets), *Hairenik* (an Armenian daily published by the author during the Armistice for a very short period in Istanbul). Installments Nos. 1 and 2 (October 28/November 10; October 30/November 12, 1918).

Revue D'Histoire Arménienne Contemporaire vol. I (1995) (A collection of articles and documents dealing with the history of the Turko-Armenian conflict and the World War I genocide. R. H. Kevorkian, ed.).

Vahram S. "Ariunod Turvakner" (Bloody Episodes) *Zhoghovourtee Tzain*, February 25, 1919.

"Dzerougee Hishadagneru 1915–1918" (The Memoirs of Dzeroug 1915–1918). *Djagadamard* (namesake of *Azadamard*, organ of the Dashnak party, a daily in Istanbul, which often was closed down by the Turkish authorities and reappeared temporarily under new names) March 2, 1919 issue.

NEWSPAPERS

Turkish:

Cumhuriyet; Hadisat; Hayat; Sabah; Tanin; Vakit

Armenian

Azadamard (Ariamard); Hairenik (Armistice Daily, Istanbul); Zhamanag; Zhoghovourtee Tzain

French

Le Journal d'Orient; Renaissance

German

Berliner Tageblatt; Kölnische Zeitung; Deutsche-Levante Zeitung; Der Orient; Allgemeine Missions-Zeitschrift

American

Boston Globe; New York Times

OTHER WORKS BY THE AUTHOR

I. ON GENOCIDE AND GENOCIDE-RELATED TOPICS

BOOKS

Histoire du Génocide Arménien. Conflits Nationaux des Balkans au Caucase. Paris: Editions Stock. 1996. 682 pp., text, 19 pp. bibliography and Index. Expanded version in French of *The History of the Armenian Genocide* described next. Trans. Marc Nichanian.

The History of the Armenian Genocide. Ethnic Conflict from the Balkans to Anatolia to the Caucasus. Providence/Oxford: Berghahn Books, 1995. 446 pp. text, xxviii pp. Preface and Introduction. Extensive bibliography in Turkish, German, English, French, and Armenian with annotations to selected works used in the book. Subject and Name Index.

Autopsie du Génocide Arménien. Paris: Editions Complexe, 1995. French translation of "Genocide as a Problem of National and International Law: The World War I Armenian Case and Its Contemporary Legal Ramifications," *Yale Journal of International Law*, vol. 14. No. 2. (Summer, 1989). 244 pp. Two Annexes and Bibliography. Trans. Marc and Mikael Nichanian.

Ulusal ve Uluslararası Hukuk Sorunu Olarak Jenosid. Istanbul: Belge Publishers, 1995. Turkish translation of the 1989 monograph cited above. Trans. Yavuz Aloğan, 204 pp.

Haigagan Tzeghasbanoutiumu Khorturanayeen yev Badmakeedagan Kunnargoumnerov (The Treatment of the Armenian Genocide by the Ottoman Parliament and Its Historical Analysis). Boston: Baikar, 1995. In Armenian. 142 pp. and Bibliography in English.

MONOGRAPHS

"Genocide as a Problem of National and International Law: The World War I Armenian Case and Its Contemporary Legal Ramifications," *Yale Journal of International Law*, vol. 14. No. 2. (Summer, 1989). Printed separately with two Appendices and Bibliography.134 pp.

"The Armenian Genocide in Official Turkish Records:Collected Essays," Special issue of *Journal of Political and Military Sociology*, vol. 22. No. 1. (Summer, 1994). 208 pp.

"Documentation of the Armenian Genocide in German and Austrian Sources" in *The Widening Circle of Genocide* I. Charny, ed. New Brunswick, N.J., 1994. Expanded and published as a separate unit. 125 pp.

TRANSLATION OF BOOK

Zarevand, *United and Independent Turania. Aims and Designs of the Turks* (Leiden, 1971) (From Armenian). 153 pp. text. xxiii pp. Preface and Foreword. Index.

ARTICLES

"Egocentric Factors In Ethnocentrism—The Structural Patterns of Modern Nationalism. *Sociologus* 18, 2: 45–122 (1968).

"On the Dual Role of Social Conflicts." *International Journal of Group Tensions* 1, 4: 371–377 (1971).

"The Bi-polar Structure of Nationalism: A Conceptual Approach." *International Review of Sociology (Revue Internationale de Sociologie)* 7, 3: 121–12 (1971)

"Cultural and Social-Psychological Factors in the Study of Survivors of Genocide. " *International Behavioral Scientist* 3, 2: 48–55 (1971).

"Factors of Anger and Aggression in Genocide." *Journal of Human Relations* 19, 3: 394-417 (1971).

"Methodological Components of the Study of Genocide as a Sociological Problem" *Recent Studies in Modern Armenian History*. Cambridge MA: National Association for Armenian Studies & Research 83–103 (1972).

"Structural-Functional Components of Genocide: A Victimological Approach to the Armenian Case." in Drapkin, Israel, ed., *Victimology:* vol. III. Lexington, MA: D.C. Heath and Co. 123–136 (1974).

"Common Features of the Armenian and Jewish Cases of Genocide: A Comparative Victimological Perspective," in Drapkin, Israel, ed., *Victimology: A New Focus.* vol. 4, *Violence and its Victims.* Lexington, MA: D.C. Health and Co. 99–120 (1975).

"A Typology of Genocide." *International Review of Sociology* 5, 2: 201–212 (1975).

"Some Determinants of Genocidal Violence in Inter-Group Conflicts with Particular Reference to the Armenian and Jewish Cases." *Sociologus* 26, 3: 130–149 (1976).

"The Victimization of the American Indian." *Victimology: An International Journal* 1, 4: 513–537 (1976).

"An Attempt at Defining Victimology." in Viano, Emilio, ed., *Victims and Society* Washington, D.C.: Visage Press. 40, 2 (1976).

"An Oral Testimony and a Written Analysis of the Sociological Factors Involved in the Armenian Genocide before an American Congressional Panel, along with the Submission of a Set of Policy Recommendations." in *Hearings on Genocide, 94th Congress, Second Session* Washington, D.C.: Government Printing Office 6–21 (1976).

"The Naim-Andonian Documents on the World War I Destruction of the Ottoman Armenians: The Anatomy of a Genocide." *International Journal for Middle East Studies* 18: 311–360 (1986).

"The Role of Turkish Physicians in the World War I Genocide of the Ottoman Armenians." *Holocaust and Genocide Studies* 1, 2: 169–192 (1986).

"An Interview with Vahakn N. Dadrian: An Expert on the Armenian Genocide. Conducted by Harry James Cargas." *Social Science Record.* Special Issue on Genocide. Issues, Approaches, Resources 24, 2: 23–27 (1987).

"The Anticipation and Prevention of Genocide in International Conflicts. Some Lessons from History." *International Journal of Group Tensions* 18, 3: 205 214 (1988).

"The Circumstances Surrounding the 1909 Adana Holocaust." *Armenian Review* 41, 4–164: 1–16 (1988).

"The Convergent Aspects of the the Armenian and Jewish Cases of Genocide. A Reinterpretation of the Concept of Holocaust." *Holocaust and Genocide Studies* 3, 2: 151–169 (1988).

"Genocide as a Problem of National and International Law: The World War I Armenian Case and its Contemporary Legal Ramifications." *Yale Journal of International Law* 14, 2: 221–334 (1989).

"Rapports Médicaux Dressés après l'Examen des Cadavres des Arméniens Massacrés dans les Rues d'lstanbul en Septembre 1895." *Union Medical Armenienne de France* 56: 10–14 (1990).

"Towards a Theory of Genocide Incorporating the Instance of Holocaust: Comments, Criticisms and Suggestions." *Holocaust and Genocide Studies* 5, 2: 129–143 (1990).

"Documentation of the Armenian Genocide in Turkish Sources." in Charny, Israel W., ed., *Genocide: A Critical Bibliographic Review,* vol. 2. London: Mansell; New York; Facts on File. 86–138 (1991).

"The Documentation of the World War I Armenian Massacres in the Proceedings of the Turkish Military Tribunal." *International Journal of Middle East Studies* 23, 4: 549–576 (1991).

"A Textual Analysis of the Key Indictment of the Turkish Military Tribunal Investigating the Armenian Genocide." *Armenian Review* 44, 1–173: 1 36 (1991).

"Von Tätern und Opfern: Der Armenische Völkermord." *Flüchtlings Forum* 7,10: 32–34 (1991).

"The Perversion by Turkish Sources of Russian General Mayewski's Report on the Turko-Armenian Conflict." *Journal of the Society for Armenian Studies* 5: 139–152 (1991–1991)

"Ottoman Archives and Denial of the Armenian Genocide." in Hovannissian, Richard G., ed., *The Armenian Genocide: History, Politics, Ethics.* New York: St. Martin's Press, 280–310 (1992).

"The Role of Turkish Military in the Destruction of Ottoman Armenians: A Study in Historical Continuities." *Journal of Political and Military Sociology* 20, 2: 257–286 (1992).

"A Twist in the Punishment of Some of the Arch Perpetrators of the Armenian Genocide." *The Armenian Cause* 10, 2: 2E–5E (1993).

"The Role of the Special Organization in the Armenian Genocide during the First World War." in Panayi, P., ed. *Minorities in Wartime: National and Racial Groupings in Europe, North America and Australia during the World Wars.* Oxford: Berg. 5–82 (1993).

"The Secret Young-Turk Ittihadist Conference and the Decision for the World War I Genocide of the Armenians." *Holocaust and Genocide Studies* 7, 2: 173–201 (1993).

"Party Allegiance as a Determinant in the Turkish Military's Involvement in the World War I Armenian Genocide." *Revue du Monde Arménien Moderne et Contemporain* 1, 1: 87–101 (1994).

"The Comparative Aspects of the Armenian and Jewish Cases of Genocide: A Socio-Historical Perspective," in Rosenbaum, Alan, ed., *Is the Holocaust Unique?* Boulder, CO: Westview Press, 101–135 (1966).

II. ON FORMER SOVIET ARMENIA

MONOGRAPHS

"Nationalism Communism and Soviet Industrialization. A Theoretical Exposition," *Sociologia Internationalis* (Duncker and Hamblot, Berlin) 10, 2 (1972).

"Nationalism in Soviet Armenia—A Case Study of Ethnocentrism," *Naionalism in the USSR and Eastern Europe in the Era of Brezhnev and Kosygin*, George W. Simmonds, ed. (Detroit, 1977) 201–258.

ARTICLES

"An Apprisal of the Communist Formula, 'National in Form, Socialist in Content'," Part 1. *Armenian Review* 16, 3–63: 3–14 (1963).

"An Appraisal of the Communist Formula, 'National in Form, Socialist in Content'," Part II. *Armenian Review* 16, 4–64: 3–13 (1963).

"Major Patterns of Social and Cultural Changes of Soviet Armenians." *American Philosophical Society* 65: 375–379 (1965).

"Sources and Signs of Nationality Unrest." *Problems of Communism* 16, 5: 70–71 (1967).

"An Interpretation of the Address to the Central Committee of the Communist Party Of the Soviet Union." *Armenian Review* 20, 1–77: 64–78 (1967).

"The Events of April 24 in Moscow." *Armenian Review* 21, 2–78: 9–26 (1967).

"The Karabagh Issue." *Armenian Review* 21, 3–83: 57–84 (1968).

"The Development of the Soviet Posture on Nationalities—A Review of the Roles of Lenin and Stalin." *Indian Sociological Bulletin* 6, 11: 18–38 (1968).

"Inter-Ethnic Conflicts in the Soviet Transcaucasus." *International Review of History and Political Science* 6, 2: 79–92 (1969).

"National Communism—A Soviet Dilemma. *Political Scientist* 6, 1–2: 13–20 (1970).

"Industrialization and Recent Trends of the Ethnocentrism in Armenia." *Ukrainian Quarterly* 38, 1 (1972).

Translations from Soviet Armenian Intellectual-Activists

"Natioanal Vaingloriousness and National Self-Respect." (A speech delivered at the recent 5th Congress of the Union of Soviet Armenian Writers by Barouyr Sevag.) *Armenian Review* 20, 3–79: 43–50 (1967).

"An Appeal to the Armenians Throughout the World." (An essay by Soviet Armenian poet Hovannes Sheeraz.) *Armenian Review* 20, 3–79: 51–56 (1967).

"Who if Not Us and When if Not Right Now." (A speech delivered by Kevork Emin at the 5th Congress of the Union of Soviet Armenian Writers.) *Armenian Review* 20, 4–80: 19–27 (1967).

"On Attaining a Medium-Range Image on National Character." (by Soviet Armenian editor of the literary monthly, *Karoun*, Vartkes Bedrosyan). *Armenian Review* 20, 4–80: 27–34 (1967).

III. MISCELLANEOUS

"Kant's Concepts of 'Human Nature' and 'Rationality': Two Arch Determinants of an Envisioned 'Eternal Peace'." *Journal of Peace Research* 22, 2 82: 57–64 (1968). 5, 4: 396–401 (1968).

"The Britannica on the Armenian Atrocities." *Armenian Review* 22,2–82: 57 64 (1968).

"Recent Trends in Sociology in the U.S.A." *Annali Di Sociologia* 6: 23–31 (1969).

"Affluence as a Key Factor in American Sociology." *International Review of History and Political Science* 7,1: 23–34 (1970).

"The Cyprus Episode: Some Lessons from Turkish History." *Journal of the Hellenic Diaspora* 2, 1: 36–2 (1975).

"The Relationship of Subcultures to Individual Motivations of Drug Use. A Review of the Case of Marihuana." *Annali Di Sociologia* 7: 23–30 (1971).

SUBJECT & NAMES INDEX

SUBJECT INDEX

Abdul Hamit, Sultan
  bribery practice, 15, 172
  -era massacres, 8–9, 11, 183
  -era tortures, 197 n 238
Anti-Armenian repercussions, 165
Anti-Russian ideology, 165
Armenia
  Caucasian, 40
  Russian, 16, 59, 60
Armenian
  angle of, 238, 248
  Patriarch (Istanbul), 27, 114, 117
  Patriarchate (Istanbul), 115, 153, 155, 212
  Patriarchate (Jerusalem), 212
  Problem, 47, 115, 147, 177
  Provocation (the claim of) in Van, 25, 84, 274
  Question, 12
  Reform, 109
  Reform Agreement, 107–108, 109, 115, 129
  Republic, 2
Armenian(s)
  deportations, 5, 17, 19–24, 27, 29–30, 40, 42–44, 46,48, 50, 59, 61–64, 64, 71, 73, 75, 79, 81–82, 86–87, 90–93, 111, 113–118, 122–123, 126–127, 131–136, 148, 152–154, 156, 159–160, 163, 165–166, 179–180, 182–185, 209–216, 229–230, 232–233, 236, 246, 250, 252, 275
  labor battalions (annihilation), 17, 19, 28, 119
  massacres, 8,12–13, 15,21, 56, 59, 61–63, 66, 70–71, 73, 76, 82, 86, 88, 91–92, 119, 134, 138, 145, 147–148, 163, 168–169, 170, 173, 182.
  genocide (liquidation, mass murder, extermination, elimination), 1, 3, 9, 15, 22, 26, 29, 44, 48, 53, 68, 74, 135, 143, 148, 157, 159, 161–162, 165–166, 168, 170, 174–175, 179, 183–184, 186, 199, 206, 209, 214, 216, 227, 248– 249
Armenian genocide,
  compared to Dante's inferno, 195 n 179
  denial, 1, 4
  designation as holocaust, 206
  obfuscation (by revisionists and deniers), 4
  premeditated nature, 216
  the role of power (in its enactment), 1, 184
  relationship to the Black Sea incursion by the Turko-German armada led by German admiral Souchon, 187 n 5
Armenians
  conversion (forcible) to Islam, 81, 143
  as indigenous population of Turkey, 3
  relocation (the deceptive claim of authorities), 22, 135, 184

Balfour Declaration, 246, 255
Balkan War, 49, 107, 115, 172, 228
Bank Ottoman, 239
Barbarism, 198 n 242
Bassiouni, M. C. confirms Hague Conventions prohibiting wartime deportations, 93
Black Eagle Order, 21; *see also* Prussian
Breslau, German light cruiser, 54, 134, 146, 202, 218
Gen. Bronsart's role in the destruction of Armenians, 116–118

Central
  Empires, 19
  Powers, 227, 245
çetes (irregular brigands), 26, 45, 47, 62, 126, 229
Christian(s)
  Armenians, 52, 70
  Europe, 233
  Powers, 11
  of Turkey, 73
Cihad (holy war), 52–53, 67, 246
Circassians, 32, 80, 151

Dashnak(s), 26, 30–31, 47, 116, 239
Deutsche Bank, 7, 132
Deutsche Orientbank, 69
Dönmes, 240–241, 243

Emniyeti Umumiye (Sureté Nationale, National Security Bureau), 49, 194 n 159, 211
Entente Powers (France, England, Russia), 1–3, 19, 51, 54, 66–68, 70–71, 79, 90–94, 141, 151, 167, 170, 206, 223, 227, 229, 232, 245–246, 251, 265

Expeditionary Force, 27, 54–55, 64, 77, 136, 162

Freemasonry, 242–243
Freemasons, 244

Gallipoli Expedition, 247
German(s)
  agents, 15
  censorship (on Armenian gonocide), 157–158, 195n 181
  complicity (in the genocide), 3, 16–17, 19, 89, 157, 163, 170, 184–185
  consuls, 3, 15–16, 21, 23, 27, 85
  consuls (benevolent and critical of genocide, officials included), 3, 5, 16, 58–62, 85
  Experts of criminal law, 169
  General Headquarters, 113, 154, 157, 173, 207
  General Staff, 148, 158, 172, 207
  High Command, 56, 92, 129, 154, 157–158, 167, 172, 182, 207, 254
  involvement (in the genocide), 3, 16, 18, 23, 173
  liability, 20, 89, 90, 120
  liability, financial, 22–23, 157
  military officers, 3, 5, 20–21, 23, 28–29, 35, 37, 52, 56, 58, 61, 63–64, 92–94
  official documents, 2, 5
  officials, 1, 3, 5, 17, 21, 91, 152, 182, 185, 205, 208, 227
  Orientalists, 148
  responsibility, 3, 20, 175
  pro-forma protests, 82–83
  "Turkified," 124, 127
  Turkey policy, 8
  Turkophiles, 37, 115, 127, 140, 161
German Military (Mission to Turkey), 4, 7, 20, 25, 29, 52, 61, 63, 92–93, 109–112, 117, 121, 131, 136, 138, 140, 146, 149, 157, 207, 209–210, 217
German-Turkish League (*Deutsch-türkische Vereinigung*), 115
Goeben (battle cruiser), 53, 134, 146, 218
Marshal Goltz's role in the destruction of the Armenians, 116–118
Greece, 2, 90, 223, 228–230, 241
Greeks of Turkey, 228

Hague Conventions
  First (July 29, 1899), 18, 93
  Fourth (October 18, 1907; The second Peace Conference), 18, 93, 97n 30
  the prohibition of wartime deportations, 93

International Law (and the Armenian genocide), 2, 16–19, 22, 89–91, 93–94, 95n, 96n, 97n, 169–171, 235, 239
International Law and criminal law, 185–186
Iron Cross (German military medal), 210–211, 214–215, 217
Islam, 36, 49, 51–53, 66–68, 70–71, 81, 113, 124, 143, 226, 233, 235, 240, 265–266
Islamic Union, 45
Ittihad Party (C.U.P.), 30, 37, 41, 44–45, 61–62, 123, 135, 159, 172, 209–210, 212, 216, 226, 229, 240, 242
Ittihadist Young Turks, 26, 50, 123, 167, 175, 214, 240–241, 245

Jewish
  dispersion, 233
  Holocaust, 16
  Ingathering, 236, 238, 244
  Legion, 247
  Masonic, 242
  spies, 261
Jews, 121–122, 246–247
  of Almohade, 234
  of America, 256
  of East Europe, 254
  of Europe, 15
  of Germany, 245–246, 253
  of Palestine, 246, 254, 257
  of Russia, 144
  of Turkey, 235–236
Jewish military operations against Turkey, 244

Lepsius, Johannes
  volume, 5–6, 30, 71, 154–156, 174
  deletions, 5, 58, 83, 128, 137
  trips to Turkey (to investigate massacres), 154
  negotiations (with German Foreign Office to exonerate Germany), 155–156

"military necessity" doctrine, 24, 28, 87, 144, 169, 174, 201, 230, 253
Muslims, 51, 53–54, 68, 235, 240

Nazi(s), 91, 199, 201–202
  Foreign Service, 199
  Germany, 199–202
  Reich, 199

Okhrana, 166
Ottoman
armies: IIId, 27–28, 35–37, 41–43, 46–47, 62, 64
IVth, 72, 201, 211, 250, 252, 257
VIth, 57
VIIIth, 40, 201
Chamber of Deputies, 33, 42
Constitution, 83, 235
General Headquarters (*Umumi Karargâh*), 17, 19, 20–21, 36, 39, 90, 92, 116, 120, 122, 131, 134, 153–154, 158–159, 182, 201, 214–215
General Staff, 17, 59, 120, 159
High Command, 21, 30, 35, 42, 64, 127, 215
Senate, 135, 214
War Office, 50

Palestine, 7, 40, 65, 135, 143–144, 211, 223, 232, 234–240, 242–248, 250–254, 256–257
Palestine Issue, 240
Pan (isms)
German, 8
Islam, 51–52, 135
Turk, 167
Turan, 44, 165, 169
Peace Conference (Paris), 18
Perpetrators (decorations of the), 205–218
Prussian Orders
the Black Eagle, 217
the Red Eagle, 209, 213–214, 217
the Royal Crown, 209, 213–214

Railways, 7–8, 19, 58, 80, 114, 126, 248–249
Revolution, 26, 51, 84, 139, 166, 240, 243, 258
Russo-Turkish (rivalries, wars), 11, 47, 115, 134, 146, 202, 225

Special Organization, 29, 38, 41–46, 47–49, 53, 54–57, 61, 79, 158–159, 170, 182, 214–215, 229–230
Special Organization convicts (felons), 29, 42–43, 61, 73, 154, 159–162, 214

Tanzimat (19th century twin Ottoman Reform Acts), 226
Temporary Law of Deportation, 90
Treaty of Paris, 212
Turkish
Court-Martial, 39, 55, 166, 209–210, 250
doctrine of domination, 223, 225
Historical Society, historiography, 120, 224
legal history, 2
military officers, 75, 93
Military Tribunal, 2, 22, 38, 40, 44, 46, 79, 92–93, 123, 209
"mimosaic sensitivity," 128, 155
Republic, 17, 123, 241
drive for Turkification of Turkey, 44, 175, 250
Turko-German Joint Initiatives, 54, 163
Turko-German Solicitousness, 249
Turkophile Germans, 37, 115, 127, 140, 161

United Nations, 91, 94
Urfa Uprising, 56, 58–59, 68–69, 74–77
U.S.A., 18, 119, 122, 144, 150, 199, 256

Van Uprising, 28–29, 31–34, 36, 76, 84–85, 87, 211

William II, German Emperor
architect of Germany's Turkey policy, 171
his creation of German Military Mission to Turkey, 110, 121
his decrials of Abdul Hamit, 12
his praises of Abdul Hamit, 113
his reported approval of Turkey solving Armenian problem at its discretion, 139
World War I, 1, 3, 5, 7, 9–10, 29, 35, 48–49, 66, 68–69, 89, 107, 116, 123, 127, 137, 165, 167, 182, 199–200, 202, 206–208, 212, 216, 223, 231, 235, 242, 244–245, 251, 257
World War II, 15, 116, 164, 200

Yıldız Palace, 12, 14
Yozgat Verdict, 105 n 281

Zionist(s), 83, 144, 237–241, 243–248, 251–253, 255–257
Movement, 144, 236, 242, 245, 248, 256
of Berlin, 244
Organization, 240, 251

NAMES INDEX

Abdul Hamit, 8-15, 49, 66, 107, 109, 112, 118, 125, 129-130, 139, 145, 154, 171-172, 183, 214, 224, 237, 240, 243, 245, 265
Abdul Kadir, 78
Abdulhalik, Mustafa, 209
Adana, 45, 69, 82, 126, 211
Adrianople, 164, 209; *see also* Edirne, 69, 244
Aegean, 134, 228, Aegean Sea, 230, 250, Aegean Sea Littoral, 230
Ahmed Çerkez (Major), 33
Akçam, Taner, 197–198
Akçura, Yusuf, 166-167
Akif Paşa, Reşit, 191
Aleppo, 16, 58, 68-69, 73-74, 77-80, 82, 115, 119, 126, 156, 209, 266
Alexandrette, 74-75
Alexandria, 247
Alexandropol, 59
Ali Ihsan, *see* Sabis
Ali Şükrü, 152, 227
Allenby, Sir Edmund, General, 247
Alp, Tekin, 167, 235
Amasya, 151
Anatolian, 8, 132, 228
Andonian, Aram, 80,
Angora, 8, 209
Antranig, 48
Ardahan, 45
Ardanus, 45
Arvas, Ibrahim, Van deputy, 34, 84
Asım, Foreign Minister, 149–150
Askeri, Maj. Süleyman, 67
Atatürk, Mustafa Kemal, 234
Athens, 230, 258
Auschwitz, 202
Avcıoğlu, Doğan, 48, 152, 241
Avni Paşa, 41, 126,
Avram, 240
Axenfeld, Karl, 86
Aydemir, Şevket, 203n
Azerbaijan, 167
Azmi, Hüseyin, 208

Bafra, 231
Baghdad Railroad, 139
Baghdad Railway Project, 7–8, 132
Bakalian, Eghia, 40
Baku, 54–55, 57, 60, 135, 151
Bakuba, 250
Ballin, Albert, 200
Baltic, 162
Basle, 237
Bassiouni, M.C., 18, 93–94
Bathurst, A. Harvy149–150
Batum, 54
Bayar, Celal, 229, 258
Bayburt, 43
Bedri, Osman, Police Chief, 212–214
Behiç, (Erkin), Colonel, 45–46, 214
Beirut, 103n, 208
Belen, Gen. Fahri, 58, 136, 248
Belgium, 19, 113, 202, 264
Bentheim, Maj. von, 124
Berg, Lt.,154
Bergfeld, Dr. Heinrich, 163, 231
Bern, 102n, 192n
Bernstorff, Ambassador J. Heinrich,128, 172, 230, 254–255
Beşikçi, Ismail, 166
Bieberstein, Marshall Baron Adolf, Foreign Minister, Ambassador, 9, 103n, 191n,
Bihl, Wolfdieter, 156
Bismarck, 7–11, 14, 131
Bitlis, 27, 29, 31, 33, 38, 46, 57, 115, 209–211
Black Sea Littoral, 231
Black Sea, 54, 110, 142, 202, 218, 228, 231
Boettrich, Lt. Col., 19, 131, 184, 185
Bosphorus, 53, 133, 145, 172
Botho, Wedel, 171
Britain, 67, 245–246
Brode, Heinrich, 253
Bronsart, von Schellendorf, Gen. Fritz, 17–21, 23–25, 29–30, 35, 64, 67, 90, 93, 116–118, 120–126, 128, 131–132, 134, 138, 143, 146, 148, 157, 159–160, 182, 185, 230
Budapest, 202
Büge, Dr. Eugen, 211
Bülow, Bernhard von, 10, 20, 66, 140
Burian, Stephan Baron, 163, 227
Bursa, 38

Cahid, Hüseyin, 226
Cairo, 66, 68
Cambon, Paul, 9
Canbolat, Ismail, 212
Carasso, Emmanuel, 240–242, 244
Cardashian, Vahan, 149
Cavid, 129, 152, 243–244, 256
Cemal (Djemal) Paşa, 41, 65, 72, 80, 123, 136, 139, 209, 250–255, 257
Cevdet (Djevdet), Tahir, Governor of Van, 31, 33, 99n., 81, 211, 213
Cezire, 57
Chabur, 68

Colley, Dr., 210
Constantine I, 227, 230
Czechoslovakia, 199

Damascus, 68, 72, 113, 237
Dardanelles, 54, 133, 144, 218, 255
Daurri Bey, (Dürri Bey), 80–81
Dinkel, Christoph, 63
Diyarbekir, 21
Dönitz, Admiral Karl, 202
Dörtyol, 75

Egypt, 66, 69, 135, 153, 247, 250
Elkus, Abram, 256
Enver, 14–15, 21, 36–37, 39, 42, 44, 60, 64, 67, 77, 88, 92, 96n, 111, 116–117, 120, 122–123, 125, 127, 129, 131, 134–139, 142, 145–148, 151, 154–155, 159, 161, 172, 182, 187n, 189n, 201, 207, 211, 228–231, 254
Erzincan, 42–43, 210–211
Erzurum, 24, 26, 29, 31–32, 34, 37–38, 40–42, 45, 47–48, 57, 61–62, 64, 69, 82, 84–85, 87, 115, 118, 163, 200, 208, 215, 231
Euphrates, 263–264, 266

Faber, Dr., 174
Falkenhausen, Gen. Alexander, 202
Falkenhayn, Gen. Erich von, 110, 133, 254
Fehmi, Hasan, 152
Feldmann, Lt. Col., 124, 131, 185
Feyzi, 78–79, 151
Fischer, Fritz, 68, 218
Franckenstein, Georg Freiherr (Baron), 60
Friedman, Isaiah, 253–254,
Fuad Paşa, Keçecizade, Grand Vizier, 224

Gani, Abdul, 210
Gaza, 253
Giumri, 59
Gökalp, Ziya, 37, 42, 226
Gollnick, Attorney General, 170
Goltz, Colmar von der, Marshal, 7, 20, 56–58, 67, 68, 78, 109–110, 114–116, 124–132, 140, 146, 165, 182, 185, 216, 230–231
Göppert, Dr. Otto, 5, 22, 125, 156
Gottlieb, Wolfram W., 138, 192n
Grey, Sir Edward, 256, 258
Grovenstein, Maj., 209
Gulkevitch, Russian Chargé, Istanbul, 108
Günther, Otto, 160
Guse, Felix, 29–30, 35–37, 39, 63–64, 84, 93
Gustav, Karl, 162

Haci Adil (Arda), 209
Hafız Hakkı, 37
Hakkı, Ibrahim, 155, 244
Hâlet, Erzincan Deputy, 42–43
Halil, (Menteşe), 65, 212
Halil, (Kut), 55, 60, 215–216
Halit, (Deli), 55
Harden, Maximillian, 157
Harput, 29, 38, 46
Hayret Paşa, 38
Hedjaz, 136
Herbert, Aubrey, 117, 143–144, 188
Herzl, Theodor, 236–239, 242, 245, 252
Hilmi, Filibeli, 42, 47–48, 61–62
Hitler, Adolf, 199–202
Hitler, Testament, 209
Hoffmann, Hermann, 58, 74–76
Hohenlohe, Ambassador Gottfried, 129
Hohenlohe, Ernst Langenburg, 81–82, 88, 129, 206
Hohenlohe–Schillingsfürst Chlodwig, 11
Holland, 139, 155–156
Hollweg, Dr. Bethmann,(Chancellor), 14, 26, 66, 71–73, 77, 81, 84, 86, 104, 128, 137, 140, 199–200, 206, 231, 252
Höss, Rudolf, 202
Hötzendorf, Gen. Conrad von, 128
Humann, Hans, 14, 20–21, 35, 20, 145–146, 161, 182, 185
Humann, Karl, 146
Hüseyin Celal, 79
Ibrahim, Hakkı, Ambassador(later Grand Vizier), 155

India, 51, 54, 58, 260
Iran, 54–56, 200
Iraq, 57, 69, 127, 231–232
Ismail Hakkı, 244
Ittihad, 93
Izmir, 27, 87, 229, 250
Izmit, 87
Izzet Paşa, Ahmet, 215
Izzet, Ahmed Paşa, Grand Vizier, 111, 158–159, 215, 220, 224,
Izzet, District Gov. of Jerusalem, 253

Jäckh, Ernst, 115, 146, 161
Jacobson, Victor, 256
Jaequemeyns, Rolin, 19
Jagow, Dr. Gottlieb, Foreign Minister, 19, 57, 81, 101n, 104n, 133, 140, 155
Jodl, Gen. Alfred, 202

Kâmil, Gen. Mahmud, 24, 37–42, 47, 62–64, 215, 208
Karabekir, Gen. Kâzım, 159–160

Kelekian, Diran, 66
Kemakh, 211
Kemal, Kara, 37, 213
Kemal, Yusuf, 46, 214
Kharput, 50
Koch, Martha, 78–79
Konya, 8, 191, 208, 210
Kressenstein, Gen. von Kress,16, 40, 59, 64, 159, 201–202, 252, 254
Kühlmann, Dr. Richard, Ambassador, Foreign Minister, 27, 65, 133, 146, 217
Künzler, Jacob, 77, 104, 191
Kurdish, 26, 78, 120
Kuşcubaşı, Eşref 67, 228–229
Kwiatkowski, 162–163, 185, 231

Lansing, Secretary of State, 18
League of Nations, 19
Lebanon, 65, 69, 72
Lepsius, Johannes, 5–6 30, 58, 70–71, 83, 98n, 128, 137, 154–156, 174, 189n, 193n–195n
Leverkuehn, Paul, 162
Lewis, Bernard, 206
Lichtheim, Richard, 236, 256
Lithuania, 201
Locock, G. H., 149
Lossow, (Col., later Gen.) Otto, 16, 50, 59, 64, 142, 154, 201
Lüttichau, Count von, 133, 164–165

Mackensen, Fieldmarshal August von, 134, 207
MacRury, Captain E., 78
Malatya, 165
Malta, 40, 213, 234
Mandelstam, André, Russian Official, Legist., 108
Mardin, 22, 78
Marquart, Dr. Joseph, 70
Medina, 136
Mehmed Memduh, 210
Mehmed Asım, 28
Mertem, Admiral, 110
Meskene, 266
Metternich, Paul Count von Wolff, Ambassador, 16, 81, 87–88, 127, 148, 154, 200, 206–207, 216, 252
Mil, A. Special Organization Leader, Memoirs, 42–44, 47–48, 100n, 118, 121, 124, 136, 138, 140, 194n, 196n
Mittwoch, Dr. Eugen, 70, 161
Moltke, von Helmuth (the elder), 7,
Moltke, von Helmuth (the younger), 51, 128, 172
Mordtmann, 84, 114
Morgenthau, Ambassador Henry. 82, 114, 119, 122, 134, 138, 141, 143–145, 147, 176–177, 185, 213, 218, 229, 258
Morocco, 171
Mosel, Louis, 55–57
Mosul, 22, 57–58, 68, 80, 82, 126, 210–211
Muammer, Ahmed, 41, 210–211
Mühlmann, Carl, 92
Müller, Admiral Georg Alexander von, 141
Munich, 139, 201–202
Mussa Dagh, 58, 74–75, 136
Musul, 41
Muş, 27, 33, 46, 162

Nadamlenzki, A. C., 164
Nadolny, Rudolf, 55, 200, 203
Nahum, Chief Rabbi of Turkey, 240–241
Nail, Yenibahçeli, 41–42, 55, 61,164
Naumann, Friedrich, 10, 13, 15, 112, 135
Nazım, Dr. Mehmed, 42, 44, 52–53, 123, 142, 161–162, 208, 240–243
de Nogales, Rafael, 29, 32–33, 52
Neratof, Deputy Foreign Minister, Russia, 108
Nesim Masliyah, Ottoman–Jewish deputy, 240
Nesim Russo, Ottoman–Jewish deputy, 240, 244
Nesimi, Foreign Minister, 255
Neurath, Baron Konstantin von, 77, 85, 137, 199, 202, 252
Niemeyer, Dr., Defense Counsel, Berlin, 170
Nuremberg, 91n.
Nuri, 60
Nusuhi, Colonel,38, 41

Odessa, 240
Okyar, Fethi, Interior Minister, 123, 125, 189n, 194n
Ömer, Naci, 27, 42, 55, 57–58, 162
Oppenheim,Baron Max von, 65–81
Orbay, Admiral Rauf, 116–117
Ormanian, Patriarch Malakia, 183

Pallavicini, Ambassador Johann Markgraf, 163, 227
Papen, Franz von, 199, 202
Parsons, Talcott, 50, 139
Patterson, Henry J., 247
Pera, 178–181
Persia, 27, 31, 33, 56
Pertev Paşa, 39–40, 126, 210
Pfeifer, Lt., 158

Pinon, René, 114
Pohl, Admiral Hugo von, 142
Pomiankowski, Joseph, Vice Marshal, 21, 32, 124, 143, 211
Pontus, 152, 228
Portugal, 233
Posseldt, Maj. Gen., 85
Pourtalés, Fredrich, 50

Radowitz, Wilhelm, 65
Raphael Lemkin, 15
Ras–el–Ain, 68, 70, 73, 80
Razzuk Chelebi, 78
Rebeur–Paschwitz, Admiral Hubert von, 124
Refik, Ahmed, (Attınay), 100
Reinhard Heydrich, 199
Reinhard Mannesmann, 151
Reshid Bey, Dr., Diyarbekir Governor, 80
Rhine, 199
Rintelen, Franz von, 172
Riza, Ahmed, Young Turk leader, 46
Riza, Tevfik, 159
Riza, Yusuf, 44, 55, 61, 164
Rohrbach, Paul, 114, 130
Rosen, Friedrich, 155
Rosenberg, Frederic Hans von, 200
Rössler, Dr. Walter, 16, 58, 73, 119, 156, 209
Rothschild, Edmond, 242
Rumania, 200, 258

Sabis, Gen. Ali Ihsan, 40–41, 55–56, 67, 159
Sadık, Colonel, 242–243
Said Halim, Grand Vizier, 117, 168
Salisbury, Lord, Prime Minister, 12, 107
Saloniki, 240–242
Sanders, Marshal Limann, 29, 52–54, 61, 78, 110, 116, 121–122, 127, 140, 144, 209, 217, 230–231
Sarıkamış, 37, 87, 120
Schellendorf, *see* Bronsart
Scheubner Richter, 23, 25, 32, 38, 45, 55, 58, 64, 84–85, 115, 118, 162–163
Schmidt, Edmund, 252
Schmidt, Oswald von, 55–56, 160, 185
Schraudenbach, Ludwig, 157, 208
Schulenburg, F. W., 42, 56, 58, 64, 118, 160, 162, 199
Schwarzenstein, Alfons Mumm, 11
Seeckt, Gen. Hans Friedrich, 59, 64, 92, 112, 123, 127–128, 134–135, 159, 200–201
Serbia, 134, 258
Sertel, Zekeriya, 241
Seyfi, Colonel, Chief of Department II, General Headquarters, 50, 111–112, 154, 214
Seyfullah, Deputy, 42, 62
Sievert, Lt. Col., 112
Smyrna, 27, 87, 229, 232, 250, 261
Solf, Wilhelm, Foreign Minister, 5, 156, 200, 275
Sonyel, Salahi, 118, 120, 189n 35
Souchon, Admiral Wilhelm, 21, 110, 134, 140, 146, 185
Spain, 224, 233, 240
Stange, Colonel, 16, 38, 55, 60–64, 164, 216
Stoffels, Dr., 162
Stürmer, Dr. Harry, 179–180, 182, 128n, 228
Suad, Ali, 80
Sudi, Deputy, 42, 208
Süleyman Faik Paşa, 38
Switzerland, 63, 102, 180
Syrian, 253
Şahabeddin, Colonel Cenab, 148
Şakir, Dr. Behaeddin, 42–43, 47, 61, 153, 163–164, 215–217, 252
Şükrü, Mithat, General Secretary of Ittihad Party, 44, 260
Sykes, Mark, 93

Tahsin, Hasan (Uzer), Governor of Erzurum, 24, 34, 41, 84–85
Talât, Küçük, 44
Talât, Paşa, Interior Minister, Grand Vizier, pary boss, 123, 136, 148, 216
Teheran, 149
Teilerian, Soghomon, 52
Tekirdag, 112
Tel Aviv, 250, 253
Tell Halaf, 68
Tercan, 43, 62
Tevfik Hadi, 212
Tevfik Paşa, 239–240
Thauvenay, 112, 131
Tiflis, 59
Tirpitz, Admiral, 12, 113, 146
Toynbee, Arnold, historian, 206, 229, 258
Trabzon, 29, 40–42, 46–47, 55–57, 61–62, 82, 152, 162–164, 185, 209, 215, 231
Transcaucasus, 31, 55, 59, 114, 135
Treue, Wilhelm, 68, 77
Tripoli, 258
Trumpeldor, Joseph, 246
Trumpener, Ulrich, 53, 132, 156, 206, 216

U. S. A., 18, 119, 122, 144, 150, 199, 256

Usedom, Admiral Guido, 21, 110, 133–134, 140, 185
Ussher, Dr., U.S. Physician in Van, 31

Vasfi, Colonel, 40
Vartkes, 79
Vehib, General, Commander of IIId Army, 37
Venizelos, Greek statesman, 227–230
von Diest, 114
Vramian, Armenian Deputy from Van, 32–33

Waldersee, Gen. Alfred von, 130–131
Wangenheim, Baron Hans von, 14, 20–21, 23–24, 35, 51–52, 56, 81, 83, 85–88, 107, 138, 141–147, 165, 168, 172, 174, 185, 199, 218, 232, 252
Washington, 149, 172, 185, 199, 256
Weber, Frank G., 53, 206
Wegner, Armin T., 263,
Weizman, Chaim, Jewish scientist, statesman, 245–246
Werthauer, Dr. J., Defense Counsel, Berlin, 170–171
Wesendonck, Otto Günther, 160–161
Wetzell, Colonel Wilhelm, 128
White, Dr. G., Anatolia College President, 210
Wildenbruch, Pfeffer von, S.S. General, 202
William II, German Emperor, 8–13, 15, 20, 51, 66, 68, 86, 107, 109, 111, 113, 121, 137–142, 171–172, 183, 185, 207, 212, 216, 218, 230–231, 237, 255, 261, 275–276
Winston, Churchill, WWI Lord of Admiralty, 54
Wolffskeel, Maj. Eberhard, 56, 58–59, 76, 136–137, 192n 105, 276

Yakub, Cemil, 55, 163
Yemen, 234
Yerevan, 59

Zechlin, Egmont, 255
Zeitoun, 74
Zimmer, Dr. Max, 151
Zimmermann, Dr. Arthur, Undersecretary, Foreign Minister, 52, 67, 81, 83, 85–87, 104, 172, 174, 218, 245, 254
Zohrab, Armenian Deputy and Prof. of Law, 79